# Venice's Hidden Enemies

# Venice's Hidden Enemies

## Italian Heretics in a Renaissance City

## John Jeffries Martin

The Johns Hopkins University Press
Baltimore and London

Hardcover edition published by University of California Press, 1993
Johns Hopkins Paperbacks edition, 2004

The Johns Hopkins University Press
2715 North Charles Street
Baltimore, Maryland 21218-4363
www.press.jhu.edu

Library of Congress Cataloging-in-Publication Data

Martin, John Jeffries, 1951–
    Venice's hidden enemies: Italian heretics in a renaissance city /
John Jeffries Martin.
        p. cm.
Originally published: Berkeley : University of California press, 1993,
in series: Studies on the history of society and culture.
Includes bibliographical references and index.
    ISBN 0-8018-7877-2 (pbk. : alk. paper)
    1. Heresies, Christian—Italy—Venice—History—16th century. 2.
Renaissance—Italy—Venice. 3. Reformation—Italy—Venice. 4. Venice
(Italy)—Church history. 5. Venice (Italy)—Intellectual life. 6.
Venice (Italy)—History—1508–1797. I. Title.
  BR878.V4M37 2003
  273'.6'094531—dc22

                                            2003015037

A catalog record for this book is available from the British Library.

*for*
*Mary Ellen*
*with love and admiration*

# Contents

# Preface to the Johns Hopkins Edition

When in 1572 Giovanni Antonio Facchinetti, the pope's ambassador, warned the Venetian government that heretics were the "hidden enemies" of the state, he expressed a widely held fear. The rulers and magistrates of Florence, Milan, Naples, and Rome, after all, had to look no farther than Germany for evidence of the political turmoil that heresy brought in its wake. Yet the words the ambassador chose—*hidden enemies*—especially suited the case of Venice. For while most Venetians who articulated their hopes for religious reform saw themselves as friends of the republic, gradually both Roman and Venetian authorities came to think of them as enemies. And once they were so labeled or defined, it became imperative for them to hide—to conceal their own beliefs and convictions, to exercise discretion when discussing the books they read, equally to keep quiet about their relationships with others suspected of heresy, and even, at times, to run from the law. In their hiding, they were assisted both by the relative anonymity of such a large maritime center as Venice and by the government's diplomatic and commercial concerns that made it reluctant to admit, officially at least, the existence of religious tensions in the city. As a consequence, despite the best efforts of the Inquisition, the heretics of Venice were largely successful in their subterfuge.

When I undertook this project in the late 1970s and early 1980s, I had three objectives in mind. First, I was eager to cast some light on a period of Italian history that many scholars simply ignored. At the time, most historians paid far more attention to Italy in the

Renaissance—that is, Italy in the fourteenth, fifteenth, and early sixteenth centuries—than in the early modern era as a whole. Consequently, the scholarship (in the English language at least) that focused on Italian matters after the death of Machiavelli (1527) was decidedly thin. This historiographical situation, happily, is no longer the case, and the study of early modern Italy has now emerged as a major field. *Venice's Hidden Enemies* certainly did not the cause this shift in emphasis, but it has been part of a trend in historical research that has devoted more and more attention to sixteenth– and seventeenth–century Italy—a subject of growing interest to scholars.

My second objective was ideological or political. In college I found myself turning to the study of history largely because of my conviction—one broadly shared in my generation—that we have, in our approach to the past, paid far too little attention to the ideas and beliefs of those who were excluded from cultural, political, or economic power and influence. In graduate school—first through a reading of Emmanuel Le Roy Ladurie's *Montaillou* and then through the study of Carlo Ginzburg's *The Cheese and the Worms*—it became clear to me (as it did to many others) that studies of Venetian inquisitorial documents could bring to life the experience and beliefs of "ordinary" men and women by excavating the social conditions of the time as well as the prevailing cultural beliefs and ideas. As I learned more and more about Venice, moreover, I became convinced that the rich and well-preserved inquisitorial documents in its archives could be used to illuminate not merely one eccentric individual as Ginzburg had done in *The Cheese and the Worms* but also broad popular movements, in which hundreds, if not thousands of individuals were involved. To be sure, a measure of youthful romanticism played a role in this quest. But I remain convinced that the cultural, religious, and intellectual lives of workers, artisans, and merchants of the early modern (and modern) world must be examined with the same interest as those of well-known writers and artists. If anything, calling for such an emphasis has become even more important now than when this book first appeared in 1993. The last decade has witnessed a disconcerting shift away from social history and therefore away from the study of the lives of non-elites—a turn in the historiography that I see as limiting our vision of the past's richness and of the roles that all social classes played in shaping history.

My third overriding concern stemmed from a desire to

understand the connections that might exist between religion and social life. To me, this was and remains a central question in both the humanities and the social sciences. In a general sense I accept both the Marxist premise that religious notions are largely determined by the social location of believers and the Weberian view that religion can shape social life and institutions. The cultural anthropologist Clifford Geertz nicely captured the interactive nature of religion and society by observing that religion, as a cultural system, is not only a reflection of society but also a way of ordering the mundane as well as the religious life. Nonetheless, while I recognize that religion and society exercise a reciprocal influence over one another, I find both in my research and in my own experience that social forces are generally the more decisive—that the social world tends to shape religion rather than the other way around.

Certainly the primacy given to the sociological analysis of heresy in this book was apparent to many reviewers. Yet the study of reform movements in sixteenth–century Italy has remained oddly detached from sociological questions. Scholars have in fact been primarily concerned with theological subjects, such as unpacking the varied threads of Valdesian and Erasmian, Lutheran and Calvinist, Anabaptist and Socinian ideas, and with illuminating the spiritual itineraries of particular individuals. Unlike other studies of Christian reform in the late medieval world—especially those on the Reformation in Germany, Switzerland, and France—the scholarship on Italian reform movements remains overly isolated from the more theoretically informed questions. I can only hope that the re-issuance of this text in paperback may encourage new studies of the sociology and anthropology of religious beliefs and practices in early modern Italy.

After a decade of hindsight, some of this book's shortcoming have become apparent. First, this study gives too little attention to the elites of the city. Not that I would de-emphasize the role of workers and artisans in the Venetian reform movements, but the historiography of individuals such as patricians, friars, priests, and humanists would provide a crucial connection between the local story I tell here and the broader religious currents in Europe at the time—though admittedly the relation of educated elites to non-elites in early modern society is still not well understood. Certainly the relationship was not merely top-down but involved a number of complex interactions between the rich and poor, priests and the laity, and the educated and the less educated (since most of the heretics were, in fact, literate).

Secondly, I would now do even more to emphasize the instability and provisional nature of religious beliefs in the age of the Reformation. The religious situation in sixteenth-century Italy was far more fluid than the categories of dissent introduced in this book might suggest. There was something so malleable, restless, and individualistic about many of the Italian reformers or heretics that to line individuals up on one side or another of the religious battle lines of the sixteenth century would be to oversimplify the situation. Individuals very often passed over those lines, drifting from heresy to heresy (what St. Augustine centuries earlier in his *Confessions* had called the "*circuitus errori mei*"). What needs to be explained, therefore, is not how the social location of a particular group of individuals made it more likely than another to accept a certain set of religious views but rather how social experience in the early modern world often led individuals to move from one religious position to another with relative ease. This "religious" mobility may have been particularly characteristic of Italy, though it was probably not confined to Italy. Long ago, the great French historian Lucien Febvre remarked that a "fertile, elementary age was bound to produce something more than an opposition between a well co-ordinated Protestantism on the one hand and a well-expurgated Catholicism on the other."

Finally, I would now approach the history of heresy by focusing on how Venetian heretics presented themselves in public and in private. The use of the term *hidden* in my title refers to the dual or even multiple identities religious dissenters in early modern Venice (if not in Europe as a whole) had to assume to avoid prosecution—a development that we still understand imperfectly. Apart from the few who were willing to die or be exiled for their convictions, the majority had to decide whether and to what degree they should dissimulate their own beliefs and/or simulate or adopt the beliefs of the Catholic society in which they lived. That this was a difficult choice is clear, especially since many of the heretics sought, in their newly acquired religious beliefs, membership in a community that served to reinforce their own sense of identity as individuals. Those who were able to represent themselves publicly as Calvinists or Anabaptists were, in the emerging modern sense of the term, "sincere." Yet the political and religious situation of the time often dictated, especially to those with businesses and families, that they present a public identity as Catholic—that they attend mass and make their confessions—in order to protect themselves and their loved ones from the suspicions of their neighbors and from the force of the Inquisition. As a result, many heretics were often anything but sincere in their actions; to the contrary, they were often deliberately "prudent" about what and how much they would reveal about themselves. The tension between these two ideals—sincerity and prudence—helped to shape new notions of identity in the early modern world.

It is a special pleasure to acknowledge here the advice and encouragement of the many good friends and colleagues who had a role in the making of this book. Among those who played an essential role were my teachers Caroline Walker Bynum, Giles Constable, Felix Gilbert, Myron Gilmore, David Herlihy, and Simon Schama. But I am equally indebted to Albert Ascoli, Marino Berengo, David Broussard, Antonio Calabria, Linda Carroll, Francesca Meneghetti Casarin, Sam Cavaglione, Stanley Chojnacki, Gaetano Cozzi, Tom Cragin, Michela dal Borgo, Nicholas Davidson, Andrea del Col, James R. Farr, Joanne Ferraro, Francisco García-Treto, Paul Gehl, Carlo Ginzburg, Edith Gladstone, Eunice Herrington, Lynn Hunt, Gary Kates, Marion Kuntz, Nanette Le Coat, Sheila Levine, Richard Mackenney, John A. Marino, Maria McWilliams, Char Miller, Stephanya Miller, Edward Muir, Deanna Perez, Lilly Peterson, Stefano Pillinini, David Robertson, Dennis Romano, Guido Ruggiero, Kris Ruggiero, Alessandra Sambo, Silvana Seidel Menchi, John Tedeschi, Cynthia Truant, Rose Vekony, and Sharron Wood. To each of these individuals I am more grateful than I can easily say. It is also a pleasure to thank Henry Tom and Courtney Bond at the Johns Hopkins University Press for helping shepherd this book to a paperback edition.

Nor would this book have been possible without the support of several institutions and foundations for whose generosity and assistance I remain deeply appreciative: the *Archivio di Stato* (Venice), the Faculty Development Commission (Trinity), the Fulbright-Hays Commission, the Danforth Foundation, the Krupp Foundation, the Coates Library (Trinity), the *Marciana* (Venice), the National Endowment for the Humanities, and the Newberry Library

(Chicago). I wish to thank my former and present colleagues, faculty and staff, in the Department of History at Trinity for their warmth, their enthusiasm, and their willingness to share their expertise with me.

Parts of this study appeared previously, albeit in substantially different versions. I am grateful to the University of Chicago Press for permission to republish portions of my article, "Salvation and Society in Sixteenth-Century Venice: Popular Evangelism in a Renaissance City," which appeared in the *Journal of Modern History* 60 (1988): 205-33; to the editors of *Quaderni storici* for granting me the right to use parts of my essay, "L'Inquisizione romana a la criminalizzazione del dissenso religioso a Venezia all'inizio dell'eta moderna," *Quaderni storici* n.s., 66 (1987): 777-802; and finally to Croom Helm for the use of brief selections from my chapter, "Popular Culture and the Shaping of Popular Heresy in Renaissance Venice," in Stephen Haliczer, ed., *Inquisition and Society in Early Modern Europe* (London: Croom Helm, 1987), 115-128.

Above all, it is a pleasure to thank my family—my parents Dorothy and Junius, whom I now greatly miss, for their unfailing support and encouragement; my wonderful brother William Thomas Martin for his love and warmth; and my formidable children Margaret and Junius, who have enriched my life more than either can ever know. But I take special pride in re-dedicating this book to Mary Ellen. Ten years ago I wrote that being with her makes it plain that grace and good fortune are not mere intellectual abstractions; she brings me an abundance of both. Now it is an honor to reaffirm these words—truer than ever.

# Salvation and Society
# in Sixteenth-Century Venice

*A fertile, elementary age was bound to produce something more than an opposition between a well-co-ordinated Protestantism on the one hand and a well-expurgated Catholicism on the other.*

Lucien Febvre

Few places in the history of the western world seem so unlikely a setting for an examination of the conjoined themes of repression and dissent as Renaissance Venice. For Venice has almost always been perceived as a place apart, and not only because of its watery location, so splendid and so strange. In the fourteenth century, for example, when most of the other cities and states of Italy were torn by violence and civil conflicts, this peaceful island republic, "solidly built on marble but standing more solid on a foundation of civil concord," appeared to the visiting Florentine humanist Petrarch as "the one refuge of honorable men." But it was in the sixteenth century that Venice's unusual destiny provided an especially striking counterpoint to the general course of Italian and other European developments. It was in that century that the city survived not only the invasions of Italy first by the French and then by Spanish troops but even preserved, despite all odds in an age of princes, many of the internal liberties of republican institutions. Thus, in what was to become a famous and influential book, *The Commonwealth and Government of Venice*, the Venetian humanist Gasparo Contarini boasted that no state could be found in history or his own times "that may bee paragond with this of ours, for institutions & lawes prudently decreed." And to the French political philosopher Jean Bodin, also writing in the sixteenth century, Venice was virtually synonymous with political freedom. "Whereas other cities and districts are threatened by civil wars or fears of tyrants or harsh exactions of taxes or the most annoying inquiries into one's activities," Bodin observed, "[Venice] seemed to me to be nearly the only city that offers immunity and freedom from all these kinds of servitude."[1] To contemporaries, Venice was indeed a republican island in a sea of monarchies. In such a free and serene city, what reason was there for dissent? And what excuse was there for repression?

1. The quotations come, respectively, from *Letters from Petrarch*, ed. and trans. Morris Bishop (Bloomington: Indiana University Press, 1966), 234; Gasparo Contarini, *The Commonwealth and Government of Venice*, trans. Lewes Lewkenor (London: John Windet, 1599), 5 (first published as *De magistratibus et republica Venetorum* [Paris: M. Vascosani, 1543]); and Jean Bodin, *Colloquium of the Seven about Secrets of the Sublime*, trans. Marion L. Kuntz (Princeton: Princeton University Press, 1975), 3.

---

*Opposite.* The myth of Venice was able to capture the imagination of sixteenth-century Europeans not only through literature and works of political theory but also through such stately images of the city as Jacopo de' Barbari's perspective of the city, printed in Venice about 1500. (Museo Correr; courtesy of Osvaldo Böhm)

Yet Venice never really was, of course, a place apart. As a major port and commercial center on the crossroads of the trade routes that connected east with west and Europe with the Mediterranean, Venice stood at the center of things—and not only the world of merchants. Venice was also an intellectual center. In the early sixteenth century the city claimed the largest publishing industry in the world; and its university, in nearby Padua, attracted students from all over Europe. Indeed, Venetian history has always been tied to the fortunes of Europe and the Mediterranean. It is thus no surprise that, in the age of the Reformation, religious tensions made themselves felt in this northern Italian city.

Although these religious tensions and in particular the development of religious dissent in sixteenth-century Venice have been marginal concerns to most scholars who have made the city the focus of their research, this book is by no means the first to examine the history of Venetian heresy. It has now been over a century since Karl Benrath published his *Geschichte der Reformation in Venedig* (History of the Reformation in Venice); the second volume of Emilio Comba's *I nostri Protestanti* (Our Protestants), which appeared in 1897, was devoted to the same subject; and Paul Grendler's *Roman Inquisition and the Venetian Press*, published in 1977, is but one of scores of related studies that have appeared in recent years.[2] And yet the field has been cultivated in such a way that it risks enclosure in one of those intellectual hothouses of subspecialization—by no means rare in academia—in which the possibility of cross-pollination with social and political history, for example, or with other dimensions of intellectual history has become increasingly remote. This study, by contrast, is an effort to carry at least a few of the seedlings out into the open air. My central goal is both to offer a general picture and to do so with attention to the larger social, political, and intellectual contexts.

The problem of context has not been an easy one for students of religious dissent in sixteenth-century Italy. At first, of course, the backdrop seemed obvious. Efforts at religious reform that the Catholic church defined as heretical scholars considered to be extensions or

2. Karl Benrath, *Geschichte der Reformation in Venedig* (Halle: Verein für Reformationsgeschichte, 1887); Emilio Comba, *I nostri Protestanti*, vol. 2: *Durante la Riforma nel Veneto e nell'Istria* (Florence: Claudiana, 1897); and Paul Grendler, *The Roman Inquisition and the Venetian Press, 1540–1605* (Princeton: Princeton University Press, 1977). For a comprehensive overview of the literature on the Italian reform movements, see the essay on sources and bibliography.

echoes of the Protestant Reformation to the north. They searched for signs of Lutheran or Calvinist sympathies; and, given what were for the most part their own Protestant or liberal commitments, they lamented the failure of the reform to take root—a failure they generally attributed to Rome's reaction and the dogged aggressiveness with which it suppressed the new ideas.[3]

In the 1930s two eminent Italian historians—Delio Cantimori and Federico Chabod—offered new frameworks for the study of the Italian heresies. In his *Eretici italiani del Cinquecento* (Italian heretics of the sixteenth century), published in 1939, Cantimori redefined both the context and the character of the contributions of the Italian reform movements.[4] In Cantimori's view, the Italian reformers were not especially influenced by Luther or Calvin. To the contrary, they were often as hostile to the teachings of the Lutheran and Reformed churches as they were to Roman doctrine. The significance of the *eretici* became particularly plain in their refusal ultimately—after abandoning the Roman church—to make the new Protestant confessions their home. As Cantimori put it, they were "rebels against every form of ecclesiastical organization."[5] To be sure, there was a time when many of them hoped to find their ideas realized in the new Protestant confessions and, during the 1540s especially, fled to Geneva, Basel, Bern, Zurich, and other Swiss cities with some optimism. But after the execution of the Spanish antitrinitarian Michael Servetus in Geneva in 1553—an execution

3. Among the major early studies on the Italian Reformation (including Benrath and Comba, cited above), see Thomas M'Crie, *History of the Progress and Suppression of the Reformation in Italy in the Sixteenth Century, Including a Sketch of the Reformation in the Grisons* (1827; Edinburgh: Blackwood and Sons, 1856); and Cesare Cantù, *Gli eretici d'Italia: Discorsi storici*, 3 vols. (Turin: UTET, 1865–1866). Useful overviews of the early scholarship on the Italian heretics appear in Frederic C. Church, "The Literature of the Italian Reformation," *Journal of Modern History* 3 (1931): 457–473; and in Delio Cantimori, "Recenti studi intorno alla Riforma in Italia e ai Riformatori italiani all'estero (1924–1934)," *Rivista storica italiana* 8 (1936): 83–110; but see also Adriano Prosperi, "Riforma in Italia, Riforma italiana?" preface to Manfred Welti, *Breve storia della Riforma italiana*, trans. Armido Rizzi (Casale Monferrato: Marietti, 1985), vii–xvi [the original German edition, cited in the essay on sources and bibliography, lacks Prosperi's preface].

4. *Eretici italiani del Cinquecento: Ricerche storiche* (1939; reprint Florence: Sansoni, 1967). Cantimori's work decisively shifted the emphasis of studies on the Italian Reformation away from the earlier preoccupation with the influence of Luther and Calvin on thinkers in Italy, but Frederic C. Church's work anticipated many of Cantimori's conclusions. See Church, *The Italian Reformers, 1534–1564* (New York: Columbia University Press, 1932), which Cantimori himself translated into Italian: *I Riformatori italiani*, 2 vols. (Florence: La Nuova Italia, 1935); Cantimori's important review of this work appeared in *La Nuova Italia* 3 (1932): 333–342.

5. Cantimori introduces the phrase "ribelli ad ogni forma di comunione ecclesiastica" in the preface to his *Eretici italiani del Cinquecento*.

Calvin himself encouraged—the Italian heretics realized that the gulf between their values and those of Calvin was irreconcilable. Many sought refuge in Poland and Moravia where the political regimes were tolerant of religious diversity. Among the exiles were figures such as Bernardino Ochino, Giorgio Biandrata, and Lelio and Fausto Sozzini. Cantimori's argument made it clear that the patently radical and often antitrinitarian ideas expressed by these and many other Italian reformers belonged to a context quite different from that of the magisterial Reformation. In formulating their views these men drew, he argued, not on the writings of Luther or Calvin but rather on several currents of syncretism and religious rationalism that originated in Renaissance Italy. Thus they looked with particular interest to the works of the humanist Lorenzo Valla and the Platonist Giovanni Pico della Mirandola. Cantimori's formulation of a specific definition of heresy had the merit of stressing the contribution that Italian radicals and Socinians made to the ideas of tolerance and freedom of conscience that seemingly foreshadowed many of the most notable achievements of the Enlightenment.[6]

Shortly before Cantimori completed *Eretici italiani*, Chabod published a remarkable study on the history of religious life in the Duchy of Milan during the sixteenth century.[7] In this work, part of his comprehensive examination of the duchy in the age of the emperor Charles V, Chabod viewed the reform movements of the sixteenth century in relation to the specific political context in which they developed. The invasions of Italy by France and Spain that began at the end of the fifteenth century, he argued, precipitated a crisis that was both religious and political; they provoked not only anger and hostility against those princes who had allowed the "barbarians" back into Italy but also, as Chabod emphasized, a sense of outrage "against the Church

6. Socinianism (involving antitrinitarian views and a denial of Christ's divinity) derives from *Socinus*, the Latinized form of Sozzini. These remarks on Cantimori are not meant to be exhaustive. His writings on the Italian Reformation spanned forty years, and it would be absurd to suggest that his views remained consistent. Here I wish merely to stress that Cantimori's *Eretici italiani del Cinquecento* best represents the break between earlier studies on the reform movements in Italy and subsequent research. For an analysis of Cantimori's significance that focuses on his later work and in particular his *Prospettive di storia ereticale italiana del Cinquecento* (Bari: Laterza, 1960), see Anne Jacobson Schutte, "Periodization of Sixteenth-Century Italian Religious History: The Post-Cantimori Paradigm Shift," *Journal of Modern History* 61 (1989): 269–284.

7. Chabod's study (pt. 1 on the Catholic church and pt. 2 on the Reformation) is "Per la storia religiosa dello Stato di Milano durante il dominio di Carlo V: Note e documenti." This 1937 essay is now most accessible in his collected works: *Opere*, vol. 3: *Lo Stato e la vita religiosa a Milano nell'epoca di Carlo V* (Turin: Einaudi, 1971), 227–516.

and the clergy, who were incapable of either consoling or exalting the faithful, so anxious in this period, and who seemed instead, with their bad examples, to invoke the wrath of God. This was the environment in which Machiavelli launched his bitter condemnation of princes and in which Ochino, Vergerio, and the other Italian reformers mounted their condemnations of the Roman church. . . . Thus together were political and religious protests born."[8]

In contrast to the formulation of Cantimori (whose interests led him to emphasize the most original dimensions of Italian reform thought), Chabod's analysis underscored the affinities that existed between the various reform movements in Italy and those north of the Alps. To be sure, he was conscious of certain radical and Anabaptist tendencies among the heretics he studied, but his emphasis fell primarily on those who had been influenced by Luther and by Calvin. This was especially apparent in his discussion of reform movements in the easternmost parts of the duchy, at Cremona and Casalmaggiore. In Cremona, Chabod uncovered a large and well-organized community that adhered to the reform—a community he described as *nettamente calvinista* (clearly Calvinist).[9] Thus like Cantimori's, Chabod's work represents a watershed in the study of the reform movements in sixteenth-century Italy. For unlike the earlier focus of scholars such as Benrath, Chabod's interest never led him to mourn the failure of the reform. More decisively, his analysis made it clear that context—the social experience but especially the political environment—was decisive in the development of reform ideas in Italy.[10]

The studies of Cantimori and Chabod have animated much of the very best research into the history of the Italian reform movements. Scholars following Cantimori's lead continue to uncover evidence of radicalism (antitrinitarianism; anabaptism; spiritualism), while those following Chabod draw attention to the widespread diffusion (both geographical and social) of reform ideas—often moderate, philo-Protestant ideas—in sixteenth-century Italy.[11] Indeed, the current re-

8. Ibid., 302.

9. Ibid., 360; on Casalmaggiore, see 337–349; on Cremona, 357–361.

10. Chabod emphasized the political context and discussed the social environment, but in a profoundly non-Marxian sense. He rejected any correlation of class and religious experience; see "Per la storia religiosa dello Stato di Milano," 345, where he writes: "vano sarebbe il voler istituire correlazioni—inesistenti—fra desiderio di rinnovamento religioso e determinate situazioni economico-sociali, il voler ricercare, allo slancio verso una diversa fede, una 'sottostruttura' di classe."

11. Though I cannot list here all those scholars who followed either Cantimori's or Chabod's lead, for several examples of works in Cantimori's tradition, see Antonio Ro-

searchers on the Italian Reformation often point to the presence of reform ideas among the *popolo*, especially merchants and artisans.[12] The
view, widespread only a generation ago, that reform ideas in Italy were
confined to the aristocratic circles of the Italian courts no longer
holds.[13] Still no one has attempted to analyze the relative participation
of different social groups in the various reform movements of the age.
Moreover, given the now rather long-term coexistence of the research
traditions initiated by Cantimori and Chabod, surprisingly little has
been done to bring them together—to see, that is, the interplay of
religious ideas with social and political experience. Accordingly, in this
book I seek—through an exploration of the reform movements in Venice—to offer a new characterization of the heresies of sixteenth-century
Italy. I do so, above all, by trying to understand the various currents
of reform ideas in the city and their relation to one another. This "intellectual" history is never divorced from its social and political contexts. The approach of this book, therefore, is methodologically inclusive, perhaps even eclectic. It is my conviction that a balanced picture
of the history of heresy in early modern Venice must take as many ideas
and as many social groups as possible into account.

tondò, *Studi e ricerche di storia ereticale italiana del Cinquecento* (Turin: Giappichelli, 1974);
Aldo Stella, *Dall'anabattismo al socinianesimo nel Cinquecento veneto: Ricerche storiche* (Padua:
Liviana, 1967); and Carlo Ginzburg, *Il nicodemismo: Simulazione e dissimulazione religiosa
nell'Europa del '500* (Turin: Einaudi, 1970). For examples of scholarship that continued
Chabod's lead, see especially Salvatore Caponetto, "Origini e caratteri della Riforma in
Sicilia," *Rinascimento* 7 (1956): 219–341; and Domenico Maselli, "Per la storia religiosa
dello Stato di Milano durante il dominio di Filippo II: L'eresia e la sua repressione dal
1555 al 1584," *Nuova rivista storica* 54 (1970): 317–373. It is important not to exaggerate
the differences between these two scholars. Chabod cites several of Cantimori's articles
approvingly, and Cantimori incorporates Chabod's findings into his research.
    12. On Lucca, see Marino Berengo, *Nobili e mercanti nella Lucca del Cinquecento* (Turin:
Einaudi, 1965), chap. 6; and Simonetta Adorni Braccesi, "La repubblica di Lucca fra
Spagna ed Impero: Il mercanteggiamento della libertà (1557–1558)," *Nuova rivista storica*
67 (1983): 345–366; as well as the other articles by Adorni Braccesi cited in the essay on
sources and bibliography. On Modena (where the passage from the Accademia to the
community of *fratelli* offers an exemplary case of the diffusion of evangelical teachings
among shopkeepers and artisans), see Susanna Peyronel Rambaldi, *Speranze e crisi nel
Cinquecento modenese: Tensioni religiose e vita cittadina ai tempi di Giovanni Morone* (Milan:
Franco Angeli, 1979); and Cesare Bianco, "La communità di 'fratelli' nel movimento
ereticale modenese del '500," *Rivista storica italiana* 92 (1980): 621–679. On Siena, see
Valerio Marchetti, *Gruppi ereticali senesi del Cinquecento* (Florence: La Nuova Italia, 1975);
on Bologna, Antonio Rotondò, "Per la storia dell'eresia a Bologna nel secolo XVI," *Rinascimento* 13 (1962): 107–154; and on Cremona, again Chabod, "Per la storia religiosa
dello Stato di Milano," 357–361.
    13. For the older view, see especially Eva-Maria Jung, "On the Nature of Evangelism
in Sixteenth-Century Italy," *Journal of the History of Ideas* 14 (1953): 511–527.

Given these goals, it makes little sense for me to begin my research with a specialized interpretation of *eretici*. Cantimori's definition in particular is much too restrictive. I therefore begin with a decidedly conventional use of the term. When I refer to *heretics* in a general sense, I mean first and foremost those individuals whose ideals for the reform of church and society placed them at odds with the interests of both the Roman curia and the Venetian state. Admittedly, at times these individuals made no conscious effort to break, even in matters of detail, with the teachings of Rome or with arrangements in Venice. As long as no clear line was drawn between dissent and orthodoxy—roughly down to the year 1550—such figures were not uncommon. If they were defined as heretics, it was not so much because they saw themselves as dissidents but rather because (as I try to show in the first two chapters of this book) the interest of both the papal curia in Rome and the ruling elite in Venice had narrowed the options for acceptable approaches to reform.

But both the political and religious climate as well as the meaning of the term heresy changed markedly after the middle of the sixteenth century. For after 1550 or so, those men and women who participated in the reform movement were increasingly conscious that their ideals diverged from the dominant values of their society. Heresy became (as the etymology of the word suggests) a matter of choice. To be sure, some reformers were extremely moderate in their views; but others were uncompromisingly radical. In this perspective Cantimori's *eretici*, as we shall see, constituted only one group among many.

But how do we determine the nature of the beliefs held by those involved in the various heretical currents of the time? Certainly, the reformers themselves offer little assistance. They established no permanent institutions and left few records. At the very most, they belonged to underground conventicles; more often than not they were merely occasional participants in more informal and therefore more elusive gatherings. The reformers lamented their inability to organize. As early as 1540 one sympathetic observer wrote that "the Christians of Italy"—and by "Christians" he meant those who rejected the Roman church—"are like dead, dispersed limbs without a head, without direction, for the Italian churches are neither congregated nor regulated according to the Word of God." In one of his Venetian sermons Bernardino Ochino, among the greatest of the Italian reformers, drew the attention of his listeners to the *gran confusione* of his time. "Almost everyone," he asserted, "has his own set of beliefs. Articles, sects, heresies, faiths, and religions have so multiplied that everyone wishes to treat faith after his own manner. Similarly, insofar as works are concerned, everything is up in the air, with so many precepts, decrees, decretals, sanctions, rules, statutes, human traditions, rites, ceremonies, and ways of living, that we risk losing our heads." In 1542 another reformer—a layman by the name of Baldassare Altieri, who was active in dissenting circles in Venice—in a letter to Martin Luther reiterated Ochino's concern. "We do not have public churches," he lamented, "everyone is a church unto himself, according to his own individual whim and will. . . . There are many apostles, but no one is properly sent. Everything is done here without order, without decorum."[14] And in 1570 Alessandro Trissino—a Vicentine nobleman who lived in Venice from 1558 to 1561 and who, after his trial for heresy in 1563, fled to Chiavenna where he eventually became pastor—echoed these views. "But observe, most dear brothers, that by remaining outside of God's church, you are still deprived of the Word of God . . . See how many Anabaptists, how many Arians, how many Servetans, Libertines, and other heretics there are among you."[15]

But by far the most significant difficulty in the analysis of the heresies of the sixteenth century derives from the character of the most extensive sources at the disposal of the historian: the archives of the Inquisition. How can historians use an archive of repression to reconstruct the history of dissent? Is not such an archive by its very nature so distortive that we cannot trust it at all? Or, to ask the same question in its most extreme form, does heresy exist outside the act that suppresses it?[16]

Certainly hazards are involved in the use of inquisitorial documents to analyze the beliefs of those the Holy Office was designed either to

14. The sympathetic observer was Giulio da Milano, and the passage is from his *Esortazione al martirio*, cited in Comba, *I nostri Protestanti* 2:174; the quotation by Bernardino Ochino is from his sermon, "Del modo di liberarsi dalla confusione di tante fedi, sètte e modi di vivere," in Giuseppe Paladino, ed., *Opuscoli e lettere di riformatori italiani del Cinquecento* (Bari: Laterza, 1913), 1:263; and for Altieri, see Martin Luther, *Werke: Briefwechsel* (Weimar: Hermann Böhlaus, 1947), 10:204–205.

15. "Ragionamento della necessità di ritirarsi a vivere nella Chiesa visibile di Gesù Cristo, lasciando il papesimo, d'Alessandro Trissino a fratelli d'Italia," ed. Achille Olivieri, "Alessandro Trissino e il movimento calvinista vicentino del Cinquecento," *Rivista di storia della Chiesa in Italia* 21 (1967): 100–101.

16. Carlo Ginzburg raised these and other related questions with characteristic cogency in the preface to the Italian edition of *The Cheese and the Worms: The Cosmos of a Sixteenth-Century Miller*, trans. John and Anne Tedeschi (1980; reprint New York: Penguin, 1982), xvii.

reconcile or repress. For one thing, in many trials it seems impossible to retrieve the voice of the heretic at all. The inquisitor leads, and the defendant follows right along, with the hope perhaps that cooperation will result in merciful treatment by the judges. In such cases, we can hardly trust the testimony, the confessions, or the abjurations. Each may have been merely the expression of a frightened and humiliated individual. In a revealing sixteenth-century literary typology, the Paduan humanist Carlo Sigonio even used the term *inquisitio* to describe those dialogues in which one interlocutor (usually representing the author) "in a somewhat roundabout fashion, in the process of interrogating others, makes clear the innermost feelings of his own mind." Tellingly, he recognized the subtle power relations that underlay the unfolding of such exchanges and, drawing on a famous Platonic metaphor, referred to such works also as *obstetrici dialogi* (midwife dialogues) in which "the imprudent man is led from what he had conceded to what he did not wish to concede." [17]

Not all trials conform to this type. Just as the literary dialogue included those (especially the Ciceronian *in utramque partem*) in which conflicting views came to the fore, heresy trials as well exhibit discord. Sigonio's slightly younger contemporary Sperone Speroni made this clear in his *Apologia dei dialoghi* (Apology for his dialogues). Book 1 of the *Apologia* represents Speroni's encounter with the Inquisition in Rome: in 1574 a collection of his youthful dialogues, which he had

17. Carlo Sigonio, *De dialogo liber* (Venice: Apud Iordanum Ziletum, 1562). The use of the term *inquisitio* is introduced on 40v; the citations—"ille interrogandis aliis, aliquanto obscurius intimum animi sui sensum patefacit" and "Quare ratione rogationis imprudens ab eo, quod concessit, ad id, quod non vult concedere, deducendus est"—are from 41r and 45v respectively. My interpretation of this dialogue follows Jon R. Snyder, *Writing the Scene of Speaking: Theories of Dialogue in the Late Italian Renaissance* (Stanford: Stanford University Press, 1989), 39–86, and reflects his translation of the first passage quoted (ibid., 69). But see also Peter Burke, "The Renaissance Dialogue," *Renaissance Studies* 3 (1989): 3; Burke cites the second passage and gives the midwife metaphor. For a general introduction to Sigonio, see William McCuaig, *Carlo Sigonio: The Changing World of the Late Renaissance* (Princeton: Princeton University Press, 1989).

I do not claim that Sigonio had in mind the judicial meaning of *inquisitio*; this term generally denotes a search or inquiry and even in its judicial applications referred primarily to a procedure used by lay and religious tribunals in which "the court itself compiled the case against the suspect." On this procedure, see John H. Langbein, *Prosecuting Crime in the Renaissance* (Cambridge, Mass.: Harvard University Press, 1974), 120–139; and Bruce Lenman and Geoffrey Parker, "The State, the Community and the Criminal Law in Early Modern Europe," in V.A.C. Gatrell, Bruce Lenman, and Geoffrey Parker, eds., *Crime and the Law: The Social History of Crime in Western Europe since 1500* (London: Europa Publications, 1980), 29–30.

published some thirty years earlier, was denounced for various passages now judged scurrilous in the increasingly puritanical climate of the Counter-Reformation. Speroni's work begins, that is, with a judicial *inquisitio*, but it is one that turns Sigonio's characterization on its head. In the *Apologia*, it is Speroni (the defendant) and not the Master of the Sacred Palace (the inquisitor) who has the upper hand. To be sure, the inquisitor has the power, and at first it seems that he might silence the author, but Speroni is able to take control of the interview. He repeatedly insists that the Master of the Sacred Palace hear him out. And by craftily referring to the Avogaria di Comun, a secular court in Venice in which a good defense, even on behalf of the most despicable of criminals, was an expected and honored part of the judicial process, Speroni makes it clear that he expects no less in an inquisitorial setting. "Let those who would interrupt me keep quiet," he writes. He is sharply critical of "those who accuse the innocent without listening to them or giving them a space to defend themselves (*uno spazio per difendersi*)." [18] In the end, the very representation of the interchange between the Master of the Sacred Palace and Speroni (the audience actually took place, but who knows which of the two in fact had the upper hand?) serves to reinforce Speroni's primary purpose—namely, that of demonstrating that disagreement and discord (what Speroni refers to as *il contrasto delle persone*) are "the heart and soul of dialogue." [19] "We must remember dialogue's privilege of having men and women of various conditions and backgrounds," he continues, "speak plausibly of every subject and dispute in their own way." [20] Speroni's substantive arguments therefore offer a theory of dialogue—and significantly even of dialogue developed in the context of an inquisitorial proceeding—that contrasts sharply not only with Sigonio's notion of *inquisitio* but also with his understanding of the art of dialogue in general. In Speroni's mind, dialogue is greatly impoverished if its conflicting views are either suppressed or taken out of context. Sigonio's largely monologic or monophonic view of dialogue gives way to the expansive, inclusive, comic polyphony of Speroni.

Many of the heresy trials held in sixteenth-century Venice were the courtroom equivalent of the type of dialogue that Sigonio described as *inquisitio*. It is not surprising that men and women suddenly confronted

18. *Opere di M. Sperone Speroni degli Alvarotti*, eds. Natal dalle Laste and Marco Forcellini (1740; reprint Rome: Vecchiarelli, 1989), 1:276. My interpretation of Speroni also owes much to Snyder's excellent work (*Writing the Scene of Speaking*, 87–133).

19. Speroni, *Opere*, 1:282.

20. Ibid., 293–294.

with an accusation of heresy resorted to a rich array of popular tropes by which they sought to escape the charges leveled against them. The inquisitors were certainly aware of this practice. One of the most widely read inquisitorial manuals of the period, Francisco Peña's edition of Nicolau Eymeric's *Directorium Inquisitorum*, first published in Rome in 1578, listed a variety of ways "in which heretics seek to hide their errors," from equivocation to the pretense of insanity.[21] And the trials were full of examples of evasion. Many individuals claimed ignorance of why they had been summoned or arrested. They suffered lapses of memory or remembered imperfectly. They told lies. They surmised that an enemy (perhaps a debtor) had denounced them out of spite. They admitted that, yes, they might have said something that could be construed as heretical, but that they hadn't meant it; they were only reporting what they had heard a fellow worker or perhaps even a priest say. Or they confessed to having had certain doubts but denied ever wishing to hold any beliefs that were not those of the Holy Mother Church. But they also frequently complied with the inquisitor and went out of their way—as Sigonio's example of *inquisitio* suggests—to say what they believed the Inquisition wanted to hear.

Yet many other trials, by contrast, rather resemble Speroni's portrayal of dialogue—in which the accused were able to carve out "a space to defend themselves" (much as Speroni does in his representation of his encounter with the Master of the Sacred Palace in Rome).[22] For one thing, though admittedly atypical, there were several trials in which the accused did defend themselves. They talked back to

21. Nicolau Eymeric, *Directorium Inquisitorum . . . cum commentariis Francesci Pegnae . . . in hac postrema editione iterum emendatum et auctum, et multis litteris apostolicis locupletatum* (Venice: Apud Marcum Antonium Zalterium, 1595), 430–431: "De modis decem haereticorum, quibus errores suos obtegere student." On Peña's edition of Eymeric, see Edward M. Peters, "Editing Inquisitors' Manuals in the Sixteenth Century: Francisco Peña and the *Directorium inquisitorum* of Nicholas Eymeric," *The Library Chronicle* 40 (1974): 95–107; and Agostino Borromeo, "A proposito del *Directorium Inquisitorum* di Nicolás Eymerich e delle sue edizioni cinquecentesche," *Critica storica* 20 (1983): 499–547.

22. Carlo Ginzburg emphasized the dialogic character of inquisitorial trials. Drawing on the insights of the Russian literary critic Mikhail Bakhtin, Ginzburg distinguished between two genres of trials: monologic (in which "the defendant's answers were quite often just an echo of the inquisitors' questions") and dialogic ("exceptional cases" in which "we have a real dialogue: we can hear distinct voices, we can detect a clash between different, even conflicting voices"); Ginzburg, *Clues, Myths, and the Historical Method*, trans. John and Anne Tedeschi (Baltimore: Johns Hopkins University Press, 1989), 160. In my view, the contrast between Sigonio's and Speroni's theories of the dialogue allows us to make critical use of a broader range of trials. For further observations on Ginzburg's method, see my "Journeys to the World of the Dead: The Work of Carlo Ginzburg," *Journal of Social History* 25 (1992): 613–626.

the inquisitor. They made their dissenting views heard. Some freely admitted that they held beliefs at odds with those of the Roman church. They argued that it was they and not the inquisitors who were true Christians. They cited Scripture as their authority or recalled a sermon that they had heard. That trials often assumed this quality of debate should not be surprising. The inquisitorial tribunal was subject to a myriad of legal regulations, including the stipulation that each individual was entitled to a defense, that gave certain defendants an opportunity to speak their minds.[23] Moreover, to some of those accused of heresy, the experience must have been less intimidating than we might at first suspect. At times, after all, the defendant and the inquisitor were peers who simply held opposing views about how their shared culture should be expressed within its religious institutions.[24] Additionally, the defendants were able to demonstrate considerable resourcefulness in the context of the trials. Once, in Udine, a town subject to Venetian control, a heretic managed to have his abjuration (originally prepared by the inquisitor) rewritten by a fellow reformer to turn what was meant to be a public apology into an open act of defiance and propaganda.[25] Finally, the trials are not only dialogic; they are polyphonic. The reformers and heretics, we learn, were not only engaged in a struggle against Rome but also in debates, often heated ones, among themselves. And the trials are also filled with the voices of neighbors and shop mates, family members, and parish priests—none of whom was under suspicion of heresy.[26]

For the historian, then, these transcripts open a window onto the world of the heretics in sixteenth-century Venice. But in the exploration of this world, we are by no means limited to the trials alone; indeed, there are ample external sources. Many of those brought to trial, after all, were relatively well known figures. Reformers like the bishop Pier Paolo Vergerio, the priest Bartolomeo Fonzio, the humanist An-

23. John Tedeschi, "The Organization and Procedures of the Roman Inquisition: A Sketch," in *The Prosecution of Heresy: Collected Studies on the Inquisition in Early Modern Italy* (Binghamton: Medieval and Renaissance Texts and Studies, 1991), 135–139.

24. Silvana Seidel Menchi, "Inquisizione come repressione o inquisizione come mediazione? Una proposta di periodizzazione," *Annuario dell'Istituto storico italiano per l'età moderna e contemporanea* 35–36 (1983–1984): 53–77.

25. Andrea del Col, "L'abiura trasformata in propaganda ereticale nel duomo di Udine (15 Aprile 1544)," *Metodi e ricerche: Rivista di studi regionali* 2–3 (1981): 57–72.

26. My argument here is informed by Wayne A. Meeks, "The Polyphonic Ethics of the Apostle Paul," *The Annual of the Society of Christian Ethics* (Washington, D.C.: Georgetown University Press, 1988), 17–29. Meeks deftly draws on Bakhtin's insights into the nature of texts.

tonio Brucioli, the prophet Guillaume Postel, and the poet Alessandro Caravia were not only tried by the Inquisition, they also left writings expressive of their views. Others made their commitments clear by the actions they took. Perhaps the most famous of these was the Venetian patrician Andrea da Ponte, who chose in 1560 or so to leave his native city and live in Calvin's Geneva instead. And many reformers underwent more than one trial; some were brought before the Inquisition as many as three or four times, providing considerable opportunity to compare the testimonies offered on different occasions. Finally, few of those tried were isolated individuals. It is thus possible to trace the contacts that most defendants had with one another, to learn something of the social networks of which they were members, and even at times to stumble into the gathering of a conventicle. Gradually, therefore, it becomes possible to glimpse the contours of the various currents of dissent in the city.

Thus, while it may not be entirely misleading to argue that heresy did not exist outside the act that suppressed it, it is absurd to assume that the reformers had no existence outside the Inquisition. On the contrary, without them the surviving transcripts of inquisitorial proceedings would have none of the rich dialogic or polyphonic texture that in fact they have. Not only is there something outside the text; all texts (whether humanist dialogues, papal edicts, or dusty archival documents such as trial transcripts, wills, and tax records) are at least in part products of social and cultural life.[27]

Accordingly, in this early modern Babel, it has been possible to learn something of the nature of the beliefs held by many of the men and women who were tried by the Inquisition. In my analysis, I discern three currents of reform ideas. The most prominent and the most widely diffused is what students of Italian religious life have come to

27. I do not entirely deny many claims of poststructuralist theorists that texts are the products of linguistic structures, but such arguments—especially Derrida's claim that "il n'y a pas de hors-texte"—result in absurd reductions of all historical experience to text. For a thoughtful response to what she aptly calls the "semiotic challenge," see Gabrielle M. Spiegel, "History, Historicism, and the Social Logic of the Text in the Middle Ages," *Speculum* 65 (1990): 59–86. Bakhtin, however, makes the strongest theoretical case for the presence of social ("metalinguistic") forces in texts. See, for example, his *Problems of Dostoevsky's Poetics*, trans. Caryl Emerson (Minneapolis: University of Minnesota Press, 1984), 184: "logical and semantically referential relationships, in order to become dialogic, must be embodied, that is, they must enter into another sphere of existence: they must become *discourse*, that is, an utterance, and receive an *author*, that is, a creator of the given utterance whose position it expresses."

call *evangelism*. In essence, evangelism shared many of the fundamental tenets of Protestantism, including the doctrine of salvation by faith alone, though Italian evangelicals, naively perhaps, did not always believe it necessary to break with the Roman church in order to hold these beliefs. But as the hopes of the first generation of evangelicals foundered, various breakaway sects, often holding more radical beliefs, formed. In northern Italy, in particular, there were a number of well-organized Anabaptist communities, and Venice was the site of a clandestine Anabaptist synod in 1550. But just as we should not confuse the Italian evangelicals (despite numerous overlaps) with German or Swiss Protestants, so we should not conflate the Italian *anabattisti* with their northern counterparts. There was a rationalistic vein in the teachings of the Italian radicals, and a tendency to deny the divinity of Christ, viewing him as fully human though filled with virtue and worthy of emulation. Finally, there was a strong millenarian current in Italy—one that, rooted in the writings of the twelfth-century Calabrian abbot Joachim of Fiore, was particularly enduring. It was at the close of the fifteenth century, for example, that Girolamo Savonarola actually came to rule Florence by preaching that the millennium was at hand; and both Joachim's and Savonarola's ideas continued, as we shall see, to exercise considerable influence throughout the sixteenth century. In general, though these millenarian ideas tended to lie dormant, they would surface with considerable force at times of crisis and they too did much to give shape to the history of religious dissent in sixteenth-century Venice. While these three currents were often quite distinct, it should nonetheless be noted that they did at times flow into one another. On occasion, a heretic would pass from evangelism to anabaptism, and then subsequently abandon his Anabaptist commitments to embrace millenarian ideas.[28] This is an additional reason why it has proven necessary to avoid an overly restrictive definition of heresy.

But what of the relation of these various currents of dissent to social experience? The trials offer rich information about such factors as the status, the occupation, and the nationality of those accused of heresy. Certainly, the analysis of such factors would help us understand better

---

28. For a celebrated example of such a figure, see the testimony of Benedetto Florio in Domenico Berti, "Di Giovanni Valdes e di taluni suoi discepoli secondo nuovi documenti tolti dall'Archivio Veneto," *Atti della R. Accademia dei Lincei* 275 (1877–78), 3d series, *Memorie della classe di scienze morali, storiche e filologiche*, 2:61–81.

why certain men (and women) chose to dissent from the received religious traditions of their society—to understand, in other words, how tensions in the social, cultural, and political life of Venice acted to predispose many Venetians to listen attentively to the new religious ideas they encountered in diverse places: in church or in the workshop, in the piazza, or in the barber's chair, or even in bed with a spouse or a fellow apprentice. And indeed my findings on the social context of heresy—which I present in chapter 6—suggest certain correlations between social experience and religious beliefs.

It is not, however, my argument that social forces were determining. Many scholars, especially those who define themselves as social historians and who tend to view religion as a collective phenomenon, stress the primacy of social forces. To these scholars, the Reformation was much more than a reflection of the ideals of its intellectual proponents, as more "traditional" students of Luther and Calvin often claim; far more decisive was the fact that early modern Europe was in transition. New religious ideas took hold, they argue, because individuals and groups stood in new relations to one another or because the new ideas responded more directly to new needs. The historian's task, then, is to explore changes in religious ideology in light of transformations in the workplace, say, or in geographic mobility, economic status, and family life, and then to try to explain the predisposition of certain types of municipalities or the receptivity of certain social groups to popular Reformation theology. The writings of Marx and Durkheim especially provide these scholars (though often by an indirect route) with their theoretical underpinnings. And while Marxist historians are more likely to portray religion as an ideology—as a set of illusory beliefs that either mask or express social relations—and the followers of Durkheim are more likely to stress the functional dimensions of religious constructions and the way in which they reinforce social solidarities, both agree that social change defined the religious conflicts and underlay the religious revolutions of the sixteenth century.[29]

29. Classical Marxist accounts of the Reformation may be found in Frederick Engels, *The Peasant War in Germany*, trans. Moissaye J. Olgin (New York: International Publishers, 1926); and Karl Kautsky, *Communism in Central Europe in the Time of the Reformation*, trans. J.L. and E.K. Mulliken (London: Unwin, 1897). For more recent examples of Marxist approaches to the Reformation, see Rainer Wohlfeil, *Reformation oder frühbürgerliche Revolution*, 5 (Munich: Nymphenburger Verlagshandlung, 1972); and Thomas A. Brady, Jr., *Ruling Class, Regime and Reformation at Strasbourg, 1520–1555* (Leiden: Brill, 1978). An especially influential Durkheimian approach informs the essay by Lucien Febvre, "The Origins of the French Reformation: A Badly Put Question," in *A New Kind*

Although I share many of the presuppositions of these scholars, I try to avoid some of the reductions implicit in their approach by giving religion somewhat greater autonomy. It is in the irreducibility of culture to society, after all, that the possibility for change and for cultural criticism has always been located. Our search therefore should be less for a "fit" than for a dialectic, for those tensions that can render religion not only a reflection of the social order but also a critical vantage point from which to view and ultimately change it. Clearly this emphasis applies in a study of dissent or heresy, since, by definition, heretics were out of step with at least the broader values of their society. Moreover, as anthropologists have taught us, religion, conceived as a "cultural system," is not only a reflection of society but also a model for society, a way of ordering the mundane as well as the religious life.[30] And this is especially true in periods of intense religious debate such as occurred in the Reformation, when men and women argued so heatedly about the role of works in the economy of salvation. For whether those involved in the debate were conscious of it or not, the conclusions they reached were to be heavily consequential for the various types of societies and, indeed, the political and economic systems that eventually came to characterize early modern Europe.

This point is essential. In our world we are more likely to separate religious and social issues. Indeed, many historically informed social theorists argue that this compartmentalization of experience is a fundamental attribute of modernity (of late nineteenth- and twentieth-century western culture). But in the Italian cities of the Renaissance, there was no such compartmentalization, and religion was manifestly a public and civic affair. To be sure, the Renaissance was, in a certain sense, an age of secularization. A mercantile elite formed the public of a learned lay culture, and urban governments exercised considerable control over religious institutions. But secularization in these spheres by no means entailed a decline in spiritual feeling or the restriction of religious ideas and rituals to the sphere of private life. On the contrary: in the Italian republics of the Renaissance religion ceased to be, as it had been in the Middle Ages, the preserve of specialists. It left the

---

*of History: From the Writings of Lucien Febvre*, ed. Peter Burke and trans. K. Folca (New York: Harper and Row, 1973); the 1927 essay provides this chapter's epigraph (86).

30. Clifford Geertz, "Religion as a Cultural System," in *The Interpretation of Cultures* (New York: Basic Books, 1973), 87–125.

monastery and entered the public and civic arena. The process began as early as the eleventh and twelfth centuries with the rebirth in Italy of urban life. In these young cities the very first popular lay religious movements in European history took place. Some were entirely orthodox; others, because they challenged the received order of things, became or came to be labeled heretical. But there can be no question that the rebirth of the city occasioned a fundamental transformation in the history of Christianity. Indeed, the Reformation itself can be seen, at least on one level, as a consequence of this quickening of urban life in the late Renaissance and the broadly felt need of early modern Christians to find ways to sacralize their new occupations and their new, increasingly complex communities.

Less ascetic than its medieval antecedents, the spirituality of the Renaissance focused on the problems of urban life: on issues of poor relief, for example, or on public health and public morality. It had become a "civic" Christianity.[31] Its proponents were both clerical and lay—artisans, merchants, and members of the professions—who found in their guilds and in their confraternities or spiritual brotherhoods a means of participating directly in the religious life. Each guild, each confraternity, and each parish had its patron saint or saints, its special festivals and religious holidays. This elasticity within the fabric of the religious life appealed to merchants and artisans. They were able to fashion their sense of identity as neighbors or as members of a common trade or brotherhood and derive thereby a sense of belonging to a special group that made the relative anonymity of the city more endurable. Thus, citizens found a myriad of ways to express their piety. As members of guilds and confraternities, they sponsored processions and built hospitals; they participated in devotions and listened to preachers invited to address their membership; and they were the guardians of valued relics and the patrons of religious art. To be called "religious"

---

31. For the concept of a "civic" Christianity, I am most indebted to David Herlihy, *Medieval and Renaissance Pistoia: The Social History of an Italian Town, 1200–1430* (New Haven: Yale University Press, 1967), chap. 10. These introductory remarks on the religious life of the Renaissance city have been shaped by the works of more scholars than I can mention here, but see esp. Lester K. Little, *Religious Poverty and the Profit Economy in Medieval Europe* (Ithaca: Cornell University Press, 1978); Brian Pullan, *Rich and Poor in Renaissance Venice: The Social Institutions of a Catholic State, to 1620* (Cambridge, Mass.: Harvard University Press, 1971); Richard Trexler, "Florentine Religious Experience: The Sacred Image," *Studies in the Renaissance* 19 (1972): 7–41; and John Bossy, *Christianity in the West, 1400–1700* (Oxford: Oxford University Press, 1985).

no longer meant, as it had in the Middle Ages, that one was a member of the clergy or a monastic order—for now, religion could be an attribute of the lay population as well.[32]

Given this intense public and popular quality of religion, the Italian states of the Renaissance found it necessary to grapple constantly with religious issues. On one level, the religious life of the Renaissance city was, we see, markedly particularistic. And this particularism could threaten the peace and unity of the city as a whole. Magistrates and religious leaders alike were compelled to find ways to channel the religious sentiments of their citizens and subjects into manifestations of loyalty. They took care to organize processions and festivities that involved as many guilds and confraternities as possible in citywide celebrations. The relations between the state and the miniature republics of the guilds or parishes were never perfect. There were conflicts between corporations and constant danger of charismatic religious expressions that, in moments of acute social tension and special spiritual fervor, threatened to break outside the safer institutional framework of religious life. For instance, political revolts in the Renaissance almost always had religious legitimation. The leaders of the Ciompi revolution in fourteenth-century Florence flirted openly with the radical Franciscans known as the Fraticelli. And in 1494 when Savonarola, the Dominican friar and prophet, took political control of the city, he did so by fostering and pandering to popular millenarianism. Thus we might best imagine the Renaissance city not, following the suggestion of the great nineteenth-century Swiss historian Jacob Burckhardt, as a secular stage but rather as a theater of virtually uninterrupted religious drama. Its backdrop was formed by the churches and monasteries whose towers dominated the urban skyline. Space was defined largely by the diffusion of the sacred (relics in holy places) and time was punctuated by the daily and yearly rhythms of religious observances. And it was a stage animated not only by itinerant preachers, mendicants, flagellants, and penitents, but also by the lay population whose access to the sacred was assured in a variety of ways.

This civic and public quality of Renaissance Christianity, therefore, makes it necessary to see religion as a dynamic and shaping force and not merely as a reflection of social life in early modern Europe. It was not possible to attack the cult of saints, for example, without also at-

---

32. Charles Trinkaus, *In Our Image and Likeness: Humanity and Divinity in Italian Humanist Thought* (Chicago: University of Chicago Press, 1970), 2:674–682.

tacking the most potent symbol at the center of guild and confraternal life, nor was it possible to attack any of the sacraments without also calling the authority of priests as key members of the moral hierarchy into question. And, while this had been true throughout the Renaissance, it became especially apparent in the sixteenth century as the urban Christian culture of the fourteenth and fifteenth centuries began to undergo certain severe strains in response to social and political crises alike. The collapse of republican institutions or at least, as in the case of Venice, their profound modification made rulers suspicious of those institutions such as the guild, the confraternity, and even the parish that had made the sacred so familiar to the laity of the city. In a political climate preoccupied with centralizing authority in the hands of the few—whether a family as in Florence or the members of the papal curia as in Rome or a restricted oligarchy as in Venice—both secular and religious rulers found it expedient to discourage all signs of particularism. Cults that expressed the interest of a particular group or that seemed to give the laity excessive authority in religious matters were suppressed, while cults that served the interests of the ruling groups were encouraged. The sacred, once such a familiar attribute of a merchant's or an artisan's life, became something rather distant, something that fell under the protection of priests and specialists. The reform movements of sixteenth-century Italy, therefore, were not only a response to political and social change, they were also a response to genuinely religious tensions as well.

The history of the Inquisition must be approached with a similar sense of the dialectic between cultural and social history. For while the perceived threat of Protestantism to Italy was the most manifest motivation of those Italian prelates who pushed so hard for the restoration and refurbishing of the Inquisition in the 1540s, the tribunal of the Roman Inquisition that was reorganized in Venice in 1547 also had its roots in the variable social and political ground of Italian life. The tribunal, as we shall see, was able to establish itself as a viable institution because it gave ordinary men and women institutional means of resolving religious conflicts with neighbors, fellow workers, and even spouses in a society where more traditional means of social control appear to have broken down. The consequences of social change in Renaissance Venice, therefore, were contrapuntal, with the tensions that stemmed from the social and economic changes of the sixteenth century encouraging dissent and repression alike.

Finally, the story of the Venetian heretics should contribute not only to our knowledge of Renaissance Venice but also to our understanding of the relation of social to cultural life. While I share the view of many contemporary scholars that we might best dispense with those metaphors—such as the allegedly Marxist image of the ideological as "superstructural"—that seemingly always give priority to social and economic life, I consider those more fashionable approaches that refuse to accept the importance of a world beyond language to be equally distortive. In sixteenth-century Venice, at least, both social and cultural factors were at work in the shaping of a tradition of religious dissent. Perhaps then the historian's best hope to understand the past is to keep both aspects of experience—the cultural and the social—in balance. To be sure, there may be times when the scales tip rather more to one side than the other. Nonetheless, the art of history, it would seem, lies in the effort to capture something of the constant interplay between worlds imagined and worlds inhabited—to focus, that is, on those fascinating and often elusive dimensions of human experience that are shaped both by words and by those no less palpable realities of economic, social, and political life.

## CHAPTER ONE

# A Republic Between Renaissance and Reform

*Every religion has some political opinion linked to it by affinity.*
Alexis de Tocqueville,
*Democracy in America*

In 1545 Pope Paul III warned the Venetian ambassador to Rome that Lutheranism was epidemic. Not only had this disease, the pope continued, already infected "persons of every order" in the Venetian republic itself but it risked contaminating other Italian states as well. Indeed, many of the pope's contemporaries assigned to Venice a special place on the religious map of sixteenth-century Italy. As the capital city of a republic whose borders stretched for several hundred kilometers along Germanic lands and as a mercantile city with ports open to traders from all over the world and a population of well over one hundred thousand, Venice was doubly exposed to the influence of the ideas concerning religious reform that were so prevalent in that century of upheaval. Moreover, as the center of one of the largest publishing industries in Europe and as a neighbor to Padua, where many German Protestants were enrolled in the university, Venice seemed not only exposed but even receptive—possibly more so than any other city on the peninsula—to Reformation ideas.[1] Thus, while the pope and others like him feared that Venice would become the source for heresy in Italy, such leading Italian reformers as Bernardino Ochino, exiled in Geneva, could look to Venice with optimism, and pray that it would become the source for reform. "Already Christ has begun to penetrate in Italy," he wrote in a letter in 1542, "but I would like Him to enter in glory and openly, and I believe Ven-

1. On the pope's warning to the Venetian ambassador to Rome, see Fulvio Tomizza, *Il male viene dal nord: Il romanzo del vescovo Vergerio* (Milan: A. Mondadori, 1984), 237; see B. Fontana, ed., "Documenti vaticani contro l'eresia luterana in Italia," *Archivio della società romana di storia patria* 15 (1892): 398–400, for further evidence of the pope's concern over heresy in the Venetian republic. On Venice's setting and mercantile character, see Frederic Lane, *Venice: A Maritime Republic* (Baltimore: Johns Hopkins University Press, 1973). On the city's population, Karl Julius Beloch (*Bevölkerungsgeschichte Italiens* [Berlin: W. de Gruyter, 1937–1961], 3:17) and Daniele Beltrami (*Storia della popolazione di Venezia dalla fine del secolo XVI, alla caduta della Repubblica* [Padua: CEDAM, 1954], 59) agree that the number of inhabitants in 1509 was over 100,000 (Beloch: *etwa* 105,000; Beltrami: 115,000) and place the population at 168,627 in 1563; the total probably reached 175,000 before the plague of 1575–77. On Venetian printing, see Horatio Brown, *The Venetian Printing Press, 1469–1800* (New York: G. P. Putnam's Sons, 1891); and on its significance within the European book economy, Lucien Febvre and Henri-Jean Martin, *The Coming of the Book: The Impact of Printing, 1450–1800*, trans. David Gerard (London: NLB, 1976).

---

*Opposite.* Venice, its mainland dominions, and its neighbors, around 1550. Despite the Alps, several major trade routes linked Venice by land to the center of Europe; the most famous was the Brenner Pass from Verona through Trent to Augsburg. Each city shown within the Venetian republic was a center of heretical activity.

ice will be the door."[2] And in Germany, reformers in the circle around Philip Melanchthon, Luther's closest associate, also recognized the special position of the city. "As your city is the only one in the world which enjoys a genuine aristocracy, preserved during many ages and always hostile to tyranny," they wrote in a 1538 letter to the Venetian Senate, "it becomes it to protect good men in freedom of thinking, and to discourage that unjust cruelty which is exercised in other places. Wherefore, I cannot refrain from exhorting you to employ your care and authority for advancing the divine glory, a service which is most acceptable to God."[3]

Indeed, as early as 1520 the ideas of no less a reformer than Martin Luther had made themselves felt in Venice. In the spring of that year, several copies of one of his treatises were discovered in a bookshop in the parish of San Maurizio. Some months later, when the friar Andrea da Ferrara preached to a large crowd congregated in San Stefano Square and openly attacked the pope and his court, many believed him a follower of Luther.[4] The presence in Venice of the Fondaco dei Tedeschi, a permanent colony of German merchants, many of them self-acknowledged Lutherans, made the importation of religious ideas into the city relatively easy.[5] By the late 1520s such heresies appear to have found a popular audience. Ruzante, the Paduan playwright whose comedies were the rage of patrician circles in both Venice and Padua in these years, made this clear in a pun, characterizing Luther as a luteplayer, a *laútuolo*, whose tune many followed. There were those,

2. Paolo Piccolomini, ed., "Due lettere inedite di Bernardino Ochino," *Archivio della società romana di storia patria* 28 (1905): 207.

3. Cited in M'Crie, *History of the Progress and Suppression of the Reformation in Italy*, 66. This letter, though not by Melanchthon himself, came from circles close to him; see Cantimori, *Eretici italiani del Cinquecento*, 36.

4. These events are reported by Marino Sanuto, *I diarii*, ed. Rinaldo Fulin et al. (Venice: F. Visentini, 1879–1903), vol. 29, cols. 135 and 492. On Sanuto's interest in Luther, see the selections from his diaries published as Marino Sanuto, *Martin Luther und die Reformationsbewegung in Deutschland vom Jahre 1520–1532 in Auszügen aus Marino Sanutos Diarien* (Ansbach: C. Brugel, 1883).

5. Henry Simonsfeld, *Der Fondaco dei Tedeschi in Venedig und die deutsch-venetianischen Handelsbeziehungen*, 2 vols. (Stuttgart: Scientia Verlag Aalen, 1887). On the Lutheranism of the Germans at the Fondaco, see the remarks of the papal nuncio Alberto Bolognetti, "Dello stato et forma delle cose ecclesiastiche nel dominio dei signori venetiani, secondo che furono trovate et lasciate dal nunzio Alberto Bolognetti," in Aldo Stella, ed., *Chiesa e stato nelle relazioni dei nunzi pontifici a Venezia* (Vatican City: Biblioteca Apostolica Vaticana, 1964), 279; and Theodor Elze, *Geschichte der protestantischen Bewegungen und der deutschen evangelischen Gemeinde . . . in Venedig*, rev. ed. by Eugen Lessing (Florence: B. Coppini, 1941).

he noted, "who do not wish to go to confession anymore, who no longer keep vigils, who never go to church, and who give heed to no other images but those on their [tarot and playing] cards."[6] At about the same time Luther himself, on hearing of the responsiveness of the Venetians to his teachings wrote in a letter to his friend Gabriel Zwilling that it gave him great joy to learn "of the Venetians receiving the Word of God."[7] And in the early 1530s several Venetian artisans and shopkeepers began to assert publicly a variety of heretical ideas. A certain Antonio, a master carpenter, was especially outspoken, buttonholing fellow craftsmen and brazenly mocking the piety of his elders. He and his followers—among them a tutor, a tailor, a notary, a poulterer, an egg vendor, a knife grinder, an instrument maker, a weaver, a number of silk merchants, and a friar—would frequent the sermons at the Dominican church of San Zanipolo and at the parish church of Santa Ternità, and they eagerly drank in the emphasis which the preachers there placed on the teachings of Saint Paul. They came to deny the cult of saints, the saying of rosaries and Ave Marias, the use of votive offerings, and the miracles of Our Lady of Loreto, whose shrine on the Adriatic coast, just south of Ancona, was an especially popular pilgrimage center in the late Renaissance. Antonio and his followers placed their faith not in works but in God's mercy.[8]

Luther then did exert a significant influence on the development of heresy in Venice. Even the word *luterano* would come to be the most popular designation for heretic.[9] Years later the Tuscan Pietro Carnesecchi, a famous heretic, would recall that he had once been in the habit of calling Luther "the ocean," since, in his view, the German reformer

6. Angelo Beolco, called Ruzante, "Seconda Oratione," in Ludovico Zorzi, ed., *Ruzante: Teatro* (Turin: Einaudi, 1967), 1211. On the place of Ruzante's theater in Venetian culture, see Linda Carroll, "Carnival Rites as Vehicles of Protest in Renaissance Venice," *Sixteenth-Century Journal* 16 (1985): 487–502.

7. Cited in Karl Benrath, *Geschichte der Reformation in Venedig*, 4.

8. Franco Gaeta edits and introduces the trial of the carpenter Antonio in "Documenti da codici vaticani per la storia della Riforma in Venezia," *Annuario dell'Istituto storico italiano per l'età moderna e contemporanea* 7 (1955): 5–53.

9. Elisabeth Gleason's remarks are useful: "After Luther's death Italian writers usually referred to him as the father of later heresies, until eventually any form of religious dissent came to be called Lutheranism. For instance, the word 'Protestant' is not used in the register of men and women brought before the Venetian Inquisition between 1541 and 1600; suspicious people were called 'Lutherani.' Even Calvin is spoken of as a 'Lutheranus haeresiarcha' in a tract as late as 1559. For the Church of the Counter-Reformation there was only one meaning attached to the name of Luther—it was the symbol of religious rebellion" ("Sixteenth-Century Italian Interpretations of Luther," *Archiv für Reformationsgeschichte* 60 [1969]: 167).

had been the source of all other heresies, of "the Zwinglians, the Calvinists, the Anabaptists, and so on."[10] Nevertheless we must be cautious about attributions made in an age that thought of heresy as a contagious disease, the cause of which could be isolated.[11] For not only were the Italian heresies far too diverse to be in any direct sense produced by Luther's teachings, they also expressed quite specific political, social, and cultural developments in Italy itself.

Certainly one key factor in the development of heresy in Venice was its openness. Indeed, this city was as open and as cosmopolitan as any other city in either the Mediterranean or European world. As a commercial center, the city teemed with merchants from other lands, with pilgrims and travelers, and various immigrant communities, among which the most conspicuous were the German, Jewish, Greek, and Turkish colonies.[12] In Venice, therefore, religious diversity was something of a given, and the republic's commitment to commerce rendered most Venetians relatively tolerant. And, as always, tolerance bred tolerance. Outsiders were living reminders of the actual existence of alternate religious arrangements; they became part of the mental horizon of many Venetians, heretics and orthodox alike. They brought news and told stories about the differences between lands subject to Catholic and those subject to Protestant or non-Christian rule. Widely diffused in Venice at this time, for instance, was the legend of the three rings— a story that held there was no way of discerning which of the three great Mediterranean religions (Judaism, Christianity, or Islam) was the true faith.[13] And it was largely this gift for tolerance in Venetian culture that would attract the French conciliarist Guillaume Postel to the city in the 1540s and that would lead Jean Bodin to select Venice as the setting for his *Colloquium of the Seven about Secrets of the Sublime*, a dia-

---

10. Giacomo Manzoni, ed., "Estratto del processo di Pietro Carnesecchi," *Miscellanea di storia italiana* (Turin: Fratelli Bocca, 1870), 10:326.

11. On sixteenth-century perceptions of heresy as an infectious disease, see Berengo, *Nobili e mercanti nella Lucca del Cinquecento*, 399–400.

12. On the Jews in Venice, see Cecil Roth, *History of the Jews in Venice* (New York: Schocken Books, 1975); and Brian Pullan, *The Jews of Europe and the Inquisition of Venice, 1550–1670* (Totowa, N.J.: Barnes and Noble, 1983); on the Greeks, Giorgio Fedalto, *Ricerche storiche sulla posizione giuridica ed ecclesiastica dei Greci a Venezia nei secoli XV e XVI* (Florence: Olschki, 1967); and on the Turks, Agostino Sagredo and Federico Berchet, *Il Fondaco dei Turchi in Venezia* (Milan: G. Civelli, 1860).

13. On this legend, see Archivio di Stato, Venice (hereafter ASV), *Sant'Uffizio*, busta (hereafter b.) 46, dossier (hereafter doss.) "Contra Antonium Aurificem," denunciation of 18 October 1580; and Ginzburg, *The Cheese and the Worms*, 49–51.

logue that examined not only the major religions but also the major opinions about religion held in sixteenth-century Europe. Catholicism, Lutheranism, Calvinism, Judaism, and Islam, as well as skepticism and natural religion are each represented. And Venice was the ideal place for such a dialogue, Bodin told his readers in an important variant of the myth of Venice,

not only because the Venetians delight in receiving strangers hospitably, but also because one can live there with the greatest freedom. . . . This is the reason why people come here from everywhere, wishing to spend their lives in the greatest freedom and tranquillity of spirit, whether they are interested in commerce or crafts or leisure pursuits as befit free men.[14]

Ultimately, however, it was in the larger context of the political crises of the first half of the sixteenth century that Venice's special place on the religious landscape of Italy was defined. For Venice, it turns out, would emerge virtually unscathed from the upheavals of that century. As a consequence, this city was to become a haven for many Italians who dreamt not only of preserving certain republican traditions, values, and institutions but of bringing about religious reform as well.

When Italians of the first half of the sixteenth century sought to explain the origins of the turmoil that characterized their tragic era, it was the invasion of Italy by the young French king Charles VIII that stood out as the source of their continuing social and political miseries. Nearly a millennium had passed since the peoples of Italy had faced such a redoubtable foreign force. Then in the fall of 1494 Charles, like a new Hannibal, crossed the Alps with thirty thousand well disciplined troops and forty impressive cannon. Before his march, virtually all Italy from Milan to Naples submitted. Even in his retreat the following year, Charles was able to claim victory in a battle on the outskirts of Parma, at Fornovo. Many Italians could recall omens that seemed, in retrospect, to warn them of the catastrophes they were about to confront. In Puglia men had observed three suns in the skies above them;

14. Bodin, *Colloquium of the Seven about Secrets of the Sublime*, 3. On the importance of Bodin and Postel in the history of religious toleration, see Quentin Skinner, *The Foundations of Modern Political Thought*, vol. 2: *The Age of the Reformation* (Cambridge: Cambridge University Press, 1978), 244–249. For Postel's relation to Venice, see William James Bouwsma, *Concordia Mundi: The Career and Thought of Guillaume Postel (1510–1581)* (Cambridge, Mass.: Harvard University Press, 1957); and Marion L. Kuntz, *Guillaume Postel, Prophet of the Restitution of All Things* (The Hague: Martinus Nijhoff, 1981).

in Tuscany armed horsemen had swished or clamored through the air; and throughout Italy the birth of monsters both human and nonhuman had been widely noted.[15]

The French invasion ushered in a new era in Italian history, one in which foreign powers, above all France and Spain, would come to dominate the internal politics of most Italian states. For the myriad of independent duchies and city states that checkered the peninsula were no match for the new monarchies of the early modern world. But the most dramatic shift was the defeat of republicanism, especially in Florence, where the Florentine republic, renewed first by Savonarola in 1494 and then heroically in 1527, finally collapsed in 1530, while throughout the peninsula more oligarchic and monarchical regimes emerged. Great states such as the Kingdom of Naples and the Duchy of Milan were reduced to virtual pawns in the power struggle between the Valois kings of France and the Spanish Hapsburgs. In 1527 the sack of Rome by imperial troops dealt a stunning blow to Italian self-confidence.

These same decades saw a change in social attitudes and values. The ideals of civic humanism, of the *vivere civile*—the active engagement in political life that earlier Renaissance humanists, drawing on classical authors such as Aristotle and Cicero, had articulated—gave way to an increasingly aristocratic conception of politics and society. The cultivation of the ideal of citizenship and, with it, the corollary notion that an individual's merit derived from virtue and not from birth, had been especially fitting in the Italian city republics (dominated by merchants and bankers) of the fourteenth and fifteenth centuries. But the sixteenth century was to become the age of the courtier. The eclipse of republicanism simultaneously elevated individual families to positions of dominance in many Italian states and reduced others to the role of supplicants and clients, seeking favors and prestige from the princes around whom they orbited—from the Medici of Florence (who finally set themselves up as the dukes of Tuscany in the 1530s) or from the Sforza of Milan, the Estensi of Ferrara, the Gonzaga of Mantua, or the pope

---

15. For a detailed overview of the crisis of the early sixteenth century, see Francesco Guicciardini, *Storia d'Italia* (1561), ed. Silvana Seidel Menchi, 3 vols. (Turin: Einaudi, 1971); Guicciardini discusses the apparitions and the monsters in 1:74 (Sidney Alexander's splendid English abridgement, *The History of Italy* [Princeton: Princeton University Press, 1984], refers to the apparitions and monsters on 44). Guicciardini remains the best introduction to the political history of this period, but for a recent overview see Lauro Martines, *Power and Imagination: City-States in Renaissance Italy* (New York: Knopf, 1979), 277–337.

himself whose court, crowded as it was with a myriad of cardinals, was the most sumptuous in Europe. In this world, politics was radically circumscribed, and the offering of counsel to one's prince—as Baldassare Castiglione made plain in his *Book of the Courtier*, first published in Venice in 1528—was the sole political privilege remaining to most members of the Italian upper classes. It was a privilege gained, moreover, only through the rigorous cultivation of certain social graces and the strict observance of the rules and genteel rituals of the court.[16]

To be sure, changes in both society and the economy played an important role in the creation of this increasingly aristocratic conception of life. The shift to despotism had been under way for some time. Already in the fifteenth century the economic elites of the Italian cities had begun to invest more heavily in land, with the result that by the sixteenth century they constituted a rentier class of petty gentry and great *signori*. In many places an urban patriciate, active in commerce and the civic life, had ceased to exist. Thus the invasion of Italy by France and Spain, both by reducing the opportunities for trade and by closing off numerous avenues for political initiative, only hastened a transformation of the Italian ruling classes that was already in progress. The sixteenth century, therefore, quickly became an age of conspicuous consumption—of *pompa* and *estravaganza*. Noble families competed for the most splendid *palazzi* or the most ostentatious villas, and they began to seek with a new enthusiasm all the trappings of the gentleman—they concerned themselves with heraldry and they fabricated fantastic genealogies. Inevitably, the civic humanists' ideal of virtue in which merit outweighed birth found itself reversed, and an increasingly hierarchical notion of the social order made men and women unduly sensitive to questions of position and prestige. Indeed, the foundations of baroque Italy, with its stress on hierarchy and formalism and the ensuant widening of the gulf between rulers and their subjects, as well as the foundation of the Counter-Reformation church, with its

16. On civic humanism, see Hans Baron, *The Crisis of the Early Italian Renaissance* (Princeton: Princeton University Press, 1955; rev. ed. 1966). On the transition from civic to courtly culture see Benedetto Croce, "A Working Hypothesis: The Crisis of Italy in the Cinquecento and the Bond Between the Renaissance and the Risorgimento" in Eric Cochrane, ed. and trans., *The Late Italian Renaissance, 1525–1630* (London: Macmillan, 1970), 23–42. On the political thought of Castiglione, see V. Cian, "Il perfetto cavaliere e il perfetto politico della Rinascità: B. Castiglione e F. Guicciardini," in *Francesco Guicciardini nel IV centenario della morte (1540–1940)*, supplement no. 1 of *Rinascità* (1940): 49–95. George Bull's translation of *The Book of the Courtier* (Harmondsworth: Penguin, 1967) is excellent.

studious ostentation and the occasional resemblance of popes to generals and cardinals to princes, were cast largely by the transformations of Italian politics, both secular and religious, that occurred during the first half of the sixteenth century.

Yet, miraculously in this age of courts and princes, the Venetian republic endured. To be sure, there were republicans elsewhere in Italy. In Rome, for example, the humanists who met together at the Academy of Pomponio Leto were committed to republican government, and it was in Florence especially, in the first few decades of the sixteenth century, that Italy witnessed a most remarkable series of reflections on the nature of political and especially of republican institutions. There in the Orti Oricellari, the private gardens of the Florentine patrician Cosimo Rucellai just inside the city's third wall, a circle of men—of humanists and aristocratic opponents of the Medici regime that had been restored in 1512—regularly gathered to discuss history and politics in light of events recent and distant. Here the Florentine Niccolò Machiavelli, in dialogue with others, developed the ideas he was later to publish in his *Discourses on the First Ten Books of Livy*. This work was the most rigorous argument for republicanism and for the preservation of political liberties written in the entire Renaissance. But Machiavelli was only one of a number of republican theorists who met in the shade of the Rucellai gardens. Francesco Guicciardini, the greatest of the sixteenth-century historians, also frequented the gardens, as did Donato Giannotti, whose *Florentine Republic*, published in the 1530s, was a celebratory swan song to Renaissance and particularly Florentine liberty. Present also was Antonio Brucioli, who would participate in the anti-Medici conspiracy of 1522 and then, while in exile in Lyon, complete several important dialogues on republican culture and institutions. The conversations in the Rucellai gardens, therefore, were to have far-reaching implications, and, although the men gathered there were unable to arrest the changes overtaking their fatherland, their discussions explored and set the context for modern political theory. It was, in short, an especially creative moment, as men who lived in the last decades of the Florentine republic sought to forge a language that could both account for political change and preserve political freedom.[17]

But while republican theory reached new heights in Florence, it was

17. Here I follow Quentin Skinner, *The Foundations of Modern Political Thought*, vol. 1: *The Renaissance* (Cambridge: Cambridge University Press, 1978), 153–155; and Felix Gilbert, "Bernardo Rucellai and the Orti Oricellari: A Study on the Origin of Modern Political Thought," in *History: Choice and Commitment* (Cambridge, Mass.: Harvard Uni-

in Venice that republican institutions actually survived. This achievement should not surprise us. Even before the French and Spanish intrusions into Italy, Venice had enjoyed a reputation for unusually stable political arrangements; humanists and scholastic authors alike had praised it for its mixed government that—in the uniquely Venetian institutions of the Maggior Consiglio or Great Council, the Senate, and the doge—appeared to embody an Aristotelian vision of the ideal state as one that combined the best elements of democracy, aristocracy, and monarchy.[18] Nonetheless, with the defeat of republicanism elsewhere on the peninsula, the Venetian reputation for stability was greatly magnified. And, as we have seen, the first few decades of the sixteenth century proved decisive in the creation of the myth of Venice—the view that the republic was unparalleled in the stability of its constitution and the freedoms and peacefulness of both its subjects and its citizens. In these years several humanists, Florentines as well as Venetians, explored the reasons underlying the fortune of Venice. Donato Giannotti offered the most detailed account, but the Venetians Gasparo Contarini and Pier Paolo Vergerio—both bound to be important figures in the religious reforms of 1530s and 1540s—also wrote treatises on the republic.[19]

---

versity Press, 1977), 215–246—both stressed the seminal role of the Rucellai gardens in the creation of modern political theory. On Brucioli's participation in the discussions there, see Giorgio Spini, *Tra rinascimento e Riforma: Antonio Brucioli* (Florence: La Nuova Italia, 1940).

18. On medieval praise for the stability of the Venetian constitution, see Frederic Lane, "Medieval Political Ideas and the Venetian Constitution," in *Venice and History: The Collected Papers of Frederic C. Lane* (Baltimore: Johns Hopkins University Press, 1966), 285–308. For the fortune of the Venetian constitution in the Renaissance see Gilbert, "The Venetian Constitution in Florentine Political Thought," in *History: Choice and Commitment*, 179–214; and Skinner, *Foundations*, 1:140.

19. Giannotti, *Libro de la Republica de Vinitiani* (Rome: Antonio Blado d'Asola, 1540); Contarini, *The Commonwealth and Government of Venice*; and Vergerio, *De Republica Veneta liber primus* (Toscolano: Paganini, 1526). On Contarini and Giannotti, see Gilbert, "Religion and Politics in the Thought of Gasparo Contarini," and "The Venetian Constitution," in *History: Choice and Commitment*, 204–214, 247–267; and Felix Gilbert, "The Date of the Composition of Contarini's and Giannotti's Books on Venice," *Studies in the Renaissance* 14 (1967): 172–184. See also Skinner, *Foundations*, 1:140–142. Finally, on Vergerio, see Anne Jacobson Schutte, *Pier Paolo Vergerio: The Making of an Italian Reformer* (Geneva: Librairie Droz, 1977); and Tomizza, *Il male viene dal nord*, 67–501. The literature on the myth of Venice is extensive but see esp. Franco Gaeta, "Alcune considerazioni sul mito di Venezia," *Bibliothèque d'humanisme et Renaissance* 23 (1961): 58–75; Edward Muir, *Civic Ritual in Renaissance Venice* (Princeton: Princeton University Press, 1981), 13–61; and James Grubb, "When Myths Lose Power: Four Decades of Venetian Historiography," *Journal of Modern History* 58 (1986): 43–94.

The myth had religious significance as well. First, Venice had long been independent from Rome on religious matters. The Venetian patriciate exercised considerable autonomy in its control of the Church. Most of the bishops appointed to Venetian sees (there were forty-four bishoprics in the republic) were natives, not foreigners. The state oversaw monasteries and both taxed and subjected the clergy to its courts. And propertied parishioners enjoyed the privilege of electing their own priests. This subordination of the Church to the state was manifest in the central location of the Basilica San Marco, the dogal chapel that served as the focal point for ritual and religious activity, while the episcopal church of the patriarch was placed on a small island off the easternmost end of the city—an arrangement that symbolized the state's desire to keep Rome at bay.[20]

In light of the special place that Venice occupied on both the political and religious landscapes of Italy, it is hardly surprising that the republic would come to exercise a powerful, almost magnetic attraction upon those Italians, in Venice and elsewhere, who had grown dissatisfied with the direction of change in the Roman church, with its increasingly princely and worldly nature and its seeming inability either to reform itself or to meet the spiritual needs of the difficult times. Indeed, in these years papal corruption reached such heights that Machiavelli once noted, with some credibility, that "owing to the bad example set by the Court of Rome, Italy has lost all piety and religion." And Guicciardini was to remark at the end of a devastating diatribe against recent papal customs that "reverence for the papacy has been utterly lost in the hearts of men."[21] But Venice seemed—through the preservation of its republican government and the relative autonomy of its ecclesiastical institutions—to offer a counterpoint, a vital exception to the general drift of things. Again and again the Italian reformers (many, moreover, in sympathy with the Protestant leaders to the north) would look to Venice for both moral and political leadership.

20. Innocenzo Cervelli, *Machiavelli e la crisi dello stato veneziano* (Naples: Guida, 1974); William James Bouwsma, *Venice and the Defense of Republican Liberty: Renaissance Values in the Age of the Counter Reformation* (Berkeley: University of California Press, 1968), 71–83; and Paolo Prodi, "The Structure and Organization of the Church in Renaissance Venice: Suggestions for Research," in John R. Hale, ed., *Renaissance Venice* (London: Faber and Faber, 1973), 409–430.

21. Machiavelli, "Discorsi," in *Il Principe e Discorsi sopra la prima deca di Tito Livio*, ed. Sergio Bertelli (Milan: Feltrinelli, 1960), 165 (in the English version, *The Discourses*, ed. Bernard Crick, trans. Leslie J. Walker, rev. Brian Richardson [New York: Penguin, 1970], 144); Guicciardini, *Storia d'Italia*, 1:428 (*History of Italy*, 149).

The movement for religious reform existed throughout Europ reached from England to Naples and from Spain to Poland. The pro ponents of this Christian humanist movement included men as diverse as John Colet in England, Jacques Lefèvre d'Etaples in France, Cardinal Francisco Ximénes de Cisneros in Spain, Juan de Valdés in Naples, and the Dutchman Desiderius Erasmus (whose European itinerary and publications would soon make of him an international figure). These men drew in new and creative ways on their humanist educations to reinterpret the writings of the New Testament and of St. Paul in particular. Behind them stood the example of the fifteenth-century Italian humanist Lorenzo Valla whose *Annotations on the New Testament* pointed the way toward a more historical treatment of Scripture—one that, moreover, seemed to promise a means of capturing the original intent and the genuine meaning of the Gospels. In the place of a religion apparently corrupted by tradition they sought a simplified faith, one that made Scripture and especially the Gospels the central authority of the Christian life. None of these individuals, however, could have anticipated the revolutionary conclusions to which later reformers, the German Martin Luther above all, would push the same methods. But in their ideas was implicit a potentially explosive contrast between the Church of their day and the Church of the apostles.[22]

Nonetheless, within Italy it was in Venice that this movement found its most articulate spokesmen and that the question of religious reform was most poignantly and imaginatively posed. We see an example of this development in the spiritual struggles of the youthful Venetian patrician and humanist Gasparo Contarini. Born in 1483, Contarini studied philosophy and theology at the University of Padua before 1509, when he came into close contact with Tommaso Giustiniani and Vincenzo Quirini, like him members of prominent Venetian families. All three young men felt profound malaise over the spiritual values and religious institutions of their society. Whereas Giustiniani and Quirini chose finally to leave Venice and enter the monastic life in a Camaldolensian house near Arezzo, in Tuscany (where they would write their celebrated proposal on the reform of the Church, the *Libellus ad Leonem X*), Contarini searched rather for a new spirituality that would allow the Christian to remain in the world, and he found it—in ways strikingly similar to those that Luther was about to discover and to render

---

22. On the pre-Reformation reforming efforts of the Christian humanists, see Myron P. Gilmore, *The World of Humanism, 1453–1517* (New York: Harper and Brothers, 1952), 204–228.

his recognition that his own efforts alone would never
ιim to achieve salvation even if, as he wrote in a letter
iustiniani, "I did all possible penance and much more

ɪ, Contarini continued, was above all else a gift from
de manifest in the sacrifice of his Son. It was not some-
re, that an individual could gain through merit or
through works. The shift in emphasis was significant; in his stress on
the primacy of grace (or on God's unconditional love) in the economy
of salvation, Contarini's view was more than a little disruptive to a faith
that generally stressed the primacy of works. In both theory and practice, late medieval Catholicism had been more Pelagian than Augustinian; that is, it had generally minimized the role of grace, while holding
that an individual's own spiritual efforts—in such activities as prayer
and fasting, confession and communion, and even vigils and pilgrimages—were necessary and vital aspects of the human quest for salvation. Late medieval religious culture was, therefore, a culture of works,
and it was against this culture, together with its theological foundations, that the young monk Martin Luther was to react so forcefully.
Not surprisingly, as Luther's writings became available in Italy in the
1520s, Contarini read them with more than a little sympathy but never,
in contrast to Luther, denied the necessity for works entirely. Nonetheless, his emphasis on grace would eventually seem to some as an
attack on the Church and on Catholic devotions. Yet, like his contemporaries Thomas More and Desiderius Erasmus, Contarini never denied the efficacy of the human will altogether in the spiritual economy,
and—like them and so unlike Luther—he never wavered in his loyalty
to Rome.

Despite the depth of his concerns and his gifts in articulating them,
Contarini's life might well have been spent exclusively in service to

23. Contarini, letter to Paolo Giustiniani, 24 April 1511, in Hubert Jedin, ed., *Contarini und Camaldoli* (Rome: Edizioni di Storia e Letteratura, 1953), 14 (in the English
version, "Three Letters of Gasparo Contarini," in Elisabeth Gleason, *Reform Thought in
Sixteenth-Century Italy* [Chico, Calif.: Scholars Press, 1981], 25). The literature on Con-
tarini is extensive—see James Bruce Ross, "The Emergence of Gasparo Contarini: A
Bibliographical Essay," *Church History* 41 (1972): 22–45, but my discussion follows esp.
Franz Dittrich, *Gasparo Contarini, 1483–1542: Eine Monographie* (Braunsberg: Druck und
Verlag der Ermländischen Zeitungs- und Verlagsdruckerei, 1885); Elisabeth Gleason,
"Cardinal Gasparo Contarini (1483–1542) and the Beginning of Catholic Reform" (Ph.D.
diss., University of California, Berkeley, 1963); Gilbert, *History: Choice and Commitment*,
247–267; and Gigliola Fragnito, *Gasparo Contarini: Un magistrato veneziano al servizio della
Cristianità* (Florence: Olschki, 1988).

Venice (which, in the 1520s, he served in prestigious ambassadorial appointments, first to the imperial court of Charles V and then to Rome), had it not been for a growing concern in the papal curia—after some two decades of floundering and political blunders—over the question of how best to respond to the challenge that Luther posed to the Church. In the first dozen years after Luther's protest, Rome, while condemning him as a heretic, had not fully recognized the gravity of his teaching and, caught up in worldly ambitions, had been either too harsh or too soft in its responses. The Medici pope Leo X had excommunicated Luther when he might have listened to him; his cousin and successor Pope Clement VII had ignored Luther when he might have curtailed him. But in 1534, the Church selected as its leader Alessandro Farnese, a man the cardinals judged capable of constructive action and a possible resolution of the conflict with the Protestants. While some hoped that this pope, who assumed the name Paul III, would be able— through a universal council or through compromise—to effect a reconciliation with the Lutherans, others looked to him as a man who would at last take decisive action in the repression of heresy. Paul himself, it turned out, was open-minded about the need for both institutional and theological change. And his first actions seemed largely reconciliatory. In 1535, for example, he appointed as cardinals a number of men who seemed both in touch with the spiritual currents of the age and capable of tackling the issue of reform honestly and effectively. Not surprisingly, in this effort to appoint the best men he turned to Contarini, whose reputation as a diplomat, a political thinker, and a theologian was unsurpassed in the Catholic world. Indeed, when word reached Venice that Contarini was to be cardinal, a fellow nobleman on the floor of the Great Council reacted by shouting, "These priests have robbed us of the best gentleman this city has." [24] But many of the others selected by the pope at this time were equally concerned with the need to close the gap between the institutional structure of the Church and the spiritual concerns of the day. The more prominent among them included the studious and reconciliatory Jacopo Sadoleto, the bishop of Carpentras, and the Englishman Cardinal Reginald Pole, later papal governor at Viterbo.

But Paul showed other signs of interest in reform. Recognizing the danger that Protestantism posed to Christendom, he called for a coun-

---

24. Gilbert, *History: Choice and Commitment*, 267. On Paul III, see Ludwig von Pastor, *The History of the Popes*, trans. and ed. Frederick Ignatius Antrobus and Francis Kerr (1923–33; reprint Wilmington, N.C.: Consortium, 1978), vols. 11 and 12.

cil and in 1536, to prepare its way, appointed a distinguished group of prelates and cardinals to draft a report on ecclesiastical reform. Contarini, Sadoleto, and Pole were to serve along with a number of others, including Gian Matteo Giberti, the learned bishop of Verona; Gregorio Cortese, the abbot of the Benedictine monastery San Giorgio Maggiore in Venice; Tommaso Badia, the Master of the Sacred Palace; and Federigo Fregoso, the former archbishop of Salerno—all of whom were sympathetic with the ideals of Contarini. But Paul also hedged his bets. For in addition to these moderates he appointed the austere hard-liner Gian Pietro Carafa, founder of the Theatines and the bishop of Chieti, as well as Girolamo Aleandro, the archbishop of Brindisi, who had been among the first to call for the repression of Luther. These men completed their report, the *Consilium de emendanda ecclesia*, in 1537. In it, they encouraged the pope to reform the institutional structure of the Roman church, "to bring her back to her pristine beauty," and agreed in calling for an end to the more conspicuous abuses—pluralism or the holding of multiple benefices, simony or the purchase of church offices, the establishment of dynastic sees, and the appointment of unqualified men to the clergy—though most of its proponents (with the noted exceptions of Carafa and Aleandro) also worked privately to encourage doctrinal reform as well.[25] Like Contarini, these members of the commission had more than a little sympathy with an emphasis on the Gospels as the center of the Christian life and a stress on faith and grace, rather than on works, in the economy of salvation. Known as the *spirituali*, these men, whose religious orientation epitomized Italian evangelism in these years, genuinely believed it possible, with certain limitations, to accept Lutheran teachings about the relative roles of faith and works in salvation and yet remain loyal to Rome.

Despite the apparent prominence of the *spirituali* in the papal curia, however, their influence was limited. On the one hand, few of them

25. "Consilium delectorum cardinalium et aliorum praelatorum de emendanda ecclesia S.D.N. Paulo III iubente conscriptum et exhibitum" in *Consilium Tridentinum: Diariorum Actorum Epistularum Tractatuum nova collectio*, ed. Societas Goerresiana, vol. 12 (Freiburg: Herder, 1929), 131–145. On the behind-the-scenes work of Contarini, Pole, Sadoleto, and Giberti, see the works cited in note 10; Dermot Fenlon, *Heresy and Obedience in Tridentine Italy; Cardinal Pole and the Counter-Reformation* (Cambridge: Cambridge University Press, 1972); R.M. Douglas, *Jacopo Sadoleto, 1477–1547: Humanist and Reformer* (Cambridge, Mass.: Harvard University Press, 1959); and Adriano Prosperi, *Tra Evangelismo e Controriforma: G.M. Giberti, 1495–1543* (Rome: Edizioni di Storia e Letteratura, 1969).

were members of the Sacred College. In the increasingly courtly climate of sixteenth-century Italy, connections and patronage still counted more than commitment and piety in the elevation of a man to the office of cardinal. To be sure, Paul had demonstrated his ability to make a few good appointments, but his power was limited. Knowing this, Sadoleto had cautioned Contarini against raising his hopes. "In the Pope," Sadoleto wrote, "we have an extraordinary leader, intent upon worthy ends. But he is no stronger than the depravity of the times."[26] Moreover, not all reformers shared the goals of the *spirituali*. Some—especially Gian Pietro Carafa, the future Pope Paul IV, but also Girolamo Aleandro, Marcello Cervini, and Lorenzo Campeggi—constituted an opposition party of *zelanti*, believing that reform meant not accommodation with the Protestants but an increase of discipline in the Church and the swift, resolute repression of dissenters. They had long taken a hard line toward heresy. As early as 1532, for example, Carafa made it clear that he viewed reform of the Church and repression of dissent as closely linked. In a memorial he prepared for the pope on the state of the Church in Venice (where he had been living for several years), Carafa admitted that heresy was, in part, the outgrowth of a deep institutional crisis. He pointed to the failure of the Church to provide competent confessors and preachers, and he listed a number of abuses in church discipline such as the failure of bishops to keep residence as causes of dissent. But his language also betrayed the hard line he took toward dissenters. Having located the origin of much of the heresy in Venice among the conventual Franciscans, he dubbed them "that cursed nest of conventual friars minor" and, like many of his contemporaries, spoke of heresy as a "plague."[27] The implied solution, therefore, was not only more church discipline but also more repression. As Pope Paul IV, Carafa was to be viewed with more dread than any other pontiff in the sixteenth century.

Nonetheless, until the 1540s the *spirituali* managed to hold their own. Their position was bolstered by the doctrinal confusion of the times. Religious language, always potentially ambiguous, was especially so then. *Extra ecclesiam nulla est salus*—there is no salvation outside the Church—this was the traditional teaching upon which both

26. Cited in Douglas, *Jacopo Sadoleto*, 97.
27. Ioannes Petrus Carafa, "De Lutheranorum haeresi reprimanda et ecclesia reformanda ad Clementum VII" in *Consilium Tridentinum: Diariorum Actorum Epistularum Tractatuum nova collectio*, 67.

the *spirituali* and the more intransigent members of the curia could agree. But what did these words mean in the midsixteenth century when, several decades after Luther unleashed a revolution in the interpretation of Christian teaching, the very nature of salvation was itself a matter of debate? If human beings are saved by faith alone, what place did the sacraments—those traditional guarantors of salvation—have in the Christian life? And if they had no place or even, as in Luther's teaching, a much reduced place, what role was there for the Church? Moreover, what did one mean by church? Did authority lie, as some claimed, with the pope, or did it rest, as others argued with equal fervor, with a council of duly ordained representatives from all Christendom? Was the Church, as many held, the visible Church of Rome or was it something less tangible, a union of the faithful? There can be no doubt that this doctrinal uncertainty, while disconcerting to many, fed the hopes of the *spirituali* for compromise and reform, since, from the 1520s down to the early 1540s, it remained possible for many to accept Luther's doctrine of salvation by faith alone and yet not deduce from it that the traditional beliefs and practices of the Roman church were superfluous. Indeed, it would take no less than the Council of Trent, which met from 1545–1563, to eradicate this view. Only in the later half of the sixteenth century did the irreconcilable differences between Protestants and Catholics become clear to all.

Moreover, the *spirituali* benefited from the ambiguities inherent in the religious language of the day and from their social position as well. They were, in general, aristocrats, drawn from the wealthiest and most influential circles of society, and in a world so conscious of status as was sixteenth-century Italy, the views of such men carried weight. Sadoleto's background may have been bourgeois, but Cardinal Gasparo Contarini, as we have seen, was a Venetian patrician, a diplomat, a man with considerable experience in the highest offices of the state. Cardinal Reginald Pole, soon to be appointed papal governor at Viterbo, was an English nobleman and cousin to the king. In Naples, too, the group that gathered around Juan de Valdés, the Spanish humanist, whose teachings deemphasized questions of dogma and simultaneously maintained that divine grace was necessary for salvation, consisted almost entirely of aristocrats, including Vittoria Colonna, the widow of the marquess of Pescara. Thus, while the *spirituali* did not constitute a party in the modern sense of the term, the social prestige they enjoyed, the frequent contacts among them, and their shared sympathies and ideals gave them considerable clout.[28]

The late 1530s and the first years of the next decade represented the heyday of their confidence. Paul III seemed supportive, and a council was promised. It was in this period, furthermore, that the *spirituali* felt sufficiently powerful to begin to proselytize their views. They did so primarily by offering their patronage and their protection to outstanding preachers who shared their evangelical commitments, above all to fra Bernardino Ochino, the vicar general of the Capuchin order (a reformed and austere branch of the Franciscans), and to the Augustinian Pier Martire Vermigli. Both were superb speakers (the Emperor Charles V said of Ochino that he could make stones weep), and both were in constant demand as preachers in the towns and cities of central and northern Italy. It was these preachers and others like them who would first bring the new evangelical ideas to a large and diverse public.[29]

But the greatest hope for the *spirituali* came in 1541 when the papacy agreed to give its official support to a final effort to reach a compromise with the Protestants at a colloquy in the German city of Regensburg. To be sure, much of the pressure for reconciliation came from the Emperor Charles V who sought every avenue he could to pacify Germany. There were humanists on both sides of the divide between Catholic and Protestant Europe who believed that an accord between Rome and the Lutherans was possible. Protestant humanists such as Martin Bucer and Philip Melanchthon were the mirror images of individuals such as Pole and Sadoleto. All of them hoped that the unity of Christendom could be restored. Moreover, the *spirituali*'s hopes quickened when the pope appointed Contarini as papal legate to the colloquy. It was a brilliant choice, for Contarini's position on justification might, some

28. Historians have seen the aristocratic makeup of the Italian evangelicals as a major reason for its absence of popular appeal—see, for example, Jung, "On the Nature of Evangelism in Sixteenth-Century Italy." But Massimo Firpo has turned this argument on its head, maintaining that the evangelicals' key positions in Italian society gave them enormous influence—see his "Juan de Valdés e l'evangelismo italiano: Appunti e problemi di una ricerca in corso," reprinted (from the 1985 article) in *Tra Alumbrados e "spirituali": Studi su Juan de Valdés e il valdesianesimo nella crisi religiosa del '500 italiano* (Florence: Olschki, 1990), 127–153.

29. Roland Bainton, *Bernardino Ochino: Esule e riformatore senese del Cinquecento, 1487–1563*, trans. E. Gianturco (Florence: Sansoni, 1940); and Philip McNair, *Peter Martyr in Italy: An Anatomy of Apostasy* (Oxford: Clarendon, 1967).

hoped, serve as a bridge between the two faiths. Indeed, because of Contarini's mediation, the Protestants and Catholics at Regensburg were able to agree, almost miraculously, on a doctrine of justification. But their talks broke down over the issue of transubstantiation, and the colloquy was immediately declared a failure by those unsympathetic to its goals.[30]

With compromise between the Catholics and Protestants no longer a possibility, the position of the *spirituali* weakened quickly. The *zelanti*, it turned out, were already well positioned. In 1540 the pope had been persuaded to give official recognition to the Jesuit order, an organization that would rapidly take charge of many aspects of the Counter-Reformation. Moreover, the *zelanti* knew that it was only a matter of time before the *spirituali* lost credibility. Knowing that the colloquy at Regensburg would fail, they saw their advantage in it; as soon as word reached Rome of the impasse, they made their move. On 4 July Pope Paul III, at the urging of those members of the papal curia who had long hoped for a more aggressive stance by the papacy against heresy, appointed a commission of six cardinals to serve as Inquisitors General, and three weeks later, on 21 July, he established, through the bull *Licet ab initio*, the Roman Congregation of the Holy Office, or the Inquisition.[31] The papacy had finally become convinced that the threat of Protestantism was real, even in Italy. And the new Inquisition, which claimed authority throughout all Christendom on matters of the orthodoxy of religious doctrine (to which authority, in theory, even the Spanish Inquisition was subject and which continues, albeit in a much modified form, down to our own time), centralized the authority to make judgments concerning the orthodoxy of religious beliefs and practices in Rome itself. In fact, its powers were for the most part limited to the Italian states. But its official adoption was nonetheless a clear signal of a far more intransigent policy toward Protestantism.

This, in itself, was a devastating setback to the *spirituali*. Indeed, many of them would soon find themselves among those suspected of heresy. But it was a setback much compounded when, at the end of August, Cardinal Gasparo Contarini died. The humanist poet Marcantonio Flaminio described the loss of this cardinal as "the cruelest of blows." The Veronese bishop Gian Matteo Giberti knew it meant the

30. Peter Matheson, *Cardinal Contarini at Regensburg* (Oxford: Clarendon, 1972), 122–144.

31. The text of the bull is found in B.J. Kidd, ed., *Documents Illustrative of the Continental Reformation* (Oxford: Clarendon, 1911), 346–350.

passing of an era. Reginald Pole, papal governor at Viterbo, felt the burdens of leadership pass to him. Even the pope was heard to remark publicly that the College of Cardinals had not suffered a comparable loss in over a hundred years.[32] Contarini had been the most prominent and effective of those Italian churchmen committed to finding a compromise between Rome and the Lutherans. Upon him had rested the hopes of those who, in this most divisive age, prayed that the Reformation, begun in earnest some twenty-five years before, would not sever the unity of western Christendom and that Luther and the papacy could be reconciled. Those in Italy who had hoped for compromise felt the floor fall out from under them. They had lost, in a crucial moment, the best man they had. They could try to regroup, but now they had little room to maneuver. Some of Contarini's colleagues believed he and his followers had gone too far. Even some of his defenders had difficulty distinguishing his views from Luther's. Moreover— while Contarini was in his sickbed—both Ochino and Vermigli, when summoned back to Rome, chose to abandon Italy altogether and to cast their lots with the Protestants. Their most ardent supporters had been Contarini and his friends. Their flight and their breach with Rome cast a shadow over those who hoped, perhaps in vain, for reconciliation. Contarini's friends found themselves surrounded by men sensitive to the subtlest hints of dissent, and figures of great stature were suddenly and unexpectedly denounced as heretics. Religion, which should have been a cause of trust, had become instead a source of suspicion.

To many evangelicals, this change in climate signaled defeat. Giberti seemed especially cautious. "With the deaths of some of our *spirituali* and the exile of others," he wrote soon after learning of the fates of such men as Ochino and Contarini, "I believe that it would be best to leave their company."[33] And not surprisingly Sadoleto, who always preferred his studies to controversy, sought permission to return to Carpentras, to his diocese and his leisures.[34] After all, Carafa had the up-

---

32. On Flaminio's reaction, see Carol Maddison, *Marcantonio Flaminio: Poet, Humanist, and Reformer* (Chapel Hill: University of North Carolina Press, 1965), 135; on Giberti's, Prosperi, *Tra Evangelismo e Controriforma*, 314; on Pole's, Fenlon, *Heresy and Obedience*, 52–53; and on the pope's, Pastor, *The History of the Popes*, 11:585.

33. "Poiché questi nostri spirituali ne dan sì poca consolatione parte col morire parte con andar profugi, credo che sarà bene lassare la loro compagnia," E. Solmi, "La fuga di Bernardino Ochino secondo i documenti dell'Archivio Gonzaga di Mantova," *Bullettino Senese di Storia Patria* 15 (1908): 76; cited in Prosperi, *Tra Evangelismo e Controriforma*, 314.

34. Douglas, *Jacopo Sadoleto*, 178–179.

per hand in the curia. The Jesuit order was gaining sway, and the Inquisition had been established.

Yet despite the resignation of such men as Giberti and Sadoleto, not all hope for reform in Italy was lost. To be sure, the enormous influence of Spain on the peninsula and the increasingly courtly character of Italian politics rendered the Church less and less likely to push for reform in the direction that the *spirituali* had hoped. But not all conditions were antithetical to the goals of the *spirituali*—especially not in Venice, a republic that occupied a special place between Renaissance and Reformation. For in the context of sixteenth-century Italy, Venice stood out as a survivor. It was a city where Renaissance republican institutions and ideals endured, despite the growing hegemony of France and Spain in Italian politics. This is not to say that there were no princes who gave their support to the Protestant or evangelical ideas. There most certainly were: the success of the Reformation at times depended on King Henry VIII of England or Duke Frederick the Wise in Germany. Moreover, even in Italy Duchess Renée of Ferrara, though her power was limited, gave her support to the evangelicals. But there were nonetheless deep affinities between the ideals of Renaissance republicans and those of the evangelicals. Both opposed hierarchy, if not absolutely, at least in its more exaggerated forms. The antihierarchical sentiment of the *spirituali* was especially evident in the *Consilium de emendanda ecclesia*, where they envisioned the Church, although headed by the pope, as a republic of laws. Perhaps, given the provenance of many of its authors, the *Consilium* reflected the model of Venice and its mixed government.

In their concern for their community and for the poor, moreover, the evangelicals blended the charitable, spiritual ideals of Christianity with those of civic humanism as it had developed in the Italian Renaissance republics. There was thus no contradiction between republican and Christian virtues. On the contrary, unlike more modern forms of republicanism (which, since the time of the English philosopher John Locke, have by a strange alchemy relied on the private vice of self-interest as the source of public virtue), Renaissance republicanism viewed personal and civic virtue as intimately connected, and jointly essential to the character of the citizen. While humanism and the reading of classical texts undoubtedly instilled certain pagan ideals in a few of the republic's elites, Christianity served as the fount of virtues and of the citizen's moral commitments to the state. In the fourteenth and fifteenth centuries, this ideal had been clearly articulated in the writings of humanists such as the Florentine Coluccio Salutati, who had argued that charity "lights the mind for virtue . . . [and that it alone] fosters the family, expands the city, and guards the kingdom," and in the writings of the Venetian Giovanni Caldiera, who had held faith, charity, and hope to be the most solid foundation of civic virtue.[35]

Yet in the sixteenth century the evangelicals became the most conspicuous representatives of this tradition. The vision was perhaps most pronounced in Contarini, whose work *The Commonwealth and Government of Venice* saw Christian virtue as an essential foundation of political responsibility. But this conjoining of republican and evangelical commitments was by no means unique to Contarini. We find it also in Antonio Brucioli. As is clear from his *Dialogues*, first published in Venice in 1526, Brucioli's republicanism ran deep. It had been formed in Florence, and his reflections on it were shaped to a large degree by his participation in the conversations in the Rucellai gardens where such men as Machiavelli and Guicciardini were also present. But by the 1530s Brucioli had also become one of the leading figures in Italian evangelism. During his exile from Florence after the anti-Medici conspiracy of 1522, he traveled to France, and it was likely while he was in Lyon, where he first came into contact with Protestant ideas, that he decided to return to Italy—to Venice—and to devote himself to translating the Bible into Italian. Indeed, it was Brucioli's Bible that was to serve as the basis for much popular evangelism. Yet in Brucioli as in Contarini, political and religious commitments were often interwoven. In his *Dialogue on the Laws of the Republic*, he wrote, "In order for the republic to flourish in all things and to remain safe and powerful, it is necessary that its citizens be learned, wise, and good men, filled with reason and properly educated, and in their actions, dedicated to God."[36] Finally, it hardly seems accidental that the Venetian Pier Paolo Vergerio also wrote treatises in praise of the republic before occupying himself in the 1530s and 1540s with more explicitly religious questions.[37]

This is not to say that Venice was the only center of evangelism in

35. On Salutati, Trinkaus, *In Our Image and Likeness*, 1:75. On Caldiera, Margaret L. King, *Venetian Humanism in an Age of Patrician Dominance* (Princeton: Princeton University Press, 1986), 105–109.

36. *Dialogi*, ed. Aldo Landi (Naples: Prismi; Chicago: Newberry Library, 1982), 202; for the interrelatedness of Contarini's religious and political convictions, see esp. Gilbert, "Religion and Politics," in *History: Choice and Commitment*, 247–267.

37. Again, see Vergerio, *De Republica Veneta*.

Italy. In fact, the movement was diffused through much of northern Italy. After the death of Contarini, several of the most prominent reformers—Cardinal Reginald Pole, for example, and his associate the humanist poet Marcantonio Flaminio, as well as Cardinal Giovanni Morone, bishop of Modena—dedicated themselves to campaign for the view that the role of faith was primary in the economy of salvation. They did so, not because they were crypto-Protestants, as some of their later detractors believed—all three would be accused of heresy—but rather because they believed that evangelism offered the best hope for a unified Christendom. What they could not foresee was the disfavor their dream would earn from the council soon to meet at Trent. Nor perhaps could they recognize the radical potential in the doctrine of salvation by faith alone. Whereas they themselves saw no contradiction between Luther's teaching and loyalty to Rome, the line dividing evangelism from heresy was quite thin. Nonetheless, they composed and urged others to compose and publish sermons, pasquinades, poems, letter collections, devotional tracts, catechisms, and commentaries on the Gospels to spread their views. And as a consequence, in the course of a few years, they created a stream of literature (of which the *Beneficio di Cristo* was the most eloquent expression) that diffused to a broad and diverse public, already somewhat familiar with such views from the preaching of Ochino and Vermigli, the evangelical ideal that an individual's relationship to God was direct and immediate. As they spread their message, they hoped that the Church would approve it, and that their strategy would result in unity, not division.[38]

The response was widespread, and there can be no doubt that their efforts struck a chord in a large cross section of the urban population of the cities and towns of northern and central Italy. But it was in Venice especially that a popular movement developed, and it did so primarily because of the city's reputation for liberty. Since the sack of Rome in 1527, after all, Venice had served as a haven for those Italians who sought religious or artistic freedom. It was then, for example, that Tommaso Badia, one of the leading *spirituali*, fled Rome to take refuge in Venice. And soon thereafter figures as diverse as the satirist Pietro Aretino, the "scourge of princes," and the humanist Antonio Brucioli, no longer able to return to Florence, chose Venice as the ideal setting for their undertakings. During the 1540s, however, following the establishment of the Inquisition elsewhere—as authorities clamped down in such cities as Rome and Naples—the major movement of re-

---

38. Firpo, "Juan de Valdés e l'evangelismo italiano."

formers to Venice occurred. Some of the more prominent figures arrived in a group of heretics from Rome (Guido Giannetti da Fano, the Brescian physician Girolamo Donzellino, and Francesco Strozzi), but scores of others came as well, such as the evangelical Baldassare Altieri and the Bolognese *condottiero* Ludovico dall'Armi. And many thought not only to escape persecution at home but also to achieve, because of Venetian political freedom, certain religious reforms in Venice as well.

Thus it was inevitable that Venice became a center of religious reform. One of the leading figures in this movement was the bishop of Capodistria, Pier Paolo Vergerio. For over a decade he had struggled to reform his diocese from within the received structures of Catholicism. But in the early 1540s Vergerio, like Pole, Flaminio, and Morone, recognized that the religious climate had changed; in contrast to these *spirituali* who continued to hope that Christian unity could be preserved, Vergerio believed that his goals could no longer be met from within the Church: he initiated an intensive, though clandestine, effort to bring about a reformation of the Church in Venice. He did not act alone. Over the years, Vergerio—first as a student, then as a lawyer, and finally as a churchman—had cultivated close ties with patricians, priests, and printers who shared his goals. Several were native Venetians, but others were recent exiles to the city who, like Vergerio, now believed that the time had come to work for a genuine reformation in Italy. They never believed it possible to transpose mechanically the teachings of Luther or Calvin or the institutional arrangements of the Protestant churches to Venice. Their ideals for religious reform were sensitive to local needs and conditions, and their readings were cast broadly. Certainly Luther, Melanchthon, Calvin, Zwingli, and Bucer were among their key texts, but they also read extensively in New Testament and biblical criticism. They doubtless benefited from the presence in Venice of the Florentine exile and humanist Antonio Brucioli, whose translations of and commentaries on the Bible were well known in Venetian culture at the time. And they relied as much on the writings of Italian as they did on northern reformers.[39]

But political circumstances provided these reformers with their

---

39. On Vergerio's contacts in Venice, in addition to Schutte (*Pier Paolo Vergerio*), the researches of Andrea del Col are essential. See esp. del Col, "Lucio Paolo Rosello e la vita religiosa veneziana verso la metà del secolo XVI," *Rivista di storia della Chiesa in Italia* 32 (1978): 422–459; and del Col, "Il controllo della stampa a Venezia e i processi di Antonio Brucioli (1548–1559)," *Critica storica* 17 (1980): 457–510. A further portrait of Vergerio's circle in Venice is provided in ASV, *Sant'Uffizio*, b. 39, doss. "Donzellino, Girolamo," in a memorial, "Reverendi et illustrissimi signori. Da principio che io ritornai in questa città," presented by Donzellino to the Inquistion in November 1561.

greatest hopes. The 1545 election as doge of Francesco Donà, a patrician widely believed to be sympathetic to their ideals, was especially encouraging. Vergerio composed a congratulatory letter to Donà calling on him to reform the Church. The republic is peaceful and prosperous, Vergerio argued, and now—given the nearly universal recognition of abuses in the Church and the humanistic recovery of the theological and pastoral foundations of Christianity—is the ideal occasion to carry out such a reform.[40] Then, in 1546–1547, international circumstances gave the reformers even more hope. It appeared that Venice might be convinced to enter into at least a covert alliance with the Protestant Schmalkaldic League in its struggle against the emperor Charles V. The key activists in this maneuver were Guido Giannetti, the former secretary to the English ambassador to Rome; Baldassare Altieri, now the secretary to the English ambassador to Venice; and Ludovico dall'Armi. Together they hatched a wild scheme, requiring Venetian cooperation, for an insurrection in the Romagna timed to make it impossible for pontifical forces to come to the aid of the emperor in his crusade against the Protestants. Like Vergerio, they hoped that a return to the true Gospel was still possible in Italy and, like the Lucchese *gonfalonier* Francesco Burlamacchi, who had planned and then attempted a similar insurrection in Tuscany the previous year, they dreamt of simpler times and of a revival of Italian republicanism. As Guido Giannetti wrote in a letter to Duke John Frederick of Saxony, one of the leaders of the Schmalkaldic League, they hoped to restore not only "the ancient liberty of Italy" but also to create conditions that would allow for the free preaching of the Gospel. But, like Vergerio, with whom Altieri was in contact, their hopes for political support were dashed, at first by the quiet diplomacy of the pope who got wind of their plans, then definitively by the duke of Alba, Charles V's commander, who defeated the Protestant troops at Mühlberg in April 1547.[41]

40. Pier Paolo Vergerio, "Oratione al Doge Francesco Donado per il suo ingresso, esortatione alla riforma della chiesa," in Aldo Stella, "L'Orazione di Pier Paolo Vergerio," *Atti dell'Istituto veneto di scienze, lettere ed arti, classe di scienze morali, lettere ed arti* 128 (1969–1970): 25–39.

41. Aldo Stella, "Utopie e velleità insurrezionali dei filoprotestanti italiani (1545–1547)," *Bibliothèque d'humanisme et Renaissance* 27 (1965): 133–182. On Francesco Burlamacchi, see Berengo, *Nobili e mercanti nella Lucca del Cinquecento*, 191–218. Finally, for a recent examination of the Schmalkaldic League, see Thomas A. Brady, Jr., "Phases and Strategies of the Schmalkaldic League: A Perspective after 450 Years," *Archiv für Reformationsgeschichte* 74 (1983): 162–181.

## CHAPTER TWO

# The Coming of the Inquisition

*Since Venice is so large and so open and a place where all peoples,*
*especially the Germans, are welcomed, much vigilance is needed.*

Pope Gregory XIII's instruction to his
ambassador to Venice, 1581

Menfa Inquifitionis.

On 22 April 1547 the Venetian doge Francesco Donà, declaring that he knew of "nothing more fitting a Christian prince than zeal in religion and the defense of the Catholic faith," and acting on the advice of his councillors, established a new magistracy of state, the Tre savi all'eresia. To this office the doge appointed three nobles, each a layman, charged to cooperate with the patriarch, the local inquisitor, and the papal legate in the formation of trials against those men and women who were either accused or suspected of heresy.[1]

Part compromise and part assertion of Venetian independence, the doge's decree was a work of art. The Venetian government had not welcomed the news in 1542 that the pope had reorganized the Inquisition. This revamping had centralized the direction of the Inquisition in Rome and placed its activity directly under the authority of the papacy and a College of Inquisitors General, in which Carafa, always intransigent in his demands that heresy be harshly repressed, was the most influential presence. This innovation, it was widely believed, could not but threaten the sovereignty of any state in which a tribunal subject to the Roman Holy Office was to function, though in Venice—because of a certain pride in local traditions that tended to subordinate the Church to the state—members of the governing elite felt they had special cause to be concerned. It was not that the Venetian government took a laissez-faire attitude toward heresy. Indeed, over the previous

1. "Conoscendo niuna cosa esser più degna di Principe Christiano che l'esser studioso della relliggione [sic] e difensore della fede cattolica"—the entire decree is printed in Giovanni Sforza, "Riflessi della Controriforma nella repubblica di Venezia," *Archivio storico italiano* 93 (1935): 195–196. For an overview of the establishment of the Inquisition in Venice, see Grendler, *The Roman Inquisition and the Venetian Press*, 35–42; Pullan, *The Jews of Europe and the Inquisition in Venice*, 3–57; and Ruth Martin, *Witchcraft and the Inquisition in Venice, 1550–1650* (Oxford: Basil Blackwell, 1989), 9–33; these works should be read in light of Andrea del Col, "Organizzazione, composizione e giurisdizione dei tribunali dell'Inquisizione romana nella repubblica de Venezia (1500–1550)," *Critica storica* 25 (1988): 244–294; and Andrea del Col, "L'Inquisizione romana e il potere politico nella repubblica di Venezia (1540–1560)," *Critica storica* 28 (1991): 189–250. Del Col's meticulous research alters the received understanding of the relation of the Venetian government to the Sant'Uffizio. On del Col's contribution, see the essay on sources and bibliography.

*Opposite.* This engraving captures something of the routine business of the Inquisition. The empty chairs show that the full tribunal is not in session though an interrogation continues while the notary, at the far left, records the testimony. (Adrian Schoonbech, "An Inquisitorial Interrogation," from Limborch's *Historia Inquisitionis* [Amsterdam, 1692]; courtesy of the Rare Book Room, The Library, Syracuse University)

two decades the Venetian government had on occasion taken an active role in the repression of religious dissent.[2] But the ruling elite was frankly worried about the possibility of Roman interference in trade, and with good reason, for—as much as any state in Europe—Venice depended on commerce. In fact, over the years it had based its relations with other nations more on economic than on religious grounds. Commercial interests had even made it possible for sizable communities of Jews, Turks, Greeks, and Germans to live and do business right in the heart of the city. Furthermore, in an age when the Hapsburgs had grown so powerful in Italy (Charles V had been crowned Holy Roman Emperor at nearby Bologna in 1529) the Venetians wisely sought good relations with other powers; in this sphere, as in the world of commerce, religion was often secondary to questions of security. Accordingly, the Venetians sought to cultivate close ties not only with the Most Christian King of France, the Catholic Francis I, but also with Protestant princes such as King Henry VIII in England and even the leaders of the Schmalkaldic League; they hoped to balance these powers off against the Hapsburg empire whose Italian claims also threatened Venetian independence. Therefore, by establishing a local magistracy of lay judges, who were—in the words of the decree—"to assist in the formation of trials against heretics," the doge in fact met Rome's challenge head-on. Whenever possible, the Venetian government would provide its support to the pope's efforts to preserve orthodoxy, but the presence of Venetian patricians on the local tribunal of the Roman Holy Office would also serve as a check against any actions of the papacy that might damage Venetian sovereignty and its interests, political or economic.

Some in Venice had hoped, of course, to keep the Roman Inquisition out of the city altogether, but the papacy's pressure on the Venetians to fall in step with the other Italian states had been relentless. In an age when heresy was thought of as a contagion, many members of the papal curia had reason to believe that Venice, precisely because of its trading ties, could easily act as a conduit of heretical ideas, ultimately infecting much of the rest of Italy. As Italy's greatest commercial center, how could Venice not be receptive to the ideas of the reformers? Not unexpectedly, by the 1540s the new ideas had made considerable headway. "There is a new spirituality here," the papal

2. Del Col, "Organizzazione, composizione e giurisdizione dei tribunali dell'Inquisizione romana," 247–264.

nuncio to Venice, referring to the desire for reform, wrote to his superiors in Rome in 1543, "which men of some influence, in their academies and their gatherings, are finding ways to encourage. And, as surely as water runs to a mill," he continued, "the people here are drawn to these hypocrites and malcontents."[3] In 1545 Pope Paul, increasingly frustrated by the lack of cooperation with Rome on the part of the Venetian government, echoed a common concern of the age of Reformation and warned the Venetians that a revolution against the faith meant a revolution against the state as well.[4] And in 1546 Cardinal Jacopo Sadoleto—who, despite his sympathy with evangelism, was concerned by the possibility of a popular movement—registered a complaint to the Venetian ambassador, noting that the city of Venice was "poisoned by this Lutheran plague."[5]

Rome's pressure was not merely rhetorical. In 1544 the pope had commissioned Monsignor Giovanni della Casa, the dean of the Camera Apostolica and the archbishop of Benevento, as the nuncio to Venice with the specific charge to serve as the official representative of the Holy Office of the Inquisition in Venetian territory and to obtain the republic's cooperation in the repression of heresy. It was a superb appointment. The Florentine della Casa—a humanist and a lawyer by training as well as a close friend to the Farnese (the pope's family)—was, despite his bourgeois background, at home in the company of aristocrats and yet, as his writings and especially his famous manual on manners, *The Galateo*, were to show, supremely loyal to his friends and his superiors. He would be certain to represent Rome's interests as effectively as anyone.[6]

Indeed, soon after his arrival in Venice della Casa tested the waters, and he proved himself a man who chose his battles wisely. He made it his policy to concentrate on those heretics who made not only Rome but also the Venetian state uncomfortable. His first case, therefore, involved Ambrogio da Milano, an outspoken Augustinian whose ser-

3. Cited in Oddone Ortolani, *Pietro Carnesecchi* (Florence: Le Monnier, 1963), 43.

4. Fontana, "Documenti vaticani contro l'eresia luterana in Italia," 398–400.

5. Sadoleto's remarks to the Venetian ambassador are reported in Antonio Santosuosso, "The Moderate Inquisitor: Giovanni della Casa's Venetian Nunciature, 1544–1549," *Studi veneziani* n.s. 2 (1978): 152.

6. These and my following remarks on della Casa follow the discussions of both Santosuosso, cited in note 5, and Lorenzo Campana, "Monsignor Giovanni della Casa e i suoi tempi," *Studi storici* 16 (1907): 3–84; 17 (1908): 145–282, 381–606; and 18 (1909): 325–513. On Ambrogio, see Ugo Rozzo, "Vicende inquisitoriali dell'Eremitano Ambrogio Cavalli (1537–1545)," *Rivista di storia e letteratura religiosa* 16 (1980): 223–256.

mons had recently stirred up trouble on Cyprus. Because this eastern Mediterranean island, moreover, was a Venetian dependency in what was becoming an increasingly Turkish sea, the Venetian government was especially sensitive to problems of social unrest there and more than willing to allow della Casa, with the assistance of the local inquisitor, to carry out his investigation. The Venetian government even provided the guards who arrested Brother Ambrogio in January 1545. But success in this case did not blind della Casa to the underlying issues of his day, and he continued to weigh his options carefully. Thus, despite numerous accusations against the Capodistrian bishop Pier Paolo Vergerio, who was so well connected to many of the leading proponents of evangelism in Venice itself, and considerable pressure from Rome to bring him to trial, the nuncio recognized that the grounds for the case against Vergerio (motivated largely by personal animosities between the Farnese and the bishop) were flimsy at best, and that the Venetian government (including a number of Vergerio's friends) was not likely to give its support to his prosecution. Nonetheless, when another case—one in which the state was almost certain to be helpful—developed in 1546 and in the early part of 1547, della Casa did not hesitate to take decisive action.

The case involved the surprising and, to some, disconcerting popularity of the sermons of Angelico da Crema, a friar whose success in the pulpit at the parish church of San Barnabà convinced the Venetian government (possibly because many nobles of that parish were among the poorest in the city) that heresy posed a threat to Venetian stability as well, so much so that on this occasion it was the Venetian government that sought della Casa's assistance (rather than the papal nuncio who sought the government's, as in an earlier case). The zeal of the government was so great, in fact, that for a while some members of the Collegio (the executive council of the Senate) were calling for Angelico to be burned before the populace, while della Casa believed that it would be enough simply to cut out the friar's dangerous tongue. "The lords here," della Casa wrote Farnese, "began last year to show that they want to take some action against the heretics who, to tell the truth, have increased their numbers considerably, both in the city and in the Dominio."[7] At this same time, the international atmosphere was also propitious for greater Venetian cooperation in the repression of heresy. In January Henry VIII died, and two months later Francis I suc-

---

7. Cited in Sforza, "Riflessi della Controriforma nella repubblica di Venezia," 194.

cumbed after a long illness. Moreover, the forces of Charles V—under the command of the duke of Alba—were on the offensive in the emperor's struggle against the Schmalkaldic League. Thus the delicate balancing act in foreign affairs that the Venetian government had pursued over the last few decades was no longer possible. Although in the end tempers evidently cooled and Angelico was spared any corporeal punishment, it was in this environment that the doge and his councillors moved in 1547 to create a tribunal that would accommodate both Venetian and Roman interests. And while the direct participation of three laymen on the tribunal of the Roman Holy Office was not precisely what the pope and the Cardinal Inquisitors had in mind (the inquisitors would have preferred greater clerical independence), the nuncio was pleased. As della Casa assured his superiors, it was a reasonable compromise: the Venetian senators who were appointed meant business and their participation was likely to facilitate the repression of heretics.

And a formidable tribunal it was. Not only were there three impressive senators (the original appointees, Nicolò Tiepolo, Francesco Contarini, and Antonio Venier, all had outstanding reputations for piety and vast experience in the Venetian government behind them) and two ecclesiastics: the nuncio Giovanni della Casa, of course, and the inquisitor, the Franciscan fra Marino da Venezia (the Venetian patriarch did not become a regular member of the tribunal until 1559 or 1560); but a number of other officials as well. The more prominent of these were the nuncio's auditor Gherardo Busdraghi who, especially in the early years, often sat in for his superior; the fiscal Giovan Maria Buccello whose task it was to serve as chief prosecutor before the Inquisition; the notaries; and Alvise Scortica, who served as della Casa's commissary (*messo giurato*). Finally, around these principals circled a number of lesser figures: guards and petty bureaucrats who were, then as now, part of the inevitable buzz of the courtroom.[8] By law, moreover, the court was required to keep a record not only of the denunciations received and the sentences issued but of the testimonies of the accused and witnesses as well. At times it must have been exceedingly

8. On the organization of the Venetian tribunal, see esp. del Col, "Organizzazione, composizione e giurisdizione dei tribunali dell'Inquisizione romana nella repubblica de Venezia"; and Anne Jacobson Schutte, "Un inquisitore al lavoro: Fra Marino da Venezia e l'Inquisizione veneziana," *I Francescani in Europa tra Riforma e Controriforma*, Atti del XIII Convegno internazionale (Assisi, 17–19 October 1985) (Perugia: Università degli Studi di Perugia, 1987), 167–196.

tedious work. In 1580, for example, the papal nuncio Alberto Bolognetti complained how bothersome he found it to "sit and listen to so
many mutterings while every single word is written down (*mentre si
scrivono di parola in parola*)."[9] But this was the lament of a bureaucrat.
Others—those who were the targets of the Inquisition or who feared
that they might become so—had far more serious complaints. "The
repression grows harsher everyday," the reformer Baldassare Altieri
wrote his friend Heinrich Bullinger in 1549. And he continued: "Many
are apprehended and condemned to the galleys or to jail for life. Some
are convinced to recant for fear of punishment. . . . Many are banished
with their women and children; others take refuge in flight."[10]

While to many observers such a tribunal must have seemed out of place
in Venice, with its reputation for liberty and tolerance toward others,
there was nothing at all incongruous about the presence of an active
inquisitorial court in the republic, for piety was widely perceived as a
linchpin in the preservation of the political order. Machiavelli himself,
for example, was acutely aware of the deep interconnections between
religious and political life. "The rulers of a republic or the prince of a
kingdom," he wrote in his *Discourses*, "should maintain the basic prin-
ciples of the religion that they hold, and, if this be done, it will be an
easy matter for them to keep their republic religious, and, in consequence, good and united." And this was advice that the Venetians—
though, in general, they held a less instrumental view of religion than
did Machiavelli—heeded with special fervor.[11] As the majority of their
contemporaries did, sixteenth-century Venetians perceived a deep in-
terconnection between piety and the destiny of the state. On the one
hand, the myth of Venice stressed the freedom of Venetian citizens and
the openness of the city; on the other, it assumed and even recurrently
celebrated the piety and the orthodoxy of the populace as fundamental
to the stability and the prosperity of the state. Venetian legend, for
example, held that the city itself had been founded long before, on the
Feast of the Annunciation (25 March) in the year 421; this feast was
only one of some score of religious holidays in which the Venetians

9. Bolognetti, "Dello stato et forma delle cose ecclesiàstiche nel dominio dei signori
venetiani," 291.
10. Cited in Santosuosso, "The Moderate Inquisitor," 191.
11. Machiavelli, *Discorsi*, 163 (*The Discourses*, 143). See also Cervelli, *Machiavelli e la
crisi dello stato veneziano*, 20.

celebrated the close connection between their piety and the state. Some of the feasts were shared with all Christendom; others, such as the feast of Saint Mark, the city's patron saint, were celebrated to give special honor to the republic itself. But the message of the ritual year and the popular legends of the city was plain. Venice was a Catholic state, and its subjects' loyalty was closely intertwined with their piety.[12] Furthermore Venice, like other Renaissance city-states, had long shown a concern for religious conformity in the local population. As in other Italian cities, the medieval inquisition had established itself there in the thirteenth century, and, although Venice officially discontinued the inquisitor's stipend in 1423, there is some evidence of sporadic inquisitorial activity in the late fifteenth and the early sixteenth centuries—activity that appears to have intensified in the 1530s and 1540s even before Rome began to apply pressure.[13] In late medieval and early modern Europe, therefore, there was not so much freedom of religion as freedom in religion.

Moreover, as the papal nuncio Giovanni della Casa worked to bring the Venetian government around to Rome's view on the need for a new Holy Office in the city, his task was eased by a gradual erosion of participatory republicanism and a concomitant growth of hierarchy, both social and political, that had taken place in Venice in the first half of the sixteenth century. To be sure, Venice maintained the form of a republic and even preserved the majority of its republican institutions. But the republic was not altogether immune from the general shift toward hierarchical arrangements that was gradually concentrating power in the hands of a few prominent families. The political character of the city began to change most markedly during the War of the League of Cambrai, when an alliance consisting of the papacy, France, Spain, and a number of other European powers—formed to check Venetian expansion in northern Italy—managed, at least temporarily, to strip Venice of virtually all its holdings on the mainland. For Venice the costs were enormous, not only because of the large number of refugees who sought haven in the city or because of its loss of control of

12. Muir, *Civic Ritual in Renaissance Venice*; on the Feast of the Annunciation, see Rona Goffen, *Piety and Patronage in Renaissance Venice: Bellini, Titian, and the Franciscans* (New Haven: Yale University Press, 1986), esp. chap. 5.

13. On the activity of the Inquisition in this period, see the Archivio della Curia Patriarcale, Venice (hereafter APV), *Criminalia Sanctae Inquisitionis*, busta (hereafter b.) 1; and the articles by del Col cited in note 2.

the overland routes to much of western and northern Europe but also and above all because the war lasted so long, nearly eight years, from 1509 to 1517.[14]

There is little question that this war, so costly and lengthy, hastened the tendency within Venetian politics toward oligarchy. On the institutional level, its salient effect was to transform office into a commodity. When the war broke out, the Venetian nobility was already so large that all those who sought offices or sinecures could not easily gain one. Many of the traditional outlets in Eastern commerce had been sealed off both by economic competitors such as the Portuguese, who had recently established a route to India around the southern tip of Africa, and by social unrest in many of the eastern markets, which included the Levantine rebellions of the 1510s. But the War of the League of Cambrai, by stripping Venice of its mainland territories, reduced the number of offices dramatically. The rectorships and captaincies of Verona, Brescia, Vicenza, and Udine, which Venetian noblemen had traditionally occupied, simply vanished. Office, in these circumstances, became a valuable commodity. It is not surprising, therefore—given this pressure to obtain office and the state's increasingly desperate need for money—that offices soon went up for sale.

At first, the process was a passive one. In 1509 nobles were forced to make good on their debts; if not, they would lose political privileges. But in the following year, offices became purchasable. The process began with minor ones, those for which *cittadini* or Venetian "citizens" (a special and privileged class of subjects) also were eligible. Scribes, notaries, and accountants could buy their positions. But both the financial desperation of the government and the number of those who sought sinecures continued to grow. In the same year, the Senate allowed ten to thirty men to enter its number in return for loans. In 1515, the Quarantia or Court of Appeals also lifted its age limits for candidates who could provide a loan of one hundred ducats, and, in the Great Council, the names of those who had made financial contributions were announced prior to elections. Finally, in 1516 one of the most prestigious positions within the state, that of the Procurator of San Marco, went to the highest bidder. "The State became an object of commerce."[15]

14. Gilbert, "Venice in the Crisis of the League of Cambrai," in *History: Choice and Commitment*, 269–291.

15. This sentence is Robert Finlay's apt summation of political developments in these years; see his *Politics in Renaissance Venice* (New Brunswick: Rutgers University Press,

Inevitably, the commercialization of the state favored the wealthier members of the aristocracy. And indeed it was they who more and more occupied the key positions within the Venetian government, who filled the Senate, the Collegio, and, most decisively, the Council of Ten, leaving the poorer members of the state with access only to the Great Council. Thus, while Venice doubtless deserved the praise of such humanists as Contarini whose portraits of the republic in these years tended to idealize its government, there was nonetheless a clear drift toward the concentration of power in the hands of a few. Donato Giannotti, with analytical acumen characteristic of the late Florentine republican theorists, recognized this. Power, he noted in his treatise on the Venetian republic, was not spread evenly throughout the Venetian aristocracy but tended to be concentrated in the Senate and in the circle of advisers surrounding the doge.[16] Finally, on this matter, Ludovico dall'Armi, Altieri's associate who longed for the creation of an evangelical republic, was even more pointed. In a letter he wrote in 1547 to the doge and the Council of Ten, he contemplated the apparently inevitable collapse of republican governments and their replacement by monarchies.

As much affection as I have felt and shall always feel for this once most holy republic, I cannot help but grieve, Your Majesty, over the fortune of this republic, seeing how for the last few years it has—through ambition, through interests, and through the passions of individuals—rapidly begun to move toward that end to which all preceding republics have come. I say this because I see through experience how two or three citizens, who are enemies of their fatherland and the common freedom, have authority to have their way with the most excellent and venerable Council of Ten; and I say this because the wicked man finds more supporters than the good, the liar more than the truthful, and the unjust more than the just.[17]

Venice may have been, therefore, one of the few republics that survived the invasions of Italy in the early sixteenth century, but it did not do so without its own considerable narrowing of the circle of men who actually exercised political power.

---

1980), 173. These transformations have been analyzed in depth by Gaetano Cozzi, "Authority and the Law in Renaissance Venice," in John R. Hale, ed., *Renaissance Venice* (London: Faber and Faber, 1973), 293–345.

16. Gilbert, "The Venetian Constitution," in *History: Choice and Commitment*, 207.

17. Cited in Aldo Stella, "Guido da Fano eretico del secolo XVI al servizio dei re d'Inghilterra," *Rivista di storia della Chiesa in Italia* 13 (1959): 215.

Changes in the structure of government were not the only consequences of the war. Equally important was a shift in the perception of
the function of government whose role, more and more Venetians
agreed, included the preservation of morality, both public and private.
The result was that the sixteenth-century Venetian state, already quite
sophisticated in its legal bureaucracies and its police force for the control of such crimes as murder, rape, robbery, and larceny, now began
with special fervor to regulate the moral lives of Venetians as well. To
the nobleman Girolamo Priuli, scion of an important banking house in
Venice, for example, the suddenness with which Venice had lost its
possessions on the Italian mainland at the outbreak of the War of the
League of Cambrai was a confirmation that the state's well-being and
the virtues of its citizenry were tied together. The league, Priuli argued, was nothing other than divinely ordained punishment for a republic that had lost sight of the values of its ancestors. Priuli found his
contemporaries arrogant and irresponsible, and he chastised them for
their dissolute morals. He pointed a disapproving finger at the sexual
license of nuns whose convents had become notorious brothels (often
frequented by young nobles of the city) and at the prevalence in Venice
of homosexual practices, which he judged even more widespread in his
city than in Florence.[18]

Priuli was, in all likelihood, peculiarly sensitive to the inseparability
of morality and politics. But his contemporary Doge Loredan, in an
address delivered to the Great Council, touched on similar concerns.[19]
Moreover, during the War of the League of Cambrai the government
acted on precisely this assumption, passing numerous laws intended to
regulate public morality. In 1509 new and more exacting legislation
attempted to control the behavior of the more licentious nuns in the
city. In 1512 a new magistracy, the Provveditori sopra le pompe, was
created to curtail the use of overly expensive clothing, lavish palatial
decorations, and festivities. And in the period 1514 to 1517 the penalty
for blasphemers—those who, in their speech or acts, offended God—

18. On Priuli's reaction to the events of these years, see in particular Gilbert, "Venice
in the Crisis," in *History: Choice and Commitment,* 269–291. For an overview of the relatively sophisticated judicial institutions of late medieval Venice and the republic's efforts
to control crime, see Guido Ruggiero, *Violence in Early Renaissance Venice* (New Brunswick,
N.J.: Rutgers University Press, 1980). The fourteenth-century Venetian government's
efforts to control sexual activity, Ruggiero suggests, show a similar concern with moral
purpose (*The Boundaries of Eros: Sex Crime and Sexuality in Renaissance Venice* [Oxford: Oxford University Press, 1985]).

19. On Loredan, see Cervelli, *Machiavelli e la crisi dello stato veneziano,* 11–15.

was increased to five hundred lire and five years of exile.[20] If only the excesses could be brought under control, many in Venice argued, then perhaps Venice might once again benefit from divine favor. Doubtless, nonreligious factors had a role in such legislation: the acute need to raise funds to finance military campaigns made the conspicuous consumption of many nobles particularly unpalatable. Yet like other early modern governments, the Venetian magistracies perceived themselves as invested with a special moral purpose.

Nor did this special sense of moral purpose come to an end with the cessation of the war. Shifting social conditions did not allow it. The population was growing rapidly. The city was repeatedly struck by famine and was often filled with the poor and the hungry. Further, Venice was becoming an increasingly industrial city. There were new forms of work, which brought with them new social problems. The Arsenal, the state shipyard, and the textile industry, in particular, were all expanding quickly.[21] Finally, the growth of the Ottoman empire and the constant threat of war imposed heavy social and political costs. Thus those who did manage to monopolize power within the city faced a more and more difficult task of preserving their authority. It was necessary to develop laws and institutions that could control the poor, maintain a large naval force in a state of preparedness and, as in Priuli's generation, preserve public morality. These shifts, which began during the War of the League of Cambrai, therefore continued well into the sixteenth century. They were characterized above all by a hardening of social policy. In 1527, for example, the Council of Ten insisted on tighter supervision in granting the imprimatur of books and in the following year took control of the Provveditori sopra i monasteri. Then in 1537, on learning that Corfu, a Venetian colony, had been seized by Ottoman forces, it created the Esecutori contro la bestemmia—a magistracy with authority over blasphemers. While such institutions as

20. On the legislation concerning the nuns, see Gilbert, "Venice in the Crisis," in *History: Choice and Commitment*, 269–291; on the Provveditori sopra le pompe, see Giulio Bistort, *Il magistrato alle pompe nella republica di Venezia* (Bologna: Forni, 1969); and on the 1514 penalty for blasphemy, see Gaetano Cozzi, "Religione, moralità e giustizia a Venezia: Vicende della Magistratura degli Esecutori contro la bestemmia" (Typescript, Cooperativa libraria editrice degli studenti dell'Università di Padova, n.d.), 8; and Renzo Derosas, "Moralità e giustizia a Venezia nel '500–'600: Gli Esecutori contro la bestemmia," in Gaetano Cozzi, ed., *Stato, società e giustizia nella repubblica veneta (sec. XVI–XVIII)* (Rome: Jouvence, 1980), 431–528.

21. On these economic developments, see my more detailed discussion in chapter 6 below.

these were in many ways traditional, there was an important novelty. They were now tied more than ever to the most powerful governmental bodies within Venice and to the Council of Ten especially. They were its satellites and, as such, represented an effort to develop a more rationalized means of social control.[22]

But the new poor laws, in particular, were the clearest manifestations of the changing tone of Venetian society. Essentially these Venetian laws (enacted in 1529, but first systematically enforced in 1545) sought to eradicate begging and other highly personalized forms of charity, replacing them with more institutionalized forms of relief. As much as its Protestant counterparts, this Catholic state began to subsidize shelters and hospitals; it carefully controlled the price of grain; and it actively called on a wide variety of preexisting institutions, most notably the parishes, the guilds, and the confraternities, to assist in the execution of these policies.[23] Moreover, in Venice as in the Protestant countries, the development of new forms of poor relief derived both from the harsh social, economic, and demographic realities of the sixteenth century as well as from new religious sensibilities.[24] Charity was rationalized in Venice, but it remained a religious act and often flowed through traditional institutions. It was meant to improve not only the benefactors but also the recipients and to inculcate in them the ways of piety.[25]

A similar sensitivity to new social conditions and a remarkably similar sensibility to the importance of the poor were manifest also in the new regulations concerning conscription. Until the sixteenth century conscriptions, much like charity, had been organized primarily by neighborhood, with each parish providing a certain number of men in times of military need—much as each parish had assumed responsibility for its own poor. But in the sixteenth century the guild replaced the parish as the basis for naval levies. Yet there were more than structural parallels between the changes in conscription and in the establishment of new forms of poor relief. Both had similar moral goals as well. When in the early 1540s the levy by guild proved itself to be inadequate,

---

22. Stressed by Cozzi, "Authority and the Law." On the Esecutori contro la bestemmia, see Derosas, "Moralità e giustizia a Venezia."

23. Pullan, *Rich and Poor in Renaissance Venice*, 239–326.

24. On comparable developments elsewhere in Europe, see Natalie Zemon Davis, "Poor Relief, Humanism, and Heresy," in *Society and Culture in Early Modern France* (Stanford: Stanford University Press, 1975), 17–64, esp. biblio. on 59.

25. Pullan, *Rich and Poor in Renaissance Venice*, 631.

Cristoforo da Canal, admiral of the fleet, advocated the institution of convict labor on the galleys. In the treatise *Della milizia marittima* he presented arguments on the unsuspected benefits that the use of convict labor on the galleys would bring.

It is pious work, pleasing to God, that some of these rogues be condemned either for life or for time [to the galleys] in order that, recognizing their faults, they might return to Christ. . . . And such men as these, in addition to rendering themselves useful to us, become—almost through force—good men, because blasphemy, games, robbery, luxuries, and gambling and other vices, if there be any, are severely prohibited.[26]

Here, too, a reform in social policy was meant to have religious benefits.

In such a climate, it is hardly surprising that many members of the Venetian ruling class would ultimately reach an agreement with Rome concerning the Inquisition. For it represented, in a society in which religious tensions were no less palpable than social ones, one further turn of the screw. Unlike the poor laws and the creation of the new means of conscription, however, the Inquisition was less exclusively a Venetian creation, with the initiative for the intensification of its activity coming from Rome. There the leading figures of the Curia came to acknowledge that hope of reconciliation with the Protestants no longer existed. Consequently they began a counteroffensive. And while the Venetian ruling group may at times have acted to protect its trading interest, it was by no means adverse to supporting the Holy Office as a means of enhancing its own social control. For the Inquisition was, in its objectives and its procedures, fully consonant with the increasingly watchful and moralistic tone that Venice had gradually assumed during the first half of the sixteenth century.

Thus in Venice two powers, the Church and the state—the first preoccupied primarily by the threat of Protestantism but not unconcerned with the political turmoil that religious reform often brought in its wake, and the second focused primarily on the public order but aware too of the religious issues involved—came together to cooperate in the prosecution of heresy. Since their motives were different, certain tensions and disagreements between them were inevitable. But these

26. Cited in Alberto Tenenti, *Cristoforo da Canal: La marine vénitienne avant Lépante* (Paris: S.E.V.P.E.N., 1962), 91; see also Andrea Viaro, "La pena della galera: La condizione dei condannati a bordo delle galere veneziane," in Cozzi, ed., *Stato, società e giustizia*, 377–430.

tensions were for the most part family matters, mere squabbling. On the fundamental issue of the need to maintain orthodoxy, they agreed. But to do so, they needed to enlist the support of the faithful subjects of Venice. Accordingly, an essential objective of the Holy Office was the criminalization of religious dissent. The Inquisition sought, that is, to redefine certain forms of religious behavior and the expression of certain types of religious ideas—ones that the *popolo* had traditionally viewed as disconcerting or disruptive perhaps, but by no means as criminal—as heresy, as crime. The tribunal needed, in short, both to establish and to legitimate its function in Venetian society. But how did the Holy Office do this? What means did it have at its disposal?

The process of legitimation was not easy. To be sure, there was opposition to heresy on a popular level. Dissent from the dominant religious beliefs of a culture was after all likely to bring sharp disapproval from a wide spectrum of society, lay and clerical, rich and poor. But the mere existence of such opposition was no guarantee that the residents of Venice would turn to the Inquisition as a means of adjudicating religious disputes they had with their neighbors and their fellow workers. In part, this resistance to the court stemmed from a certain resentment against the efforts of the Church and the state to intervene in matters that had not traditionally been the concern of these institutions. There were thus numerous occasions, from these years of inquisitors on the defensive, when members of several Venetian communities they visited challenged their authority—shouting obscenities at them and even, on occasion, beating them up.[27] Feelings such as these doubtless led many residents of Rome—in a celebrated moment of popular hostility to the Counter-Reformation—to burn and pillage the Holy Office on the via Ripetta in 1559 on the occasion of the death of the Carafa pope, Paul IV.[28] The Venetians had their own more communal and informal means of handling religious disputes, without appeal to either the Church or the state. In the early 1530s, for example, when the carpenter Antonio began to proselytize his neighbors in the parish of San Giacomo dall'Orio with his new ideas—his "heresies"—many of them were scandalized and did not hesitate to reprove him and tell him to

27. Seidel Menchi, "Inquisizione come repressione o inquisizione come mediazione?" 56–61.
28. Pastor, *The History of the Popes*, 14:414. Pastor's work also furnishes this chapter's epigraph (19:300 n.2).

mind his own business.[29] But in addition to the neighborhood, the workplace and the family also provided contexts in which it was possible to chastise a seemingly irreverent and disruptive individual, a blasphemer, or an iconoclast. Workers, for example, could simply turn a deaf ear to an individual whose views they found offensive. The fellow workers of the journeyman silk weaver Antonio da Bologna did precisely this in protest of his proselytizing and his continual derision of Catholic beliefs and practices, especially the appeal to saints for divine favor and the consecrated host that, in his eyes, was nothing more than a "piece of pasta." In 1561 Nicolò da Cherso, a master at the Arsenal, explained how he and his co-workers would warn Isepo Zanco—a worker at the Tana or rope factory who was given to blasphemy and heretical assertions—that he was not welcome at their work site, at least not if he insisted on denigrating their beliefs. "We kept him out of our docks, and even if he did come by once in a while, we wouldn't put up with him talking about [his religious ideas]."[30]

The family was an especially effective informal means of discipline. Families, as the Venetian humanist Giovanni Caldiera had argued in the fifteenth century, were like miniature states, in which the father served as a kind of prince or doge within the household. And this patriarchal model extended into the popular world of shopkeepers and artisans as well, with husbands maintaining or at least theorizing that it was they who commanded and their wives who obeyed. It is hardly surprising that the family tended to reinforce religious conformity. "Never have I known my wife to have bad or heretical opinions," the tailor Francesco would tell the Inquisition. "She told me she was married before, and I told her, 'If you have gone astray, I want you to be an upright woman under me (*sotto di mi*).'" And similarly, Dominico di Albori would explain to this tribunal how he had reformed his bride, the daughter of a dissenter. "It is true that he never taught her how to say her prayers," he said. "And I really had to work to get her to say them, but at least now she does say them."[31] The enforcement of or-

29. Franco Gaeta, ed., "Documenti da codici vaticani," *Annuario dell'Istituto storico italiano per l'età moderna e contemporanea* 7 (1955): 5–53.

30. "Noi perciò el fessemo privar de quel squero donde che lavoravemo noi. Et se ben el vien qualche volta, non el sopportemo chel parli più delle cose sopra ditte" (ASV, *Sant'Uffizio*, b. 19, doss. "Zanco Giuseppe," testimony of 8 July 1561). On Antonio da Bologna, see ibid., b. 7, doss. "Contra Antonium Bononiensem."

31. "Mai ho sapudo che mia moglie sia stata de cative opinioni, la me ha detto che la è stata mogier de un, et mi ghe ho detto se ti è stata una trista, voglio che sotto di mi ti

thodoxy, therefore, could take place in the privacy of the home, far from the intrusions of the Holy Office. Later in the sixteenth century Carlo Borromeo, the archbishop of Milan who did so much to implement the decrees of the Council of Trent, would exploit this special and pious function of the family, and he recommended that "on all the first Sundays or other solemn days of the month, the heads of families [by which Borromeo doubtless meant the male heads of households] should assemble in their parishes with the parish priest, to discuss together the measures which must be taken to regulate properly and govern their families."[32] Piety and discipline were inextricably interwoven, and the family was guardian of both.

Nonetheless, the Inquisition was able to develop a gradual hold over the Venetian population. The Inquisition in Venice was—like similar tribunals elsewhere—part of a complex web of ecclesiastical institutions that reached all the way from local parishes to Rome. Through the publication of edicts, through sermons, through public rituals, and especially through confessors, the Holy Office sent the message to the faithful that it was their duty to denounce whomever they suspected of heresy to the Inquisition. At first, however, it was not a message that the laity, despite this formidable array of inducements, embraced. And by necessity therefore, the Inquisition relied largely on special groups of the population, to whom it appealed directly for assistance in identifying "heretics." On 4 June 1547, less than two months after the Venetian doge had established a lay magistracy to aid the Church in the repression of heresy, della Casa wrote to his superiors in Rome:

My auditor meets daily with the Lord Deputies concerning cases of heresy; and they have had all the parish priests and the schoolmasters called together and they have admonished them to be on the lookout for anyone in their charge or their parish who seems to be a heretic, and if they notice anyone who might be a heretic, they should denounce him; and also they put out a public edict on this same matter.[33]

---

sii una dona da ben" (ibid., b. 37 doss. "Gemma Gio. Battista," testimony of 22 October 1575); and "ho habudo gran fadiga a farga [ = farghe] dir oration. Ma adesso la le disse" (ibid., b. 40, doss. "Paolo di Albori," testimony of 5 January 1576).

32. Cited in Jean Louis Flandrin, *Families in Former Times: Kinship, Household, and Sexuality*, trans. Richard Southern (Cambridge: Cambridge University Press, 1979), 121.

33. Cited in Campana, "Monsignor Giovanni della Casa e i suoi tempi," 203.

There is even evidence that the Council of Ten promised to provide a monetary award to informants.[34] The Inquisition, therefore, immediately sought allies who could serve as its familiars and spies. It could not count on the spontaneous cooperation of the people.

And, in fact, in at least two of the three largest trials that the Venetian Inquisition held in 1547 and 1548—the first two years of its activity—the clergy initiated the proceedings. It was the parish priest of San Raffaele who brought to the attention of the Holy Office a group of women who were accustomed to making the rounds of various neighborhood churches where they listened to the new evangelical preachers and challenged the practices of the traditionally Catholic women they encountered. Similarly, a Dominican friar brought another group of evangelical *popolani* to the attention of the Holy Office, while the parish priest of San Moisè likely presented the denunciation against a large group of heretical artisans, a veritable *scuola dei luterani* in his neighborhood.[35] During the first stage of the Inquisition's operation, therefore, prosecution tended to come from a special quarter, and from a well-defined hierarchy: the clergy. Here was a classic case of *inquisitio* or inquest so characteristic of the courts, religious and secular, of the sixteenth century. In the early modern world, that is, it was increasingly common for prosecution to be initiated by an official juridical institution—responsive to official concerns, in this case, of both Church and state—rather than by the community itself.[36]

Moreover, della Casa was able to rely on example as well. His very first case (held in 1545 against the Augustinian Ambrogio da Milano) had ended with the spectacle of the friar publicly abjuring his heresies in the church of Santa Maria Formosa, located not far from the piazza San Marco. One of his first cases after the local tribunal of the Holy Office had been reorganized in 1547 also ended in a public abjuration.

34. ASV, *Sant'Uffizio*, b. 7, "Contra Franciscum Stella," report of 16 January 1550. Father Anastasio Jordano collected 12 ducats for his denunciation of Francesco Stella.

35. For the accusation brought against the group of women, see ibid., b. 7, doss. "Contra Franceschinam uxorem Joannis Samitarij et al.," report of 3 May 1548; on the group denounced by the Dominican friar, ibid., doss. "Boccalaro Gio. Maria et al.," denunciation of 1 June 1548; and, on the heretics of San Moisè, see ibid., doss. "Contra denuntiatos pro hereticis de contracta Sancti Moysis," passim. Although these cases represent only about a quarter of all the proceedings in 1547–1548 (against residents of Venice), most other cases involved individuals or at least not large groups.

36. On this procedure, often called *Inquisitionsprozess*, see Langbein, *Prosecuting Crime in the Renaissance*, 120–139; and Lenman and Parker, "The State, the Community and the Criminal Law in Early Modern Europe," 29–30.

Religion—as these public events made clear—was no longer to be seen as a purely private matter but became instead a matter of state. As della Casa himself made plain, he favored the staging of more impressive spectacles, even those ending in public execution.[37]

Della Casa had cause for optimism that the Venetian government would support him. On 14 May 1547 Ludovico dall'Armi—that brash *condottiero* who, together with Baldassare Altieri and others, had plotted an uprising in the Romagna with the hope of restoring republicanism and purifying the Gospel—was publicly decapitated between the two columns of justice on the piazza San Marco. The event drew, one report read, "as large a crowd as ever."[38] On the books, dall'Armi's crime was murder. Loyalty to a friend and an exaggerated sense of honor led him, he confessed, to take the life of a Venetian nobleman, and although the dead nobleman was a scoundrel whose loss the Venetian rulers did not mourn, they were nonetheless more than pleased to have a pretext to execute his murderer. Few had found dall'Armi trustworthy. Moreover, his actions made it plain that heresy could have political implications. He posed a clear threat to the state. Thus the spectacle of dall'Armi's decapitation, by making it clear to many in Venice that certain ideas had no place, was useful to the Venetian ruling group. And together with the formal support given to the local tribunal of the Roman Inquisition by the Venetian government the following month, it represented a turning point in the republic's policy toward heresy. Dissent had become a serious matter.

Yet when della Casa later that same year pressed for the public decapitation "between the two columns" of the heretical Franciscan fra Baldo Lupetino (whom his predecessor had arrested in 1542 and who had already spent five years in prison), with the expected excuse that "his punishment would serve as an example to others,"[39] the Council of Ten refused to have the sentence carried out. Instead fra Baldo was to remain in prison for life. Unfortunately, we cannot know the full reasons for this refusal, though the debates were heated, and fra Baldo came close to following Ludovico dall'Armi to death by decapitation. It is even possible that Vergerio, who had friends on the council, was able to intervene on the friar's behalf. The more intransigent guardians

37. Campana, "Monsignor Giovanni della Casa e i suoi tempi," 204–207.
38. Stella, "Guido da Fano eretico del secolo XVI al servizio dei re d'Inghilterra," 216 n.74.
39. "Talmente che la pena sua sia exempio ad altri" (ASV, *Sant'Uffizio* b. 10, doss. "Lupetino fra Baldo," sentence of 27 October 1547).

of orthodoxy were undoubtedly disappointed. Alvise Lippomano, for example, a former nuncio to Portugal, speaking of the related case of Vergerio who remained at large, complained of the leniency of the Roman Inquisition. "It is said that the Inquisitions in Spain and Portugal are too severe, and I reply that they are very useful, for at least they have the effect that this most pestilent disease [of heresy] has not penetrated into those regions. And he went on to add that "if a hundred or two hundred had been punished" in Italy, then perhaps heresy would be a less serious problem.[40]

Yet eventually the Roman Inquisition, even in Venice, would grow stern. When in 1556 fra Baldo was found guilty of proselytizing his fellow inmates, the government finally agreed to his execution, as long as it was carried out in secret, by drowning. Indeed, drowning was to be the only method of executing recalcitrant heretics in Venice throughout the sixteenth century. Accompanied by a priest or two, officers from the night watch would row the condemned man out of the lagoon and into the Adriatic before dawn. There, they would mutter a few prayers and drop the heretic, who was weighted with a stone, into the sea. Some twenty-five heretics were dispatched in this manner in sixteenth-century Venice.[41]

But why did Venice devise such a different means to execute heretics than it used for common criminals—murderers and thieves—whose deaths were often the focus of public spectacles outside the dogal palace? In part, the difference was a consequence of the ruling group's desire to protect its reputation for tolerance and openness with those Protestant nations with whom it traded. The ruling group, that is, understood the diplomatic value of the fiction of toleration. Such a policy also allowed the ruling groups in Venice to deny to the papacy that heresy constituted a significant threat to the city. But at the same time these secret dawn executions were designed to induce fear in the local population. From the vantage point of the Venetian public, a man summoned to the Inquisition, especially for a second time, might seemingly vanish into thin air. There was no public accounting. And if the individual was executed, the victim's friends and relatives must have relied on horrible rumors, with their potent capacity to intimidate still others. In 1567 a certain Giacomo Lucengo would testify to the Inqui-

40. Schutte, *Pier Paolo Vergerio*, 229.
41. Grendler provides a listing of most of those executed in *The Roman Inquisition and the Venetian Press*, 57 n.92.

sition that he had heard "that in this city of Venice, there is a large number of Huguenots, but they make every effort they can not to reveal themselves in order not to be arrested by the authorities and drowned."[42]

The use of drowning as the means of execution in such cases stemmed also from Venice's own complex relation to the sea, and as much as any spectacle of execution, this nonspectacle was meant to be didactic. Above all, it served as a horrifying reminder to Venetian subjects that their republic was very fragile and that the ruling group was willing to be pushed only so far. For this republic was maritime, and the sea was both the city's blessing and its curse. On the one hand, the Mediterranean and more specifically the Adriatic was the republic's lifeblood. It was that essential artery that tied Venice to markets in the east and west; it was the source of fish that enriched the diet of the city's artisans and merchants; it was part of the air they breathed; and its waters acted, with the movements of the tides, to cleanse the city of its waste. Nothing then was more essential than the sea to the identity of this maritime republic. On the other hand, the sea meant that Venice was open and vulnerable. Its waters could flood the *calli* and the *piazze*; and it could take the lives of Venetian fishermen and merchants when they sailed out upon it to find food or to trade. The ships that arrived in the city's ports, moreover, brought all kinds of men, many of whom were outsiders not only to the polity but to the religious foundations of Venetian life as well. To send heretics to the sea, then, was to recognize this duality. For it was precisely because heretics so threatened the identity of the republic and because they abused the openness of the city and polluted it, that the sea became the most fitting means of purifying the republic—protecting the community from the menace that heresy represented. The drownings, therefore, embodied an exquisite logic. The waters that made Venice the Catholic and maritime republic it was would also kill to keep Venice pure and to keep the community prosperous and united.

42. "Che in questa città di Venetia era una grande quantità della setta de Ugonotti, ma che loro si sforzano a non scoprirsi per non essere presi dalla giustitia et anegati" (ASV, *Sant'Uffizio*, b. 22, doss. "Lucengo Giangiacomo," testimony of 31 January 1567).

## CHAPTER THREE

# Evangelism and the Emergence of Popular Reform

*Ignorant men act like doctors.*
*They talk about Scripture constantly*
*In smithies, at the tailors', in barbershops—*
*Theologizing beyond all measure.*
                                    Alessandro Caravia,
                                    *Il sogno dil Caravia,* 1541

# ❧TRATTATO❧
## VTILISSIMO

## DEL BENEFICIO DI
## GIESV CHRISTO
## CROCIFISSO,
## VERSO I
## CHRI-
## STIANI,

Venetiis Apud Bernardinum
de Bindonis. Anno Do.
M.D.XXXXIII.

Despite the public decapitation of capitano dall'Armi and the increased support of the republic for the Roman Holy Office in Venice, not everyone in Venice was intimidated. Dall'Armi, after all, was a victim of secular justice; apart from some occasional posturing and much bluster, the Holy Office was in reality a moderate tribunal, at least in the early years of its activity. Della Casa may have wished otherwise, but in fact those found guilty of heresy generally received no more than a slap on the wrist. They might be instructed to make a small donation to a charitable institution, for example, or to make sure they attended mass and said their confessions, or merely to say a few extra prayers. Bishop Pier Paolo Vergerio, who had as much cause as anyone to complain about the Inquisition, cautioned a Protestant friend against exaggerating the level of repression. "You say that a hundred are burned here every day. It is not true. Not even one has been so punished, though in some places a certain light persecution has developed."[1]

Things could hardly have been different. For while the Venetian government acknowledged in principle that it must begin to cooperate with Rome in controlling heresy, nonetheless many members of the aristocracy in Venice, as elsewhere in Italy, either sympathized with or embraced evangelical teachings and were hesitant therefore to give della Casa's more repressive tendencies free reign. Evangelical ideas had made their way early into elite circles in Venice. The progression was perhaps inevitable, since young Venetian noblemen customarily rounded out their educations at the nearby University of Padua where many of their fellow students were German Lutherans and where, from his pulpit at Santa Giustina, Marco da Cremona had begun to teach Scripture in ways strikingly similar to the approaches of men such as John Colet and Desiderius Erasmus. But there were other avenues of evangelical influence as well. Not only did Gasparo Contarini have many close friends in the city, but after the Sack of Rome Venice became the leading center for those Italians most concerned about religious reform. It was there that men like Contarini, Alvise Priuli, Gian

1. Vergerio to Bullinger, 1553, cited in Pastor, *The History of the Popes*, 13:219 n.2.

---

*Opposite.* Frontispiece of the *Beneficio di Cristo*, published in Venice in 1543; of this work—the masterpiece of the Italian Reformation—Vergerio claimed that over forty thousand copies were sold. (The Library, St. John's College; by permission of the Master and Fellows of St. John's College, Cambridge)

Matteo Giberti, Gregorio Cortese, Marcantonio Flaminio, and, on occasion, Reginald Pole came together for study and for conversation about some of the most pressing religious problems of the day. And these articulate and engaging men could not but influence their friends and their hosts with their novel ideas. In these years, moreover, their views were not yet labeled "heretical"; many in the noble circles of Venice, with their Paduan degrees and their anti-Roman traditions, must have been more than a little receptive.[2] Thus we readily understand why the papal nuncio Andreassi (one of della Casa's predecessors), attempting in August 1540 to arrest fra Giulio da Milano for sermons that had caused some scandal, found himself complaining that fra Giulio was receiving support from certain of the "first gentlemen of this republic." Only a few years later the nuncio Mignanelli would observe that the new religious teachings were fostered by *huomini grandi*.[3] But who were these anonymous *primi gentiluomini* and *huomini grandi*, these aristocratic evangelicals in Venice?

For the most part, we simply cannot know. Indeed, we generally know the names of only those figures, like Contarini and Giberti, who achieved prominence outside the city. In part diplomacy explains this gap in our knowledge. To pursue those local patricians who supported the new ideas, the papal nuncios realized, would only alienate the Venetian government, ultimately making it less willing to cooperate in the repression of heresy. Only later, in the mid–1560s as repression intensified, would nobles constitute a legitimate target of investigation. But there was another reason for this silence. In the 1540s, in the eyes of the Inquisition, the noble evangelicals seemed anything but threatening and entirely unlike Ludovico dall'Armi. Apart from a few limited and patently paternalistic efforts to organize charity for the poor who shared their religious views, the Venetian nobles who expressed sympathy for the new religious teachings made little active effort to popularize their beliefs. There was a certain stuffiness to the evangelical commitments of these Venetian nobles—to them, as to Contarini (after all, he was one of their own), salvation was a purely personal

2. On Marco da Cremona and Venice as a center of evangelism, see Fenlon, *Heresy and Obedience in Tridentine Italy*, 31–35.

3. Giorgio Andreassi, letter to Cardinal Alessandro Farnese, 13 August 1540, in Franco Gaeta, ed., *Nunziature di Venezia* (Rome: Istituto Storico Italiano per l'Età Moderna e Contemporanea, 1960), 2:261. Mignanelli's concern is cited in Ortolani, *Pietro Carnesecchi*, 43.

matter.[4] The evangelism of the elites was an ideology of the internal spiritual renewal of the individual, not a gospel for social reform. Indeed, social reform was to be avoided at all costs, since the new interpretations of the Gospel that reformers such as Luther and Bernardino Ochino were propounding could easily lead not merely to religious reform but, as Luther's teaching had in Germany, to political and social upheaval as well.

Nonetheless, the evangelical nobles of Venice did offer umbrage and, albeit unwittingly, hope for another group of evangelicals who saw in the new teachings not only a message of personal salvation but also a vehicle for the transformation, or rather reform, of the Venetian church. We have already encountered Baldassare Altieri, Antonio Brucioli, and Pier Paolo Vergerio, who in these increasingly intolerant days were drawn to the city by its reputation for liberty and made Venice a center for their reforming efforts. But scores of others like them made similar choices. Pietro Carnesecchi, for example—a Florentine humanist who had served Pope Clement VII as apostolic protonotary before his conversion to evangelism under the influence of Juan de Valdés and Reginald Pole—came to Venice in 1542. The Brescian physician Girolamo Donzellino—a recent and promising graduate of the medical faculty at Padua who also spent a year in evangelical circles in Rome—arrived in 1546. And in these same years Venice became a center of activity for such men as Francesco Stella, a reforming lawyer from nearby Portobuffale, and the humanist priest Lucio Paolo Rosello.[5] Moreover, local humanists and professionals became caught up in the excitement of the new religious ferment as well. They included such figures as the outspoken notary Girolamo Parto, the goldsmith and poet Alessandro Caravia, his friend Paolo Crivelli, also a goldsmith, the lawyer Rafaele de Covis, and the nobleman Pietro Cocco.[6] Even the non-nobles among them, moreover, moved easily in

4. The best expression of Contarini's moderation is his *Modus concionandi*, published in Franz Dittrich, *Regesten und Briefe des Kardinals Gasparo Contarini* (Braunsberg: von Huye's, 1881), 305–309.

5. Ortolani, *Pietro Carnesecchi*; Colleen Linda Redmond, "Girolamo Donzellino: Medical Science and Protestantism in the Veneto" (Ph.D. diss., Stanford University, 1984); and, on both Stella and Rosello, del Col, "Lucio Paolo Rosello e la vita religiosa veneziana verso la metà del secolo XVI," 422–459.

6. ASV, *Sant'Uffizio*, b. 37, doss. "Parto Girolamo," denunciation of 27 March 1572; b. 13, doss. "Caravia Alessandro," testimony of 8 July 1557; for Crivelli, b. 6, doss. "Fra Benedetto da Genova," testimony of 3 September 1546; for Rafaele, b. 11, register "1553

the most elite social circles of the city. They had attended the same schools and universities as had their noble counterparts; they read the same books and often had the same professions. It was, doubtless, a time of excitement and optimism for the evangelical humanists. In a memorial prepared for the Venetian Inquisition in 1561, for example, Girolamo Donzellino would look back on the mid–1540s with a certain nostalgia. To Donzellino, Padua, Rome, and Venice had been places that, "since they were so full of people and visitors, of various social standing, and especially of writers, [provided him with a special opportunity in those years] to make many friends and get to know many people." And he conveyed something of the flavor of the discussions of those times. "Now, our own age is so curious about religious questions," he continued, "that we are neither satisfied with nor able to settle down into the beliefs of our elders, and this is especially true of those of us who are well educated and interested in books—we are constantly seeking out new teachings."[7] Another humanist concurred: in Rome in 1567 at the trial that led to his execution, Carnesecchi spoke frankly of the *conversatione continua* that he held in the Venice of the 1540s with others, like Vergerio and Altieri, who shared his views.[8] Moreover, as a group, it was precisely this cluster of the non-noble humanists and professionals who, because they had less stake in the received order of things or in the privileges of the Venetian hierarchy, sought to propagandize the new views. That they were able to do so effectively resulted from the presence in Venice of the largest and most advanced printing industry in Europe, an ideal instrument for the propagation of their ideas.

Printing had come early to Venice, brought by the German Johann von Speyer in the late 1460s. And almost at once, because of the privileged location of the city and the commercial contacts it enjoyed, the pub-

---

primo," testimony of 22 August 1553; and for Pietro Cocco, b. 9, doss. "Contra Bonifacium Emilionum," report of 18 June 1551.

7. "Le quali città per esser populose, piene di forestieri, di varie conditioni di persone, et massime di letterarie, danno occasione di far molte amicitie et conoscenze. . . . Hora essendo questa nostra età tanto curiosa nelle cose della fede, che non si contentando né si quietando nella fede de suoi maggiori, va cercando nove sette, et massime gli huomini dotti et letterati" (ibid., b. 39, doss. "Donzellino, Girolamo," memorial, "Reverendi et Ill.mi Signori. Da principio che io ritornai in questa città," presented by Donzellino to the Inquisition in November 1561).

8. Ortolani, *Pietro Carnesecchi*, 48.

lishing and book trade took hold. By the 1480s Venice had become "the capital of printing."[9] To a large degree, the book industry prospered because of the business skills of several families who had the capital to launch this new sector of the economy. From the beginning the publishers operated on an international scale. The Florentine Lucantonio Giunti, for example, who set himself up as a publisher in 1489 in Venice, was a brother of the most prominent publisher in Florence, and his nephew opened an important house in Lyon. The Giunti family continued its activities well into the sixteenth century. Additional international networks were established as others migrated to Venice in the hope of prospering there. In the 1530s the Frenchman Vincent Vaugris—who would italianize his name as Vincenzo Valgrisi and who would also be a source of continual irritation to the Venetian Inquisition—closed down his shop in Lyon and moved to Venice where he established one of the most active houses in the city. Valgrisi, moreover, operated shops in Padua, Bologna, Macerata, Foligno, Recanati, and Canciano. Another prominent publisher, Gabriel Giolito, with shops in Ferrara, Bologna, and Naples, belonged also to an international network of publishers and printers—one that would prove especially difficult for the authorities to hem in.[10]

The presence of such publishers as these along with the capital they were willing to invest in the book trade transformed the city. Around them grew a thicket of smaller publishers, printers, and book vendors. By the midsixteenth century, the thriving Venetian printing industry employed some five hundred men in approximately fifty shops.[11] A small operation might have two compositors who set the type, two pressmen, one corrector, and one collector who gathered the sheets into a book. These six men might print only one or two editions a year, while a large house with twenty or more employees, such as those of Giunti and Aldus, might print over two dozen. The Giolito press, the largest in the city, managed one year to print twenty-four editions. The flood of books that came from the Venetian presses was enormous: probably some 17,500 editions or seventeen to eighteen million individual copies of books were printed in Venice in the sixteenth century

9. Febvre and Martin, *The Coming of the Book*, 183.

10. On the Giunti, see ibid., 123; and on Valgrisi and Giolito, see Grendler, *The Roman Inquisition and the Venetian Press*, 16.

11. These figures are derived from an analysis of Ester Pastorello's listing of publishers and printers in Venice; see her *Tipografi, editori, librai a Venezia nel secolo XVI* (Florence: Olschki, 1924).

alone. They were both exported and sold locally. Scores of bookshops flourished in such central parishes as San Zulian and San Paternian, and book carts and stalls were common sights on the Rialto, along the Merceria, and in the piazza San Marco.[12]

The degree to which this industry altered Venetian culture cannot be exaggerated. Printing gave vernacular literature—in which Italians had been experimenting since the time of Dante—its first real flowering. On the one hand, these books, as we shall see, clearly fed a strong Venetian appetite for new ideas. They diffused a humanist and a classical culture to at least the middling strata, and they also gave reformers an efficient means of spreading their views. And on the other, the new technologies of print offered an outlet to an entirely new class of writers—to men who now had the opportunity, so novel in the sixteenth century, to make a living—as the famed playwright and satirist Pietro Aretino began to do—as writers. Like Aretino, who was a cobbler's son, many members of this new class of literati who came to Venice in the sixteenth century were the sons of artisans. They dreamt of making fortunes with their talents in letters. They included Anton Francesco Doni (whose father was a scissors maker), as well as Nicolò Franco, Ortensio Lando, and Girolamo Ruscelli (all of modest backgrounds). As Aretino did, they would climb the social ladder of the very world they mocked. Since with the possibility of profits from the sale of books, individuals no longer needed to be patricians in order to write, privilege came under attack with a new vehemence. Doni, Franco, and Lando attacked priests and princes; they took aim at pomposity wherever they found it; and they developed a critique of private property and the unequal distribution of wealth—ideas that the more radical reformers would also embrace.[13]

12. The Venetian publishing industry has been the subject of considerable analysis. In addition to the work of Grendler and Pastorello (see notes 10 and 11), see Brown, *The Venetian Printing Press*; Martin Lowry, *The World of Aldus Manutius: Business and Scholarship in Renaissance Venice* (Ithaca: Cornell University Press, 1979); and Claudia di Filippo Bareggi, *Il mestiere di scrivere: Lavoro intellettuale e mercato librario a Venezia nel Cinquecento* (Rome: Bulzoni, 1988). In her work on Strasbourg, Miriam Usher Chrisman has written a model book: *Lay Culture, Learned Culture: Books and Social Change in Strasbourg, 1480–1599* (New Haven: Yale University Press, 1982); unfortunately Venice in this period has nothing comparable to Chrisman's study.

13. Paul Grendler, *Critics of the Italian World, 1530–1560: Anton Francesco Doni, Nicolò Franco, and Ortensio Lando* (Madison: University of Wisconsin Press, 1969). It is no exaggeration to say that the Venetian Grub Street anticipated that of eighteenth-century Paris. See Robert Darnton, "The High Enlightenment and the Low Life of Literature," in *The Literary Underground of the Old Regime* (Cambridge, Mass.: Harvard University Press, 1982), 1–40.

To be sure, both civic and ecclesiastic authorities did try to regulate the publishing and selling of books. As early as 1491 the papal legate to Venice decreed that episcopal authorization was necessary before books touching on matters of faith could be printed.[14] At about the same time the Dominican Filippo di Strata, himself a copyist in the scriptorium of San Cipriano on Murano, saw nothing but trouble coming from this novelty, the book. He observed that the human race had got along just fine since the Creation without printing. He complained how hawkers would thrust inexpensive works, some costing as little as two or three *grossetti*, into the arms of passersby. The book was an invention that could have the most serious consequences, he warned. And he urged the burning of books, especially books on matters of faith—otherwise, the whole world might go to heresy.[15] Over the course of the first half of the sixteenth century these admonitions were taken more and more seriously. Both the Council of Ten and the Esecutori contro la bestemmia tried to regulate what could be printed and sold. But their efforts were intermittent. It was only in 1547, with the reorganization of the Venetian Inquisition, that more systematic efforts could be made. Della Casa was again the leading proponent of control. In July 1548 he set up great bonfires of confiscated books on the piazza San Marco and near the Rialto. He harassed Brucioli (whom he managed to get exiled from the city for two years) and Francesco Stella; in 1549 he published the first Venetian catalogue of prohibited books and managed to get the publishers organized into a guild.[16] The Venetian government, however, well aware that the book trade brought considerable business and wealth to the city, decided to leave enforcement for the most part to the publishers themselves.

In any case, the total control of production and distribution within such a large industry in a mercantile city would have been impossible. First, books were, as Filippo di Strata complained, downright cheap. They were hawked for prices that put them within the reach of many artisans who earned in only two or three days' labor the equivalent of an edition of the *Beneficio di Cristo*, for example, or of Ochino's *Sermons*.

14. Febvre and Martin, *The Coming of the Book*, 244.

15. Arnaldo Segnazzi, "Un calligrafo milanese," *L'Ateneo veneto: Rivista bimestrale di scienze, lettere, ed arti* 32 (1909): 63–77.

16. For a modern critical edition of the 1549 catalogue, see J. M. De Bujanda, ed., *Index des livres interdits: Index de Venise 1549; Venise et Milan 1554* (Sherbrooke, Québec: Centre d'Etudes de la Renaissance; Geneva: Librairie Droz, 1987). See also Grendler, *The Roman Inquisition and the Venetian Press*, 76–89, though Grendler's observations should now be read in light of del Col, "Il controllo della stampa a Venezia."

And to the authorities, this widespread availability of books was a perennial problem. In the mid–1550s, for example, Alessandro Caravia's most explicitly evangelical poem, *La verra antiga ovvero la morte di Giurco et Gnagni* (The ancient war or the deaths of Giurco and Gnagni), sold for a mere six *soldi*, and this book, written in Venetian dialect, was something of a best-seller. Many booksellers carried it; one, Ludovico Avanzo, told the Inquisition that he had stocked as many as fifty to sixty copies.[17] And in the early 1580s a butter vendor from the Rialto was picked up by the Inquisition for having purchased not the whole of Boccaccio's *Decameron* (which, in addition to being on the *Index of Prohibited Books*, might have been too expensive) but rather a single *quinterno*, containing the seventh novella.[18] These capillary movements of books would have been beyond the control of all but the most totalitarian of states.

Furthermore, the ownership of a book was not a prerequisite for reading it. Books made the rounds among friends. Enthusiasts readily lent and borrowed books, treatises, and poems on a variety of topics. They were inexpensive but precious items, opening up new worlds and providing resources for the criticism of given arrangements. And finally, when the state did try to intervene between the reader and the text, the heretics themselves readily found ways of circumventing the laws. In 1547 Francesco Stella, a close associate of Vergerio, was holding two bundles and a case of heretical titles in the home of a friend in Venice, probably for distribution in the city.[19] Merchants and others often brought contraband titles, hidden in bales of cloth or other wares, to Venice.[20] But the heretics were not casual about smuggling. Their key supplier was Pietro Perna, a Lucchese printer residing in Basel, with republican sympathies and strong Protestant convictions. Shrewdly, by way of an elaborate network of connections and con men, Perna managed to ship the heretical works into Venice (and other Ital-

17. On the price of books in Venice and their relation to wages, see Grendler, *The Roman Inquisition and the Venetian Press*, 14. On the diffusion of Caravia's poem, see ASV, *Sant'Uffizio*, b. 13, doss. "Caravia Alessandro," testimonies of 8 July 1557 and 25 February 1558. This chapter's epigraph comes from his poem *Il sogno dil Caravia*: "Molti ignoranti che fanno i dottori/Parlano ogn'hor de la sacra scrittura/Per barbarie, da favri, da sartori/theologizzando fuori d'ogni misura" (Venice: Giovann'Antonio di Nicolini da Sabbio, 1541), B iii. Caravia's trial has been published: Enrica Benini Clementi, "Il testo del processo di Alessandro Caravia," *Nuova rivista storica* 65 (1981): 645–652.

18. ASV, *Sant'Uffizio*, b. 49, doss. "Semolino Guidone," testimony of 29 May 1582.

19. ASV, *Sant'Uffizio*, b. 7, doss. "Contra Franciscum Stella," denunciation of 16 November 1549.

20. Grendler, *The Roman Inquisition and the Venetian Press*, 75.

ian cities as well) despite the efforts of the authorities to prohibit the import of certain titles. The system—with its scattered correspondents and the subterfuges that Perna set up—worked, and it worked well for over two decades.[21] Once the clandestine titles cleared inspection at Venetian customs, they were delivered by another insider (at times the physician Girolamo Donzellino) to a bookshop that served as a kind of holding house for the contraband volumes. Later they were distributed to a variety of local bookshops. One such shop was that of Andrea Arrivabene, a publisher with strong commitments to religious reform. Already in the mid–1540s he had begun supplying evangelicals in Viadana, a town near his father's native Mantua, with such works as the *Beneficio di Cristo* and the *Sommario della Santa Scrittura*. He too was close to Vergerio, who visited his shop during this decade, as well as to other key figures in Venetian evangelism such as Francesco Stella, Girolamo Donzellino, Lucio Paolo Rosello, and Comin da Trino, Rosello's publisher. But other shops (those of Paolo Avanzo, Pietro Longo, Bonifacio Emilione, the Valgrisi, and the Ziletti) also sold heretical works.[22] Thus books expounding heretical doctrines filtered into Venice and, once there, given the ubiquity of shops in the city, allowed the authorities few chances to control their sale.

The propaganda, however, would have been unsuccessful without readers. The most striking aspect of the culture of the heretics—even at the popular level—was that it was a literate one—hungrily so. There was an appetite for religious works. The book was not only appealing to the university educated and to professionals; it also reached an audience of artisans and shopkeepers. The book, that is, entered the shop in sixteenth-century Venice. In part, this was the ideal of some of the leading reformers. But the very atmosphere of the shops also encouraged reading, for the artisans of the elite crafts and trades were, by and large, citizens of the republic of letters. Very few were illiterate in the absolute sense of being unable to read at all.

21. Leandro Perini, "Note e documenti su Pietro Perna, libraio-tipografo a Basilea," *Nuova rivista storica* 50 (1966): 145–200; "Ancora sul libraio-tipografo Pietro Perna e su alcune figure di eretici italiani in rapporto con lui negli anni 1549–1555," ibid., 51 (1967): 363–404; and Andrea del Col, "Il Nuovo Testamento tradotto da Massimo Teofilo e altre stampate a Lione nel 1551," *Critica Storica* 15 (1978): 658–661 and 670–671. See also Antonio Rotondò, "Pietro Perna e la vita culturale e religiosa di Basilea fra il 1570 e il 1580," in *Studi e ricerche di storia ereticale*, 273–391.

22. Del Col, "Il controllo della stampa a Venezia."

In general, the Venetian artisans appear to have been much like their counterparts in other European cities where, as historians have been able to show, literacy was not "distributed evenly"; rather it was, not surprisingly, most diffused among those occupations that required the greatest skills—for example, among apothecaries, printers, musicians, metalworkers.[23] Patterns in which levels of literacy varied from one social group to another were common in early modern Europe, and, indeed, some evidence, albeit impressionistic, shows that this was the case in Venice also. Illiteracy appears to have been a recurrent problem within the Venetian navy; many petty officers in the fifteenth and six-teenth centuries alarmed their superiors by their inability to read. The Venetians themselves were conscious that literacy and class were linked. Until the sixteenth century illiteracy—in this case a shield against the leaking of state secrets—was even a prerequisite for candi-dates for the office of *bullator*, the keeper of the dogal seal. But in 1501 the Maggior Consiglio rescinded this requirement, on the grounds that persons who were illiterate were not the sort to be present in the apart-ments of the doge.[24] But if literacy was not evenly distributed through-out the population, it was nonetheless on the rise. The Venetian patri-cian and political philosopher Giovanni Maria Memmo encouraged artisans to learn to read, and in their books of trades Ludovico Fiora-vanti and Tommaso Garzoni noted that printing itself had made books accessible to the poor. "Before [the invention of] this marvelous art of printing," they wrote (with Garzoni plagiarizing Fioravanti), "there were many fewer literate men than there are today—a consequence of nothing other than the intolerable cost of books these days."[25] A

23. Natalie Zemon Davis, "Printing and the People," in *Society and Culture in Early Modern France*, 210. On patterns of literacy in Europe see, for England, Lawrence Stone, "Literacy and Education in England, 1640–1900," *Past and Present* 42 (1969): 69–139; for France, François Furet and Wladimir Sachs, "La croissance de l'alphabétisation en France, XVIIIe-XIXe siècles," *Annales: Economies, sociétés, civilisations* 29 (1974): 714–737; and for Italy, Piero Lucchi, "La Santacroce, il Salterio e il Babuino: Libri per imparare a leggere nel primo secolo della stampa," *Quaderni storici* 38 (1978): 593–630; Anne Jacobson Schutte, "Teaching Adults to Read in Sixteenth-Century Venice: Giovanni Antonio Ta-gliente's *Libro Maistrevole*," *Sixteenth-Century Journal* 17 (1986): 3–16; and now Paul Gren-dler's *Schooling in Renaissance Italy: Literacy and Learning, 1300–1600* (Baltimore: Johns Hopkins University Press, 1989).

24. Carlo Cipolla, *Literacy and Development in the West* (New York: Penguin Books, 1969), 57–58.

25. Giovanni Maria Memmo, *Dialogo . . . nel quale dopo alcune filosofiche dispute . . . un perfetto Prencipe, & una perfetta Republica, e parimente un Senatore, un soldato, et un mercante* (Venice: Gabriele Giolito, 1563), 122–123; and Tommaso Garzoni, *Piazza universale di tutte le professioni del mondo* (Venice: Gio. Battista Somascho, 1585), 833. Garzoni draws

modern quantitative historian has compiled statistics that seem to prove that this impression of a rapidly growing literacy rate was accurate.[26] In Venice, therefore, as in the French cities of Lyon and Montpellier, the culture of the book could set readers apart from their neighbors, fellow workers, and even family members on religious matters.[27]

But even those who were unable to read appreciated the nearly magical power of the book. Franceschina, the wife of a silk weaver, had her husband's apprentice read to her and her spouse from the Bible on Sunday mornings.[28] Alberto da Gesuy, a sword smith who resided in Bergamo, when asked by the inquisitors if he could read, responded that he was unable but added, "I wish to God that I could!"[29] And the Anabaptist Valerio, a Venetian dyer, explained how a friend, on learning that he could not read, bought him a copy of the *New Testament* and urged him to learn to do so.[30] Thus those on the margins of literacy hoped to or actually did find ways to penetrate the world of books. By contrast Francesco Cagnolo, an *ormesiner* or silk weaver, argued that his inability to read was evidence that he was no heretic. When asked if he knew why he had been arrested, he responded that he had no idea, adding, "I am not a heretic, because I have no letters, if I have said anything, I have said it *semplicemente*, and it will never be shown that I am a heretic."[31] The problem is thus not simply to establish a correlation between literacy and heresy. They stood in a dynamic relation to each other. Not only could ability to read incline a man or a woman to heresy, heresy could incline a person to learn to read. Moreover, it is clear that the book did not supplant their traditions and culture but

---

on a passage in Leonardo Fioravanti, *Dello specchio di scientia universale* (Venice: Vincenzo Valgrisi, 1564), f. 61v.

26. Cipolla, *Literacy and Development*, 22–23 and 57–58.

27. On some religious consequences of literacy, see Davis, "Strikes and Salvation in Lyon," in *Society and Culture*, 5; and Emmanuel Le Roy Ladurie, *The Peasants of Languedoc*, trans. John Day (Urbana: University of Illinois Press, 1974), 149–171.

28. ASV, *Sant'Uffizio*, b. 7, doss. "Contra Franceschinam uxorem Joannis samitarij," testimony of 18 September 1548.

29. "Mi non so né legger né scriver perché fui mai a scola. Volesse Dio che savesse legger et scriver" (ibid., b. 15, doss. "Costituto de Alberto Spader milanese," testimony of 3 December 1548).

30. Ibid., b. 22, doss. "Odorico Marosella, Valerio Perosin et al.," testimony of 8 March 1567.

31. "Non son lutherano, perché io non ho lettere. Se ho detto qualche cosa, ho detto semplicemente, et non se troverà mai che sia lutherano" (ibid., b. 24, doss., "Contra Franciscum Cagnolo," testimony of 10 July 1568).

supplemented them. Reading and the discussion of texts were frequent, almost distinguishing activities of the heretics. Reading aloud, furthermore, served to bridge the gap between those who could and those who could not make their way through a complex text.

Examples of the presence of the book among those tried for heresy are endless. We have already noted how widespread the sale of a book such as Caravia's evangelizing poem could be. But especially important was the *Beneficio di Cristo*, published anonymously in Venice in 1543. Historians have long suspected that the *Beneficio* played a leading role in the Italian heretical movements. In the words of the great Italian historian and philosopher Benedetto Croce, the treatise, "barely off the press, ran swiftly like a torch through all Italy, igniting others."[32] There were at least three editions of the work published in Venice in the 1540s, and it is probable that the work was printed at Mantua as well.[33] Vergerio defended the work: "If it is evil, why was it permitted for forty thousand copies to be sold? For I know that this many have been printed and sold in Venice alone over the last six years."[34] The statistic is certainly inflated, but there is abundant evidence that the work had a remarkable diffusion both within Venice and through much of the rest of Italy. Indeed, in Venetian evangelical circles the work was central, especially in the late 1540s and early 1550s. The printer Andrea Arrivabene and the bookseller Bonifacio Emilione both distributed it, and records of Arrivabene's warm recommendation of the trea-

32. Benedetto Croce, "Il 'Beneficio di Cristo,'" *La critica* 38 (1940): 115.

33. On the editions, see Salvatore Caponetto, ed., *Il Beneficio di Cristo con le versioni del secolo XVI: Documenti e testimonianze* (DeKalb: Northern Illinois University Press; Chicago: Newberry Library, 1972), 497f. The scholarship of the *Beneficio* is vast. On its authorship, see Carlo Ginzburg and Adriano Prosperi, "Le due redazioni del 'Beneficio di Cristo,'" in *Eresia e Riforma nell'Italia del Cinquecento*, Miscellanea I [Biblioteca del Corpus Reformatorum Italicorum] (DeKalb: Northern Illinois University Press; Chicago: Newberry Library, 1974), 135–204. On the text's relation to the writings of other reformers, see esp. Ruth Prelowski, ed. and trans., "The 'Beneficio di Cristo,'" in John Tedeschi, ed., *Italian Reformation Studies in Honor of Laelius Socinus* (Florence: Le Monnier, 1965), 21–102; and Tommaso Bozza, who argues that the *Beneficio* draws primarily on Calvin's *Institutes*: Bozza, *Il Beneficio di Cristo e la Istituzione della Religione Cristiana di Calvino* (Rome: Arti Grafiche Italiane, 1961). Carlo Ginzburg and Adriano Prosperi—although they exaggerate the *Beneficio*'s Pelagian dimensions—offer an important argument for its context of popular sixteenth-century religious writings; see their *Giochi di pazienza: Un seminario sul "Beneficio di Cristo"* (Turin: Einaudi, 1975). For a recent overview of this scholarship, see Paolo Simoncelli, "Nuove ipotesi e studi sul 'Beneficio di Cristo,'" *Critica storica* 12 (1975): 320–388, and other works on this topic cited in the essay on sources and bibliography.

34. From a *commento* of Vergerio published in Caponetto, ed., *Il Beneficio di Cristo*, 444.

tise survive.[35] Certain individuals who happened on the *Beneficio* maintained before the inquisitor that they disapproved of it, destroying it as soon as they recognized the dangerous doctrines it contained.[36] But many admitted reading it. Both the goldsmith Iseppo and the turner Bernardo, members of a large conventicle of heretics uncovered in 1548, confessed to having read it. The following year, Anzolo Lion, a jeweler in his early twenties, not only confessed to reading the *Beneficio* but noted that it and other suspect works could be purchased easily and over-the-counter in Venice.[37] The work was available elsewhere as well. In this same period, the silk weaver Paolo Gaiano read the treatise in Modena and the solicitor Vincenzo Marchesio read it in Bergamo.[38] Over time, however, it became more and more difficult to come by. Andrea delle Gambarare, an itinerant merchant from Treviso, tried for heresy in 1568, admitted both that he had purchased the *Beneficio* and that it had pleased him very much, but noted that all this had taken place twelve years earlier.[39] In 1572 the jeweler Giulio di Stai, closely associated with a large group of Venetian evangelicals, confessed that he had read the treatise, but that he had done so twenty-five years earlier.[40] But the work did not disappear entirely. In the early 1570s Aquilina Loschi—though the illegitimate daughter of a Vicentine nobleman, she resided in Venice—had a copy of the *Beneficio* that she would hide under her bed, away from her husband's view.[41] The Dominican Ambrogio Catarino Politi undoubtedly felt justified in devoting an entire treatise, *Il compendio d'errori et inganni luterani* (The compendium of Lutheran errors and deceits), which he published in Rome in 1544, to refuting the theology òf the *Beneficio di Cristo*.[42]

35. ASV, *Sant'Uffizio*, b. 10, doss. "De Benedetti fra Benedetto," testimony of 8 February 1552 and b. 30, doss. "Arrivabene Andrea," testimony of 24 October 1574. See also del Col, "Lucio Paolo Rosello e la vita religiosa veneziana verso la metà del secolo XVI," 424.

36. ASV, *Sant'Uffizio*, b. 8, "Chioggia/Vescovo e canonici," deposition of 10 October 1559; and b. 10, doss. "De Benedetti fra Benedetto," testimony of 8 February 1552.

37. Ibid., b. 7, doss. "Contra denuntiatos pro hereticis de contracta Sancti Moysis," testimonies of 30 October 1548 and 6 January 1549; and doss. "Leone Angelo," testimony of 22 May 1549.

38. Ibid., b. 20, doss. "Paolo Gaiano," testimony of 1 December 1569; and b. 32, doss. "Contra Vicentium Marchesium," transcript of trial from 1552, f. 3.

39. Ibid., b. 24, doss. "Contra Andream quondam Melchioris Gambararium," testimony of 10 June 1568.

40. Ibid., b. 32, doss. "Contra Fratrem Hieronimum de Padua et al.," testimony of 19 January 1572.

41. Ibid., b. 35, doss. "Contra Aquilinam Loschi," testimony of 15 March 1572.

42. The full title of the work was *Compendio d'errori, et inganni Luterani, contenuti in*

At its heart, the *Beneficio* was a deeply Augustinian work, at once emphasizing man's radical and absolute dependence on the merits of Christ for his salvation and his utter inability to avoid offense or rebellion against God. "It is impossible," the *Beneficio* asserted, "for us to love God and to conform to his will on our own."[43] This was the result of Adam's disobedience, of the calamitous loss of the divine image in which man had been created. Through the law, however, God had rendered many painfully conscious of this condition. The final office of the law, after having uncovered man's sinfulness and the wrath of God, was to demonstrate the necessity for Christ. Christ was, moreover, the fulfillment of God's promise to Moses. Christ was a great prophet, the only begotten Son of God, who delivered man from the curse of the law, reconciled him with God, made his will capable of good works, healing the freedom of his will and restoring the divine image that had been lost.[44] With the grace of God, therefore, comes a transformation of man. He is rendered not only capable of good works but is directly incited to do them. "He is probed by a violent love to do good works and to render the sweetest fruits to God and to neighbor."[45] The stress on the transformation could not be greater. Without faith in Christ, man is incapable of good works, but through faith good works become inevitable, almost natural. "He who considers himself just through the justice of Christ," the *Beneficio* continues, "does not ask if good works have been commanded or not, but moved and incited by a violence of divine love, immediately offers himself to holy and Christian works and never ceases to do them."[46] The treatise, then, dwells

---

un Libretto, senza nome de l'Autore, intitolato, *Trattato utilissimo del benefitio di Christo crucifisso* (Rome: Girolamo Cartolari per Michele Tramezzino, 1543). A modern edition appears in Caponetto, ed., *Il Beneficio di Cristo*, 345–422, esp. 349.

43. "È impossibile che con le forze nostre possiamo amar Dio e conformarci con la sua volontà" (*Trattato utilissimo del Beneficio di Giesù Christo Crocifisso, verso i Christiani*, in Caponetto, ed., *Il Beneficio di Cristo*, 13–14).

44. I paraphrase the beginning of chap. 3 of the *Beneficio:* "Avendo adunque il nostro Dio mandato quel gran profeta che ci avea promesso, che è l'unigenito suo Figlio, acciochè esso ci liberi dalla maledizion della Legge, e reconcilii con lo nostro Dio, e faccia abile la nostra volontà alle buone opere, sanando il libero arbitrio, et ci restituisca quella divina imagine" (ibid., 19).

45. "È spinto da un violento amore alle buone opere e a rendere frutti dolcissimi a Dio e al prossimo" (ibid., 33).

46. "Colui che si tiene giusto per la giustizia di Cristo, non domanda se le buone opere sono di precetto o no, ma, commosso e incitato da una violenza di amor divino, s'offerisce prontissimo alle opere sante e cristiane, né mai cessa dal bene operare" (ibid., 44).

but briefly on sinfulness and human depravity and after the first few pages offers an optimistic anthropology. "He who believes that Christ has taken upon himself his sins becomes similar to Christ (*simile a Cristo*)."[47] Like Christ, the believer becomes, through faith, "a son of God."[48] But the transformation is not expressed only in metaphors. A genuine imitation of Christ is called for, and it is one that would have effects in the real world. "His spirit moves us . . . to humility, to eloquence, to obedience toward God, to charity, to further perfections, through which we recover the image of God."[49] And the treatise stresses, in its final paragraphs, the need for man to express his love through works, charity, and concern for neighbor. The believer is never to be made to feel entirely alone but is rather to join a brotherhood, a charitable fraternity.

Although certainly the masterpiece of Italian evangelical literature, the *Beneficio* was only one of perhaps a score of works that circulated in reform circles. The evangelicals propagated their views through a series of such treatises, catechisms, and sermon collections. In their searches of print shops and bookstores, agents of the Inquisition uncovered, alongside the *Beneficio*, other similarly devotional readings such as the *Sommario della Sacra Scrittura*, Ochino's sermons, Valdés's *Alfabeto cristiano*, and various catechisms as well as works of a more spirited genre, including Caravia's poetry, the better-known pasquinades of Celio Secondo Curione and the satirical *Tragedia del libero arbitrio*—all of which reiterated messages similar to those of the *Beneficio*. In only a few years, through intense propaganda the leading reformers had made a wide range of literature available to a broad public, eager to reinterpret their relationship to God and to the Church in significant ways.[50]

The pulpit also served as an important medium for propaganda, and Venice saw an increasing number of evangelical preachers in the late 1540s. This was not the first time such ideas had been propagated openly in Venice. A decade earlier Bernardino Ochino had mesmerized

47. "Colui, il quale crede che Cristo abbia tolto sopra di sé li suoi peccati, diventa simile a Cristo" (ibid., 27).

48. Ibid., 40–42.

49. "Lo spirito suo ci muove . . . all'umiltà, alla mansuetudine, alla ubbidienza di Dio, alla carità alle altre perfezioni, per le quali recuperiamo l'imagine di Dio" (ibid., 43).

50. Surprisingly, there is no general study of the evangelical literature; for a preliminary orientation, see Johannes Trapman's introduction to Cesare Bianco's ed. of *Il Sommario della Santa Scrittura e l'Ordinario dei Cristiani* (Turin: Claudiana, 1988).

his Venetian audience with his unambiguously evangelical emphasis. Over the next few years evangelical sermonizing intensified markedly, and the evidence suggests that this trend was part of a concentrated campaign on the part of Italian evangelicals to propagate their increasingly heretical ideas despite or, perhaps, because of their recent political defeats and the failure of the *spirituali* in Italy. Such Franciscans as fra Sisto da Siena, Antonio Pennarolo, Mariano da Crema, Giuliano "da Colle," and Sebastiano Castello as well as such Augustinians as fra Ippolito Chizzuola, Angelico da Crema, Andrea Ghetti da Volterra, and Agostino da Genova became well known for the heretical ideas they preached during the Lenten or Advent seasons—often in the Frari, the great cavernous basilica of the Franciscans, or Santi Apostoli, a parish church nestled in the center of the city.[51] Outside the churches, however, there was a less official preaching, the work of itinerant ex-friars such as Andrea di Pontremolo, Bernardino, and Paolo Furlan who preached in the open in exchange for charity but whose apparently evangelical ideas brought them first to the attention of and then stern warnings from the Venetian Holy Office.[52]

Like the book, the sermon quickly became a central resource in the development of an evangelical culture. Giovanni Antonio Clario, a gentleman from Eboli who made his living as a proofreader in the Erasmus printing shop, and Antonio Bernerio from Correggio, who worked as an illuminator in the district of San Marco, made it a practice of accompanying each other to the sermons of the evangelicals.[53] Witnesses summoned to testify about the activities of three women heretics—a silk weaver's wife and two of her neighbors from the parish of San Pantaleone—emphasized the importance of the evangelical preachers. "I've seen them go to all those preachers who have a heretical reputation," Stefano di Francesco testified, "and especially to the one at San Barnabà." A second witness agreed and made clear the significance of the new preaching to these women: "[They] go to these sermons and

51. Andrea del Col, "Due sonetti inediti di Pier Paolo Vergerio il giovane," *Ce fastu?* 54 (1978): 70–85. Compare Chabod's remarks on the importance of the Franciscans and Augustinians in the heretical movements of Milan: "Per la storia religiosa dello Stato di Milano," 304–305.

52. ASV, *Sant'Uffizio*, b. 6, doss. "Clozio fra Bonaventura," warning given 22 February 1549; b. 7, doss. "Giovanni e Bernardino," testimony of 15 January 1549; and b. 7, doss. "Paolo . . . Quaderno," sentence of 4 January 1549.

53. Ibid., b. 6, doss. "Clario Gio. Antonio," testimony of 24 May 1547 and doss. "Bernerio Antonio miniatore," also testimony of 24 May 1547.

discuss evangelical matters. They have told me they believe in the Gospel, that the Truth is being preached, and that earlier, because the Truth was not preached, we were deceived."[54] The preacher at San Barnabà—almost certainly the Augustinian fra Angelico da Crema whose tongue the papal legate Giovanni della Casa had hoped to have cut out—had a marked influence on popular opinion in Venice. In the trial of a large group of artisans from the parish of San Moisè, one witness compared the sermons of another preacher, who turned things upside down, to those of the preacher at San Barnabà. Another noted that when fra Angelico was arrested, maestro Iseppo, a goldsmith, one of the leaders of the group at San Moisè, made no effort to conceal his disgruntlement over the preacher's retention.[55] Not all the preaching was public. After being censured by his superiors for his 1546 sermons at the parish churches of San Giacomo dall'Orio and San Bartolomeo, fra Agostino da Genova nonetheless continued to make his views heard. Bartolomeo Carpan, a Venetian jeweler, invited a number of acquaintances—for the most part, fellow guildsmen from the Ruga degli Oresi—to his house in the parish of San Stai to hear Agostino preach. Though several members of the audience disagreed with the friar, he held forth in debate and in sermonizing on the subject of predestination for eight hours! Those present were doubtless men known also to Alessandro Caravia. One of them, Paolo Crivelli, was, like Caravia, an occasional poet and the man who—according to Caravia in his testimony before the Holy Office—was in part responsible for the composition and the publication of *La verra antiga*. As early as 1546, therefore, evangelical ideas were making their way into the world of the elite guilds of Venice.[56]

By the mid–1540s religious discussion had become widespread in the shops of Venice. The imputed heresies of the iron smith Battista "Bataglia," who was denounced in the fall of 1547, more likely reflected

54. "Et l'ho vedute andar diretto a tutti quelli predicatori che havevano il nome di lutherani et maxime di quel predicator di San Barnabà" (ibid., b. 7 doss. "Contra Franceschinam uxorem Joannis samitarij," testimony of 4 May 1548); and "queste done vano alle prediche et ragionano de le cose del evangelio. . . . Mi hanno ditto che esse credeno nel evangelio et che hora si predica la verità et che per avanti semo stati inganati, perché non si predicava la verità" (ibid., testimony of 7 September 1548).

55. Ibid., doss. "Contra denuntiatos pro hereticis de contracta Sancti Moysis," testimonies of 14 October and 20 November 1548.

56. Ibid., b. 13, doss. "Caravia Alessandro," testimony of 8 July 1557.

the jealousies and rumormongering of his fellow guildsmen than any proselytizing on his part.[57] But the majority of those accused had indeed found salvation in the ideas of the evangelicals and were eager to share their insights with those around them. This was doubtless the case with Bartolomeo Trentin, a cobbler, who was perhaps the first individual sentenced by the recently reorganized Holy Office—a sentence softened by the inquisitor's recognition that he was "an ignorant, common, rustic person, of lowly condition who worked at a trade."[58] The journeyman silk weaver Antonio da Bologna was especially given to proselytizing. A loom-master, he constantly derided Catholic beliefs and practices, especially the appeal to saints for divine favor, and he called the consecrated host nothing more than "a piece of pasta." He rooted his theology in the conviction that "all good work derives from God." When his proselytizing fell on deaf ears in one shop, he moved on to another where there was greater sympathy for his notions. Then, when he was denounced and the hearing against him was under way, he got wind of the proceedings and shrewdly left town.[59] Zuan di Angelo, another silk weaver, was equally outspoken while at work in the shop of Bernardino della Porta on the Rialto. His fellow journeymen there disapproved of his proclivity to argue about the faith, and Bernardino finally fired him, so he too found a workplace where there was greater tolerance for his ideas.[60] The story of the belt maker Rocco is similar. He also made the shop the center of his evangelizing. He had read the *Tragedia del Libero Arbitrio* and the *Beneficio di Cristo*. Despite his father's admonitions (he worked in his father's shop), he talked continuously about religion, attempting to convert those who worked alongside him.[61] Bernardino, a hatter's apprentice, shared his heresies with a fellow apprentice in the evenings as the two were going to bed.[62] Popular evangelism, however, was not always directed at fellow workers. Paolo Gaiano, a silk weaver from Modena, held forth on his convictions while seated in a barber's chair.[63] The musician Zuan Maria da

57. Ibid., b. 7, doss. "Battista el bataglia," denunciation of 15 September 1547.

58. "Et considerato che gli è persona ignorante, ignobile et rude et di bassa conditione et di exercitio" (ibid., b. 6, doss. "Bartolommeo Trentin," sentence of 30 May 1547).

59. Ibid., b. 7, doss. "Contra Antonium Bononiensem," testimony of 7 January 1548.

60. Ibid., doss. "Contra Franceschinam uxorem Joannis samitarij," testimony of 3 October 1548.

61. Ibid., doss. "De Mandanti Rocco, centurer," testimony of 6 February 1549.

62. Ibid., doss. "Bernardino . . . garzatore di berette," testimony of 8 January 1549.

63. Ibid., doss. "Pre Alvise de Michiel et al.," testimony of 6 May 1549.

Bologna was bold enough to challenge a Franciscan's belief in free will, arguing that we are mere instruments of God's grace. He blew on his trumpet to make his point. "If I did not blow it, it would not make any sound," he mused, suggesting that without grace we are incapable of doing good works.[64]

During the late 1540s several evangelical groups or conventicles drew their membership from a wide range of trades and from across the city. In June 1548 a friar denounced a group that included a potter who worked on the Campo San Tomà, a doctor who lived in San Marcuola, a painter, and two soap makers, one from Santi Apostoli and the other from Santa Fosca. In October of the same year a group of artisans, most of whom lived or worked in the parish of San Moisè, came to the attention of the Inquisition. Its membership was extensive and embraced some dozen craftsmen. Among others, it included several coral workers, a cobbler, a goldsmith, two turners, a carpenter, and a jeweler. Its members would gather now in the shop of one artisan, now in the shop of another, for religious readings and discussions. These meetings, though held with caution, were not entirely secretive. Neighbors knew that they took place and had at least some sense of what they were about. One man, whose shop was adjacent to that of the goldsmith Iseppo in the Frezzaria, a narrow way that snaked through the parishes of San Moisè and San Fantin, asserted that several would gather at Iseppo's every morning. Their sect seemed to him a kind of confraternity; and he referred to those who took part in its gatherings as members of "la scuola di lutherani."[65] Another witness, the armorer Lorenzo, also a resident of San Moisè, noted that the accused "meet now at the shop of maestro Girolamo, now at that of Zuanjacomo the sword smith. They discuss Scripture and the Gospels and read certain books."[66]

To a large degree, these men had come to know and to trust one

64. "Et s'io non lo sonasse da si non soneria" (ibid., doss. "Favretti . . . [due] di Bologna," testimony of 18 May 1548).

65. "Ho detto, videndoli insieme: Vedi el gastaldo et compagni della scuola di luterani" (ibid., doss. "Contra denuntiatos pro hereticis de contracta Sancti Moysis," testimony of 11 October 1548). On the group denounced by the friar in June 1548, see ibid., doss. "Boccalaro Gio. Maria; Bressan Gio. Batta; Zago Santo; Saoner Pietro; Saoner Stefano."

66. "Si riducono insieme hora dal detto maestro Hieronymo, hora da maestro Zuanjacomo spader, li parlano della scriptura sacra et delle evangelie et legono certi sui libri" (ibid., doss. "Contra denuntiatos pro hereticis de contracta Sancti Moysis," testimony of 14 October 1548).

another in the course of practicing their trades, and in both formal and informal settings from the tavern to the confraternity. A prominent member of the conventicle was the goldsmith Iseppo. When the inquisitor asked him if he knew others who had also been named as heretics, he responded that he did. Together with Antonio delle Celade, he had served as an officer in the Scuola di San Fantin or della Giustizia (the confraternity whose members accompanied the condemned to their executions);[67] he had made a gold chain for the cobbler Bortholo; exchanged services with the turner Jacomo and his son Bernardo; and purchased various goods from the jeweler Alvise dalle Crosette. Such business ties themselves provided heretics with a measure of trust. They were confident that they could discuss religious issues with one another. It was a confidence, however, that occasionally backfired. Paolo Marascotto, a doctor of law, recalled that after he came to know Iseppo, the goldsmith would boldly invite him into his shop. "And one day," Paolo testified, "I remember he showed me a letter that spoke against the authority of the pope and against the Roman prelates, and I tell you that I was amazed that master Iseppo would have dared to show and keep such a letter so openly."[68]

But Iseppo was open. Francesco, a priest from the Dominican church of San Zanipolo, had left a watchcase for repair with Iseppo. He passed by the goldsmith's shop to hasten his order. While he was there, the bells of the parish church of San Moisè rang out for the Hail Mary. "I removed my cap," Francesco reported, perhaps obsequiously, to the Inquisition, "and said the Ave Maria, and when the goldsmith asked me what I had said, I answered, 'I have said the Ave Maria.' He said—reproaching me—that I should say the Lord's Prayer, because Christ had done so and he said that Christ had ordered that when one needed to pray, one should say the Lord's Prayer, that He had not ordered the Ave Maria."[69] To challenge a priest was not out of charac-

67. Ibid., testimony of 30 October 1548. On the Scuola di San Fantin, see Pullan, *Rich and Poor in Renaissance Venice*, 33.

68. "Mi ricordo che uno giorno el mi mostrò una lettera che parlava contra l'auctorità del papa et contra li prelati di Roma et vi dico che mi maravigliai che così palesamente el detto maestro Iseppo havesse ardir mostrar et tener tal lettera" (ASV, *Sant'Uffizio*, b. 7, doss. "Contra denuntiatos pro hereticis de contracta Sancti Moysis," testimony of 20 November 1548).

69. "Et aritrovandomi una sera alla sua botega, sollicitando la esspeditio della ditta casa de horrelogio, sonò l'Ave Maria a S. Moysè et io mi chavai la beretta et dissi la oratione Ave Maria. Et alhora esso orese mi disse quel che io haveva ditto et io li rispose che io haveva ditto l'Ave Maria, et ipso orese mi disse riprehendendomi che io doveva dir

ter for this group of heretics. When the Confraternity of the Holy Sacrament passed the shop of the jeweler Girolamo, for example, he and
his fellow workers would throw their caps to the floor and turn their
backs, continuing to work.[70] Even blatant efforts at intimidation did
not seem to frighten these heretics. Soon after one of della Casa's book
burnings, Bernardo, a turner, was reported to have told a fellow artisan
that he knew where he could find more books.[71] The ties these artisan
heretics enjoyed with one another were solid, as the attitudes of the
goldsmith Iseppo, one of the more prosperous members of the group,
reveal. When asked if he enjoyed reading religious works, his response
was tantamount to a boast: "I have read the Gospels in the vernacular
and a work composed by Jean Gerson [here Iseppo refers to *The Imitation of Christ* by Thomas à Kempis] that teaches the Christian way of
life. . . . and I also have the works of Saint Augustine that are concerned with free will."[72] Later, he admitted that he had read the *Beneficio di Cristo*—a work he at least claimed to judge harshly, dubbing it a
"composition of ignoramuses"—and that he owned a copy of the *Sommario della Santa Scrittura*, as well as an edition of Ochino's sermons.[73]
The list is impressive and demonstrates the degree to which the ideas
of the heretics could be rooted—as they often were—in a medieval
tradition (Augustine and à Kempis) and in Italian writings (the *Beneficio*
and the sermons of Ochino) rather than in those of such leading
sixteenth-century reformers as Luther or Calvin. Yet Iseppo's beliefs or
convictions were far from abstract. He hoped to see a radical transformation of Venetian institutions. He did not call for the abolition of
Venetian confraternities and, as noted earlier, once served as secretary
to the Scuola di San Fantin. Nonetheless, like Caravia he was in favor

---

il Pater Noster perché l'haveva Cristo, e dissimi . . . che Cristo non haveva ordinato l'Ave
Maria" (ibid., testimony of 10 November 1548).

70. Ibid., testimony of 14 October 1548.

71. Ibid., testimony of 11 October 1548.

72. "Io ho letto li evangelii vulgari et uno libro che insegna el modo del viver christiano conposto da Gioan Gierson . . . et ho etenim li opusculi di san Agostino che trat-
tano del libero arbitrio" (ibid., testimony of 30 October 1548). For an early identification
of the text by Gerson with Thomas à Kempis's *Imitation of Christ*, see Stefano Pillinini,
*Bernardo Stagnino: Un editore a Venezia tra Quattro e Cinquecento* (Rome: Jouvence, 1989),
58: "Quamvis iste libellus dicatur Ioannis Gerson: author tum ipsius fuit Thomas de
Kempis canonicus regularis."

73. "Mi credo che le sia compositione di ignoranti" (ASV, *Sant'Uffizio*, b. 7, doss.,
"Contra denuntiatos pro hereticis de contracta Sancti Moysis," testimony of 30 October
1548).

of rechanneling their energies and resources. "So many *scuole*," he asserted, "would do better to spend their funds for something other than themselves and for religious feasts, because God does not wish for these things."[74] Iseppo hoped that the churches, too, would be transformed. One witness admitted that Iseppo had told him many times "that he has hope in God that he will see the Venetian lords know the true faith, that they will take all the images of saints and the crosses and other things from the churches, put them in a heap, and set them on fire . . . that the churches will become guild halls for preaching."[75]

In the early 1550s a group similar to the conventicle at San Moisè was active at Castello, the city's easternmost neighborhood surrounding the Arsenal. Caravia would observe in a poem published in the mid–1560s that in Castello there were no heretics; his remark was better poetry than sociology.[76] For here too, though with less intensity than in the central parishes of Venice, artisans and other workers embraced the evangelical ideas of their contemporaries. As in San Moisè, the participants in the religious discussions came from a wide variety of trades, though the majority were either silk weavers or involved in the maritime trades so characteristic of the neighborhood: one, for example, was a shipwright, another a ship's captain. A lawyer also participated in the discussions, though the central figure was a silk worker, a *bavallero* by the name of Tommaso, at whose shop the participants would gather to read and discuss the Bible. At times the crowd was large, with several persons leaning up against Tommaso's shop window to listen to the readings and debate.[77]

The ideals of this group were evangelical, and, in their interrogation before the Inquisition, several of its members demonstrated a remarkable knowledge of the Bible that they began to use as a standard for evaluating the religious customs of the Roman church. This learning is perhaps not surprising for Rafaele de Covis, the lawyer in the group. His profession guaranteed him a certain culture. Moreover, he listened assiduously to the sermons of such evangelical preachers as don Ippo-

74. "Che tante schuole faresti meglio a spender li sui dinari in altro che in schuole et in feste solenne perché Dio non vuole 'ste cose" (ibid., testimony of 21 November 1548).
75. "Più volte mi ha detto . . . che l'ha speranza in Dio di veder che li signori venetiani cognoscerano la vera fede, per el che torrano tutte le imagine di santi et le crose et altre cose da giesie et le metterano in magazeni et ghe faranno fuogo sotto. . . . [Et le giesie] saranno alberghi da predicar" (ibid., testimony of 12 November 1548).
76. *Naspo bizaro* (Venice: Domenico Nicolino, 1565), 15 verso.
77. ASV, *Sant'Uffizio*, b. 11, register "1553 libro secondo" and "1554 libro primo," testimony of 15 September 1553.

lito, fra Giuliano da Colle, fra Benedetto da San Marco, and especially a certain fra Franceschino who had preached recently at San Zaccaria.[78] Their arguments as well as the biblical commentaries of Brucioli assisted him in his study of Scripture, a study he believed essential for establishing, for example, whether or not there was a purgatory or if saints could intercede for human beings or if works, without faith, were effective. But Tommaso "Bavallero" appears to have been equally sophisticated, engaging the inquisitor in a brief debate over the authenticity of a passage from 2 Maccabees, the text on which many of the Catholic arguments for the existence of purgatory depended.[79] But for Tommaso, as for Rafaele de Covis, purgatory was only one of the many Catholic beliefs that fell within the scope of biblical criticism.

To a large degree—all the evidence points in this direction—the propaganda was successful. The ease with which printers and booksellers could distribute the new texts, the popularity of certain evangelical preachers, and the relatively high level of literacy in the city facilitated the diffusion of evangelical ideas to such a degree that, by the late 1540s and early 1550s, religious discussion and debate had developed into a self-conscious current of heterodoxy at all levels of Venetian society. Though a clear minority (I count only some 676 individuals accused of evangelical beliefs in Venice at this time), many Venetians now saw themselves as heretics in a decidedly anti-Catholic sense. That they did so cannot be explained, however, by the effectiveness of the press and the pulpit in the diffusion of evangelical ideas. Other forces, embedded in their social and culture experience, were, as we shall see, equally decisive.[80] Nonetheless, by midcentury it was clear that Venice harbored a sizable number of evangelicals. Like the Protestants in northern Europe, they replaced papal with biblical authority. They reduced the number of sacraments from seven to two or three, invariably maintaining baptism and the eucharist and, at times, including penance as the third. They denied the real presence and held that the Last Supper was to be celebrated in commemoration of the passion of Christ. They were opposed to sacerdotal confession and masses for the dead, arguing that if there was any purgatory at all, it was the experience of this life.

78. Ibid., 31 October 1553.
79. Ibid., 12 September 1553. On the importance of 2 Maccabees in Catholic arguments for the existence of Purgatory, see Jacques LeGoff, *The Birth of Purgatory*, trans. Arthur Goldhammer (Chicago: University of Chicago Press, 1984), 41–42.
80. I develop this argument in chapter 6.

They denied the intercession of saints and disparaged their neighbors who turned to the Virgin Mary or a locally popular saint for aid. The whole range of Catholic practices from vows to pilgrimages and processions came under their attack. And, insofar as possible, they ignored those Catholic distinctions that ritualized everyday experience. They worked on feast days and ate meat on fast days. But unlike the Protestants, who enjoyed the protection of princes and magistrates, the Venetians were thrown back exclusively on their own inner resources. They formed conventicles—coming together to read the Bible and to discuss religious ideas. They followed religious and political events throughout Europe, hoping for developments that would allow them to express their beliefs more openly. But while they waited, they went underground. And we know about their world only by accident, when an individual was denounced for heresy or when, under physical or, more likely, psychological torture, an accused talked, giving the names of *complici*, fellow Venetians who shared his views.

## CHAPTER FOUR

# The Humanity of Christ and the Hope for the Messiah

*We returned to the sound of our own speech, in which each word has a beginning and an ending—far, far different from your Word, our Lord, who abides in himself for ever, yet never grows old and gives new life to all things.*

Saint Augustine, *Confessions*

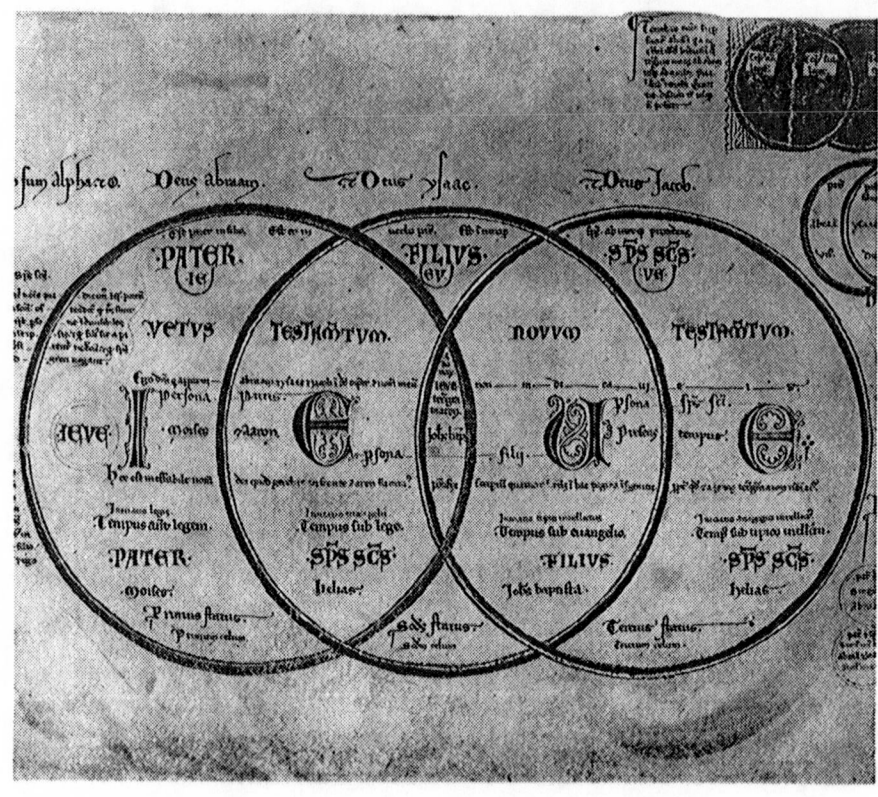

In December 1551 the Dominican Gerolamo Muzzarelli, master of the Sacred Palace, left Rome for Venice on urgent business. By some strange twist of fortune a former Catholic priest by the name of Pietro Manelfi, who was a leading member of the Anabaptist community of northern Italy, had decided earlier that fall to renounce his heresies and return to the Roman church. This personal decision led him to the Inquisition, and the Inquisition encouraged him to talk. Manelfi's revelations to the Roman Holy Office—at first in Bologna and subsequently, because of their importance, in Rome itself—confirmed the inquisitors' worst fears. A large and well-organized network of Anabaptists had recently begun to take root throughout Italy, especially in the north, reaching from Florence through Bologna, Ferrara, Padua, and Venice on into the Friuli and Istria. Muzzarelli's charge was to bring the matter to the attention of the Venetian government and to encourage swift repression of such groups in its territory. The heresies were extreme, with potentially dangerous consequences.[1]

The letter Muzzarelli carried to Venice placed particular stress on the political threat that these Anabaptists posed. The Anabaptists, so the first article of the letter alleged, "consider all Christian magistrates enemies of God and claim that no Christian can be an emperor, king, duke, or magistrate of any kind, and that the people are not obligated to obey them, and that such magistrates contradict the law of God, and

1. ASV, *Sant'Uffizio*, b. 9, dos$ș$. "Manelfi." Manelfi's celebrated revelations were first published at the end of the nineteenth century by Emilio Comba but are available in Carlo Ginzburg's much superior edition, *I costituti di don Pietro Manelfi* (DeKalb: Northern Illinois University Press; Chicago: Newberry Library, 1970). Aldo Stella demonstrated that many of Manelfi's remarks cannot have been entirely true. See esp. Stella's *Anabattismo e antitrinitarismo in Italia nel XVI secolo: Nuove ricerche storiche* (Padua: Liviana, 1969), 64–72. Nonetheless, Manelfi's revelations and Ginzburg's critical annotations remain the starting point for the history of anabaptism in northern Italy. On Muzzarelli's role in bringing the matter before the Venetian authorities, see Ginzburg, ed., *I costituti di don Pietro Manelfi*, 13; and Pio Paschini, *Venezia e l'Inquisizione romana da Giulio III a Pio IV* (Padua: Antenore, 1959), 87.

---

*Opposite.* Late medieval and Renaissance conceptions of history included the millenarian vision of the twelfth-century abbot Joachim of Fiore, depicted here in an illustration from his *Liber Figuarum*. The age of the Holy Spirit (*Spiritus Sanctus*) was to follow that of the Son (*Filius*), which had succeeded that of the Father (*Pater*); the new age was to be a new dispensation. Some followers of Joachim's teachings held that a messiah would usher in the Millennium. (Bodleian Library; by permission of the President and Fellows of Corpus Christi College, Oxford)

so forth." But the religious convictions of these Anabaptists were not less subversive, especially in their denial of the divinity of Christ. "They say," the second article continued, "that our Lord Christ is not God conceived by the Holy Spirit but is only a man born from human seed, though filled with all the virtues of God." Twenty additional articles followed, providing the portrait of a movement and a community radically opposed not only to the teachings of Rome but to the ideals of the evangelicals or Lutherans as well:

> [These Anabaptists] consider baptism worthless, and they are all rebaptized . . . they do not baptize anyone unless he or she first accepts their teaching and especially their teaching that Christ is only a man . . . they do not want lords, holders of benefices, doctors, magistrates, priests, friars, or sisters in their churches unless these have resigned their positions; they have ministers and bishops called "apostles"—these travel continuously, discussing, visiting churches, rebaptizing, and arguing; each time they have a rebaptism, they celebrate the Last Supper in their own fashion, that is, with bread and wine, in honor of their union and of Christ as a man filled with the virtues of God.[2]

Although Manelfi's revelations were alarming, they were also, in another sense, welcomed. For in them the Roman authorities saw precisely the evidence they had long needed to persuade the Venetian government, thus far temperate in its approach to heresy, to take sterner action. Unlike the evangelicals whose teaching never presented a threat to the state, the Anabaptists put forward a religious and political program that, with its denial of a role for the Christian prince or magistrate, threatened its very foundations. Yet the radical Christology—the denial of the divinity of Jesus—was even more disconcerting. For if Jesus was not God, on what divine basis would Christendom itself rest? Moreover, such radical views were extraordinary for midsixteenth-century Anabaptists. Elsewhere in Europe, Anabaptists still stigmatized by the 1535 millenarian debacle at Münster, where extremists had attempted to establish a communistic kingdom of saints,

2. ASV, *Sant'Uffizio*, b. 9, doss., "Manelfi," undated document beginning "Per tutta Italia è scoperta"; Ginzburg, ed., *I costituti di don Pietro Manelfi*, 83–84. The views of the Venetian Anabaptists were far more complex than I present in this chapter, which focuses on their Christology and their notion of salvation; for fuller discussion see Stella, *Dall'anabattismo al socinianesimo*; Stella, *Anabattismo e antitrinitarismo*; and George H. Williams, "The Two Social Strands in Italian Anabaptism, ca. 1526–ca. 1565," in Lawrence P. Buck and Jonathan W. Zophy, eds., *The Social History of the Reformation* (Columbus: Ohio State University Press, 1972), 156–207. Both Stella and Williams discuss the northern Italian Anabaptists' denial of hell and belief in the sleep of the human soul after natural death and before the Last Judgment.

had begun to moderate their views. Indeed, it was in these years that Menno Simons (the founder of the Mennonites) was working to reorganize the pacifist and separatist communities of his followers in the Low Countries. But in Italy, peculiar circumstances shaped a more radical Anabaptist culture.[3]

Because of the explicitly political implications of these heresies, the Council of Ten, not the Venetian Sant'Uffizio, took responsibility for the first strike. Late in the night of 18 December, the Ten—in conjunction with the local authorities in such places as the mainland cities of Vicenza, Treviso, and Padua—carried out a number of arrests quickly and secretly so that "one would not know of the other."[4] The operation was not a success. The authorities captured only some two dozen of the scores and scores of the men and women Manelfi had denounced. Most of the others—who must have had some warning—managed to escape. And in Venice itself, the council was able to capture only three of the local Anabaptists: a former sword smith (or *spader*) by the name of Zuanjacomo; his wife, Anzelica; and a certain Zuanmaria, a highly skilled silk weaver (*racer*). Several other figures—a certain Bortolomeo, a cobbler and one of the most prominent figures of the group; Beneto, a silk weaver; Marina, the widow of a craftsman; and possibly others—had slipped out of the city immediately before the crackdown.[5]

In Venice, as elsewhere in northern Italy, the baptisms of adult "believers" (the ritual that gave anabaptism its name) had begun only recently: in the latter part of 1549. To be sure, the earliest manifestations of Anabaptist thought in the Veneto probably reached back to the late 1520s. After the defeat of the peasant uprisings of 1525–1526 in the Tyrol and the Trentino, for example, many artisans and agricultural laborers, who had already proven receptive to religious radicalism, fled to the Venetian republic, settling in the towns and villages in the mountains and foothills that lay to the north of both Vicenza and Verona. Even Michael Gaismayr, the leader of an especially radical current of religious ideas in the Tyrol—he was a miner's son who dreamt of a rural socialist utopia, with state ownership of industry and the aboli-

---

3. For an excellent contextualization of Italian anabaptism and its relation to other radical movements in these years, see Ugo Gastaldi, *Storia dell'anabattismo*, vol. 2: *Da Münster ai giorni nostri* (Turin: Claudiana, 1981), 531–590.

4. "Che l'uno non sapesse dell'altro" (Stella, *Dall'anabattismo al socinianesimo*, 88).

5. ASV, *Sant'Uffizio*, b. 11, doss., "Processus contra Anabatistas."

tion of private property—found refuge in the Venetian republic, settling in Padua. There, until he was assassinated by the agents of the Archduke Ferdinand in 1532, he shared Zwingli's hope of inducing the Venetian government into an anti-Hapsburg league.[6] The immigration of religious radicals and especially of a figure as prominent as Gaismayr was bound to have an influence, and indeed echoes of Anabaptist ideas in Venetian heretical circles were heard as early as 1532. The Venetian carpenter Antonio, for example, while boasting to a neighbor of his religious understanding, stated that he would not have had any of his children baptized as infants "if I had known what I know now." And Zuanjacomo "Spader," who was from the Trentino, appears to have had Anabaptist leanings before 1549.[7] But Anabaptist ideas made little headway in these years. This reception is not surprising, for in general anabaptism enjoyed little success in areas of Europe where a strong Protestant movement was lacking.[8] Thus, in Venice and the Venetian republic generally, it would only be in the 1540s, after evangelical ideas had begun to acquire a sizable popular following, that the terrain would be prepared for more radical theologies.

The more significant precondition of the development of anabaptism in the Veneto, however, was not the growth of an evangelical movement per se but rather the growing frustrations and increased disillusionment of those evangelicals who, for a short while at least, had believed that the Venetian government might offer its support to a reform of the Church. This confidence in the Venetian government was not entirely without foundation. Many of the leading evangelicals, as we have seen, had connections among the most powerful groups of Venetian society. They were friends of Venetian gentlemen with whom they had gone to school and university. For some, it seemed entirely plausible that members of the ruling patriciate would support their views. In 1545, Vergerio had written a letter to the new doge, Francesco Donà, imploring his assistance for the religious reforms he and others

6. Stella, *Dall'anabattismo al socinianesimo*, 11–33. On Gaismayr, see also Walter Klaassen, *Michael Gaismair: Revolutionary and Reformer* (Leiden: E.J. Brill, 1978).

7. On Antonio, see Gaeta, "Documenti da codici vaticani," 28–29. On Zuanjacomo Spader's views of baptism, see ASV, *Sant'Uffizio*, b. 7, doss. "Contra denuntiatos pro hereticis de contracta Sancti Moysis," testimony of 14 October 1548, during which the witness noted that Zuanjacomo had not yet baptized his two-month-old son. Interestingly, the Holy Office did not pick up on this as an important detail at this time. By 1551, such information would have most likely attracted the Inquisition's attention.

8. The complexities of the relation of anabaptism to Protestantism are emphasized by Claus-Peter Clasen, *Anabaptism, A Social History, 1525–1618: Switzerland, Austria, Moravia, South and Central Germany* (Ithaca: Cornell University Press, 1972), 298–305.

like him sought. But toward the end of the decade these hopes were dashed, as the Venetian rulers decided to give their support not to reform but rather to the Roman Inquisition. To be sure, the repression was mild, but it made clear nonetheless that the evangelicals' hope for religious reform with the assistance of the secular government was no longer a possibility. In such a climate, the Anabaptist message—one that argued that salvation lay not in cooperation with the secular world but in the cultivation of small, almost holy communities of the "truly" baptized—was to exercise considerable appeal.

Thus in 1549 when an Anabaptist missionary arrived in northern Italy, the climate was to prove receptive to his teachings, especially since this missionary, a certain Tiziano, was himself an Italian, and a man of rather remarkable organizational skills.[9] Like many other Italian heretics, Tiziano had fled to the Grisons (or *Graubünden*) at some point after the establishment of the Roman Inquisition in 1542, in search of religious liberty. But while Catholics and Protestants tolerated one another in the mountain republic of the Grisons as well as in the territories of Chiavenna, Bormio, and the Valtellina that were subject to it, local authorities continually did whatever they could to discourage anabaptism or other forms of religious radicalism. Nonetheless, this miniature Switzerland that lay to the north of Brescia and Bergamo, stretching from the westernmost boundaries of the Venetian republic high into the Alps, had proven receptive to both. As early as the mid-1520s, Georg Blaurock—one of the first Swiss Anabaptists to have broken with Zwingli—had brought his teachings there, and many of the Italian evangelicals who sought refuge in this region appear to have been open to certain radical religious views.[10] The most notable of these was Camillo Renato, an exiled Italian humanist, who in 1547 argued in his *Trattato del battesimo e della santa cena* that neither baptism nor the eucharist were sacraments.[11] And Tiziano—in all likelihood frustrated by what he perceived as the exaggerated moderation of the Italian evangelicals in the Grisons—appears to have fallen under the influence of Renato in particular and the Anabaptists generally. Indeed,

---

9. Tiziano is not to be confused with Lorenzo Tizzano (alias Benedetto Florio); see Ginzburg's introduction to *I costituti di don Pietro Manelfi*, 18.

10. On the Grisons, also known as the Rhaetian League, and the early diffusion of Anabaptist teaching there, see George H. Williams, *The Radical Reformation* (Philadelphia: Westminster, 1962), 545–559.

11. Camillo Renato, "Trattato del battesimo e della santa cena," in *Opere: Documenti e testimonianze*, ed. Antonio Rotondò (DeKalb: Northern Illinois University Press; Chicago: Newberry Library, 1968), 93–108.

it is likely that Tiziano organized the first Italian-speaking Anabaptist community among evangelical refugees near Chiavenna immediately prior to his expulsion. Now in exile, Tiziano took not only his teachings but also his organizational skill into Italy. His missionary endeavors met with immediate success. In the fall of 1549 he rebaptized the first group of his followers in Italy at Asolo, a hill town to the northwest of Treviso. In turn, these men—among them the notary Benedetto del Borgo, Marcantonio del Bon, Giuseppe Sartori, and Nicola d'Alessandria of Treviso—became his "apostles," spreading Anabaptist teachings and establishing new communities of believers in Vicenza, Padua, Rovigo, Cittadella, and Gardone. Tiziano's activity, however, was not limited to the Veneto. He carried his teachings to Tuscany and into the Romagna as well.[12]

Because of the prominence of its evangelical communities, Venice too inevitably became a center of active proselytizing on the part of these men. And in Venice, as elsewhere, their approach was to identify groups of evangelicals who, they believed, might be receptive to their ideas. As Marcantonio del Bon (one of the most prominent Italian Anabaptist missionaries) would explain to the Venetian Holy Office after his arrest in 1552, it was not especially difficult to instruct their new converts, "because they were already Lutherans."[13] Almost immediately after the establishment of the group in Asolo, for example, Manelfi and Benedetto del Borgo managed to establish contact with the evangelical Pietro Speziale of Cittadella, who was being held prisoner in Venice, and convert him to their more radical views. They bribed the guards and actually rebaptized him in his prison cell![14] But this was only the most dramatic incident in a systematic effort to bring evangelicals into their ranks. In the early part of 1550, Nicola d'Alessandria— though himself quite wealthy—managed to become part of a circle of artisans who met together at the home of a prominent tailor, Francesco Poetin, in calle della Bissa, near the Rialto. Whether Francesco or any of his friends ever accepted rebaptism is not known. But with some, certainly with the cobbler Bortolomeo, with Zuanjacomo Spader, and Zuanmaria Racer, this approach was successful. Indeed, Marcantonio del Bon and Manelfi may have discovered Zuanjacomo because of his

12. Gastaldi, *Storia dell'anabattismo,* 2:567–577.
13. "Perché erano già lutherani" (ASV, *Sant'Uffizio,* b. 158, register "Libro terzo," testimony of 5 March 1552; Stella, *Anabattismo e antitrinitarismo,* 49).
14. ASV, *Sant'Uffizio,* b. 9, doss. "Manelfi," testimony of 14 November 1551; Ginzburg, ed., *I costituti di don Pietro Manelfi,* 72.

involvement in the large circle of artisan heretics active during the late 1540s in the Frezzaria and the parish of San Moisè.[15] Anabaptist propaganda was doubtless most successful on the terrain already prepared by the evangelicals.

To those evangelicals who joined the Anabaptists (certainly a minority), baptism was above all a sign of a far deeper transformation. Politically, it entailed the abandonment of the Augustinian vision of a world of two cities—in which the elect lived, as an invisible community, among the damned and in which, at least as a ideal corollary, the state would not persecute but would rather support the goals of a Christian society. And while the Venetian Anabaptists did not aspire to a total denial of the political role of the state, nonetheless, as one artisan from Vicenza, arrested for heresy in 1552, would explain to the Holy Office, there was no obligation to obey secular magistrates "in matters of faith."[16] On a religious level, anabaptism entailed placing their hope not, as did the evangelicals, in the actions of God's grace in a fallen world, but rather in an intensive effort to fulfill what they saw as the ethical commands of Christianity. In this effort, they turned with renewed fervor to Scripture as the basis of the Christian life. In Camillo Renato's view, for example, nothing else was necessary.[17] Zuanjacomo Spader echoed this sentiment before the Council of Ten, to whose lords he explained that the lives of the Anabaptists were based above all on biblical precepts. "We do not have any other decree or writing but the New Testament," he explained to the magistrates, "our life is not to take things that belong to others, to help everyone, and not to commit adultery."[18] Zuanjacomo himself could not read—at least not well—so his ideas about Scripture were influenced deeply by his fellow Anabaptist, the cobbler Bortolomeo, who read to him from the New Testament. When the members of the Ten asked him what Bortolomeo taught him, Zuanjacomo's response went to the fundamentals. "He says quite a lot about our needing to love one another and that we should never do to others things we would not wish done to ourselves."

15. ASV, *Sant'Uffizio*, b. 8, doss. "Contra Franciscum Poetinum," testimony of 23 April 1550. Ibid., b. 7, doss. "Contra denuntiatos pro hereticis de contracta Sancti Moysis," testimony of 30 October 1548; and on Zuanmaria Racer's rebaptism, see b. 158, register "Libro secondo," testimony of 11 January 1552.

16. "Nelle cose della fede" (ibid., testimony of 26 January 1552).

17. Renato, "Trattato del battesimo e della santa cena," 93.

18. "Non havemo altro decreto né altra scrittura che il Testamento Novo; la nostra vita è non tuor quel d'altri, agiutar tutti, non far adulterij" (ASV, *Sant'Uffizio*, b. 11, doss. "Processus contra Anabatistas," testimony of 22 December 1551).

It was a message that Zuanjacomo took seriously. He even gave up the crafting of swords because, as he explained to the Holy Office, "this is not a proper trade for a Christian."[19]

In their separatism, their pacifism, and their stress on the New Testament as an ethical code, the Venetian Anabaptists had many common ties to their counterparts elsewhere. Little more than language divided them from the Swiss Brethren and the Mennonites. But these were merely "the old opinions," as Manelfi called them.[20] In 1550, in a meeting of representatives from Anabaptist churches throughout northern Italy and Switzerland—a meeting held in Venice itself—the Italian Anabaptists came to accept a number of new opinions, the most shocking of which involved a denial of the divinity of Christ.

According to Manelfi's account, the origins of this radical Christology could be traced back to a discussion held in Vicenza in the early part of 1550, during which a dispute had developed, in the reading of a passage from Deuteronomy, over the question of whether Christ was "God or man." Manelfi continued in his testimony to the Inquisition:

And to resolve this issue, we decided to call together all the ministers of the various localities to a council in Venice, and therefore we chose two men who traveled everywhere, even to Basel, to call two representatives from each church or locality to come to that council. . . . And thus in September [the meeting was actually in October], sixty Anabaptist ministers and bishops met together in Venice, where for forty days they fasted, prayed, and studied the Holy Scripture.

At the conclusion of their discussions, those in attendance agreed that "Christ is not God, but a man conceived of the seed of Joseph and Mary, though filled with all the virtues of God," that Mary had other sons and daughters, that there is no such thing as an angel or angelic nature, that the only devil is human wisdom, and that no hell exists, but only eternal death to those who are not saved.[21] And while it would

19. "El dize pur assai cose, che si devemo amar insieme, et che non faciamo ad altri quello che non l'ossamo che fosse fatto a noi" (ibid., testimony of 19 December 1551). "Non volea più far quel mestier di far spade, che non è da cristiano" (ibid., testimony of 20 December 1551). Cf. ASV, *Sant'Uffizio*, b. 9, doss. "Manelfi," list of "Lutherani, anabattisti et altri heretici," presented to the Bolognese inquisitor on 2 November 1551; Ginzburg, ed., *I costituti di don Pietro Manelfi*, 48: "gli anabattisti non vogliono alchuno che facci arme, né dipintori, anabattista."

20. "L'openioni antique" (ASV, *Sant'Uffizio*, b. 9, doss. "Manelfi," testimony of 13 November 1551; Ginzburg, ed., *I costituti di don Pietro Manelfi*, 66).

21. "Et per risolvere questo dubio concludessemo che si chiamasse tutti gli ministri delle congregationi de lochi a Venetia a concilio, et però furno eletti doi che andassero

be charitable to say that Manelfi's memory was playing tricks on him—among other things, he exaggerated both the length and the size of the Venetian "synod"—other witnesses would confirm the most striking of his claims. By late 1550 with few exceptions (one, notably, the town of Cittadella), most of the northern Italian Anabaptist communities had officially accepted the radical antitrinitarian view that Christ was not God.[22]

The origins of this belief are obscure. It is possible that the antitrinitarian ideas of Michael Servetus—the Spanish physician whom Calvin would have burned at Geneva in 1553—were influential. His early books arguing against the doctrine of the Trinity circulated in Italy in the 1530s and 1540s and were undoubtedly known in Venice.[23] Yet it is certain that the development of antitrinitarian thought in these years was a complex phenomenon that could in no way be traced to one individual. Throughout the 1540s and 1550s a number of prominent Italian thinkers—most especially the Sienese Lelio Sozzini and eventually Bernardino Ochino and Camillo Renato—would also arrive at antitrinitarian positions.[24]

Nonetheless, despite its complexity, the most decisive antitrinitarian influence on the Venetian Anabaptists appears to have originated in the circle that developed around Juan de Valdés in Naples. For while Valdés's thought served primarily as the starting point for the evangelical reformers in Italy, it also contained ideas that struck at the core of the doctrine of atonement (a doctrine that made the divinity of Christ essential to the Christian view of salvation). Was not God's love for the

---

per tutto fin in Basilea a chiamare doi per chiesa over loco, che venessero a detto concilio. . . . Et così dell'anno 1550 del mese di settembre si ritrovorno sessanta fra ministri et vescovi de anabattisti in Venetia a concilio, ove per quaranta giorni digiunando, orando et studiando le scritture sacre, determinassemo così questi articoli: 1. Christo non essere Dio ma huomo concetto del seme di Ioseph et di Maria, ma ripieno di tutte le virtù di Dio" (ASV, *Sant'Uffizio*, b. 9, doss. "Manelfi," testimony of 17 October 1551; Ginzburg, ed., *I costituti di don Pietro Manelfi*, 34–35).

22. Stella has noted several inaccuracies in Manelfi's report; see esp. his *Anabattismo e antitrinitarismo*, 64–72. On Cittadella, see Ester Zille, *Gli eretici a Cittadella nel Cinquecento* (Padua: Rebellato, 1971).

23. On the fortune of Servetus' *De trinitatis erroribus libri vii*, see Earl Morse Wilbur, *A History of Unitarianism*, vol. 1: *Socinianism and Its Antecedents* (Cambridge, Mass.: Harvard University Press, 1945), 49–112; and Cantimori, *Eretici italiani del Cinquecento*, 28.

24. Cantimori, *Eretici italiani del Cinquecento*, passim; and, on the early diffusion of antitrinitarian ideas in Italy, see Antonio Rotondò, "Calvino e gli antitrinitari italiani," in *Studi e ricerche di storia ereticale italiana del Cinquecento*, 57–86.

world so great, Valdés suggested in his *Hundred and Ten Divine Considerations*, that Jesus' sacrifice was not necessary but merely a sign of God's mercy?[25] And if this were so—especially in the view of several of Valdés's followers who were of Spanish and likely of *marrano* (or crypto-Jewish) origin—why should Jesus be believed to be the Son of God?

From the vantage point of the Anabaptist communities in Venice and its territories, the key figure among these more radical followers of Valdés was a Neapolitan by the name of Girolamo Busale.[26] Almost certainly the son of a *marrano*, Busale moved in upper-class circles in Naples that would have brought him into Valdés's world. Moreover, as a young man he received as a benefice the abbacy of San Onofrio—a monastery on the outskirts of Monteleone—a position that guaranteed him a stipend of one thousand ducats annually and the leisure, therefore, to pursue his intellectual interests. In the 1530s he traveled to Padua to study philosophy and, while there, fell under the influence of Marco da Cremona, the evangelical preacher whose ideas were so influential to Contarini and his friends and whose sermons Busale attended regularly at the Church of Santa Giustina. But something—probably the fame of Juan de Valdés and Busale's desire to deepen his understanding of the Gospels—pulled him back to the south of Italy. At first he was an ordinary participant in the evangelical circle of Neapolitan aristocrats, humanists, and prelates who surrounded Valdés. Then, like others who came to Naples to listen to and study with Valdés, Busale must have experienced considerable disillusionment after the death of this Spanish humanist in 1541 and the establishment of the Inquisition the following year.

Unlike such evangelicals as Cardinal Pole, Bishop Giberti, and the poet Flaminio—who continued to place their hopes in what was ultimately a moderate evangelical reform (though it appeared threatening to the hard-liners in the Curia)—Busale would take a far more radical turn. In particular, Busale grew to share the views of the humanist Juan de Villafranca—a Spanish nobleman in the service of the viceroy—who argued that the best hope for Christianity lay in a reduction of the

25. Juan de Valdés, *Le cento e dieci divine considerazioni*, ed. Edmondo Cione (Milan: Fratelli Bocca, 1944).

26. On Busale, see Stella, *Anabattismo e antitrinitarismo*, 15–44; and Anne Jacobson Schutte, "Busale, Girolamo," in the *Dizionario biografico degli italiani*, 15:475–478. Schutte hypothesizes that Busale was a *marrano*. For a similar view, see Williams, "The Two Social Strands in Italian Anabaptism," 162–166.

Christian faith to Scripture alone. All councils, all doctors, all teachings of the Church over the last fifteen hundred years became superfluous. Clearly, therefore, not only all sacraments but also such traditional teachings as the doctrine of the Trinity and the doctrine of hell were to be swept away as mere human inventions. But even Scripture was subject to criticism. Villafranca, Busale, and their followers would argue that certain passages in the Gospels were corrupted or were interpolations. In part, these views stemmed from their own radical hermeneutics. They were extraordinarily gifted textual scholars who made the approaches of both Valla and Erasmus their own. But theirs was also a scholarship intent on demonstrating that Christ was not the Son of God. As Giovanni Laureto di Buongiorno, a former Benedictine who accepted their views, would explain to the Inquisition in Venice, Busale "doubted the divinity of Christ, and when he discussed this with me, we would begin to read and look through Scripture to clarify this point. And he was very learned in Hebrew and Greek, and he urged me to learn these languages as well, because he said they were necessary to get at the truth."[27] Perhaps Busale's Jewish background—a background that Villafranca (though this is speculation) may have shared—played a significant role in shaping their denial of the divinity of Christ. Although they developed these arguments in a Christian and in particular a Valdesian context, in dialogue with other Christians, the context was equally one in which their own Jewishness could remain hidden as they kept faith with their most basic beliefs about Jesus' prophetic yet exclusively human role in history.[28]

About 1546 Busale returned to Padua. It was here that he and several other Neapolitans who also denied the divinity of Christ—among them Girolamo's brother, Matteo Busale, Giovanni Laureto di Buongiorno, and another former monk by the name of Lorenzo Tizzano

27. "Et qui io me domesticai cum lui, et lo scopersi che egli dubitava della divinità di Christo; et ragionando cum mecco di questo comenzamo a lezer et rivoltar le Scritture per chiarir questo puncto. Et lui era molto dotto nella lingua hebrea et greca, et esortò anche me ad imparar le ditte lingue, [perché] diceva che erano necessarie per haver la verità" (ASV, *Sant'Uffizio*, b. 11, register "1553 libro terzo et 1554 libro primo," testimony of 2 October 1553; M.E. [ = Edouard] Pommier, "L'itinéraire religieux d'un moine vagabond italien au XVIe siècle," *Mélanges d'archéologie et d'histoire de l'Ecole française de Rome* 66 (1954): 318). On Villafranca, see also Seidel Menchi, *Erasmo in Italia*, 206–207.

28. I have no firm evidence for the view that either Busale or Villafranca were *marranos*. But they were both of Spanish origin; both lived in the Kingdom of Naples under Spanish rule, where men and women still needed to conceal their Jewish backgrounds; and both adopted theologies that minimized the fundamental doctrinal differences between Christians and Jews.

(also known as Benedetto Florio)—would eventually encounter the Anabaptists of northern Italy. In part, the encounter was a foregone conclusion. Both groups, after all, were most at home in evangelical circles. But the radicalism of their groups provided an even greater affinity between the two movements. Not surprisingly, in 1550 Girolamo Busale accepted rebaptism from the Anabaptist missionary Nicola d'Alessandria. The alliance that this rebaptism represented was to prove consequential for the emerging Anabaptist movement as well. As Marcantonio del Bon would explain to the Holy Office in 1552, the Neapolitans imposed their views concerning Christ on the group as a whole.[29] The Neapolitans and the northern Anabaptists, in other words, ended up proselytizing one another and, in so doing, carved out a new and radical position within the complex patchwork of the heretical movements of sixteenth-century Italy.

To some, the acceptance of Busale's view appears to have developed from his remarkable gift at inducing doubt concerning received Christian doctrine. But this method assumed among the members of the community a certain humanistic culture or at least a certain comfort in textual discussions that not all the Venetian Anabaptists could have mastered. Thus, while Marcantonio del Bon and Nicola d'Alessandria may have arrived at an antitrinitarian position on textual grounds, the motivations that underlay the wider acceptance of such a view could not have been purely intellectual: the majority of the Anabaptists in the Veneto were artisans (weavers, cobblers, tailors) and petty merchants—men and women with little formal education. Yet they too came to accept the antitrinitarian views of Busale and others. As the silk weaver Zuanmaria explained to the Holy Office, before he was rebaptized, the others "taught me the principal matters in which we are in disagreement with the Roman church: and the first concerns the birth of Christ, who, our church maintains, was born of human seed, just as are all other men."[30] Whereas Zuanmaria, like many other Venetian craftsmen, was literate—he admitted having read the New Testament and Celio Secondo Curione's *Pasquino in estasi*—not all the Vene-

29. ASV, *Sant'Uffizio*, b. 158, register "Libro terzo," testimony of 3 March 1552; Pommier, "L'itinéraire religieux d'un moine vagabond," 305.

30. "Mi insegnorno tre cose principali che discordano dalla Chiesa romana, la prima è del nascimento di Cristo, il quale la chiesa nostra tiene che sia nato di seme humano secondo che nascino tutti gli altri huomini" (ASV, *Sant'Uffizio*, b. 158, register "Libro Secondo," testimony of 11 January 1552).

tian Anabaptists were. As we have seen, Zuanjacomo Spader, who also accepted that Christ was born of human seed, could barely read.[31]

To a large degree, then, this popular antitrinitarianism (or Josephism) was less a theological than an ethical matter. Several of the *anabattisti popolari* had a grasp of theological issues—an understanding that no doubt deepened as they came together in one another's shops to read and discuss Scripture. But what mattered to them fundamentally were the ethical dimensions of their religious convictions. In Jesus, who was the son of Joseph, they saw not a mediator (as both the Catholic and the Protestant churches portrayed him) but a teacher; like other Anabaptists, they placed special emphasis on Jesus' Sermon on the Mount as the basis for a Christian life. Christ was no longer a mystery, a figure whom only the doctors of the Church could interpret. Whereas both Catholics and evangelicals accepted the received tradition that Christ was God and made man, the Venetian Anabaptists argued instead that Christ was a man just like all others. Even though this view must have shocked many contemporary theologians, it was not altogether surprising in a Renaissance culture that had come to emphasize the humanity of Christ in its devotions, its art, and the stories it told about the life of Jesus. Under the influence first of Tiziano and his apostles and then of Girolamo Busale and his Neapolitan friends, the Venetian Anabaptists simply carried this aspect of Renaissance culture to what they deemed a logical conclusion. Ultimately, it seems, this popular antitrinitarianism was a way of making Jesus their own. It was a popular Christology, moreover, that could lead the Anabaptists to an extreme identification with Jesus himself. When the officers of the Ten arrested Zuanjacomo Spader, for example, this young man—seemingly as a pure reflex—compared himself and his own experience to that of Jesus. "O Christ, it is for you that I bear this pain," he shouted, adding, "and I am persecuted just as you were persecuted, and I, like you, am taken in the garden of the Pharisees."[32]

Thus by the early 1550s Venetian heresy had taken more than one radical turn. To be sure, only a minority of evangelicals passed over to

31. Ibid., b. 11, doss. "Processus contra Anabatistas," testimony of 19 December 1551.

32. "Christo per ti porto questa pena, et son persequitado come fossi persequitado anco ti, et son sta presso . . . come ti fosti presso nell'horto delli faresei" (ibid., report of the arresting officer, 19 December 1551).

Anabaptist and, almost immediately afterwards, to antitrinitarian teachings. But the suddenness of this shift in the nature of popular heresy in Venice and its surrounding communities alarmed the Venetian lords. After all, even though the Venetian inquisitors had come to see the evangelicals as heretics, at least with these they shared the Augustinian view of the nature of the relation of the religious to the political order, and Catholics and evangelicals alike based their faith on the view that Jesus was the Son of God. Both recited the Nicene Creed. By contrast, with the spread of Anabaptist and antitrinitarian teachings, heaven and earth seemed imperiled by the new heresies in the Venetian republic.[33] Not surprisingly, repression—even in the relatively moderate republic of Venice—intensified. At Rovigo on 17 March 1551 Benedetto del Borgo was decapitated, and his body publicly burned. And only two years later in Venice an Anabaptist (whose name we do not know) was sentenced to death. After a public condemnation and with the support of the Council of Ten, the Holy Office sent him to be drowned.[34]

Yet the Josephite Anabaptists were not the only ones in Venice and northern Italy during these years who developed an alternative interpretation of the role of Christ in human salvation. The period witnessed an intensification of yet another current of popular religion—a millenarian current—a stream of beliefs that stressed the realization of God's kingdom on earth in the one thousand years before the Last Judgment. And, like the Venetian Anabaptists, these millenarians (though they thought of their beliefs as entirely orthodox) developed an image of Christ and his role in history that easily crossed the boundaries of orthodoxy.

There was nothing necessarily heretical in Christian theology about millenarianism, for at its very origins Christianity had been a religion of expectation, of hope for a "second coming." Moreover, like other millenarian movements of the late Middle Ages and the Renaissance, the Venetian movement derived its primary impulse from the teachings

33. As the nunzio Ludovio Beccadelli reported to Cardinal del Monte on 19 December 1551: "Parendo a questi signori [the rulers of Venice] com'è, che questa fosse una coniura de ribaldi contra il stato del paradiso et del mondo" (Franco Gaeta, ed., *Nunziature di Venezia* [Rome: Istituto Storico Italiano per l'Età Moderna e Contemporanea, 1967], 5:330).

34. On Benedetto's execution, see Stella, *Anabattismo e antitrinitarismo*, 79. On the execution of the Anabaptist in Venice, see Gaeta, ed., *Nunziature di Venezia*, 6:285.

and writings of the twelfth-century Cistercian Joachim of Fiore. Joachim had developed an elaborate conception of history. Drawing on a mystical, allegorical, and trinitarian reading of the Bible, this Cistercian theologian divided human history into three great ages. The first had been the age of the Father. In that time, which reached from the Creation of the first man to the birth of Christ—so Joachim argued—human society had been subject to the law of the patriarchs. But with Christ a new era of human history had come into existence. This age, in whose last days Joachim and many of his followers over the next several centuries believed they lived, was an age not of the patriarchs but of the priests. In it, grace had come to replace the law, and wisdom had replaced knowledge. But these two ages pointed to a third, the age of the Holy Spirit. In this era, the Church would no longer be a carnal church but a spiritual one; the rulers would not be priests but monks; and the age would be characterized by a more ample grace and a fullness of understanding.[35]

Joachim rarely related his prophecies to the troubles of his own day, but many of his followers would draw revolutionary conclusions from his teachings. They were eager to find in this third age "a new 'testament,' a new authority, and new institutions."[36] Like modern Marxist ideologies, millenarianism often saw history as progressive and believed that a better world would come into existence within human history. Its adherents yearned for the total transformation of the social order and the advent of an age of universal peace, justice, and equality. They were, therefore, radical critics of the received social order. The Millennium was to be a this-worldly paradise. All humanity—Catholics, Protestants, Jews, and Muslims—would be united into one sheepfold. The realization of the dream would be the consequence of divine intervention. A new emperor, together with a new pope, would enter the world's stage and the messiah would then return (or come). Present sufferings would pass. The terrestrial utopia was possible. Finally—as interpreters of their political worlds in the light of Scripture—they saw the Millennium as imminent and as the final "moment" of historical

35. On Joachim, see Marjorie Reeves, *The Influence of Prophecy in the Later Middle Ages: A Study in Joachimism* (Oxford: Oxford University Press, 1969); and Reeves, *Joachim of Fiore and the Prophetic Future* (New York: Harper and Row, 1977), as well as Bernard McGinn's overview of medieval apocalyptic thought in his introduction to *Visions of the End: Apocalyptic Traditions in the Middle Ages* (New York: Columbia University Press, 1979), 1–36.

36. Reeves, *Joachim of Fiore*, 8.

time. Deeply sensitive historically, millenarians often concluded that history itself was about to end. Moreover, the potency of Joachim's ideas seemed continually reinforced by political developments both within the Church and in society as a whole. Many in the generation immediately following Joachim's death viewed the new mendicant orders of the Franciscans and the Dominicans as the heralds of the age of the Spirit. In later centuries Joachimism fueled the political dreams of monarchists and republicans alike, culminating in Italy in fra Girolamo Savonarola's ability to adapt Joachim's concepts to the Florentine crisis of the late fifteenth century.

Although Savonarola was burned at the stake in 1498, his ideas and those of Joachim found many supporters in the sixteenth century.[37] The very events of the time rendered men and women receptive to a prophetic language that claimed to make sense of the turmoil about them: the emergence of a German friar who challenged papal authority and initiated the Reformation, the sack of Rome in 1527, the fall of the last Florentine republic in 1530, and the continuing threat posed to Christendom by the rise of the Ottoman power in the Mediterranean all served to keep millenarian expectations alive. Moreover, it is not surprising to encounter the dream of a golden age in Venice, given the crises the republic confronted. Joachim's views had enjoyed considerable fortune in late medieval and Renaissance Venice. As early as the thirteenth century, legend had it that Joachim had personally overseen the depiction of religious history in the mosaics of the Basilica San Marco; in the fourteenth century, it became fashionable among Venetians, rich and poor, to visit the basilica and to read the mosaics in a prophetic key.[38] In the fifteenth century Joachimism appears to have captured the imagination of a more elite circle of Venetians. In the monastery of San Cipriano a compilation of his prophecies (as well as those of his followers) was made and, over the course of the late fifteenth century, expanded. Understandably, as Venice once again faced the political crises precipitated by the War of the League of Cambrai in the early sixteenth century, Joachimism again broke out of mo-

---

37. On Savonarola's influence in the sixteenth century, see Donald Weinstein, *Savonarola and Florence: Prophecy and Patriotism in the Renaissance* (Princeton: Princeton University Press, 1970), esp. the final chap.; Cesare Vasoli, *Profezia e ragione: Studi sulla cultura del Cinquecento e del Seicento* (Naples: A. Morano, 1974); and Ottavia Niccoli, *Prophecy and People in Renaissance Italy*, trans. Lydia G. Cochrane (Princeton: Princeton University Press, 1990).

38. Otto Demus, *The Mosaics of San Marco in Venice* (Chicago: University of Chicago Press, 1984), 1:10, 256.

nastic walls. The fashion of reading the mosaics in San Marco as a key to current events and the meaning of history was widespread in noble circles. And in 1516 Silvestro Meuccio, an Augustinian friar at San Cristoforo della Pace, began publishing Joachim's works. He sustained this activity for more than a decade, and though only a small circle of friars shared directly in this enterprise, they must have believed that there was a receptive public for the works. In all likelihood they were right. In these same years Paolo Angelo was to publish his largely Joachimite *Profetie certissime* (Most certain prophecies); the Franciscan Francesco Zorzi was writing his cabalistic *De harmonia mundi* (On the harmony of the universe); and Savonarola's writings especially were gaining popularity—in the first half of the sixteenth century, several hundred editions of his works were printed in Venice alone.[39]

It was virtually inevitable, therefore, that the rapid shifts in popular religion in the Venice of the 1540s would find expression in a millenarian key. To many Venetians—especially those who longed for a world that was religiously unified—the proliferation of new sects, of evangelical conventicles, and small groups of Anabaptists could only cause anguish. And indeed toward the end of the decade millenarians in Venice began to look to the local heresies of the city as a sign that a new dispensation was both necessary and imminent. The most famous of these millenarians was the enigmatic and eccentric humanist Guillaume Postel.[40] A Frenchman with a seemingly superhuman gift for languages and recently expelled from the newly founded Jesuit order, Postel fetched up in 1547 at Venice, where his long-held dream of religious unity was to reach a new level of intensity. Like most who shared his religious hopes, Postel was distressed by the proliferation of heretical sects (which were the very antithesis of religious unity) and, in a sermon he delivered at the Church of Santa Maria dei Miracoli in 1548, warned his listeners of the danger that heresy presented to their society. "Pray to God a Lord's Prayer for this city, for it has not been in greater distress since the time of Tiepolo," Postel warned, in an exquisitely Venetian reference to the attempted uprising of Baiamonte Tiepolo at the start of the fourteenth century—one of the greatest po-

39. On the interest in Joachim in early sixteenth-century Venice, see Reeves, *Joachim of Fiore*, 96–125; and Reeves, *The Influence of Prophecy*; on Savonarola's influence, see Roberto Ridolfi, *The Life of Girolamo Savonarola*, trans. Cecil Grayson (New York: Knopf, 1959), 303; on Zorzi, see A. Foscari and M. Tafuri, *L'armonia e i conflitti: La Chiesa di San Francesco della Vigna nella Venezia del '500* (Turin: Einaudi, 1983).

40. On Postel, see Bouwsma, *Concordia Mundi*; and Kuntz, *Guillaume Postel*.

litical emergencies the city had ever confronted. "One cannot but take precaution," Postel continued, "seeing that in this city there is a great abundance of Lutherans, sacramentarians, and others who lack piety."[41] But Postel, who received support for his crusade from the Council of Ten, was not the only millenarian who believed that the heresies of the day must be repressed. At about the same time that he gave his sermon in the Church of Santa Maria dei Miracoli, a certain armorer (*corazzaro*), a Venetian artisan by the name of Benedetto, was extending his own millenarian teachings to include an attack on heresy.[42]

Like Postel, Benedetto spoke out against the heresies of his time, and he sought to place himself on the side of the religious and political authorities. In Benedetto's case too, the authorities cooperated. The Council of Ten seems to have believed that Benedetto might be a more effective and certainly less politically risky opponent of the popular evangelical heresies in the city than the Roman Holy Office, and accordingly its members arranged for a number of the evangelicals from the large heretical circle at San Moisè—already under investigation by the Venetian Inquisition—to hear his teachings. Thus at some point in the fall of 1548 an officer of the Ten escorted the heretics to the home of Benedetto.[43]

Once all were present, Father Iseppo Bressan, a priest who officiated regularly at Santa Maria dei Miracoli (and who therefore undoubtedly moved in the same circles as Postel himself), began reading from Benedetto's works. At first those the officer of the Ten had brought to hear the reading were confused. Perhaps they had been told that Be-

41. Cited in Stella, *Anabattismo e antitrinitarismo*, 116.

42. Benedetto remains an obscure figure in Venetian history, but for a preliminary orientation, see Carlo Ginzburg, "Due note sul profetismo cinquecentesco," *Rivista storica italiana* 78 (1966): 184–227; Adriano Prosperi, "Intorno a un catechismo figurato del tardo '500," in Ernst Ullmann, ed., *Von der Macht der Bilder* (Leipzig: E. A. Seemann, 1983), 99–114; and Ottavia Niccoli, "'Prophetie di Musaicho': Figure e scritture gioachimite nella Venezia del Cinquento," in Antonio Rotondò, ed., *Forme e destinazione del messaggio religioso: Aspetti della propaganda religiosa nel Cinquecento* (Florence: Olschki, 1991), 197–227. Niccoli's analysis of this group is closest to my own, though she focuses on the role and significance of images in popular religious sensibilities.

43. ASV, *Sant'Uffizio*, b. 7, doss. "Contra denuntiatos pro hereticis de contracta Sancti Moysis," testimony of 23 November 1548. Although the scholars cited above missed this reference to Benedetto Corazzaro, he had come to the attention of the Venetian authorities in spring 1540 when the Council of Ten arrested him and two fellow artisans "per motivi di ordine publico" (del Col, "L'Inquisizione romana e il potere politico nella repubblica di Venezia," 195).

nedetto was one of their own. But when Father Iseppo began to read from Benedetto's writings about the necessity of works for salvation, they realized that they could not accept Benedetto's teachings. To the evangelicals, salvation was clearly not the result of works but of grace. A hunchback priest who had come with them and shared their views began to argue with Father Iseppo Bressan. At this point Benedetto "Corazzaro" joined the fray. He attacked the evangelical clergyman: "You are a priest, a minister to us laymen," adding that it was his role to urge the laity to do good works, not to harden people's hearts against them.[44] More words were exchanged, and the encounter ended with a threat Benedetto drew from Psalms. God, the armorer maintained, would dash his enemies with an "iron rod." Judges, he warned, would use force to make people follow them. In this instance, Benedetto's powers of prophecy were to be confirmed. About a week after the meeting, one of the heretics who was present—the goldsmith Iseppo, a leading figure in the evangelical circle of San Moisè—was arrested for heresy. A tailor who admired Benedetto's teachings saw this event as a fulfillment of Benedetto's admonition, interpreting the arrest as "the iron rod"; Benedetto's reputation as a prophet was undoubtedly enhanced.[45] To many Venetians Benedetto's teaching must have held appeal—an outcome that did not escape Manelfi's attention. "There are also in Venice," he noted in a list of heretics provided to the Inquisition, "some thirty or forty persons who have started a new confraternity (*schola*) or sect, called the sect of the Corazzaro. [And this Corazzaro] says he is that man of whom St. Paul says, 'I know a man in Christ' [who fourteen years ago was caught up to the third heaven (whether in the body or out of the body I do not know, God knows) (2 Cor. 12:2)]."[46]

Ironically, given their explicit opposition to the heresies of the late 1540s, both Postel and the followers of Benedetto would eventually come under suspicion for heresy and would be tried and punished.

44. "Digando che è sacerdote, ministro di nui laici" (ASV, *Sant'Uffizio*, b. 7, doss., "Contra denuntiatos pro hereticis de contracta Sancti Moysis," testimony of 23 November 1548).

45. "Et questo è stato la verga ferea" (ibid.).

46. "Sono etiandio in Vinegia da trenta o quaranta persone quali hanno comminciato una schola o setta nova detta del Corazzaro, quale dice essere quello huomo di cui dice san Pavolo: 'Scio hominem in corpore etc.'" (ASV, *Sant'Uffizio*, b. 9, "Manelfi," list of "Lutherani, anabattisti et altri heretici," presented to the Bolognese inquisitor on 2 November 1551; Ginzburg, ed., *I costituti di don Pietro Manelfi*, 49).

Whereas they opposed the heresies of their day as vigorously as the authorities did, their opposition stemmed from conceptions of salvation that troubled the Inquisition and eventually came into sharp conflict with Catholic orthodoxy. Indeed, not only would both Guillaume Postel and Benedetto Corazzaro elaborate millenarian visions of salvation that would, as Joachim's and Savonarola's did, call the religious and the political arrangements of their times into question, but they would also, as the Venetian Anabaptists under the influence of Girolamo Busale did, develop a theology that much reduced the role of Christ in history. In particular, they did not see Christ as sufficient for human redemption but rather looked forward to the coming of a new messiah who would usher in a new age.

Postel's vision of this new age—what he would come to call "the restitution of all things"—was elaborate. At the center of his millenarianism was the idea of the *concordia mundi*, a spiritual and political harmony that would resolve all tensions. Christians would rediscover their Jewishness; reason and emotion would be brought into a new equilibrium; and, as a universal truth would be made known to all, there was to be "one sheepfold and one shepherd." In this vision Venice was to assume a special role. The city, though plagued by heresy, was graced by a special divine favor. God had preserved its political institutions for over one thousand years. But of even greater value in demonstrating to Postel's satisfaction that Venice was the New Jerusalem was the presence there of a female mystic, a certain Madre Zuana— whom Postel came to view, both because of her commitment to the care of the poor and because of her spiritual intensity, as a sign of God's favor toward the city and also as a prophet in her own right and one who would reveal to Postel deeper truths than he could find in his studies alone.

In Madre Zuana's eyes, Postel was to serve as the new Elijah and specifically as the prophet of "the restitution of all things." Evidently she found in this strange Frenchman a figure from her own millenarian dreams. She was convinced that a carving in the Basilica San Marco depicting a woman with her young son—an image popularly believed to be inspired by the abbot Joachim of Fiore—was a prophetic depiction of her spiritual relationship with Postel. Yet this relationship was to prove most meaningful to Postel. Indeed, as he deepened his study of Jewish prophetic writings in these years, his connection with Madre Zuana, who chose him as her confessor but who also acted as Postel's spiritual adviser, pushed him to new levels of millenarian frenzy. Postel came to equate Madre Zuana (whom he called the Venetian Virgin) with the Shechinah or divine presence of the *Zohar*, the masterpiece of Spanish Kabbalism.[47] This identification in turn only strengthened Postel's belief that he was in fact the prophet that Zuana had told him he was. The conviction stayed with him after his departure from Venice in 1549 and after Madre Zuana's death (which occurred soon after he left). And in Paris in the early part of 1552, it became the basis for the decisive spiritual experience in Postel's life. "After about two years," Postel wrote, "[Madre Zuana's spirit] came to find me in Paris" and there her spirit replaced his. To Postel this mysterious experience—which he would call an "immutation" and which penetrated him, burning away his old self, to his very marrow (*usque ossa transfundens*)—was a rebirth, in which his former self was purified and in which he was made new by Zuana's indwelling. The experience intensified Postel's hopes for a new dispensation and led to an outpouring of one treatise after another, each of which announced Postel's truth that a new age or order was about to break in upon the present.[48]

The armorer Benedetto stood in a similar tradition. He too claimed certain prophetic powers, at least as early as 1548, after predicting that the heretics would be punished by "an iron rod." By 1551 he claimed, albeit enigmatically, as Manelfi testified, that he had been to the "third heaven." Moreover—and here some direct contact with Postel seems almost certain—both men used strikingly similar metaphors in the elaboration of their prophecies. For Benedetto's sect also harbored a belief that a new dispensation was imminent. A book written out by hand that circulated among the members of his sect contained—so the Inquisition would eventually learn from one of his followers—"proph-

---

47. On the *Zohar*'s place in Spanish Kabbalism, see Gershom Scholem, *The Messianic Idea in Judaism and Other Essays on Jewish Spirituality* (New York: Schocken Books, 1971), 39–42; and Moshe Idel, *Kabbalah: New Perspectives* (New Haven: Yale University Press, 1988).

48. This account of Postel and Madre Zuana is deeply indebted to the research of Marion L. Kuntz, especially her *Guillaume Postel*, which brings a once shadowy Madre Zuana (or Johanna or the Venetian Virgin) and a number of other spiritual women of sixteenth-century Venice to the foreground (for Postel's immutation see ibid., 102 n.328). In addition see Kuntz, "The Myth of Venice in the Thought of Guillaume Postel," *Supplementum Festivum: Studies in Honor of Paul Oskar Kristeller* (Binghamton: Center for Medieval and Early Renaissance Studies, 1987), 505–523; and Kuntz., ed., *Postello, Venezia e il suo mondo* (Florence: Leo S. Olschki, 1988). Bouswma, *Concordia Mundi* is characteristically insightful. The many studies on Postel by François Secret, cited by Kuntz, have good bibliographies on the Kabbalists and on Postel's intellectual contacts but a highly inaccessible style.

ecies that the Turks were to be defeated, that the Austrian empire was to meet its ruin, that Constantinople was to be taken, and that the Turks were to convert to Christianity and that there was to be one sheepfold and one shepherd."[49] Moreover, Benedetto also appeared to have placed his faith not in Jesus but in the imminent coming of a new messiah. Like Postel, therefore, Benedetto represented a further radicalization of heretical thought in Venice. Indeed, just as several of the Venetian evangelicals had first passed from their rather moderate Protestant convictions to anabaptism and antitrinitarian views, so now it was possible for those who were antitrinitarian to pass over to the messianism of a Postel or a Benedetto Corazzaro. Benedetto Florio, a prominent figure in Busale's antitrinitarian circle in Padua, may have been among Benedetto's earliest followers.[50]

Moreover, the language of Postel and Benedetto was remarkably similar. Both appear to have been indebted to Jewish Kabbalah. In his treatise the *Restitution of All Things*, Postel argued that while Christ had acted "for the priesthood in the conversion of Cain," the next messiah "acts for the kingdom in the conversion of Abel." And although neither messiah "has been called priest or king," Postel continued, "still the First Born was ordained for the priesthood, the second for the kingdom."[51] The new messiah, in other words, was to complete in the political realm what Jesus had accomplished in the spiritual. Redemption, in Postel's view, was to take place in this world and not, as in Augustinian Christianity, in some unseen realm. The single surviving fragment of Benedetto's writings used the same metaphor, though in a less explicitly political key. Benedetto recalled that God had accepted the sacrifice of Abel but not that of Cain, who had been conceived out of wedlock. Yet "in the present," Benedetto wrote, "most sacrifices are those of Cain; only a few are those of Abel"—by which he meant (as one of his followers would explain to the Inquisition) that it was the habit of the Venetian lords to make priests of their illegitimate sons,

49. "Conteneva solo di Profecie cioè che haveva da essere la rotta del Turcho, la finitione dell'Imperio in Casa d'Austria, et che s'haveva a pigliare Constantinopoli, et che il Turcho haveva a venire alla fede christiana et che haveva ad essere uno solo Ovile et un sol Pastore" (APV, *Criminalia Sanctae Inquisitionis*, b. 2, doss. "Contra Joannem Baptistam Ravajoli Friulanum," testimony of 6 October 1573).

50. This admittedly speculative possibility exists if Benedetto Florio (alias Lorenzo Tizzano) can be identified with Benedetto Florian, an important figure in the circle of Corazzaro's followers.

51. Cited in Marion L. Kuntz, "Guillaume Postel and the World State: Restitution and the Universal Monarchy," *History of European Ideas* 4 (1983): 306.

and for this reason their sacrifices were not pleasing to God.[52] This perversion of the proper nature of priestly sacrifice was to Benedetto and to his followers a clear sign that a new dispensation and a new messiah were necessary to ensure salvation. Moreover Benedetto appealed to many, developing as Postel did in his sermons and his writings a sizable following in Venice. Manelfi asserted that Benedetto had gathered some thirty or forty followers. Perhaps he had. We know for sure that as late as the early 1570s, long after Benedetto died, a group of some half-dozen men still adhered to the teachings of this charismatic armorer.

In Venice, the crisis of the religious reform in Italy—signaled by the death of Contarini and the flight of Ochino as well as the establishment of the Roman Inquisition in the early 1540s—did not result in a simple return to Catholic orthodoxy. On the contrary, the ensuing decade proved itself to be one of creative and rich searches for alternative understandings of the nature of redemption. Only a very few Venetians were involved in the various currents that the Holy Office would define as heterodox. Yet the strength of these currents was impressive. By far the broadest of the three was that of the evangelicals. But the Anabaptists and the millenarians (both struggling in fundamental ways with the problem of the role of the messiah in human history) also made their presence felt in Venetian culture in these years. The popular religious discussions in this late Renaissance city, therefore, were never limited to the problem of the relative importance of faith and works in the economy of salvation. The figure of Jesus became a central part of the debates about the nature of redemption. To the evangelicals, Jesus' sacrifice was the cornerstone of human salvation. Salvation was a benefice, a gift, over which individual men and women could exercise little or no control. The Anabaptists disagreed and emphasized a view of salvation that was, despite its radicalism, more traditionally Catholic or Pelagian in its insistence on merit and the ability of ordinary men and women to create Christian utopias whose citizens would be saved. To these *anabattisti*, Christ was a man like all others. Jesus was not God; rather he was filled with divine virtue; therefore the imitation of Christ seemed a real possibility to those who clung to the hope that individual Christians might achieve salvation on the basis of their mer-

---

52. "Che adesso son tutti sacraficii de Cain, et pochi sono quelli di Abel," APV, *Criminalia Sanctae Inquisitionis*, b. 2, doss. "Contra Jo: Baptistam Ravajoli Friulanum," manuscript treatise, f. G.

itorious acts. To others, neither the hopes of the evangelicals nor the hopes of the Anabaptists were sufficient. Agreeing with the evangelicals that salvation was not in their hands but accepting the Anabaptists' belief that Jesus was not God, they placed their hope in the only place that was left: in divine intervention, in the coming of a new messiah. In so doing, these Venetians brought the Christian dream of redemption full circle, from the interior transformation of the individual believer to the radical transformation of the political order itself.

The Inquisition's function was as variegated as the heresies it sought to police. As we have seen, the first evangelicals were brought to trial in the early 1540s, and the reorganization of the Inquisition in 1547 sharpened its focus. The first trials against the Anabaptists came in 1551, intensifying after Manelfi's denunciation in that same year. The attention of the Inquisition turned to millenarian teachings at about this same time, and to the works of Postel in particular. Postel returned to the west from Jerusalem in 1551, with no intent to reduce the controversies that surrounded him. Experiencing a rebirth in which he claimed that Madre Zuana took possession of his body, he threw himself into a frenzy of publishing. His ideas began to stir up more and more controversy. His teachings were condemned by the Sorbonne in 1553 and placed on the *Index of Prohibited Books* in 1554. In January 1555 he left Vienna (where he held a chair in religious studies) for Venice. His hope was to convince the Inquisition there that his views were orthodox and that his name should be removed from the *Index*. Characteristically, Postel placed his hope in rational argument but made little progress with the authorities, who believed his views were too contradictory and who were convinced that this mad Frenchman had denied the divinity of Christ. Frustrated after nearly a year of argument before the tribunal, Postel finally declared that he would rather be executed than retract his views. The Holy Office pronounced him insane, and the Venetian government extradited him to Rome where he was to be confined to prison for life.[53] But in 1559, when Paul IV died, the Inquisition prisons were emptied during the celebratory rioting that followed the news of the death of the pope. Postel, a lucky man, made his way back to France.[54]

---

53. Aldo Stella, "Il processo veneziano di Guglielmo Postel," *Rivista di storia della Chiesa in Italia* 22 (1968): 438; see also Andrea del Col, "Il controllo della stampa a Venezia," 464–476.
54. Bouwsma, *Concordia Mundi*, 24; and Kuntz, *Guillaume Postel*, 135.

## CHAPTER FIVE

# Hiding

---

*Non omnis simulatio peccatum est.*
Fausto Sozzini, 1601

I n 1547 Francesco Spiera, a lawyer and a leading figure in the evangelical community of Cittadella, a town just outside Vicenza, became one of the first heretics to be denounced before the newly reorganized Holy Office in Venice. Spiera held no doubt about his own guilt. He had, in fact, spoken out as a critic of the Roman church; and this was widely known among his neighbors and acquaintances. But Spiera was anxious and uncertain about how he should present himself to the Inquisition, as we learn from Pier Paolo Vergerio's account of Spiera's ordeal:

> At times he seemed to want to declare his opinions openly and hide nothing. At other times he thought rather of saving himself from this danger by going as soon as possible out of the country, leaving his property and children behind. Finally, after a long internal battle, he decided upon dissimulation. He would keep his opinions firmly but secretly in his heart and with his mouth say something else, namely, exactly what the legate wished him to say.[1]

Spiera, we discover, was only one of many members of the evangelical community in the Republic of Venice who, after the intensification of inquisitorial activity in the late 1540s, decided to lead a dual life. This increasingly repressive climate turned some evangelicals to more radical views, to Anabaptist and even antitrinitarian ideas, or to millenarian hopes. Yet most of the evangelicals—at least those who chose not

1. Pier Paolo Vergerio, *La historia di M. Francesco Spiera* in Emilio Comba, ed., *Biblioteca della Riforma italiana: Raccolta di scritti evangelici del secolo XVI* (Rome-Florence: Claudiana, 1883), 2:112–122. Spiera's trial is located in ASV, *Sant'Uffizio*, b. 9, doss. "Spiera Francesco." For further information on Spiera and on heresy in Cittadella, see Giuseppe De Leva, *Degli eretici di Cittadella* (Venice: Grimaldo, 1873); and Zille, *Gli eretici a Cittadella nel Cinquecento*. The Spiera case generated considerable discussion in sixteenth- and seventeenth-century Europe; see Celio Secondo Curione, ed., *Francisci Spierae, qui quod susceptam semel evangelicae veritatis professionem abnegasset damnassetque, in horrendam incidet desperationem, historia* (Basel: Pietro Perna, 1550). See also the treatise of Giorgio Siculo, cited in note 11. The story was well known in England: Nathaniel Bacon, *A Relation of the Fearful Estate of Francis Spira, after he turned Apostate from the Protestant Faith to Popery* (1638; London: Printed for G. Terry, Paternoster-Row, 1793).

---

*Opposite.* The bustle of activity, both religious and secular, at Venice's Rialto was famous: here at the center of the city merchants from all over the world met to do business. Given the constant comings and goings, it must have been easy not only to pick up new ideas but to hide one's convictions as well. In the 1580s the present stone structure replaced the older wooden Rialto bridge shown here. (Vittorio Carpaccio, *The Healing of a Possessed Man*, ca. 1495 [Accademia, Venice]; courtesy of Osvaldo Böhm)

to flee Italy and who shunned martyrdom—shifted less in the substance of their religious convictions than in their manner of expressing them. They came, in other words, to understand the necessity of concealing their true beliefs from the authorities, even if duplicity might weigh heavily on their consciences. Outwardly, they would do all they could to mask their heretical views. They would attend mass, give their confessions to a priest, and baptize their children in the parish church. But inwardly, they would cultivate a different faith. They came to view public ceremonies as meaningless in themselves, but they continued to hope for the day when they might express their evangelical ideals openly.

To those men and women who became committed to reform, whether moderate or radical, such dissimulation was no doubt painful in itself. In many ways, the decision to make religious convictions a purely private matter and to recognize that the most individuals could hope for was compromise with a culture they could do little to change was itself a kind of defeat. Furthermore, the leading reformers outside Italy—from Zwingli and Bullinger to Bucer, Oecolampadius, and Melanchthon, but most especially Calvin—provided no comfort at all. These theologians found dissimulating behavior reprehensible. "Nicodemites," Calvin disparagingly called those who temporized in their faith, after the Pharisee Nicodemus who, according to the Gospel of John, had come to Jesus by night in order that his new faith not be known by others.[2] And while Calvin's strictures were directed primarily against his fellow Frenchmen who also found such compromises necessary, they applied to the Italian heretics as well. The only hope for salvation, Calvin argued, lay in flight or in martyrdom. He rejected unequivocally the argument that belief within was what mattered.

2. Of Calvin's several works on the subject see esp. *Excuse . . . à Messieurs les Nicodemites, sur la complaincte qu'ilz font de sa trop grand' rigueur* (1544) in John Calvin, *Three French Treatises*, ed. Francis M. Higman (London: Athlone Press, 1970), 131–153. Italian scholars have given considerable attention to Nicodemism. Cantimori defined the phenomenon in *Eretici italiani del Cinquecento*, 70, 134–139, and 392–405. For a rich overview of this problem, see Antonio Rotondò, "Atteggiamenti della vita morale italiana del Cinquecento: La pratica nicodemitica," *Rivista storica italiana* 79 (1967): 991–1030; Albano Biondi, "La giustificazione della simulazione nel Cinquecento," in *Eresia e Riforma nell'Italia del Cinquecento*; and Paolo Simoncelli, *Evangelismo italiano del Cinquecento: Questione religiosa e nicodemismo politico* (Rome: Istituto Storico Italiano per l'Età Moderna e Contemporanea, 1979). Ginzburg, *Il nicodemismo* should now be read in light of Carlos M.N. Eire, "Calvin and Nicodemism: A Reappraisal," *Sixteenth-Century Journal* 10 (1979): 45–69. For a survey of Calvin's views on Nicodemites, see Eire, *War Against the Idols* (Cambridge: Cambridge University Press, 1986), 234–275.

"The inward worship of the heart," he preached, "does not suffice unless it is accompanied by outward profession among men."[3]

Indeed, the critique of such behavior would develop into one of the most often repeated refrains of the second half of the sixteenth century. There was a continual barrage of disapproval; numerous authors, in addition to Calvin, attacked such behavior. Thus in the 1553 preface to one of Calvin's most forceful anti-Nicodemite works, *Del fuggire le superstitioni*, the translator (whose identity we do not know, but certainly an Italian) urged his readers to flee Italy:

And it would have been pleasing to God if all those in Italy who have already known the truth of the Gospels had left sooner and come to those places [such as Geneva] where they might have more readily preserved it; for, in this way, one would see a greater number of the truly faithful from that nation [that is, Italy], but these are almost all lacking, since some have allowed themselves to be corrupted by vices and the evil conceptions that have rendered them impious and profane, without God and without religion; others have been seduced by some new heresy; others, by contrast, have been induced to renounce their beliefs out of fear.[4]

At about this same time Giulio da Milano argued against Nicodemism with equal fervor, although in his view flight itself was an "act of weakness"; he urged instead the open profession of faith, exhorting his readers to martyrdom.[5] The concerns over deception by the Italian evangelicals would continue for an entire generation. As late as 1570, Alessandro Trissino observed that "many still go about concealing [their true beliefs] after the example of Nicodemus, saying that although he was a disciple of Christ, nonetheless he went secretly at night to find Him lest he allow his views to be known, and they add that one can be a good Christian and still live in one's house by remaining silent and keeping within oneself that truth which one knows."[6]

Even in the late 1540s the "outward profession" of one's faith, of which Calvin spoke, was no longer possible in Italy, though dissimulation too was not easy. Indeed it was the ethical burden of concealing

3. Cited in William James Bouwsma, *John Calvin: A Sixteenth-Century Portrait* (New York: Oxford University Press, 1988), 216.

4. *Del fuggire le superstitioni che repugnano a la vera e sincera confession de la fede* (N.p., 1553), 4. Delio Cantimori first discussed this work in "Spigolature per la storia del nicodemismo italiano," in Cantimori et al. eds., *Ginevra e l'Italia* (Florence: Sansoni, 1959), 177–190; see also Cantimori, *Prospettive di storia ereticale italiana del Cinquecento*, 37–49.

5. Cantimori, *Prospettive di storia ereticale italiana del Cinquecento*, 52.

6. Trissino, "Ragionamento della necessità di ritirarsi a vivere nella Chiesa visibile di Gesù Cristo, lasciando il papesimo," 109.

one's evangelical commitments that drew Spiera to Vergerio's attention. For while Spiera did conceal the depths of his evangelical commitments from the Inquisition, he nonetheless confessed to wavering a bit in matters of faith and was forced to abjure his heresies. This act of renunciation did not rest easily on his conscience. Increasingly he grew depressed in the belief that he had now lost all hope of salvation. "I am cursed forever among the reprobate because I have denied Christ and the known truth." And to prove his point Spiera became his own prosecutor, drawing on his lawyerly skills and on Scripture to make his case. "Whoever denies me before men," Christ had said, "I also will deny before my Father who is in heaven" (Matt. 10:33). It was a warning reiterated in Paul's Epistle to the Hebrews: "For if we sin deliberately after receiving the knowledge of the truth, there no longer remains a sacrifice for sins, but a fearful prospect of judgment and a fury of fire which will consume the adversaries" (Heb. 10:26–27).[7] The case he made against himself plunged him into despair. He could hardly bring himself to eat or to sleep; his sons turned to the best medical advice available in nearby Padua; Vergerio himself, who spent much time at Spiera's bedside, struggled to convince him of God's saving grace but failed, and Francesco Spiera died convinced he was going to hell.

Yet Nicodemite behavior may not have been so difficult for everyone who sought to conceal his or her beliefs from both the authorities and the neighbors. Certain aspects of the evangelical tradition—especially as it developed in Italy—seemed to provide some justification for dissimulation. The writings of Juan de Valdés, one of the most influential theologians of the Italian reform, argued that the external manifestations of one's faith mattered little. What counted were the conversion and commitment of the individual believer. Many of Valdés's more aristocratic followers, in the Italian courts especially, appear to have been attracted to this interpretation of the religious life because it allowed them to cultivate evangelical ideals in absolute privacy, with no political risks at all. Similar ideas occurred to Erasmus who, like Valdés, played down the importance of external signs of piety and whose works circulated through sixteenth-century Italy, not only among schoolmasters and humanists but among artisans and shopkeepers as well. And from

7. In addition to these passages, see Heb. 6:4–6 and 2 Pet. 2:21. On Spiera's use of Scripture, see Schutte, *Pier Paolo Vergerio*, 241 nn.119–122.

them a variety of heretics would find some justification in the cautious religious posturing that Nicodemite behavior entailed.

But more explicit justifications of the legitimacy of religious dissimulation were readily available. In the compendious *Pandectae veteris et novi Testamenti* of Otto Brunfels—first published in Strasbourg in 1527 but widely diffused in Italy—the attentive reader could find passages justifying the decision to conceal one's convictions. "Among unbelievers and the obstinate," Brunfels wrote, "we can dissimulate and feign, especially if there is no hope, because God will weigh our hearts." And later he added, "It is permitted to feign and to simulate before the impious in order to avoid or to prevent danger. We can also humble ourselves considerably before them in order to glorify God, and pray nonetheless in our hearts that God might abandon them to the destruction of the flesh."[8]

Moreover, in the late 1540s, just as the Roman Inquisition was beginning to clamp down on religious dissidents, Lelio Sozzini addressed to Calvin a letter that was clearly meant to develop a greater understanding of the legitimacy of dissimulation. Troubled by Calvin's intransigence on this issue, Sozzini tried to broach the subject with the reformer from a new angle. Was it legitimate, he wondered, for one to marry a woman who had the "true faith" but who, out of fear, continued to attend Catholic ceremonies? And could one, he asked, attend mass out of necessity?[9] Equally subtle were the observations on this problem of Celio Secondo Curione, who—after arguing against any form of simulation and urging those in Italy who accepted the evangelical message, if they could not accept martyrdom, to go into exile—did allow for simulation on the part of those whose faith was not yet strong enough to allow them to express it openly. But such simulation was acceptable, Curione insisted, only provisionally. These Christians were

8. The two key passages Ginzburg cites are "Inter incredulos et pertinaces dissimulare possumus et fingere, praesertim si non sit spes; quia Deus ponderat cor"; and "Fingere et simulare licet coram impiis propter vitandum vel praeveniendum periculum. Possumus item aliquantisper nos illis humiliare, propter gloriam Dei, et corde tamen orare, ut Deus perdat eos, ad interitum carnis" (*Il nicodemismo*, 3 and 78 n.2). Yet few sixteenth-century readers were likely to find in the *Pandectae* the manifesto for dissimulation that Ginzburg claimed it was. See Eire, "Calvin and Nicodemism: A Reappraisal," 57, which notes, "The counsels for simulation cited by Ginzburg are buried in a mass of unrelated topics and are even contradicted by other passages."

9. Ginzburg, *Il nicodemismo*, 169. Lelio Sozzini's nephew Fausto provides this chapter's epigraph (*Epitome colloquii Racoviae habiti anno 1601*, ed. Lech Szczucki and Janusz Tazbir [Warsaw: Pánstwowe Wydawnictwo Naukowe, 1966], 84).

to pray continuously for a strengthening of their faith and, when it was strengthened, must no longer conceal their convictions. Thus to Curione (a Piedmontese who had taken refuge in Basel) Nicodemite behavior was legitimate only within the most narrow limits.[10]

The most explicit Italian defense of dissimulation came from the Benedictine visionary Giorgio Siculo. Outraged by Vergerio's treatise on Spiera and the conclusions the former bishop drew from the lawyer's ordeal, in 1550 Siculo published his *Epistola . . . alli cittadini di Riva di Trento contra il mendatio di Francesco Spiera et falsa dottrina de' Protestanti* (Letter . . . to the citizens of Riva di Trento against the lies of Francesco Spiera and the false teachings of the Protestants). In this treatise Siculo made his dissent from the Protestant interpretation of the Spiera case explicit. "Now, according to . . . the doctors and teachers of the Protestant faith," Siculo wrote, "all those who consent either in fact or in person to cults that are not true, deny Christ just as [Spiera] did." But such a view, Siculo went on, had unacceptable consequences:

O what a great number of priests and friars and men and women there are, who are of the Protestant view, hidden in diverse regions and countries of the Roman church, and who, out of fear of being arrested and maltreated by the inquisitors, both consent with their words and with their own persons to cults and sacraments that they themselves believe to be false and abominable to God and his saints! What! According to Spiera's teaching—a teaching confirmed by his mendacious teachers—are all of these to be held among the reprobate for denying Christ in this way?

To Siculo this view was clearly unacceptable, and he argued that such a teaching failed to grasp the character of divine grace. In his effort to counter such an interpretation, he cast himself in a prophetic role and stressed the expansiveness of God's mercy. Surely it would reach to those in Italy who struggled with the reality of repression. Finally, drawing on Paul's circumcising of Timothy and purification of himself according to Mosaic law, he concluded that "those who accept and publicly confess the doctrines of the Roman church, like those who *propter infirmos fratres* consent to those cults which do not appear licit or true," in no way deny Christ. Ultimately, the treatise constituted a defense of

10. Mario Turchetti, "Nota sulla religiosità di Celio Secondo Curione (1503–1569) in relazione al 'nicodemismo,'" in Adriano Prosperi and A. Biondi, eds., *Libri, idee e sentimenti religiosi nel Cinquecento italiano* (Ferrara: Panini, 1987), 109–115.

dissimulation—a defense that must have enjoyed a certain success.[11] Calvin seems to have been disturbed by the large number of readers it attracted; a group of Giorgio's followers was discovered and tried for heresy a few years later.[12]

The choice to hide one's inner convictions was not therefore—as this debate makes clear—a simple decision. Yet many Italian heretics, evangelicals and Anabaptists, did lead confessionally duplicitous lives. We cannot know how many evangelicals and Anabaptists chose to conceal their true convictions, but the number was in all probability quite high; the evangelical community especially remained active, even after the Inquisition began its task of bringing men and women suspected of heresy to trial. In the late 1560s, Paolo Gaiano—a former silk weaver who now faced his second Venetian trial for heresy—informed the inquisitors that if they would let him go about the city in the company of a guard, he would show them *un mondo di eretici*—a world of heretics. Brigata, a young woman residing in Venice, attempted to persuade her mother, in Geneva, to return to this Italian city in which, she promised, the Gospel was preached as freely as it was in Switzerland. And a certain Francesco Spinola—a Genoese humanist who had been an active leader in the heretical communities of Venice—told the nuncio Facchinetti in the early 1570s that he would reveal "a large and very important conventicle of heretics" in exchange for a pardon from the authorities.[13]

Over the previous decade a significant number of those brought to trial before the Venetian Holy Office had been, in some sense, recidi-

11. *Epistola di Giorgio Siculo servo fidele di Iesu Christo alli cittadini di Riva di Trento contra il mendatio di Francesco Spiera, & falsa dottrina di Protestanti* (Bologna: Anselmo Giaccarello, 1550), 45r and 45v; 49r and 49v. The passages discussed here are prominent in Cantimori's study of Nicodemism: *Eretici italiani del Cinquecento*, 62–70.

12. See, for example, Calvin, *De aeterna Dei praedestinatione* in *Ioannis Calvini Opera quae supersunt omnia*, ed. G. Baum, E. Cunitz, and E. Reuss (Brunswick: C.A. Schwetschke, 1863–1900), vol. 8, col. 249–366; and Ginzburg, "Due note sul profetismo cinquecentesco," 184–227. Adriano Prosperi is completing a study of Siculo; his preliminary results are in "Opere inedite o sconosciute di Giorgio Siculo," *La bibliofilia* 87 (1985): 137–157; and in "Ricerche sul Siculo e i suoi seguaci," in Regina Pozzi and Adriano Prosperi, eds., *Studi in onore di Armando Saitta* (Pisa: Giardini, 1989), 35–71.

13. For Paolo's remark about "un mondo di eretici," see ASV, *Sant'Uffizio*, b. 20, doss. "Paolo Gaiano," testimony of 20 February 1570; for Brigata's letter, ibid., doss. "Tommaso Bavallero," testimony of 28 July 1568; and for Spinola's remarks, Giovanni Antonio Facchinetti, letter to Michele Bonelli, 31 August 1566, in Stella, ed., *Nunziature di Venezia*, 8:100.

vists. Like Spiera, they had had a brush with the Inquisition either in the late 1540s or at some point in the 1550s. A few of them had abjured; others had simply been given a warning to watch what they did or said. But unlike Spiera they were able to justify to themselves these early false abjurations and continue as active members of the Venetian evangelical community. Among these Nicodemites were the booksellers Andrea Arrivabene and Vincenzo Valgrisi, the jeweler Bartolomeo Carpan, the merchant Adamo dalla Crea, the lawyer Marc'Antonio d'Armano, the physician Girolamo Donzellino (though he spent much of the time in exile), the notary Girolamo Parto, a certain Vincenzo Quaiato and the silk weaver Tommaso, the scrivener Zaccaria Azzalin, the chancellor Zuanbattista Michiel, and the weaver Paolo Gaiano.[14]

These men, it seems, not only concealed their own beliefs (by dissimulating) but found it necessary as part of their deception to pretend to be practicing Catholics as well (by simulating). Before the Venetian Holy Office in 1567, for example, one suspect, a certain Marcantonio Varotto, a weaver of taffeta, reported having received advice from a

14. Andrea Arrivabene: in 1549 interrogated by the Holy Office and warned not to sell heretical books; in 1551 denounced as "lutherano" by Manelfi; questioned in 1570 (ASV, *Sant'Uffizio*, b. 7, doss. "Comino da Trino"; b. 9, doss. "Manelfi," list of Lutherani, anabattisti et altri heretici for inquisitor in Bologna, n.d. [also in Ginzburg, ed., *I costituti di don Pietro Manelfi*, 49]; b. 30, doss. "Arrivabene Andrea"); for more detail see Grendler, *The Roman Inquisition and the Venetian Press*, 105–112.—Vincenzo Valgrisi: interrogated in 1559, tried in 1570 (b. 14, doss. "Vincenzo Valgrisio"; b. 159, register "Proccesi [*sic*] 1569, 1570, 1571").—Bartolomeo Carpan: implicated in 1547, arrested in 1568 and abjured (b. 6, doss. "Fra Benedetto da Genova"; b. 29, doss. "Carponi Bartolomeo").—Adamo dalla Crea: interrogated in 1549, implicated in 1570 (b. 7, doss. "Pre Alvise de Michiel confessore nel convento delle monache de S. Lucia"; b. 20, doss. "Paolo Gaian").—Marc'Antonio d'Armano: denounced in 1559, tried (and exonerated) in 1572 (b. 16, doss. "Mario D'Armano"; b. 35, doss. "Marc'Antonio d'Armano").—Girolamo Donzellino: denounced as "lutherano" in 1551, implicated in 1552; tried and abjured in 1561, again in 1574; executed in 1587 (b. 9, doss. "Manelfi" [also Ginzburg, ed., *I costituti di don Pietro Manelfi*, 48]; b. 10, doss. "Rosello Paolo"; b. 39, doss. "Donzellino Girolamo"); Grendler, *The Roman Inquisition and the Venetian Press*, 108–110.—Girolamo Parto: abjured after trial in 1553; in 1572 denounced and tried; executed by drowning in 1575 (b. 11, register "1553 libro secondo et 1554 libro primo"; b. 37, doss. "Parto Girolamo"). —Vincenzo Quaiato: abjured in 1553, denounced in 1570 (b. 11, register "1553 secondo et 1554 primo"; doss. "Paolo Gaian").—Tommaso: abjured in 1553; tried in 1568, died in prison some two years later (b. 11, register "1553 primo"; b. 24, doss. "Bavallaro Tommaso").—Zaccaria Azzalin: implicated in 1549, accused in 1569 (b. 7, doss. "Pre Alvise de Michiel confessore nel convento delle monache de S. Lucia"; b. 20, doss. "Paolo Gaian").—Zuanbattista Michiel: tried in 1554, again in 1574 (b. 11, doss. "Processus contra Anabatistas"; b. 37, doss. "Parto Girolamo").—Paolo Gaiano: implicated in 1549, tried in 1569; executed in 1570 (b. 7, doss. "Pre Alvise de Michiel confessore nel convento delle monache de S. Lucia"; b. 20, doss. "Paolo Gaian"; b. 159, register "Proccesi [*sic*] 1569, 1570, 1571").

fellow heretic in Mantua that he maintain the greatest of caution. "If you know the truth," he was counseled, "give thanks to God, but attend to your own affairs, keep the truth within, do not go about revealing it because it is not now the time to discuss these matters." In the same year, the tribunal learned that Silvestro Semprini, his wife, and two sons were said "to go sometimes to mass not with faith but out of fear; thus they say it is necessary to attend in order not to cause the people to gossip." And the following year, a witness testified that a certain Uberto Verlato who "was in agreement with certain practices of Geneva . . . had said to [him], speaking of the mass, that it is necessary to attend to do as others do." In 1576 lawyer Michel Oldofredo's explanation to the Inquisition demonstrated the degree to which social pressure could make attendance at the mass necessary. "When I was at mass I stayed for the whole service in order not to scandalize anyone." And in 1581 the parish priest of a Zuan Grison, a pork butcher's apprentice, complained: "Every year he pretends to go to confession and take communion and he has never come to the holy sacrament, not even at Easter."[15]

The self-conscious struggle to seem orthodox but keep Protestant convictions is especially evident in the studied caution of the notary Girolamo Parto—a caution learned after his first encounter with the Venetian Holy Office in 1553. Like many others who had this experience, Girolamo was able to continue his life as an evangelical. He did so as a Nicodemite, behind the facade of a devout Catholic. He attended mass and went to confession—justifying his deception with

---

15. "Figliolo, se voi conoscete la verità, ringratiate Idio, ma fatte il fatto vostro, tenite la cosa in voi, né vi andate palesando, perché non è tempo adesso de ragionare di queste cose" (ASV, *Sant'Uffizio*, b. 22, doss. "Varotta Marcantonio," memorial of 21 January 1567; cited also in Domenico Caccamo, *Eretici italiani in Moravia, Polonia, Transilvania* [DeKalb: Northern Illinois University Press; Chicago: Newberry Library, 1970], 203); note that Barotta is a variant of Varotta.—"Item andavano alle volte alla messa non con fede, ma per timore, però dicevano fa bisogno andarli per non dar da mormorare al populo" (ASV, *Sant'Uffizio*, b. 23, doss., "Contra Silvestrum, Angelam, Stephanum et Cyprianum," denunciation of 24 November 1567).—"Assentiva in certe cose di Genevra . . . et parlando della messa mi disse che'l bisognava andar lì per far come fanno li altri" (ibid., b. 24, doss. "Boroni Francesco et al.," testimony of 1 October 1568; cited also in Ginzburg *Il nicodemismo*, 179 n.2).—"Quando io stava alla messa vi stava a tutta intera per non dar scandalo alla zente" (ASV, *Sant'Uffizio*, b. 29, doss. "Odofredo Michele," testimony of 5 June 1576).—"Ogni anno fingi di confessarsi et communicarsi et mai è venutto a sacratissimi sacramenti nella parochia et maxime alla santa Pasqua" (ibid., b. 45, doss. "Grison Giovanni," denunciation).

pragmatism: "In this city," he said, "you have to live as others do."[16] After all, he had a family to support, and certain compromises were necessary. But inwardly as well as within the contours of a clandestine network of friends and acquaintances who shared his beliefs, this Venetian notary led a different life. He often carried an evangelical text hidden under his sleeve, and he would talk quietly with those who shared his views about the need for reform. On at least one occasion his duplicity was no less than artful. He was summoned to the home of Monsignor Rocco Cataneo, who for fourteen years had served as auditor (an assistant) to the papal nuncios to Venice in matters pertaining to the Inquisition. From all outward signs, the visit was routine; Cataneo had merely summoned Girolamo to draw up a will, though the notary was likely sweating under his robes. Cataneo's instructions were simple and direct: his debts were to be paid and gifts were to be made to his parish church, to his confessor, to the Jesuits, to various servants and acquaintances, and "because of the fragility of my flesh" to an illegitimate daughter. At once a religious and civil act, this testament was an expression of Catholic piety.[17] Yet as Girolamo Parto wrote out the praise for the saints and the Virgin in the formulaic opening passages of the will, he was dissimulating; Parto was profoundly committed to evangelical teachings and in his heart rejected the saints whose praise he was compelled, on this occasion as on many others, to record. It was a compromise he could justify on the basis of Saint Paul's statement, "You are the temple of God, and the spirit of the Lord dwells in you." "God lives among us," Parto once said, "and not in rock, wood, or metal." Thus he downplayed the importance of external and material arrangements. His emphasis was decidedly on the internal world: "The spirit that has strength in us, which is the Holy Spirit, does great things in our hearts."[18] With hindsight we know that Parto's dissimulation was justified. In the mid–1570s when he momentarily let down his guard, the Inquisition had him arrested, tried, and executed.[19]

16. "In questa Terra bisogna viver al modo d'altri" (ibid., b. 37, doss. "Parto Girolamo," denunciation of 27 March 1572); on this figure, see also Seidel Menchi, *Erasmo in Italia*, 132–133.

17. ASV, *Testamenti*, b. 783, no. 1020, 12 March 1567.

18. "Noi semo l'imagine et le vive gesie de Dio et san Paulo dice 'sto medesimo: Templus Dei estis vos, et spiritus Domini habitat in vobis. . . . Iddio habita con noi, non con li sassi, né con li legni né con i metalli. El spirito che ha vigor in noi, che è il Spirito Santo, fa gran cosa nei nostri cuori" (ASV, *Sant'Uffizio*, b. 37, doss. "Parto Girolamo," testimony of 11 March 1574).

19. His execution is recorded in ibid., report of 22 March 1575.

The dissimulations of the master printer Pierre de Huchin were similar. Pierre had come to Venice from France in the mid–1540s to work in the city's burgeoning printing trade when he was sixteen years old. Hard-working and with a good head for business, he quickly found a place as a first-rate typefounder while still an apprentice in the shop of Gabriel Giolito, one of the city's largest publishing firms. Publishers and printers sought his services. Later he worked for the Bevilaqua and then for Lucantonio Giunti, also printers. Eventually he set up his own shop, where he came to employ as many as ten journeymen. He married and raised a large family, and, from all outward appearances, was part of Venetian society. He made a habit of going to mass and being seen. Yet Pierre was secretly a Calvinist. In his private library he kept a copy not only of Rabelais's *Gargantua and Pantagruel* but also of Marot and Beza's *Psalms of David;* he ate meat on Fridays and during Lent; he followed with great interest the progress of the Huguenot party in France; and finally, when repression intensified in Venice in the late 1560s, he tried to leave the city.[20] In 1567 the Lyonnais publisher Barthélemy de Gabiano, a Protestant, promised Pierre prosperity in Lyon if he would come work there.[21] But Pierre's timing could not have been worse. He took his entire family—a wife, eight children, and several servants—with him westward across northern Italy and then across the Alps to France. But just as he arrived—in September 1567—he found Lyon in turmoil. Everything was "upside down," Pierre recalled before the Venetian Inquisition eight years later; "everyone had taken up arms on account of religion. . . . and not a single shop was open. The Catholics had chased all the Huguenots out of the city . . . so I decided not to stay but to return to Venice."[22]

20. Most of these observations on Pierre de Huchin are based on ASV, *Sant'Uffizio,* b. 39, doss. "D'Ochino Pietro." I know of no studies of this printer, but he appears in Pastorello (*Tipografi, editori, librai a Venezia nel secolo XVI,* 28) as Pietro Francese Dehuchino. Pastorello counts 18 editions from his press from 1570 to 1579. Gedeon Borsa, ed., *Clavis typographorum librariorumque Italiae, 1465–1600* (Baden-Baden: V. Koerner, 1980), 126, notes that Huchin worked as a printer until 1581, when the shop passed to his heirs.

21. On Barthélemy de Gabiano, see Henri Louis Baudrier, *Bibliographie lyonnaise: recherches sur les imprimeurs, libraires, relieurs et fondeurs de lettres de Lyon au XVIe siècle* (Lyons: L. Brun; Paris: A. Picard, 1895–1921), 7:141–147. Gabiano was undoubtedly a Protestant.

22. "Io solo intrai in Lione et lassai la fameglia sei lege fuora de Lion in loco che si dimanda la Gussiera. . . . La città di Lione era tutta sotto sora. . . . In Lione erano tutti in arme l'uno contra l'altro, per conto della fede et della religione. . . . [Li Cattolici] superò" (ASV, *Sant'Uffizio,* b. 39, doss. "D'Ochino Pietro," testimony of 18 August 1575).

Despite the Inquisition, Venice was seemingly more tolerant. In his shop Pierre displayed the prints of five cities: Rome, Genoa, Geneva, Paris, and Venice—a private gallery that, with depictions of the capitals of both Roman and Reformed Christianity, gave expression to an ecumenical vision of Europe even as the confessionalism of the times rendered Pierre's Erasmian ideal obsolete.[23]

Like Girolamo and like Pierre, Vincenzo Valgrisi (born Vincent Vaugris), a member of a distinguished Lyonnais publishing family who had migrated to Venice in the late 1530s, also went out of his way to appear orthodox. After building a prominent publishing house in Venice and establishing a niche for himself in the newly formed printers' guild, he did some work for the Venetian Holy Office. It was his press that published della Casa's *Index of Prohibited Books* in 1549. In 1567 he went so far as to apply for Venetian citizenship. Yet Vincenzo's sympathies, like Pierre's, were decidedly Calvinist. He used his position in the book world to keep the book trade as free from outside interference as possible and, again like Pierre, seemed to know no boundaries: he had shops in a number of Italian towns as well as in Lyon and Frankfurt. But unlike Pierre, Vincenzo actively sought to spread the new teachings in Venice. In 1570 when word got out that he was trafficking in illicit books, the Inquisition searched his storehouse and found more than enough incriminating evidence—over eleven hundred prohibited books, including some four hundred copies of the Protestant version of the *Simolachri, historie, et figure de la morte*, cleverly disguised as editions of Cicero's *Letters*. Yet Vincenzo got off lightly. His neighbors and priest knew him as a good Catholic. He was fined fifty ducats—for a man of his wealth a mere slap on the wrist but fitting, the Venetians believed, for a foreign merchant with a good reputation.[24]

For individuals such as Girolamo Parto—with his stress on interior Pauline spirituality—and for Pierre de Huchin—with his private gallery—Nicodemism was a studied attitude that required a continuous and cautious negotiation with the demands of everyday life. Because of their relative prominence in the Venetian social order, moreover, they understood that they ran considerable risks should their views become

23. "In quella camerina sono diversi ritratti di cittadi, vi è il ritratto di Roma, di Genoa, di Venetia, di Anversa, e di Ginevra" (ibid., denunciation, not dated).

24. On Vincenzo Valgrisi see Grendler, *The Roman Inquisition and the Venetian Press*, passim; and Natalie Zemon Davis, "Holbein's *Pictures of Death* and the Reformation at Lyons," in *Studies in the Renaissance* 3 (1956): 97–130. On Vincenzo's publishing dynasty see Baudrier, *Bibliographie lyonnaise*, 10:457–464.

well known. But not all Venetian heretics felt so exposed. Further down the social ladder, in the world of highly mobile workers and tramping artisans, the heretics often found sizable pockets of tolerance within Venetian society in which no disguise for their beliefs—at least before their fellow heretics—was needed, and in which the adoption of Catholic practices was infrequent.

The life of the weaver Paolo Gaiano (or Paolo da Campogalliano as he was also called) illustrates this pattern. Like Girolamo Parto, he too would remain active in the evangelical community in Venice despite an early brush with the Inquisition. Soon after Easter 1549 a number of artisans reported to the Holy Office that Paolo regularly harangued his co-workers. He denied papal authority, decried the corruption of the Church, and stressed the sufficiency of Christ's sacrifice for salvation.[25] Given these accusations before the Holy Office, Paolo wisely fled Venice to return to Modena, but his seemingly irrepressible proclivity to talk openly about his beliefs soon earned him another accusation, probably in 1550; and he was finally brought to trial in 1555 by that city's bishop, Egidio Foscarari.[26] During his interrogation Paolo readily admitted that he believed in predestination, that he did not believe in purgatory, that he had indeed said that the pope was the Antichrist, and that he subscribed to the doctrine of the priesthood of all believers: "All faithful Christians are priests." When pressed to identify his teachers, he recalled an experience in Venice, telling the bishop that confessors there "had told him that there is no purgatory and similarly all the other things he had heard in Venice."[27] And he abjured but—again, like many who were brought to trial in these years—in no way broke with the heretical community.

To a large degree, he appears to have benefited from the cover that the textile trades provided. These crafts, after all, were virtually defined by their mobility. The evidence for itinerancy among the weavers of northern Italy—artisans who moved frequently from one city to

25. ASV, *Sant'Uffizio*, b. 7, doss. "Pre Alvise de Michiel confessore nel convento delle monache de S. Lucia," testimonies of 6 May and 10 May 1549, where Paolo is called Pier Paolo *veluder*.

26. ASV, *Sant'Uffizio*, b. 20, doss. "Paolo Gaiano," copy of the Modenese denunciation of 1550. On Paolo's encounter with the Modenese Inquisition, see Peyronel Rambaldi, *Speranze e crisi nel Cinquecento modenese*, 261.

27. "Tutti i fedeli cristiani, cioè la chiesa di Gesù Cristo, sono sacerdoti" (doss. "Paolo Gaiano," copy of the Modenese *costituto* of 22 September 1555). "Che li confessori li hanno detto che non è il purgatorio et così tutte le altre cose l'ha udito a dir a Venetia" (ibid.).

another, either in response to the demand for workers or to escape debt, or as a result of religious persecution—is considerable.[28] In addition, this mobile world was a relatively tolerant one as well. Paolo had no trouble continuing to live as a heretic, at least not until the late 1560s. At some earlier point, probably in 1559, he left Modena for Venice where he once again found work in the burgeoning textile trade, matriculating in the weavers' guild, among whose members he eventually developed the reputation as a heretic. Maestro Jacomo di Vielmo, himself a silk weaver, was called before the Sant'Uffizio in June of 1570 for questioning about Paolo, who had begun a second and what was to prove fatal trial for heresy in the previous year. When asked if he knew Paolo as a good Christian or as a heretic, Jacomo was not at all guarded. "I have heard many members of our guild say that he is a sinful heretic, and he used to be called 'Polo luteran.'" Zuane, Jacomo's son, confirmed his father's testimony. "He is called by the men of our guild and by all who know him 'Polo luteran.'"[29] Both these witnesses depicted Paolo as something of a proselytizer who frequently engaged his fellow workers in religious discussion. On the bridge at Cannaregio, these witnesses reported, Paolo had buttonholed a priest from San Geremia and a weaver's apprentice, arguing that Christ was not in the host of the holy sacrament, that it simply was not possible. And, while working at the loom in the shop of maestro Gasparo, Paolo argued the same position, holding up two spindles to drive the point home. "Suppose we have two hosts and that over one the priestly words are spoken, what difference is there between one and the other? And since they are of the same matter and form, why should [Christ] be more in one than another?"[30]

Taken by itself, such testimony suggests that Paolo—this proselytizing weaver who read broadly in such works as the *Beneficio di Cristo* and the *Sommario della Santa Scrittura*, who could also recite Petrarch,

28. Maureen Fennell Mazzaoui, *The Italian Cotton Industry in the Later Middle Ages, 1100–1600* (Cambridge: Cambridge University Press, 1981) stresses the mobility of workers in this particular textile industry—see 67.

29. "Ho sempre sentito a dir da molte persone dell'arte nostra che'l pecca da lutheran, et veniva chiamato Polo luteran" (Jacomo); "Et costui dalli huomini dalla nostra arte da tutti quelli che lo conoscano è chiamato per Polo lutherano" (Zuane) (ASV, *Sant'Uffizio*, b. 20, doss. "Paolo Gaiano," both testimonies of 22 June 1570).

30. "Presuponi che habbiamo due hostie in mano, et che sopra una siano dette le parole dal prete, che differentia è una dall'altra, atteso che le sono di una medisma materia et forma, perché dielo esser più in una che in un'altra . . . facendo questa comparatione con due spuole de quelle ch'l lavorava" (ibid.).

and who talked openly about his beliefs both in the streets and at the loom—stood out as something of an eccentric within his guild and was largely isolated from others who shared his beliefs. But the damaging and hostile testimonies of the weavers Jacomo and Zuane may be misleading. The garret workers of Cannaregio were often receptive to such debate. When the priest from San Geremia whom Jacomo had alleged was present at one of Paolo's harangues was called before the Inquisition, he denied ever having heard Paolo utter a single heresy. When the inquisitor prodded him about Paolo's reputation, he refused an unequivocal answer, noting only that he had heard from many weavers that there was considerable religious discussion in the shops, especially "in the garrets where they talk of matters against the faith."[31] The weaver Zuane, moreover, was the man who originally denounced Paolo, and the denunciation was likely motivated by extrareligious factors: by money or tensions within the guild. The mere fact that Paolo, talkative by nature, had been in Venice for so long before the Inquisition acted on a denunciation against him suggests a considerable tolerance, even sympathy for his ideas. It was a tolerance that allowed for the construction of something of an evangelical community in the city.

Indeed in Venice the evangelicals were by no means isolated one from another. To a large degree, the ability of individuals such as Girolamo Parto, Pierre de Huchin, and Paolo Gaiano to hold on to their private beliefs—something that Calvin and the other anti-Nicodemites had thought impossible—stemmed from their relationship to an invisible community of evangelicals in the city. Despite the belief of Trissino and others, quitting Italy for the more organized Protestant communities of the Grisons or of Switzerland, that the institutions and doctrines of the Italian evangelicals were fragmented, and despite the development of anabaptism and the intensification of millennial currents in Venice, the clandestine and Nicodemite world of the Venetian evangelicals was not entirely unorganized. Its members benefited both from ties to Protestants abroad and from cautious but intimate associations with one another in the city of Venice itself.

The basic level of organization was familial, for it was in the family that evangelicals were able to profess their religious beliefs with the greatest confidence.[32] Moreover, heresy had never been a purely indi-

31. "Che i rasano nelle soffite dove lavorano delle cose contra la fede" (ibid., testimony of 27 June 1570).
32. On the relation of heresy to family life, see Seidel Menchi, *Erasmo in Italia*, 178–180.

vidual matter. Once one member of a family had been "converted," others were likely to follow, or, as one local priest would explain to the Holy Office, complaining of an evangelical family into which his sister had recently married, "When one rotten apple is next to a good one, it will spoil the good one as well."[33] Yet evangelism was never reduced to a purely familial level. For one thing, the evangelical families tended to know one another, or at least they knew of one another. They had common friends and formed a kind of invisible network, within which they could freely express their views. They constituted, in other words, a cousinage of evangelicals, known only to one another, in the midst of a Catholic world.

At times the households were quite prominent. Girolamo Parto's half brother Zuanbattista Michiel shared his views, and it is likely that the two came together for devotions.[34] But perhaps the most visible of the evangelical households was that of the Gemma, who owned and managed a pharmacy, Due Colombini, in the parish of San Marcuola. Silvestro and Helena Gemma had raised their four children, two sons and two daughters, as evangelicals. And they had made their home a center for devotions. They regularly came together to read the Gospels; during the war of Cyprus, when the Venetian state sought both to celebrate and to protect itself with elaborate processions, they would lock the doors of their shop and sing Protestant litanies together. They turned their shop into a haven for a kind of counterritual. When their son Marcantonio brought home a Catholic wife, they mocked her, pressuring her to convert to their beliefs.[35]

There were many such households. Francesco and Caterina, a couple who maintained a tailor's shop in the parish of San Geremia, were both evangelicals. They went to mass together, but only to hear the Gospels, and talked continuously of Saint Paul.[36] The Semprini household, though much poorer than either that of the Gemma or of Francesco and Caterina, was much the same. Two grown sons lived under the same roof as their parents. All were carders in the textile

33. "Quando un pomo marzo è apresso el bon fa marzir anco el bon" (ASV, *Sant'Uffizio*, b. 37, doss. "Gemma, Giovanni Battista," testimony of 17 September 1575).

34. ASV, *Sant'Uffizio*, b. 37, doss. "Parto Girolamo," testimony of 16 March 1574.

35. Ibid., doss. "Gemma, Giovanni Battista." On this family, see also ibid., b. 20, doss. "Zuanbattista Gemma."

36. Ibid., b. 37, doss. "Gemma, Giovanni Battista," testimonies of 24 and 27 April 1574 esp.

industry. Again, they lived out their religious life within the home. Father Fidel Vico, an active proponent of the new religious ideas, would come there and read to them from Scripture while they listened attentively. They took communion in their home, sharing pieces of leavened bread.[37] Fidel visited several households, as did other evangelical priests like him. And while one of the more prominent of these heretical priests, the humanist Publio Francesco Spinola, a frequent visitor in the home of the tailors Francesco and Caterina, was of noble Genoese background, most—among them Father Paresin of San Geremia—tended to be of artisan backgrounds. Their educations gave them entry into a variety of homes, those of nobles as well as those of craftsmen, and they took their "heresies" wherever they could. They often served as tutors, and they developed a certain following. Both nobles and artisans trusted them. Most significantly, they kept the evangelical households of Venice from isolation in individual units. It must have encouraged such families as the Gemma or the Semprini, for example, to learn that there were others like them who shared their beliefs.[38] Indeed, it may have been because of such contacts that the Semprini, when one of their sons fell seriously ill, were able to turn to the Gemma for medication that they could not otherwise afford.[39] These priests linked the various groups of evangelicals, tying together a community that could not come together openly in the increasingly intolerant atmosphere of Counter-Reformation Venice.

But the evangelicals were not the only ones who managed to maintain their community in Venice after the refurbishing of the Inquisition in 1547. The Anabaptists did as well, though for the Anabaptists— both because of the significantly greater repression turned against them as well as their own disenchantment with the Venetian political or-

37. Ibid., b. 23, doss. "Contra Sylvestrum, Angelam, Stephanum, et Cyprianum" and b. 32, doss. "Contra Sylvestrum." On this family and Father Fidel Vico, see Karl Benrath, "Ein Inquisitionsprozess aus dem Jahre 1568," *Historisches Taschenbuch*, 6th s., 1 (1881): 157–173; and Comba, *I nostri Protestanti*, 2:603–625.

38. The role of former priests and friars, many of whom were tutors, in the development of the heresies in sixteenth-century Italy is still poorly understood, but see Pio Paschini, "Un umanista disgraziato nel Cinquecento: Publio Francesco Spinola," *Nuovo archivio veneto* n.s., 37 (1919): 65–186; and Achille Olivieri, "Il *Catechismo* e la *Fidei et doctrinae . . . ratio* di Bartolomeo Fonzio, eretico veneziano del Cinquecento," *Studi veneziani* 9 (1967): 339–452.

39. ASV, *Sant'Uffizio*, b. 23, doss. "Contra Sylvestrum, Angelam, Stephanum et Cyprianum," testimony of 24 November 1567.

der—the pressure to emigrate was much greater. Above all, they hoped to find a place to practice their beliefs openly, "to find a people who through the truth of the Gospels have been liberated from their slavery to sin and who walk in a new life." Only in the late 1550s did several Italian Anabaptists—most notably Giulio Gherlandi from Treviso and Francesco della Sega from Rovigo—discover such a place: the Hutterite communities of Moravia. There, in the small *Bruderhöfe* or communes that these Anabaptists established in eastern Europe after fleeing intensified repression in Switzerland, Germany, and the Tyrol in the 1530s, Francesco and Giulio found, as the latter explained to the Holy Office, what they were looking for: "a people that is the holy Church, immaculate, and separated from sin . . . as it was at the time of the Apostles Peter and Paul in Jerusalem."[40] Undoubtedly it was a world radically different from anything they had known in the Venetian republic. For in Moravia, as another Venetian heretic (an evangelical) would explain to the Holy Office only a few years later, "the practice is . . . that all live in a house that is something like a monastery, and they eat and drink and dress in common—the rich and the poor."[41] The Hutterites, in other words, were struggling to realize for an entire society what the Venetian Anabaptists had at first believed possible for only small conventicles of the rebaptized.

Nonetheless, Italian anabaptism was not entirely uprooted, as refugees like Gherlandi and della Sega recognized. In the late 1550s and early 1560s they—and doubtless others who fled to Moravia—began a concerted effort to convince the Italian Anabaptists left behind to join them. In part, their efforts stemmed from the Hutterites' general concern with missions. Those who gathered in the *Bruderhöfe* of eastern Europe believed it their duty, as the Hutterite *Chronicle* read, "to visit the ignorant nations, to preach to them the counsel and will of God . . . so that the number of saints will be filled."[42] But the Hutterite missions to Italy also grew out of a genuine concern over the antitrinitarian views of the Anabaptists there. In a letter that Giulio Gherlandi

40. Cited in Stella, *Dall'anabattismo al socinianesimo*, 109. On this episode, see also Henry A. DeWind, "Italian Hutterite Martyrs," *The Mennonite Quarterly Review* 28 (1954): 165.

41. "Il costume loro è che in ogni terra che si ritrovano, habitano tutti in una casa, come in uno monasterio, et mangiano et bevano e calzano tutti in comune, così li poveri come li ricchi" (ASV, *Sant'Uffizio*, b. 22, doss. "Varotta Marcantonio," memorial of 21 January 1567; cited in Caccamo, *Eretici italiani in Moravia, Polonia, Transilvania*, 212).

42. Clasen, *Anabaptism: A Social History*, 214.

carried with him to his Italian brethren on his first mission back to the Veneto in 1559, the Moravian leaders asked not only that they welcome Giulio but also that they recognize their errors. "It has also seemed a necessary matter to make some mention of certain things that you are overlooking . . . concerning the incarnation of Christ," they wrote, adding that the view of Christ as born of the seed of Joseph was Satanic; on the basis of Scripture (and in particular the first chapter of the Gospel of John) they argued that Christ was the son of God.[43] To some degree, the missions were successful. In the late 1550s Anabaptists from Padua, Vicenza, Treviso, and doubtless other localities in the Veneto responded to the Hutterites' call and decided to leave Italy for Moravia.[44] In general, they traveled in small groups, but occasionally the migration could swell: at least some thirty inhabitants of Cinto, a small village on the outskirts of Portogruaro, made their way to Moravia; in 1562 some twenty Italian Anabaptists who had met together at Capodistria for the trip to the Hutterite communities were arrested.[45] The effort was certainly well organized. On his second mission to Italy in 1561, for example, Gherlandi carried with him a list of likely sympathizers. It included over a hundred names of individuals who lived throughout the republic from Trieste to Verona. Of these, six were inhabitants of Venice: Clemente, a glover; Antonio, a blind maker; Camillo, an innkeeper at San Lio; Bastian and Pancratio Osbat, both cobblers, and their sister Christina; and finally, a certain Zuan Battista Contarini.[46] Francesco della Sega carried a similar list the following year that included among its two dozen names another half-dozen Venetians: the hatter della Vecchia, a certain Bernardin da Cittadella, a certain Zuanbattista (possibly Zuan Battista Contarini); the schoolmaster Silvio; a certain Piero Belasin; and—the only name that appears on both lists with certainty—the glover Clemente.[47]

But the most revealing evidence of the survival of anabaptism in Venice in the 1560s came from a trial against an Anabaptist conventicle

43. Stella, *Anabattismo e antitrinitarismo*, 246–247.

44. On this migration, in addition to Stella, *Anabattismo e antitrinitarismo*, see De-Wind, "Italian Hutterite Martyrs," 163–185; and Caccamo, *Eretici italiani in Moravia, Polonia, Transilvania*.

45. Stella, *Anabattismo e antitrinitarismo*, 154; see also Giovanna Paolin, "I contadini anabattisti di Cinto," *Il Noncello* 50 (1980): 91–124.

46. ASV, *Sant'Uffizio*, b. 18, doss. "Gherlandi Giulio," memorial of Gherlandi. Gherlandi's list is published in Stella, *Anabattismo e antitrinitarismo*, 249–251.

47. Stella, *Dall'anabattismo al socinianesimo*, 111 n.88.

in Padua. One of the suspects, a certain Pietro, happened to have a brother in Venice, and it was a world with which he claimed much familiarity. "But as far as Venice is concerned, there is much more to tell," Pietro told the Paduan Inquisition in the early part of 1567, "for there are those who meet every Sunday outside San Francesco della Vigna near the *scorazze*, and I know quite a few of them by sight, but I do not know their names, and they are artisans who live in several places in Venice, and this I know, for when I used to stay in Venice, many came to call on my brother."[48] Because of the importance of his testimony, Pietro was called to testify before the Paduan *podestà* the following morning. He reiterated his early statements. "There are many many in this sect in Venice, for the most part they are artisans of various ages, who meet in various places in addition to the spot near San Francesco della Vigna. . . . they are led to other places by the cobbler Piero da Modena at Santi Apostoli." This was a slip of the tongue. Piero, it turned out, was in fact the cobbler Giacomo da Sacile. But he named several others. In addition to his brother Odorico, there was a certain Valerio Perosin, a journeyman dyer, and then Antonio Colomban, the accountant at the Hospital of Santi Pietro e Paolo. At the end of his testimony he again emphasized that there were many and that they were for the most part artisans.[49]

While Pietro exaggerated neither the extent of heresy in the city of Venice nor its diffusion among artisans, it is unlikely that the Anabaptist community was as large as he suggested. Most of those whom he knew as "heretics" were evangelicals, and they were, moreover, very conscious of the doctrinal distinctions that separated them from the Anabaptists. Giacomo da Sacile was especially emphatic that his was an evangelical sect.[50] Yet in the Venice of the late 1560s, as nearly two decades earlier, anabaptism continued to find a place on the margins of

48. "Io de heretici di questa Terra [ = Padua] non so altro, ma per conto di Venetia la saria cosa longa a dire, che ghe ne sono che si riducono le feste a San Francesco dalla Vigna fuora, là dove sono quelle scovazze et ghe ne conosco purassai per vista, ma non ghe so il suo nome, et sono artesani da Venetia di più luoghi, et questo so, che quando io stava a Venetia molti venivano a chiamare quello mio fratello" (ASV, *Sant'Uffizio*, b. 22, doss. "Contra Odoricum Grisonum et complices," testimony of 6 February 1567).

49. "Ve sono molti et molti di questa congregatione in Venetia, et massime artesani di diversa generatione, quali in diversi lochi si reducono insieme, et oltre del loco di San Francesco . . . si conducono anche in altri lochi da uno maestro Piero da Modena calegaro a Santo Apostolo" (ibid., testimony of 7 February 1567).

50. Ibid., testimony of 16 May 1567.

the evangelical movement at large, attracting to it men and some women from the city's proletariat. Pietro's brother Odorico, for example—a knife grinder who worked on the campo San Bartolomeo just off the Rialto bridge—was certainly an Anabaptist and, despite Francesco della Sega's and Giulio Gherlandi's efforts, an antitrinitarian as were his friends the journeymen dyers Valerio Perosin and Zuanbattista Sambeni. And there may have been many others, but as often happened, they stayed in the shadows. Certainly caution was the order of the day. After learning that he had been denounced once again, for example, the glover Clemente (who formerly made it his practice to take his sons out in a boat with him and celebrate communion secretly, on the water) fled the city. As before, this popular Venetian anabaptism maintained certain ties with the intellectual community in Padua. There, in the home of a certain Bortolomeo da Parma, a schoolmaster, Odorico had taken Valerio to be rebaptized.[51] Some ties to the earliest period of Venetian anabaptism remained: one of those present at Valerio's baptism was Zuanmaria the silk weaver whom the Holy Office had first tried for heresy immediately after receiving Manelfi's denunciation in 1551!

Zuanbattista Sambeni, a man in his late thirties, had long been involved with heretical ideas and had been tried earlier, in 1562, in Brescia where he had abjured a number of evangelical beliefs. He was a difficult man to pin down. "I love to sing and to play the lyre," he told the Venetian inquisitor, "and I go about [doing so] here and there, in many cities." But this street musician supported himself in a trade where the demand for labor fluctuated with the seasons. Accordingly, his skill as a dyer was something he practiced in many shops in Venice alone, including one operated by Alessandro da Bologna, Valerio's uncle. He was also a street theologian. When the inquisitor asked him where he had learned his "errors," Zuanbattista answered he had learned them by "interpreting the Scriptures according to my own imagination (*seconda la mia fantasia*)."[52] Not only was his theology profoundly scriptural, he also believed that he had authority from the

51. Ibid., testimony of 13 Feb 1567; b. 159, register "Proccesi [*sic*] 1569, 1570, 1571," testimony of 7 October 1570; b. 22, doss. "Marosella Odorico et al.," testimony of 13 March 1567.

52. "Io mi son delettato di cantar in bianco et sonar di lira, et vado in quà et in là, in molte città. . . . Io ho imparato errori interpretando la Scrittura seconda la mia fantasia" (ibid., b. 22, doss. "Marosella Odorico et al.," testimony of 13 September 1568).

Holy Spirit for his interpretation. It was an authority that enabled him to withstand what must have been enormous pressure from the Holy Office to recant in a seemingly endless intellectual duel between a dyer and a doctor of laws and theology. On 25 August 1569, after more than a year of intensive interrogations, the Venetian Holy Office sentenced him to death. About a month later he was taken from his prison cell, and then by boat to the mouth of the Adriatic. There the authorities tied him to a heavy stone and dropped him into the sea.[53]

53. Ibid., report of 26 September 1569.

## CHAPTER SIX

# The Place of Heresy
# in a Hierarchical Society

*For though the artificial conception of man's activities which prompts us to carve up the creature of flesh and blood into the phantoms* homo oeconomicus, philosophicus, juridicus *is doubtless necessary, it is tolerable only if we refuse to be deceived by it. . . . A society, like a mind, is woven of perpetual interaction.*

Marc Bloch, *Feudal Society*

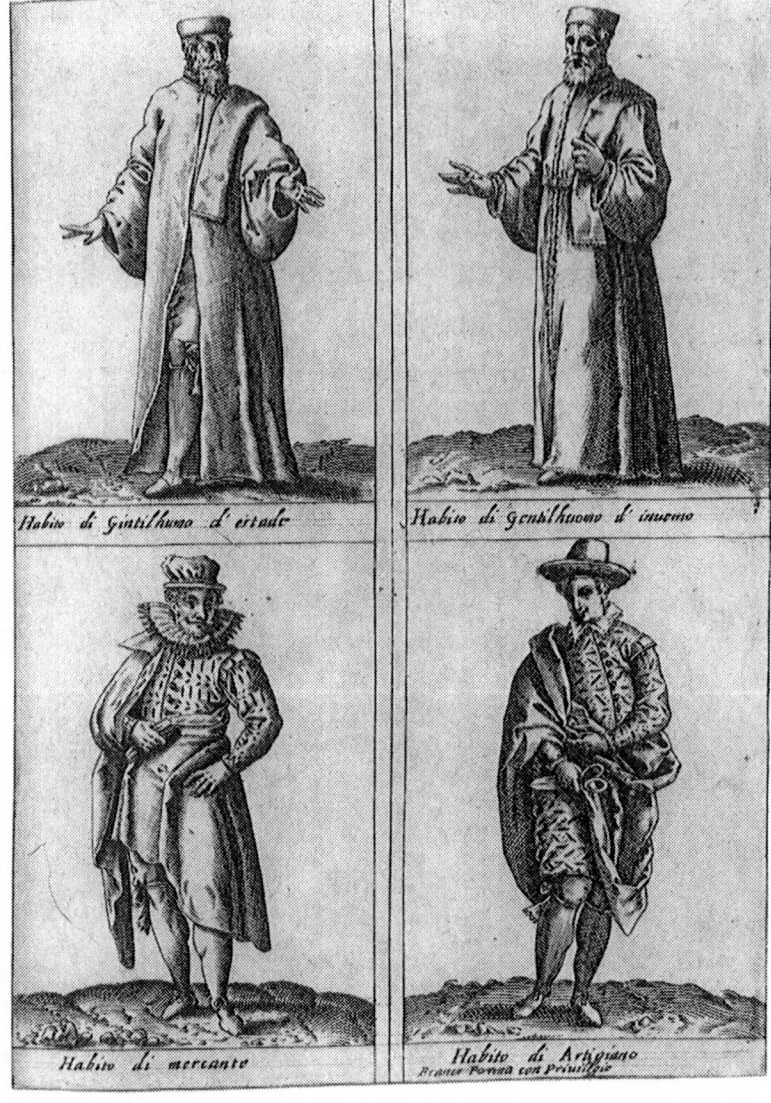

Habito di Gintilhuomo d'estade

Habito di Gentilhuomo d'inuerno

Habito di mercante

Habito di Artigiano
Franco Porna con Priuilegio

Evangelical, Anabaptist, and millenarian ideas filtered into Venice in a variety of ways. Itinerant priests and friars who had developed a sympathy for the new religious movements of the sixteenth century spoke, frequently in veiled language, on the importance of grace in the matter of salvation. Publishers arranged for the printing of books that argued in favor of the new notions, while the book vendors whose shops and stalls crowded the central parishes of the city found imaginative ways to sell them, often as under-the-counter titles. Merchants and artisans proselytized those with whom they worked or did business. Anabaptist missionaries encouraged men and women who had already embraced evangelical ideas to go further in their renunciation of what had become traditional Christianity. And, as we have seen, a millenarian armorer began to cultivate the spiritual friendship of men who, like him, hoped for a new dispensation. Thus the press and the pulpit as well as a myriad of personal contacts played key roles in the introduction of heretical ideas into sixteenth-century Venice.

What concerned such prelates as Ambrogio Catarino Politi, however, was not so much the existence of these ideas as the fact that the audience they reached was attentive. The heresies of the day were beginning to take root. "This wretched land," he wrote of Italy in the mid–1540s, "is much too disposed, too receptive to these weeds [heretical teachings]."[1] Indeed, in these same years, as we have seen, church authorities often spoke of heresy as a plague. Heresy was a contagion, and many were infected. But what accounted (to continue the metaphor) for this vulnerability? Certainly a variety of forces acted on the social and cultural medium. Different groups, depending on the particular heresy, were likely to take up the new ideas about the nature of the religious life that evangelical preachers, Anabaptist proselytizers,

1. "È questo misero mondo, terra troppo disposta a ricevere queste zizanie," Ambrogio Catarino Politi, "Compendio d'errori, et inganni Luterani," 349. The work was published in Rome in 1544.

---

*Opposite*. Like other early modern Europeans, Venetians were extremely conscious of social status, and their clothing manifested the hierarchical arrangements of the society. This illustration from Giacomo Franco, *Habiti d'huomeni et donne venetiane* (Venice, 1610) shows the summer and winter attire of the Venetian nobleman and the attire for merchants and artisans. (Courtesy of the Library, Harry Ransom Center, University of Texas at Austin)

and millenarian dreamers shared with them, and a variety of cultural experiences enflamed contemporary religious imaginations as well. This should not surprise us. Religion is never unconnected to both social and cultural life; in a period of rapid change, tensions in the religious interpretation of the world are inevitable. Moreover, the societal tensions in sixteenth-century Venice were considerable, for the city was far less harmoniously structured than its self-image would have it. Indeed, the disjunction between that self-image and the harsh social realities that many Venetians confronted threatened to exacerbate the tensions in the city.

## Evangelicals and Society

Evangelical ideals never reflected the exclusive interests of the members of one particular social group, though evangelical beliefs probably made their first real inroads in Italy within the aristocracy. Certainly many of the followers of Juan de Valdés in Naples and many of the associates of Gasparo Contarini in Venice were nobles.[2] Nonetheless, by the 1540s evangelism had acquired a popular following as well. And its adherents seemed to come from all social groups. They were women and men, natives and foreigners, young and old. Yet this does not mean that heresy had no relation to social life. On the contrary, the Venetian evangelicals were primarily—and markedly— individuals involved in the elite trades, in commerce, and in the professions of the city. They were, as we see in table 1, lawyers, physicians, notaries, merchants, mercers, publishers, printers, jewelers, apothecaries, and tailors. In absolute terms the largest number of those accused of heresy were skilled workers or those in the service guilds. At first we might assume that heresy was most widely diffused among the least prestigious crafts of the city. But such an interpretation overlooks the relative rate of accusation of heresy. Once we recognize that the total of those who belonged to the guilds for skilled trades and services outnumbered those in the professions and in commerce by a factor of ten to one and that they outnumbered those in the elite crafts by six to one, the pattern is clear: in sixteenth-century Venice, propo-

2. The classic statement of this point of view is Jung, "On the Nature of Evangelism in Sixteenth-Century Italy."

Table 1. *Persons Accused of Evangelical Beliefs and Practices*

| Occupation | Number Accused |
|---|---|
| Clergy | |
| Secular priests (17) and monks and friars (20) | 37 |
| Professions | |
| Clerks and notaries (25), lawyers (29), | |
| physicians (18), tutors and humanists (33), | |
| others (4) | 109 |
| Commerce | |
| Merchants in general (24), mercers (9), | |
| brokers (11), booksellers (10), others (28) | 82 |
| Elite Crafts and Trades | |
| Instrument makers (10), jewelers (29), | |
| tailors (22), apothecaries (23), printers (11), | |
| others (43) | 138 |
| Skilled Trades and Services | |
| Cobblers (18), silk weavers (33), workers | |
| in other textile and leather trades (26), | |
| builders (7), victuallers (15), others (56) | 155 |
| Unknown | 155 |
| *Total* | 676 |

SOURCE: ASV, *Sant'Uffizio*, b. 6–59 and 151–164; APV, *Criminalia Sanctae Inquisitionis*, b. 1–2. Of the 676 individuals suspected of evangelical beliefs or practices, I have been able to identify the occupation in only 521 cases. For a discussion of the derivation of these figures, please see the appendix, where I give the distribution of heresy in relation to the size of each occupational category.

nents of evangelical ideas found their most receptive audience among men and women who had relatively privileged positions within the social hierarchy of the city. Indeed, even among the skilled workers those artisans most likely to face an accusation of heresy were silk weavers, the traditional "aristocrats" of textile labor.

In the context of recent research into the sociology of support for the new ideas of the Reformation, this aspect of the Venetian experience does not surprise us. Members of the professions and the elite crafts were overrepresented in the Protestant movements under way in France and Germany as well.[3] Such individuals were well educated or

3. On the social distribution of similar religious movements in other European cities, see Davis, "Strikes and Salvation at Lyon," in *Society and Culture*, 1–16; Philip Benedict, *Rouen during the Wars of Religion* (Cambridge: Cambridge University Press, 1981), 71–94; Brady, *Ruling Class, Regime and Reformation at Strasbourg*, 295; and A.G. Dickens, *The German Nation and Martin Luther* (New York: Harper and Row, 1974), 140, 159. In the French cities studied by Davis and Benedict, the distribution of heresy (Calvinism) was

highly skilled; they were generally literate; and they were often especially proud or confident of their abilities. The teachings of both Luther and Calvin, dignifying the ordinary life and the work of the faithful and making Scripture central to the Christian life, appealed to them
and offered them a religious language that corresponded to their sense
of independence in civic and economic life generally. Apart from such
general attributes, these social groups were also predisposed to heresy
by their position in the social hierarchy of the city—a hierarchy that
was shifting, and whose transitions made the men and women who
belonged to relatively privileged social circles in a status-conscious age
acutely attentive to social standing.

Social life in Venice had always been hierarchically defined.
Furthermore, ever since the Great Council (the assembly of Venetians
entitled to vote on public matters) closed at the end of the thirteenth
century, Venetian social status had been allied to political power. In
1297, through an action known as the Closing (*serrata*) of the Great
Council, the members of that assembly had declared themselves and
themselves only to be Venetian nobles. Over the course of the fourteenth century, certain wealthy families of lower rank were incorporated into this charmed circle of privilege, but by the fifteenth century
the Venetian nobility (some two thousand men drawn from one hundred and sixty great families) was not only as well defined as any in
Europe but had also managed to concentrate all formal political power
in its hands.[4] Just beneath this urban aristocracy (and sometimes
wealthier) were the city's great merchant families and members of a
special class of Venetian subjects known as *cittadini* (citizens)—an elite
enjoying a variety of commercial and legal privileges that allowed its

---

comparable to what I found in Venice, though perhaps more Venetian heretics were at
the top of the guild hierarchy than their counterparts in Lyon or Rouen. In Germany
the "lower populace" and "workingmen" apparently found great appeal in Luther's ideas,
but these terms are vague. On the sociology of heresy in Germany, see Robert W. Scrib-
ner, "The Reformation as a Social Movement," in *Stadtbürgertum und Adel in der Reformation*, ed. Wolfgang J. Mommsen (Stuttgart: Klett-Cotta, 1979), 49–79.

4. On the closing of the Great Council, see Frederic Lane, "The Enlargement of the
Great Council of Venice," in J. G. Rowe and W. H. Stockdale, eds., *Florilegium Historiale:
Essays Presented to Wallace K. Ferguson* (Toronto: University of Toronto Press, 1971), 236–
274; Stanley Chojnacki, "In Search of the Venetian Patriciate: Families and Factions in
the Fourteenth Century," in John R. Hale, ed., *Renaissance Venice*, 47–90; and, for an
alternative view of the late thirteenth-century reforms, Guido Ruggiero, "Modernization
and the Mythic State in Early Renaissance Venice: The Serrata Revisited," *Viator* 10
(1979): 245–256.

members either to hold lucrative posts in the increasingly elaborate and byzantine bureaucracy of the Venetian state or to engage in long-distance trading ventures under the protection of the republic.[5] But these two groups together constituted only a small portion—less than one-sixth—of the entire Venetian population. Beneath them and next in social standing were the professionals of the city and the prosperous local merchants and artisans who worked in the elite crafts; their trades involved considerable skill, if not capital, and mastery of them entailed a certain prestige. Here too the numbers were limited. Altogether these three upper strata of Venetian society probably accounted for slightly less than a quarter of the city's population.[6] Most Venetians had much less prominent positions in this decidedly hierarchical world. Many worked in the textile and building trades, but further down the social scale were far larger numbers of men and women who struggled in poorly paying trades to make ends meet, to scrape enough together for petty investments, or to dower a daughter. Despite their relative poverty, these men and women—from stevedores to fruit vendors, and from carders to spinners—traditionally deserved a certain social respect. They clung to gainful and stable trades that set them off sharply from the very poor, the itinerant beggars and vagabonds who thronged the city during a famine, as well as from the large Venetian underclass of servants and slaves, prostitutes, common outlaws, and con men.[7]

In the sixteenth century the relations among the various strata in this hierarchy underwent a series of subtle modifications that weakened

5. On the *cittadini*, see Giuseppe Trebbi, "La cancelleria veneta nei secoli XVI e XVII," *Annali della Fondazione Luigi Einaudi* 14 (1980): 65–125; and Mary Frances Neff, "Chancellery Secretaries in Venetian Politics and Society, 1480–1533" (Ph.D. diss., University of California, Los Angeles, 1985).

6. The census of 1563 included 2,434 adult male patricians and 4,714 adult male *cittadini* in Venice from a total adult male population of 53,067 (or 13.5 percent of the total). I calculate the number of elite guildsmen on the basis of 1595 statistics as 4,406, though this number only approximates the figure for 1563. The combined number of 11,554 nobles, *cittadini*, and elite guildsmen in Venice is roughly 22 percent of the city's adult male population. On the population statistics for 1563, see Beloch, *Bevölkerungsgeschichte Italiens*, vol. 3; and Beltrami, *Storia della popolazione di Venezia*. I explain my calculation of the number of elite artisans in the appendix.

7. On these groups in Venetian society—for which unhappily we have little information—see Ruggiero, *Violence in Early Renaissance Venice*, 62–63, 95–121. Very suggestive also are Piero Camporesi's comments on this late medieval and early modern underworld in *Il libro dei vagabondi* (Turin: Einaudi, 1980), ix–clxxv; and Francesca Meneghetti Casarin, *I vagabondi, la società e lo stato nella repubblica veneta alla fine del '700* (Rome: Jouvence, 1984), with interesting pointers to sixteenth-century problems and issues.

the status of the elite artisans, professionals, and merchants of the city. Throughout the fourteenth and fifteenth centuries these highly skilled craftsmen and tradesmen together with the city's physicians and lawyers—though excluded from certain political and economic privileges—had coexisted comfortably (in a social sense) with a Venetian nobility closely involved in the political, economic, and cultural life of the city. In those centuries Venetian aristocrats, active in commerce, ran businesses from the massive front doors of their palaces that opened onto the Grand Canal. They invested in local businesses and could often be found working alongside commoners in shops and warehouses in the center of Venice, with the result that men of quite different legal status often formed friendships. Moreover, the Venetian professionals and elite craftsmen enjoyed a similarly cozy bond with the *cittadini*. This was especially apparent in the five citywide confraternities of Venice known as the *scuole grandi*. Their organizations—consisting of *cittadini* and artisans alike—were viewed as brotherhoods, as fraternities of equals, with all members participating in the ritual and charitable acts.[8] In the company of both nobles and citizens, therefore, a Venetian jeweler, for example, or a tailor, or a notary, or a physician felt quite at home.

But in the sixteenth century this close relation of professionals, merchants, and elite artisans on the one hand and patricians and *cittadini* on the other was severed. The first and most conspicuous of these changes was the growing tendency of the Venetian nobles to abandon their traditional link to commerce and to invest instead in property on the mainland and ultimately to make themselves over into a landed aristocracy. In the fifteenth century this shift was already under way, but it was greatly accelerated in the early sixteenth century by the news of the Portuguese circumnavigation of Africa. For many Venetians, the news at first engendered anxiety and incredulity, a painful unwillingness to believe that their hold on the spice trade was lost. It would be too severe a blow to the republic, the lifeblood of which was commerce, and in which the trade in spices had such a salient role. But confirmations of the first reports of the Portuguese success, which reached Venice in 1501, followed. The Venetian banker Girolamo Priuli, never optimistic, noted that "everyone knew that, in time, this would be the total ruin of the city."[9] It was, in any case, news that

---

8. Pullan, *Rich and Poor in Renaissance Venice*, pt. 1 and the conclusion.
9. "Chaduno cognosceva questa essere la total ruina dela citade veneta *cum* il tempo" (Girolamo Priuli, *I diarii* [Bologna and Città di Castello: S. Lapi, 1912–1938], 2:364).

accelerated the nobility's withdrawal of their investments from trade, encouraging them to place their assets instead in land. By the mid-sixteenth century many if not most of the great Venetian patrician families had purchased and consolidated properties on the mainland, in the Veronese, the Polesine, and the Bassa Friulana.[10] With land and villas that occupied more and more of their time, aristocrats began to develop a style of life more in keeping with the traditional ideals of the European nobility, at least as they came to construct them. It is no accident that this was the age of Castiglione and Palladio—of the ideal of the courtly life and of the architectural perfection of the villa. "The citizen gave way to the courtier."[11] By the beginning of the seventeenth century the cultural consequences of such transformations would be obvious to a foreign observer such as Dudley Carleton, English ambassador to the republic. "They here change theyr manners," Carleton wrote of the Venetian aristocracy. "Theyr former course of life was marchandising: which is now quite left and they looke to landward buieng house and lands, furnishing themselfs with coch and horses, and giving themselfs the goode time with more shew and gallantrie than was wont."[12]

The growing landed investments of the nobility had deep cultural consequences, as Carleton's observations indicated. For the commoners—even for elite artisans—it meant a loss of status. In *Il gentiluomo*, first published in Venice in 1571, Girolamo Muzio (who also composed several works against such Italian reformers as Vergerio and Ochino) argued that it was by no means fitting for a gentleman to work with his hands.[13] To be sure, the vilification of manual labor had a long history, even in Venice. Gasparo Contarini, for example, spoke disparagingly of the "very base common people, as mechanicall, & handicraftes men."[14] But the tone grew harsher and more consequential as the century progressed. To work with one's hands, formerly a mark of honor, became a stain—a gradual redefinition of manual labor that culminated in 1569 when an elaborate legal procedure was instituted in Venice to limit the rights of citizenship to those wealthy inhabitants of the city

10. Gaetano Cozzi, *Il doge Nicolò Contarini: Ricerche sul patriziato veneziano agli inizi del Seicento* (Venice: Istituto per la Collaborazione Culturale, 1958), 14.

11. Croce, "A Working Hypothesis: The Crisis of Italy in the Cinquecento," 35.

12. Cited in Cozzi, *Il doge Nicolò Contarini*, 15 n.2.

13. Girolamo Muzio, *Il gentilhuomo del Mutio Iustinopolitano* (Venice: Gio. Andrea Valvossori, 1571). On Muzio's opposition to the evangelicals, see Schutte, *Pier Paolo Vergerio*, 230–237.

14. Contarini, *The Commonwealth and Government of Venice*, 141.

who had never worked with their hands. The entreaty of a certain Sebastiano Masilio, the son of an apothecary, is illustrative. "I have lived honorably and never practiced a mechanical art"; the judges who examined his petition sought to make sure that not only he but also his father had never performed manual labor.[15] Expressing views shared by his contemporaries throughout Italy, the Venetian political theorist Giovanni Maria Memmo observed in 1563:

> In all well ordered republics, the plebes and the artisans have been excluded from the administration of the state, as they themselves are deprived of virtue . . . and in fact it is impossible that those who are occupied in the manual arts should be able to obtain any virtue.[16]

Inevitably, such changes put considerable pressure on ideas of social status at other levels of the Venetian hierarchy as well. In the *scuole grandi*, for example, the *cittadini* began to detach themselves more and more from the artisan membership. Formerly fraternal relations in which all members took equal part in ritual activities of the confraternities gave way to increasingly hierarchical arrangements in which the *cittadini* monopolized the offices while the less privileged members bore the weight of the organizations' ritual obligations (such as selfflagellation).[17]

For the elite artisans the loss of status must have been deeply felt, even resented. Alessandro Caravia, a jeweler who worked in the Ruga dei Gioiellieri on the Rialto, made his reaction clear in a poem that condemned the abuses he saw in the *scuole grandi* and called for a return

15. "Et sempre son visuto honoratamente né mai feci esertitio mechanicho" (ASV, *Avogaria di Comun, cittadinanza originaria*, b. 365/5, petition of 12 April 1578). On the esteem accorded manual labor in the fourteenth century, see Richard Mackenney, "Arti e stato a Venezia tra tardo Medio Evo e '600," *Studi veneziani* n.s. 5 (1981): 129; and on the active role of guildsmen in fourteenth-century Florentine politics—also a measure of their esteem—see John Najemy, "Guild Republicanism in Trecento Florence: The Successes and Ultimate Failure of Corporate Politics," *American Historical Review* 84 (1979): 53–71. On the 1569 legislation in Venice, see Giuseppe Trebbi, "La cancelleria veneta nei secoli XVI e XVII," 70: "Fin dagli anni settanta del Cinquecento, gli aspiranti al riconoscimento della cittadinanza originaria devono dimostrare che la loro famiglia sia astenuta, almeno da tre generazioni, dall'esercizio di 'arte mechaniche.'"

16. Memmo, *Dialogo del Magn. Cavaliere M. Gio. Maria Memmo*, 92. Berengo connects changes in the Italian economy to the nobles' growing class consciousness (*Nobili e mercanti nella Lucca del Cinquecento*, 254–263) that made wealth a prerequisite for nobility and had disdain for manual labor: "Nel diffuso declino delle attività mercantili, il volgersi del ceto nobiliare verso il godimento delle sue rendite patrimoniali e l'esclusivo monopolio degli *offici*, trovava il suo immediato riscontro nell'esclusione di ogni altro ceto dalla vita pubblica. La 'viltà' del sedere al telaio o in una piccola e media bottega assumeva cosí un significato nuovo, che al mondo comunale era rimasto sconosciuto" (257).

17. Pullan, *Rich and Poor in Renaissance Venice*, pt. 1 and the conclusion.

to the teachings of "the pure Gospel." This poem, *Il sogno dil Caravia* (Caravia's dream), first published in May 1541, was in many respects a popular version of the teachings of Contarini who, at that very moment, in Regensburg, was trying to hammer out a compromise with the Lutherans on the question of justification. The poem thus struck a middle ground, making both faith and works necessary for salvation. Like many of the *spirituali* of the time, Caravia believed that the best hope for Christians lay in abandoning their theological subtleties and returning to the simple truths of the Gospels. A bit condescendingly, therefore, he mocked the "small artisans" around him who, he said, were "theologizing beyond measure." But his evangelical faith stemmed in part at least from the changes he had witnessed. "Everyone attends to his own good," he wrote, "not caring a bit for his neighbor." He deplored the lack of charity, the unequal distribution of wealth—*le mal partite divitie*—the arrogance of the city's great confraternities, and the divisions that tore at Christendom from within. It was in this context that he called for a return to the simplicity of the Gospels and, reminding his readers of the humility of Christ, stressed the fact that all had been created equal and in the image of God.

Whereas *Il sogno* expressed sentiments that were beyond reproach, Caravia—a relatively prosperous, active, and dues-paying member of the goldsmiths' guild—would eventually get into trouble with the Inquisition on account of another poem that he published in 1550, *La verra antiga de castellani, canaruoli e gnatti, con la morte di Giurco e Gnagni* (The ancient war of the Castellani, Canaregioti, and Nicolotti, with the deaths of Giurco and Gnagni). In this work, the artisan-poet had now moved closer to a clearly heterodox position, for in describing the deaths of the two fictional friars Giurco and Gnagni felled during the popular violence of the mock battles that took place annually between young men on both sides of the Grand Canal, he seemed to favor the views of Giurco, who emerged as a spokesman for decidedly Protestant ideas. As a consequence, in 1559 he was brought before the Inquisition for questioning and a warning that the authorities did not like his ideas, though the testimony of Antonio dalla Vecchia, another rather celebrated jeweler, doubtless helped Alessandro get off the hook. Nonetheless, he seems to have learned his lesson. His final poem, *Naspo bizaro*, published in 1565, raised no religious questions at all. He died in 1568 at the age of sixty-five.[18]

18. Caravia, *Il sogno dil Caravia*; on *La verra antiga de castellani, canaruoli e gnatti, con la morte di Giurco e Gnagni, in lengua brava*, see V. Rossi, "Un aneddoto della storia della

The trajectory—the gradual radicalization of Caravia's religious views in the 1540s and then, in the 1560s, a growing moderation or perhaps privatization of his convictions—was in many ways typical of the experience of the Venetian evangelicals. But equally representative was Alessandro's social experience, for it was in this milieu of merchants and professionals and skilled craftsmen that the evangelical ideas first took root. The jewelers may have been especially receptive. The audience that gathered at the home of Bartolomeo Carpan to hear fra Agostino da Genova preach in 1546, we recall, had come mainly from the jewelers' guild.[19] And in 1548 Iseppo, a goldsmith, echoed Alessandro's more economic concerns when he argued that "it would be better to give alms than to keep oil lamps and candles burning to saints and before the images of saints."[20] Other men in different trades who moved in these same social circles—printers, tailors, jewelers, pharmacists, and silk weavers—were equally sensitive to the changes. Literate and independent, proud of their ability to make their own decisions (in both their shops and their churches) and to interpret religious issues for themselves, these artisans sought new ways to express their pride and their frustration; they found evangelism, with its denial of hierarchy and its stress on an individual's direct relationship to God, especially appealing. It reflected the essentially egalitarian and corporatist ethic of the artisans. Battista Amai, an itinerant mercer who usually worked at the Rialto bridge, railed against hierarchy. When Andrea, a belt maker who often worked alongside him, once tried to calm him, saying "it is necessary to be patient and pray to the Lord God that he help us," Battista's fury was unleashed. "These our lords are

---

Riforma a Venezia," *Scritti di critica letteraria*, vol. 3: *Dal Rinascimento al Risorgimento* (Florence: Sansoni, 1930), 191–222; see also Caravia's *Naspo bizaro*. For the Venetian Inquisition's trial of Caravia, see ASV, *Sant'Uffizio*, b. 13, doss. "Caravia Alessandro," as well as Benini Clementi, "Il processo del gioielliere veneziano Alessandro Caravia," 628–652. For a useful discussion of Alessandro Caravia as a critic of the *scuole grandi*, see Pullan, *Rich and Poor in Renaissance Venice*, 117–121; and Richard Mackenney, *Tradesmen and Traders: The World of the Guilds in Venice and Europe, c.1250–c.1650* (London: Croom Helm, 1987), 176–177. And for Caravia's relation to religious reform, see again Rossi, "Un aneddoto della storia della Riforma a Venezia"; and Ginzburg, *The Cheese and the Worms*, 22–26.

19. ASV, *Sant'Uffizio*, b. 6, doss. "Fra Benedetto da Genova," testimony of 3 September 1546.

20. "Che si faria meglio dar per l'amor di Dio che tener impezate le cesendeli et candele dinanzi alli santi et imagine di santi" (ibid., b. 7, doss. "Contra denuntiatos pro hereticis de contracta Sancti Moysis," testimony of 11 October 1548).

dogs!" he responded. "Cardinals have 40,000 to 50,000 ducats of income; they keep mules, dogs, whores; and they do not give alms as they should. The Lutherans are better, more charitable, because they love one another, give alms, and keep things in common." A blind man painted a similar portrait of the mercer's convictions. He reported that he had heard him say, "The *signori* are tyrants; they are dogs who destroy the *popolo* and the poor."[21] In a similar vein, a silk weaver argued that God had not made one "higher than another."[22] A pharmacist was more specific, directing his criticisms against the clergy. "Friars and priests," he argued, "are like nobles who deceive their peasants by telling [them] that whoever eats bread made from wheat will wind up in Hell, for they, too, make what is good appear bad." Those who refused to pray directly to Christ, a butcher's apprentice held, failed to see their own worth.[23] The idea of the dignity of individuals was recurrent.

Among more privileged commoners, evangelism provided a religious ideology and, in its devotional style, reinforced their traditional place in the Venetian hierarchy, close to the nobility. It did so in the mid–1560s for the group of some dozen lawyers, physicians, and nobles who met either at one another's home or in the room of a German nobleman at the Fondaco dei Tedeschi. At times, to avoid detection, they would gather secretly in the gardens on the Isola San Giorgio or on the Giudecca. Their devotions often began with music; afterward they read from the Psalms and the New Testament and listened to the explication of a passage or perhaps to a sermon from Ochino. Frequently the meetings would end with discussions of political events (the progress of the Huguenots in France, for example) or debates over religious issues in which they tried to resolve problems of doctrine. At the core of their group was Teofilo Panarelli, a young physician who

21. "Dicendoli io, che bisognava haver patientia et pregar il Signor Dio, che ci aiutasse, [Battista disse che] 'questi nostri signori sono cani, et che i Cardinali hanno 40 et 50 mille ducati d'entrata, et tengono muli, cani, meretrice, et non fanno limosine, come doveriano. Li lutherani sono migliori et più charitativi che noi, perché si amano insieme, et fanno delle limosine, et meteno a commun fra loro'"; and "che i signori sono cani tiranni, et che assassino i populi et i poveri" (ibid., b. 33, doss. "C. Prosperum Capellarium et Battista dalle Bambine," testimonies of 25 and 27 September 1572 respectively).

22. "Dio non ha fatto un più grande dell'altro" (ibid., b. 17, doss. "Girolamo de Luca," testimony of 11 February 1561).

23. "I frati et preti sono alla condition di nobeli, che ingannono i villani con dir che'l pan de formento che'l manzava va a Ca' del Diavolo, così anca lor ne mostra che'l ben sia mal" (ibid., b. 40, doss. "Contra Petrum a luna aromatarium et al.," testimony of 13 March 1576). For the butcher's apprentice, see ibid., b. 45, doss. "Giovanni Grison," testimony of 16 March 1579.

had grown up in an evangelical household and had studied for four years under the Venetian Franciscan and heretical leader Bartolomeo Fonzio before entering the medical school at Padua. Panarelli was one of the most committed evangelicals in Venice in these years, and he had direct contact with many *cittadini* and nobles—including Francesco Emo, Andrea Dandolo, and Marcantonio da Canal.[24] Since nobles and *cittadini* were well aware of their social superiority in Venetian society, this conventicle, with its membership drawn from a relatively wide spectrum of social groups, represented something of an anachronism in this late Renaissance city—a certain nostalgia for the more comfortable, slightly less status-conscious relations among the more privileged groups of Venetian society that had been characteristic of earlier generations.

Yet despite their evangelical views, the aristocrats and professionals made no leveling demands as did the elite craftsmen and other skilled workers. Such an evangelical was the Venetian gentleman Andrea da Ponte, perhaps the most prominent noble advocate of religious reform in Venice in the 1550s (his brother became doge in 1578). While Andrea spent some of his time propagandizing his fellow patricians on the floor of the Great Council, his most effective propaganda involved the organization of charity. In the late 1550s, da Ponte and several other Venetian noblemen who were close to Teofilo Panarelli persuaded a druggist in the parish of San Fantin to keep in his shop a small collection box where they might deposit alms for the poor. At about the same time he asked Michiel Schiavon, a Greek mercer who had a shop on the Rialto bridge, to play a similar role. Michiel was to collect alms from evangelical nobles and, under da Ponte's direction, distribute them to the poor—not indiscriminately but to those who shared their evangelical ideals.[25] The relation of these noblemen and *cittadini* to the

24. Grendler (*The Roman Inquisition and the Venetian Press*, 104–105, 134–140) stresses the role of Panarelli in the elite conventicles of Venice; I am much indebted to his discussion. I base my remarks on his overview and on the pertinent trials, esp. ASV, *Sant'Uffizio*, b. 32, doss. "Contra Theophilium Panarelli medicum et Ludovicum Abiosum" and "Teofilo, Virginia e Catherina Panarelli." See also Federica Ambrosini, "Tendenze filoprotestanti nel patriziato veneziano," in Giuseppe Gullino, ed., *La chiesa di Venezia tra Riforma protestante e Riforma Cattolica* (Venice: Edizioni Studium Cattolico Veneziano, 1991), 155–181.

25. On Andrea da Ponte, see Grendler, *The Roman Inquisition and the Venetian Press*, 134–136 and Edouard Pommier, "La société vénitienne et la Réforme protestante au XVIe siècle," *Bollettino dell'Istituto di storia della società e dello stato veneziano* 1 (1959): 7–8. On social context in the interpretation of evangelical ideals, see R. Po-Chia Hsia, ed., *The German People and the Reformation* (Ithaca: Cornell University Press, 1988), 2, which

poor was, therefore, patently elitist. Like the leading members of the *scuole grandi*, they saw themselves as moral improvers, and they used their social position to influence the less privileged members of Venetian society.

But the shift in the hierarchical structure of the city was not the only social change that encouraged a certain receptivity to the new religious ideas. Equally decisive was the growth of manufactures in sixteenth-century Venice. The city changed from the almost exclusively commercial entrepôt it had been in the Middle Ages, to the end of the fifteenth century, and expanded to become a prominent center of manufacturing. Granted, both wool and silk had been produced in Venice and in many towns on the mainland since the thirteenth century, but this activity had served primarily local needs and was, therefore, largely incidental to Venetian commerce. When merchants in the thirteenth, fourteenth, and fifteenth centuries had traded in textiles, the cloth had almost invariably been produced in Flanders, or in England, Catalonia, or Tuscany.[26] But with the disruptions of these traditional centers of textile manufacture in the sixteenth century and with the sudden growth of Venice's population, entrepreneurs began to stimulate the production of cloth that could be used as an export. The multiplication of looms in the city was startling. Between 1500 and 1565 wool production increased tenfold; in the same period silk output tripled. By 1570 at least seven thousand persons were employed in the Venetian textile industries. There were, moreover, reports of shops in which as many as twenty-five looms were working, though the silk weavers had legislation passed limiting the number to six.[27]

---

notes: "The fundamental premise of the social history of the Reformation is the belief that the religious messages of Protestants and Catholics were interpreted and appropriated by different social groups in the context and limitations of their daily existence. Only by focusing on this creative and active appropriation by various social groups can we understand the ideas of reformers, theological controversies, and political struggles in the larger cultural and historical context of the rise of confessional society."

26. Pullan, *Rich and Poor in Renaissance Venice*, 17.

27. On the expansion of the wool industry, Domenico Sella, "The Rise and Fall of the Venetian Wool Industry," in Brian Pullan, ed., *Crisis and Change in the Venetian Economy* (London: Methuen, 1970), 106–126. On the growth of the silk industry, Frederic Lane, *Venice: A Maritime Republic*, 313. And on the concentration of looms, Fernand Braudel, *The Mediterranean and the Mediterranean World in the Age of Philip II*, trans. Siân Reynolds (New York: Harper and Row, 1972), 1:431: "The law of 12th December, 1497 had forbidden any silk-manufacture to employ more than six *tellari*. The question was raised

A similar transition took place in the ship industry. As late as the fifteenth century, the Arsenal or state shipyard had competed with a large number of private yards in the city; thus it was, although the largest, only one of a number of ship construction sites in the city, an economic first among equals; as a consequence, workers could easily move from private to public employment and back again. With the growth of the Ottoman empire and the threat that it posed to Venetian commercial interests in the eastern Mediterranean, Venice expanded the state shipyard, virtually forcing the private yards out of existence. Simultaneously, the work force in the Arsenal doubled and at midcentury as many as one thousand masters would gather there to work at any given time. Enormous numbers of individuals who had worked in the Arsenal only if they needed steady employment now became state employees, dependent on government expenditures for naval shipbuilding. But economic structures alone did not reduce their independence. Precisely because their work was bound up with the naval power of the republic and with its commercial reach, the jobs were closely regulated. The Arsenal was a virtual empire. The Senate chose numerous officials from among the patriciate to govern the work force. These, in turn, selected foremen from among the master shipwrights and caulkers to supervise the work. The bell Marangona called the *arsenalotti* to work each morning and signaled the end of each working day. It was a world in which privilege came only through obedience and in which status derived from the close identification that the master artisans of the Arsenal enjoyed with the powerful of the city.[28]

Finally, less conspicuously, but as certainly, other industries expanded as well: the glassworks on Murano, the building trades, and of course printing. Venice became "a great industrial city, probably the first of Italy."[29] In the course of some fifty years, the city acquired an

---

again in 1559, when attention was drawn to 'the greed of certain persons who since they have twenty or twenty-five looms working are causing evident inequalities.'"

28. Frederic Lane, *Venetian Ships and Shipbuilders of the Renaissance* (Baltimore: Johns Hopkins University Press, 1934), chaps. 8, 10. On the size of the Arsenal workforce, see the excellent study by Robert C. Davis, *Shipbuilders of the Venetian Arsenal: Workers and Workplace in the Preindustrial City* (Baltimore: Johns Hopkins University Press, 1991), 20–21.

29. Fernand Braudel, "La vita economica di Venezia nel secolo XVI," *La civiltà veneziana del rinascimento* (Venice: Centro di Cultura e Civiltà della Fondazione Giorgio Cini, 1958), 97. On glass, see Lane, *Venice: A Maritime Republic*, 310; on building, see Deborah Howard, *Jacopo Sansovino: Architecture and Patronage in Renaissance Venice* (New Haven: Yale University Press, 1975), 2; on printing, Lowry, *The World of Aldus Manutius*, chap. 1.

industrial character that was by all standards remarkable for sixteenth-century Europe. At the eastern end of the island stood the "machine-less factories" of the Arsenal and the Tana, or rope manufactory. At the opposite end of the city, around the Rio Marin, the wool and silk workers were clustered. Printers' shops proliferated in the city's center. The soapworks and mirrormakers of the city increased the size of their operations.[30] Inevitably, in such an economy, immigrants became increasingly familiar figures of the urban landscape. "In Venice," Girolamo Priuli wrote in the early 1500s, "nearly everyone, apart from the nobles and a few *cittadini*, is a foreigner."[31] Perhaps no other place in all the Mediterranean and European worlds was as cosmopolitan. The city overflowed with merchants and artisans from other lands, with pilgrims and travelers, and supported various immigrant communities, among which the most conspicuous were the Jewish, Greek, and Turkish colonies.[32] Moreover, as Venetian manufactures expanded rapidly, the city came to rely increasingly on an immigrant and an itinerant labor force. Men poured into the city to work as weavers, as shipbuilders, as carpenters, and as printers. Certain trades attracted particular groups of immigrants. Most of the bakers and many of the cobblers and tailors were Germans; many of the butchers were from the Grisons; many of the *arsenalotti* came down from the Trentino; and many

30. The expression "machineless factory" is from Frederic Lane, "The Rope Factory and Hemp Trade," in *Venice and History* (Baltimore: Johns Hopkins Press, 1966), 270. On the wool industry and bookshops, see Richard Rapp, *Industry and Economic Decline in Seventeenth-Century Venice* (Cambridge, Mass.: Harvard University Press, 1976), 79; and Lowry, *The World of Aldus Manutius*, 8, respectively. On the soapworks and mirrorworks, see Lane, *Venice: A Maritime Republic*, 310.

31. "Dal governo in fuori dela citade et la nobeltade veneta et pochissimi citadini, tuto il resto heranno forestieri et pochissimi Venetiani" (Priuli, *I diari*, 4:101).

32. Though general studies on foreigners in Venice are lacking, for an orientation see Giorgio Fedalto, "Stranieri a Venezia e a Padova," in *Storia della cultura veneta* (Vicenza: N. Pozza, 1980), vol. 3, pt. 1, 499–535; and Stephen Ell, "Citizenship and Immigration in Venice, 1305–1500" (Ph.D. diss., University of Chicago, 1976); the insightful observations of Stanley Chojnacki, "Crime, Punishment, and the Trecento Venetian State" in Lauro Martines, ed., *Violence and Civil Disorder in Italian Cities, 1200–1500* (Berkeley: University of California Press, 1972), 202–210; and Ugo Tucci, "The Psychology of the Venetian Merchant in the Sixteenth Century," in John Hale, ed., *Renaissance Venice*, 346–378. For studies of particular communities: on the Greeks, see Giorgio Fedalto, *Ricerche storiche sulla posizione giuridica ed ecclesiastica dei Greci a Venezia nei secoli XV e XVI* (Florence: Olschki, 1967); and Deno John Geanakoplos, *Byzantium and the Renaissance: Greek Scholars in Venice* (Cambridge, Mass.: Harvard University Press, 1962). On the Jews, see Cecil Roth's classic study, *History of the Jews in Venice*; Pullan, *The Jews of Europe and the Inquisition of Venice*; Benjamin Ravid, "The First Charter of the Jewish Merchants of Venice, 1589," *Association for Jewish Studies Review* 1 (1976): 187–222; and Pier Cesare Ioly Zorattini, "Gli Ebrei a Venezia, Padova e Verona," *Storia della cultura veneta*, vol. 3, pt. 1, 537–576. Finally, on the Turks, see Sagredo and Berchet, *Il Fondaco dei Turchi in Venezia*.

of the journeymen printers came from France and the Savoy.[33] Not all of those who came prospered. Some must have been overwhelmed by the city. "Drawn by a desire for gain," Donato Giannotti observed in his *Libro de la republica de Vinitiani*, "[such men] may happen to stay here long enough, but nonetheless they only just get by or, if they make a little money, they go back to their homelands to enjoy it."[34]

Thus men like Paolo Gaiano, whose movements back and forth between Venice and Modena protected him for quite some time from the reach of the Inquisition, were by no means unusual. The itineraries, however, were often much more elaborate. The silk weaver and sometime foot soldier Francesco Cazuolo, tried for heresy in 1568, had worked in such varied places as Milan (his native city), Mantua, Bologna, Florence, Naples, and Messina before finding a spot as a journeyman in a shop in Venice. And Francesco Fontana, another silk weaver who was tried a decade earlier, provided the inquisitors with a similarly impressive itinerary. Prior to seeking employment in Venice, he had worked in Milan, Turin, Lyon, Geneva, and Brescia.[35] But many members of the more elite crafts were immigrants also, and many came from areas in Europe—such as Germany, France, and Flanders—where the Reformation had already made considerable headway. At least such was the case with several of the printers, tailors, goldsmiths, jewelers, and instrument makers who were accused of evangelical beliefs and practices.[36] Accordingly, certain patterns of immigration appear to have intersected with specifically Venetian shifts in social status in the shaping of heresy in the city. In the final analysis, it is not surprising that men such as Alessandro Caravia, no longer quite at

33. On the expansion of manufactures in the city, see Lane, *Venice: A Maritime Republic*, 308–321; and Pullan's introduction to *Crisis and Change in the Venetian Economy*, 1–21. For specific immigrant groups see specialized studies: on the bakers, Simonsfeld, *Der Fondaco dei Tedeschi in Venedig und die deutsch-venetianischen Handelsbeziehungen*, 2:269–275; on the butchers, Braudel, *Capitalism and Material Life*, 129 (which concerns the eighteenth century); on workers at the Arsenal, R. Gallo, "Maestranze trentine nell'arsenale di Venezia," *Archivio veneto* 26 (1940): 113–124. On journeymen printers, see ASV, *Sant'Uffizio*, b. 39, doss. "D'Ochino Pietro."

34. Giannotti, *Libro de la republica de Vinitiani*, 21 v.

35. On Francesco Cazuolo, ASV, *Sant'Uffizio*, b. 24, doss. "Contra Francescum Caziolo Mediolaneum," testimony of 20 August 1568. Gaetano Cozzi discusses Cazuolo's travels in "Vita avventurosa di un setaiolo eretico," *Archivio storico lombardo* 80 (1953): 244–251. On Francesco Fontana, ASV, *Sant'Uffizio*, b. 45, doss. "Fontana Francesco."

36. These data require interpretation. The Holy Office recorded the place of origin infrequently and may have underreported Venetian natives, being perhaps more interested in establishing where outsiders were from. But the statistics give a sense of the importance of foreigners to Venetian evangelism.

Table 2. *Distribution of Persons Accused of Evangelical Beliefs and Practices*

| Place of Origin | Number Accused | Percentage |
| --- | --- | --- |
| Venice | 72 | 22 |
| Elsewhere in the Venetian republic | 74 | 23 |
| Other Italian states and the Grisons | 90 | 28 |
| France, Flanders, Germany | 83 | 25 |
| Other locations | 8 | 2 |
| Unknown | 349 | |
| *Total* | 676 | 100 |

SOURCE: ASV, *Sant'Uffizio*, b. 6–59 and 151–164; APV, *Criminalia Sanctae Inquisitionis*, b. 1–2. Of the 676 individuals suspected of evangelical beliefs or practices, I have been able to identify the place of origin in only 327 cases. For a discussion of the derivation of these figures, please see the appendix.

home in their own city, would find friendships and religious camaraderie with Paolo Gaiano or Vincenzo Valgrisi, and that these strangers, in evangelical discussions in Venice, would discover something of a home away from home in an Italian city (see table 2).[37]

Cultural factors too helped shape the evangelical views of many Venetians. For in a profound sense the story of religious conflict in early modern Venice was also a struggle over boundaries, over borders setting off the sacred from the profane. To Rome and the leading proponents of the Tridentine reform, the challenge of Martin Luther and the confusions he unleashed called not only for a reinforcement of hierarchy but also for order and for a clearer delineation between the sacred and the profane. Archbishop Carlo Borromeo's pastoral letters to the Milanese are perhaps the most eloquent expression of the meaning of this concern on the level of popular piety. In his 1579 letter to the people of his diocese following the liberation of Milan from the plague, Borromeo emphasized the necessity of distinguishing sacred times and sacred places from the ordinary and the quotidian.[38] Some Venetians expressed similar concerns. The Holy Office often viewed the obser-

37. On the evangelical conventicle as a home away from home, see Davis, "Strikes and Salvation at Lyon," in *Society and Culture*, 3.

38. Carlo Borromeo, "Memoriale di Monsignor Illustrissimo e Reverendissimo Cardinale di Santa Prassede Arcivescovo. Al suo diletto popolo della Città e Diocese di Milano," in Ferdinando Taviani, *La Commedia dell'Arte e la società barocca: La fascinazione del teatro* (Rome: Bulzoni, 1969), 24–31.

vance of fasts and the reverence for holy places as evidence of orthodoxy as much as it viewed the breach of such fasts and the disdain for
holy places as signs of heresy. The inquisitors grew uncomfortable
whenever they detected a transgression of boundaries or a confounding
of categories. They frowned on lay celebrations involving music and
dance that traditionally took place inside churches, and they tried to
enforce rules keeping street merchants off the doorsteps of churches.
Confronted with a strange case of three young journeymen who had
been dressing themselves up in paper hats and makeshift vestments to
enact a religious service in the privacy of one of their flats, one heresy
they attributed to them was the "abuse of clerical vestments"—emphasizing once again the boundaries that were to prevail between clerical
and lay, between sacred and profane. Indeed, it was this attitude that
led them, in a famous trial in 1573, to chastise the Venetian painter
Paolo Veronese for including buffoons, drunkards, dwarfs, soldiers,
and other vulgarities such as a servant with a nosebleed and a clown
with a parrot on his arm in a depiction of the Last Supper.[39]

To the evangelicals, by contrast, this emphasis on boundaries was
anathema. It eroded their sense of participation in the religious life of
the city and, consequently, they rebelled. We find them ignoring distinctions between the sacred and the profane and thus confounding the
authorities. To be sure, when they were busy at work on feast days or
devoured veal, roast chicken, or pigeon on fast days, their transgres-
sions may have been prompted, as they often claimed, by economic
pressures or a weak stomach.[40] But there can be no doubt that the
evangelicals, in general, found the lines drawn between sacred and profane demeaning. They were literate and confident individuals who felt
entitled to argue about Scripture. Accordingly they took religion into
the streets and public places. They gathered in shops, in public
squares, and, after especially controversial sermons, outside churches

39. Fra Marino da Venezia, a former inquisitor whom his successors in office deemed
too lenient, frowned on such dancing; see the proceedings against fra Marino in ASV,
*Sant'Uffizio*, b. 12, doss. "Pre Marin de Venezia, detto il Zoppo," testimony of 9 August
1555; on the effort to keep merchants off the steps of a parish church, see b. 46, "Pro-
clama che niun ardisca vender cosa alcuna sotto el portego della chiesa di S. Panthaleone,"
decree of 5 May 1580; on the three journeymen, see John Martin, "A Journeymen's Feast
of Fools," *Journal of Medieval and Renaissance Studies* 17 (1987): 149–174; on Veronese,
see b. 33, doss. "Paolo Caliari"; and Sergio Marinelli, "Lo spazio ideologico di Paolo
Veronese," *Comunità* 173 (1974): 302–364.

40. For examples of working on feast days, see ASV, *Sant'Uffizio*, b. 24, doss. "Ten-
tori e chiovaroli"; b. 38, doss. "Giacomo calzolaio"; and b. 41, doss. "Tessera Costantino."

to argue over the preacher's interpretation. They resented the ringing of church bells and engaged in intermittent acts of iconoclasm. Above all, however, they argued against the idea that particular times and places were sacred. In 1555 Stefano de Ongari argued that the Sabbath was no more sacred than any other day of the week.[41] And in 1561 Costantino de Lagnasco was denounced for "denying . . . the consecration of holy places, saying that God has made the whole world sacred."[42] In 1573 the chancellor Zuanbattista Michiel maintained that it was just as useful "to say one's prayers at home or in any other place as to say them in a church."[43]

To a large degree, such new views of the place of the sacred in the religious life were yet another level of the struggle to preserve a public and inclusive religion. Many of the fundamental elements of this religious debate had been around for a long time. Crosses, images of saints, streetcorner shrines, reliquaries, elaborately decorated churches, clerical vestments, processions, the alternating rhythms of feasting and fasting—all these attributes of Catholicism had been part of the organization of the religious life in Italian cities for centuries. But in the republics of northern and central Italy in the fourteenth and fifteenth centuries, these elements of the religious life had been civic and inclusive. The sacred had been of a spontaneous and accessible character, and its relaxed diffusion throughout the city's monasteries, parishes, confraternities, guilds, and shrines guaranteed most Venetians a feeling of belonging to the greater whole that was republican Venice. To a degree that is difficult for us to imagine today, the sacred was familiar, and literally so. Nearly all Venetian noblemen had a sister in a convent and a male relative who held a benefice. Parish priests were frequently the brothers of artisans. In an advice book on the governance of the family published in the early 1400s, the great Italian preacher Giovanni Dominici had encouraged parents to foster in their children a sense of immediacy with the sacred. He invited his readers to provide their sons with toy altars and vestments, to have them learn how to celebrate the mass, and to praise them for this activity. When

41. Ibid., b. 12, doss. "Stefano De Ongari," testimony of 25 May 1555.

42. "Et nega . . . il consacrar delli lochi sacri, dicendo che Dio ha fatto tutta la terra sacrata" (ibid., b. 21, doss. "Contra Joannem de Vancimugio," denunciation of 24 May 1561).

43. Seidel Menchi, *Erasmo in Italia*, 104. My argument on the redefinition of the sacred is indebted to Seidel Menchi (esp. 100–121). See also her "Inquisizione come repressione o inquisizione come mediazione?" 58–59, as well as Natalie Zemon Davis, "The Sacred and the Body Social in Lyon," *Past and Present* 90 (1981): 40–70.

the family was not the host of the sacred, then artificial families such as the confraternity or the guilds were. Each *scuola* and every *arte* (incorporated craft or trade) had its patron saint and its particular rituals. And even as late as the 1490s—if we take Carpaccio and his generation's narrative paintings for the Venetian *scuole* as evidence—guildsmen tended to imagine the sacred as potent not because it offset the events of their everyday life but rather because it coexisted so comfortably with the ordinary and the mundane.[44] In myriad ways, the religious life of the city gave the majority of Venetians, and not merely the minority that monopolized political rights, a stake in the city's institutions. In the early sixteenth century Gasparo Contarini argued that here was a primary cause of Venice's political stability, since citizens alone could serve as officers of the *scuole grandi*.[45]

Over the course of the fifteenth and sixteenth centuries, however, the relations of the sacred to the city fundamentally altered. The sacred was increasingly set apart and subjected to the control of elites, clerical and lay. Though its familiar qualities were never eradicated, they were diminished. In an age of religious reform, critics might easily see the familiar qualities of the religious life as a source of corruption. The Venetian patriciate determined to subject the monasteries to greater and greater scrutiny; the Church pressed to enforce the celibacy of the clergy and to ensure, through the eventual establishment of seminaries in the city, their proper education. Confraternities, which had formerly coexisted comfortably with one another, now competed for honor, building increasingly elaborate halls and claiming a special connection to the sacred. Whenever the sacred did seem to appear spontaneously, moreover, the authorities were quick to control, channel, or suppress it. The beautiful fifteenth-century church of Santa Maria dei Miracoli is a monument to this dimension of the politics of the sacred. For the church was built largely to bring a popular Marian cult under patrician control. Similarly, in the sixteenth century, when a popular and possibly heretical cult developed around San Magno, the authorities again intervened and put this cult too under ecclesiastical control.[46] Finally,

44. Patricia Fortini Brown, *Venetian Narrative Painting in the Age of Carpaccio* (New Haven: Yale University Press, 1988).

45. Contarini, *The Commonwealth and Government of Venice*, 146.

46. For a comparative overview of the sacred in four Italian cities—Venice, Florence, Naples, and Udine—see Edward Muir, "The Virgin on the Street Corner: The Place of the Sacred in Italian Cities," in Steven Ozment, ed., *Religion and Culture in the Renaissance and Reformation* (Kirksville, Mo.: Sixteenth-Century Journal Publishers, 1989), 25–40. Muir ar-

and especially after the Council of Trent ended in 1563, the faithful experienced an intensification of religious supervision by their parish priests. Easter communicants were counted; marriage bans were posted; midwives were required to report all births to the local priests to ensure that each newborn was baptized.[47]

In isolation, such shifts as these might have been inconsequential, but combined with the growing elitism of the city and its increasingly hierarchical social and political arrangements, they forced many Venetians, especially those without access to political power or offices in the city's confraternities and guilds, to view the traditional manifestations of the sacred no longer as symbols of their incorporation but rather as signs of their subjugation. To many citizens, the monk, the friar, and the parish priest ceased to be the trusted and familiar friends they had been in the late Middle Ages and became instead representatives of an ideal that was at odds with their private aspirations. The miraculous was increasingly subject to elite control.

Evangelism, then, was a response not only to social change but to this crisis in the shifting character of the sacred as well. The evangelicals each sought to preserve the familiar qualities of late medieval religion. They were not, as is so often argued in traditional accounts of the Reformation, reacting against abuses; abuses had always existed. They were reacting against the barriers and walls that seemed to be under construction around their religious institutions, to hem in the sacred and to cut it off from ordinary people. In their struggle to keep religion familiar, they hoped to preserve a spirituality that made them participants in and not merely observers of the religious life of the Renaissance city.

But it was not only their resistance to shifts in the character of Venetian religious culture that made the evangelicals able—in the midst of these changes and the growing stress on hierarchy—to imagine a more egalitarian world. Their memories and their experience were important as well. For the more prosperous craftsmen, especially, could doubtless recall the more egalitarian arrangements of late medieval Venice. Many of the heretics had been born in the early sixteenth century, just long

---

gues that the Venetian government was especially able to control sacred space. On San Magno, see Flaminio Cornelio [= Cornaro], *Ecclesiae venetae antiquiis monumentis nunc etiam primum editis illustratae* (Venice: J.B. Pasquale, 1749), 6:419ff.

47. John Bossy, "The Counter-Reformation and the People of Catholic Europe," *Past and Present* 47 (1970): 51–70.

enough ago to recollect a society less prejudicial to the interests of its workers and craftsmen. But these men and women did not have to rely on memory alone. In many interstices of Venetian society—in games and rituals, in the tavern and in carnival, they enjoyed a refuge from hierarchies and a set of structures and expressions that offered alternative and decidedly more egalitarian ways of seeing the world—resources for developing a critique of "official" culture and values.

The tavern was a haven of unhampered discussion in the early modern world. A place where strangers met, it was also a place where ideas mingled. In 1549 an oar maker named Piero reported a conversation at an inn in Cadore the previous year. Several artisans from Belluno who had business there arrived at the *osteria* and one of them, a certain Prospero, felt the freedom to assert "that the true body of Christ is not in the consecrated host."[48] And several years later the boatman Stefano de Ongari recalled a similar event in the Brianza. Again, it was an individual on business, a coal porter, who spoke out with a forceful evangelism. "Christ has suffered for us and has saved us from the hands of the devil," and he concluded—this was where the heretical implications of his proclamation lay—that all ceremonies were therefore superfluous to salvation.[49]

The tavern served as a refuge from the church. It was at once its antipode and its mirror image. Both the Aquila Nera and the Leon Bianco, inns near the Rialto, were continual sources of preoccupations to the authorities, not only because of their largely German clientele but also because within such settings ideas circulated easily.[50] One morning in 1549 at the Fosseta tavern, for example, when a friar urged a group of men who were eating together to come to mass, a boatman refused, asserting, "What mass could be more beautiful than that of our sharing a meal at this table?" Paolo Gaiano would visit an *osteria* near the fish market at the Rialto in order to maintain contact with fellow heretics and natives of Modena. Paolo felt comfortable exchanging ideas in Modenese dialect with the itinerant artisans and petty merchants who had come to Venice with their wares or in search of

48. "Che nel hostia consagrasa non sia el vero corpo di Cristo" (ASV, *Sant'Uffizio*, b. 7, doss. "Prospero Battilana di Belluno," testimony of 6 July 1549).

49. "Che Cristo haveva patito per nui, et ne haveva cavato dalle mani del demonio" (ibid., b. 12, doss. "Stefano De Ongari," testimony of 28 May 1555). The Brianza is a region immediately south of Lake Como.

50. On the Aquila Nera and the Leon Bianco, see Stella, *Chiesa e stato nelle relazioni dei nunzi pontifici a Venezia*, 279.

goods.[51] And others must have felt secure in sharing their views with men whom they never anticipated seeing again. It was, after all, an especially safe environment. The Bolognese Antonio Canossi, in his testimony before the Modenese inquisitor left a vivid description of how conversation in a tavern could spill over into religious matters. "Four years ago in Modena," he testified,

It was summer, I was in a tavern. . . . A fellow called messer Cathaldo would come there on feast days. I don't know his surname, but he is a silk weaver. . . . And once I had come to know this Cathaldo, we came to discuss various matters and finally we began to discuss religion and very soon I realized that this Cathaldo held the same "Lutheran" opinions that I did; and, because of this, we became the closest of friends, and this Cathaldo told me how in this city of Modena there were many good Christians (by which he meant of the Lutheran sect) but that they went about with caution and in secret in order to avoid being accused.[52]

Games, too, could provide a structure for encounters among religious allies or between proselytizers and possible converts. In the early 1580s, for example, a vagabond priest disturbed the authorities with his chess games by which—at least from the perspective of his accusers—he was able to lure the unsuspecting into religious conversation.[53] Chess was frequently played in the apothecary of the Due Colombini, a major gathering place for the Venetian evangelicals.[54] And the mere presence of a regular spot for playing chess and cards in the shop of a certain bookseller named Vincenzo appeared to have raised suspicions. One witness, asked whether Vincenzo held heretical views, asserted, "I know nothing of his house, but in his shop . . . he has a certain little place where they play chess and various persons go there for tarots."[55] In shops, as in taverns, artisans could meet for discussions that were

---

51. For the boatman's assertion: "Lui dissi: che più bella messa è di quella che femo nui qui a tavola?" (ASV, *Sant'Uffizio*, b. 7, doss. "Domenico Canaruol e Antonio da Chioza," testimony of 4 January 1550). On the carder from Modena, ibid., b. 20, doss. "Paolo Gaiano," testimony of 29 October 1569.

52. Cited in Rotondò, "Atteggiamenti della vita morale italiana del Cinquecento: La pratica nicodemitica," 1029.

53. ASV, *Sant'Uffizio*, b. 48, doss. "Lorenzo Busnardo," denunciation of 9 December 1580.

54. Ibid., b. 20, doss. "Contra Joannem Baptistam aromatarium duarum columbarum," testimony of 22 May 1565.

55. "Di casa sua non so cosa niuna, ma nella bottega dove ch'l habita l'ha un certo luoghetto, nel quale i ghe zuoga a schachi, et lì vanno diverse persone, et anche qualche volte a Terocho" (ibid., b. 28, doss. "Contra Vicentium librarum," testimony of 14 March 1570).

virtually impossible to regulate, though in this case, too, laws to control gaming of all kinds were imposed by the authorities.

At carnival, games and the world of the tavern came together. This event was exceedingly important in Venice, and it was marked by activities in which all classes participated in a cycle of festivities ranging from the sophisticated staging of classical and contemporary comedies to the ritual slaughter of a bull and the Rabelaisian celebration of the figure of Carnival himself, acted out by a fat man, with a vat of macaroni at his side. Moreover, despite the increasing efforts of the city's magistrates to repress the excesses of the season and to bring the festivities more and more under the control of the patriciate, the popular dimensions of the celebration flourished throughout the century. In 1533, one report reads, a group of *popolani* dressed as lords, with some imitating commanders and others trumpeting as though theirs was an official procession.[56] And a heresy trial from 1571 nicely illustrates how popular and patrician dimensions of carnival could coexist. The case stemmed from a denunciation against a young nobleman and a young lawyer who, wearing clerical vestments, had been overly boisterous in their mocking of Catholic rituals the night of Giovedì Grasso (Fat Thursday, the Venetian equivalent of Mardi Gras). The testimony from the trial is rich and reveals a city filled that night with festive, indeed libidinous and even violent activities, in which the popular classes were fully involved. A certain Antonio di Piero, jeweler at the Papagallo, admitted to having masqueraded as a buffoon, and he was only part of a company that included a carpenter's apprentice, two gunners from the Arsenal, and a merchant—all in costume.[57] The festivity, moreover, with its motifs of social inversion and its mocking of social and religious hierarchy, offered a positive resource for the heretics. Not surprisingly, in his poem *Il sogno dil Caravia*, Alessandro Caravia assigned a central role to the Venetian buffoon Zanpolo Liompardi. In his representations of an intermediary between this world and the next, Zanpolo had been popular with crowds at carnival throughout the early sixteenth century. In the poem Zanpolo returns as an emissary of evangelism, curiously blending the ideas of the moderate reformers with the carnival tradition.[58]

56. Muir, *Civic Ritual in Renaissance Venice*, 176. Muir's illuminating overview of carnival festivities emphasizes the state's efforts to control the celebrations; see ibid., 156–181.

57. ASV, *Sant'Uffizio*, b. 30, doss. "Contra Jacobum Georgium et Zachariam Lombardini," *passim*.

58. Caravia, *Il sogno dil Caravia*. On Zanpolo Liompardi, see Carlo Ginzburg, *The Cheese and the Worms*, 22–5.

Finally, the very atmosphere of the artisan's shop, intimate, even secretive, was ideal for religious discussion. And much religious discussion there was. Tommaso Garzoni, for example, in his encyclopedic work *La piazza universale di tutte le professioni del mondo*, first printed in Venice in 1585, observed that cobblers were especially inclined to such discussion. Of these, he noted, "they are as Christian as anyone else, except when they argue about Scripture—an activity that belongs in the mouth of a cobbler about as much as a cap on the head of an ass."[59] In a 1548 trial of a sizable group of artisan heretics, for the most part residents of the parish of San Moisè, the gatherings in their shops emerge as a distinguishing feature of their evangelism. Speaking of these heretics, one witness, a butcher, noted that they meet now at the shop of maestro Girolamo, now at that of Zuanjacomo the sword smith.[60] Another witness was more specific:

I have seen some of them meet together in the piazza for discussion and I have seen the turner Jacomo and his son Bernardo meeting at the shop of maestro Girolamo who reads to them from a book—I don't know the title, because they keep on guard for me and also for others; that is, they withdraw to avoid letting others understand what it is they are reading among themselves.[61]

## Anabaptists, Millenarians, and Society

Much as class took a significant role in fashioning divergent religious and social views among the evangelicals—resulting, on the one hand, in a conservative and elitist movement that made no demands for changing either the social or the political order and, on the other, in a popular sentiment that appealed to the ideal of equality—so class was at work in shaping the Anabaptist vision as well. The Venetian Anabaptists came from diverse social backgrounds. Indeed, within the Anabaptist movement in northern Italy as a whole, a certain elite, made up of humanists and tutors, former priests and friars, notaries and physicians, constituted a visible and activist minority within

59. Garzoni, *La piazza universale di tutte le professioni del mondo*, 824.

60. ASV, *Sant'Uffizio*, b. 7, doss. "Contra denuntiatos pro hereticis de contracta Sancti Moysis," testimony of 14 October 1548.

61. "Ho visto in piaza alchuni di loro redursi insieme et ragionar tra loro et alchune volte ho veduto Jacomo tornidor et Bernardo suo fiol redursi dal detto m.ro Hieronimo el qual m.ro Hieronimo li lezeva sopra uno libro, non scio di che, perché si guardavano da mi et anche dalli altri, cioè, se retiravano per non lassarsi che cosa lezesero tra loro" (ibid., also testimony of 14 October 1548).

the Anabaptist conventicles. But workers formed the overwhelming majority, poorer workers, at the lower end of the social hierarchy. In Venice too, for the most part they were cobblers, textile workers, tailors, and sword smiths (or former sword smiths).[62] And many (at least in contrast to the evangelicals) were illiterate. In short, they belonged to a social world with few connections to the more powerful and privileged members of their society. Moreover, their immediate political experience made the passage from evangelical to more radical positions in the late 1540s relatively easy: the disillusionments that came with the collapse of the evangelical hopes for reform combined with an experience of poverty and a reading of the Gospel that led them to place their hope in fundamentally alternative political and religious arrangements. Salvation was to be a matter of special communities of true believers, whose baptisms would be a sign of their willingness to share with and to assist one another in every way.

The Anabaptist ideal for community was not merely spiritual. Granted, at times certain Venetian Anabaptists might take consolation in a piety that stressed spiritual as opposed to earthly expectations. The former sword smith Zuanjacomo, for example, testified before the Council of Ten that although he was poor "in this world," he was nonetheless, because of his faith in God, a rich man.[63] But in general the Venetian Anabaptists looked to more practical arrangements. Benedetto del Borgo, according to Zuanmaria Beato, used to say "that it is necessary that everyone be equal, and that things be held in common among us."[64] Matteo della Maddalena shared this view. "Christ said," he testified in 1552, virtually quoting the Gospels, "the fox has his lair and the bird his nest and the son of man has no place to rest his head. Therefore, it is necessary that the members of Christ and his servants

62. For Venice itself these observations rest on an exiguous sample of 29 Anabaptists whose occupations are identified. For general confirmation of this social world of the Anabaptists, see Ginzburg, ed., *I costituti di don Pietro Manelfi*, 25, which notes: "For now, we must limit ourselves to the observation that, for the Anabaptists, the overwhelming majority were artisans: cobblers, tailors, mercers, carpenters, and so on; next in importance were tutors, a few ecclesiastics and many friars and apostate friars. Then there were certain exceptional cases, such as that of Abbot Buzzale and his brother Bruno, a student at Padua or that of Marc'Antonio da Asola, doctor in law. The case of Francesco, lord of Cosliaco, like that of 'Antonia, wife of Antonio, agricultural laborer,' seems the exception."

63. "In questo mondo" (ASV, *Sant'Uffizio*, b. 11, doss. "Processus contra Anabatistas," testimony of 19 December 1551).

64. "Che bisogna esser tutti eguali et che la robba tra di noi fusse comune" (ibid., b. 158, register "Processus 1551 Venetiarum, libro secondo," testimony of 27 January 1552).

also be poor, because a servant ought not be greater than his master." But the logic went further. The ideal of common property was meant to solve other political and social problems. Matteo continued, "It is necessary for the rich lords and princes to possess their riches and their states as if they were not their possessions . . . in such a way that if these riches or states or lordships were taken away from a rich man or a lord or a prince that these men would not litigate or contest [such a loss] nor go to war."[65] This teaching evidently originated with Tiziano, who held—according to Giuseppe Cingano,

[that] goods should be held in common, and he argued . . . that whoever had the means and the possessions should give to who was without and, because of this, I, a poor man who had a little shop and a little capital, filled with the love of Jesus Christ, gave my part away not only to those who were of our opinion, but also to others who were in need.[66]

Finally, what of the role of class in the social makeup of the Venetian millenarians? In general, historians have seen such movements as characteristic of men and women drawn from a premodern proletariat of tramping artisans and the dispossessed rural poor, with members of a disaffected lower clergy constituting the bulk of their leadership. But perhaps this image is a mere projection of the fact that several of the ideological components of millenarianism appear unsophisticated in a political sense. After all, millenarianism in its hope for some kind of historical deus ex machina, for divine intervention in human affairs, is patently prepolitical. But in the Venetian case this view is unjustifiable on two counts. First, the millenarians, while of social backgrounds similar to the Anabaptists, were, if anything, of slightly higher social status. Almost half of them were members of the elite crafts; only a third were employed in trades such as shoemaking that had lower sta-

65. "Le volpe han le cave et li ucelli hanno il suo nido et il figliuolo dell'uomo non ha dove metter il capo; adunque bisogna che i membri di Christo et i suoi servi siano anch'essi poveri, perché non è servo maggior del suo padrone. . . . Bisognava che i ricchi et i signori et i principi possedessero le richezze et li stati loro, sì come non le possedessero . . . di modo che se ad un ricco o vero a un signore overo a un principe fosse tolte le richezze o levato il stato o la signoria che per questo non havessero a litigare né a contender né a far guerra" (ibid., testimony of 26 Jan 1552).

66. "Li beni fusseno comuni. . . . Persuadeva . . . che chi haveva facultà et robba ghe ne desse a chi non ghe ne haveva et per questo io poveromo, che havevo uno pocho de botega et de cavedal, inamorato de l'amor de Jesù Christo ho dispensato el mio a parte a parte non solamente a quelli della nostra oppinion, ma anchora ad altri bisognosi" (ibid., testimony of 14 January 1552; Stella, *Anabattismo e antitrinitarismo*, 52).

tus. Moreover, they seem to have all been literate.[67] And this second fact suggests that while such movements may have been prepolitical, they were by no means unsophisticated. On the contrary, millenarianism required a complex grasp of Scripture, one that was able to seek out subtle interrelations ("correspondences") between the New Testament and the Old. To be sure, other factors were at work. The charisma of such figures as Guillaume Postel and Benedetto Corazzaro urged them on, as did certain popular Venetian traditions concerning the interpreting of the mosaics in the Basilica San Marco. Although on one occasion a millenarian would complain about the interruption in his trade that war had brought and many appear to have been nostalgic for a time when Venice's control of the Mediterranean was not contested, their deepest concerns were less economic than religious.[68] What mattered to them most was the restoration of religious and political unity. And what led them to make this religious choice rather than the choices made by the Anabaptists was in all likelihood less their social class than their specific cultural experiences—experiences that had been informed by an Italian millenarian tradition.

Ultimately, then, class is a necessary but by no means sufficient explanation for the religious choices that men and women made in sixteenth-century Venice. For despite a social experience similar to the Anabaptists', the millenarians imagined their world in fundamentally different ways. They embraced the hierarchical arrangements of both Church and society that stood in sharp contradistinction to the Anabaptist egalitarian ethic. And—unlike such figures as Zuanmaria Beato and Matteo della Maddalena, who sought to separate themselves from the corruptions of the society around them—the millenarians hoped that through divine intervention their whole society might be made holy. To be sure, they were convinced that their own purity and devotions might help prepare the coming of a new messiah, and they too longed for a purification or a sacralization of the social and political order.

We should not be surprised by the importance of cultural experience in the shaping of religious hopes. This is certainly in keeping with a

67. As with the Anabaptists, the statistical sample is small; it includes only 13 individuals whose trades I identified.

68. The economic concerns of one millenarian are evident in a letter, beginning "Laus Deo" in APV, *Criminalia Sanctae Inquisitionis*, b. 2, doss. "Contra Joannem Baptistam Ravajoli Friulanum." On the sociology of millenarianism, see Yonina Talmon, "Millenarian Movements," *Archives européennes de sociologie* 7 (1966): 159–200, which stresses the secondary role of economic concerns.

conclusion that the social theorist Max Weber articulated with special clarity long ago. "Not ideas, but material and ideal interests," he wrote, "directly govern men's conduct. Yet very frequently the 'world images' that have been created by 'ideas' have, like switchmen, determined the tracks along which action has been pushed by the dynamic of interest."[69]

Venetian artisans who sought an alternative vision of redemption— men and women from similar social backgrounds—took three distinct courses determined by their cultural ideals—their "switchmen," Weber would say, or, to use a metaphor more suited to Renaissance Venice, their harbormasters. The evangelicals, even those in the less privileged trades, brought a certain self-confidence to their religious interpretation of the world—a confidence that made it possible for them to accept the Augustinian emphasis on the role of grace in human salvation and to locate the sacred not in special times or places but in their individual souls. By contrast, the Anabaptists held a world image colored above all by their faith in their own human virtues and by a certain healthy skepticism about the religious and political intentions of the Venetian ruling class. Finally, the millenarians took Scripture itself as their harbormaster—or had a special way of reading Scripture that led some men and women to believe that they could understand their place not only in history but in providence as well.

69. Max Weber, "The Social Psychology of the World Religions," in H.H. Gerth and C. Wright Mills, eds. and trans., *From Max Weber: Essays in Sociology* (New York: Oxford University Press, 1946), 280. Marc Bloch makes a similar case for the interplay of social and cultural life in *Feudal Society*, trans. L.A. Manyon (Chicago: University of Chicago Press, 1961); the epigraph for this chapter is from Bloch's work (1:59).

## CHAPTER SEVEN

# The Turn of the Screw

*To think of uniting Catholics and heretics is madness.*
Giovanni Botero, *Le relationi universali*, 1597

At first Michiel Schiavon, a perfume vendor at the Sign of the Pope, seemed to be a heretic like all the others. But Michiel's role in the evangelical community as a kind of beadle, who collected alms from its various members, made him an especially attractive catch for the authorities. Certainly he would know lots of names. And what particularly pleased the Inquisition was to learn the identities of the leading patrician proponents of evangelical teachings. Rumors had long held that many Venetian nobles were sympathetic to Protestant ideas, but for the most part a spirit of class solidarity seems to have prevented these suspicions from assuming the shape of a formal denunciation. To be sure, the gentleman Andrea da Ponte had been forced to flee Venice in 1560, but his case was the exception that proved the rule. Nonetheless, in 1565 Michiel Schiavon made it clear that da Ponte was only one of many noble evangelicals in the city.[1]

The patrician evangelicals Michiel identified were members of the conventicle (which included prosperous commoners as well) that had formed around the figure of Doctor Teofilo Panarelli. For the most part they were relatively young men, born in the 1530s or 1540s. They included such individuals as the lawyer Carlo Corner, Alvise Malipiero, and Giacomo Malipiero as well as Antonio Loredan, Francesco Emo, and Andrea Dandolo, each of whom would abjure his heretical beliefs. But there were also men of an earlier generation such as Marcantonio da Canal and Alvise Mocenigo, who shared their views. Fortunately, most got off with the mildest of punishments.[2] But Panarelli was not so lucky. He was viewed as the catalyst and, following his trial, was extradited to Rome. There, after undergoing torture intended to extract the names of as many of his sympathizers in Venice as possible,

---

1. ASV, *Sant'Uffizio*, b. 11, doss. "Contra Andrea de Ugonibus," testimony of 27 February 1565.

2. Grendler, *The Roman Inquisition and the Venetian Press*, 134–140; and Federica Ambrosini, "Tendenze filoprotestanti nel patriziato veneziano."

---

*Opposite.* An infrequent practice of the Venetian Holy Office before 1565, torture became a more common means of eliciting confessions and names of other heretics. The method most often used—known as *la corda* and depicted here—was to raise the victim up in the air by a rope tied to his wrists; since it pulled his arms behind him, the usual effect was to dislocate his shoulders. The tribunal's notaries kept meticulous records of the screams. (Domenico Beccafumi, *Scene of Torture*; courtesy of the Département des arts graphiques, musée du Louvre)

he was hanged.[3] Once the tribunal reached out to this noble world—in a society such as Venice where patronage counted for so much—the Holy Office inevitably found other evangelical heretics to question.

In fact, this unexpected crackdown on the noble heretics was merely an early warning of the increasingly hard line that the Venetian Inquisition was about to take. For one thing the Council of Trent, begun in 1545, had wrapped up its final session in 1563. With several doctrinal issues resolved, there was now much less ambiguity about what were to be accepted as orthodox and what were to be rejected as heretical beliefs. For another, despite the relative moderation or even a certain indifference in matters pertaining to the Holy Office on the part of Pius IV, the pope since 1559, the Dominican *zelante* Cardinal Michele Ghislieri (appointed inquisitor general in 1556 by Pius IV's predecessor, Pope Paul IV) was kept on in his post, and he was able to maintain a considerable rigor in the activities of the Inquisition. Then in 1566, when Ghislieri was chosen pope, he quickly emerged as an energetic and activist reformer, eager to implement the Tridentine decrees and to suppress heresy. During the pontificate of Pius V (the name that Ghislieri assumed) the number of executions for heresy at Rome, to which many heretics from throughout Italy were extradited, increased dramatically. The Venetian physician Teofilo Panarelli, for example, was among his victims as was the Florentine Pietro Carnesecchi, the former apostolic protonotary whom Pius IV had absolved but whose case Pius V, far sterner than his predecessor, managed to have reopened.[4]

In Venice the new pope's energies were felt immediately. As soon as the identity of the new pope was made public, the Venetian ambassador to Rome, Paolo Tiepolo, predicted that the papacy's interest in the local Holy Office would inevitably be far more engaged than it had been under Pius IV. For Pius V, as Tiepolo stressed in a lengthy report to the Venetian Senate, was a very different man. He was both profoundly religious and remarkably energetic. And, as far as the Inqui-

---

3. On Panarelli's execution, see Domenico Orano, *Liberi pensatori bruciati in Roma dal XVI al XVIII secolo (da documenti inediti nell'Archivio di Stato in Roma* (Rome: Tipolitografia Ramella, 1904), 45–49.

4. On Ghislieri, see Pastor, *The History of the Popes*, vols. 17, 18. Orano's *Liberi pensatori* gives evidence of the increased use of the death penalty in cases of heresy, though his general figures should now be modified in light of Luigi Firpo, "Esecuzioni capitali in Roma (1567–1671)," in *Eresia e Riforma nell'Italia del Cinquecento*, 307–342.

sition was concerned, Tiepolo continued, "one can say that he spends half his time in its affairs; in it he uses the greatest rigor one can imagine; and he is not satisfied with the punishment of new crimes but he busies himself with the diligent investigation of old ones as well, with cases from ten and twenty years ago—causing problems just about everywhere." [5]

To accomplish his reforms and his objectives in Venice, Pius appointed Giovanni Antonio Facchinetti as his nuncio. Facchinetti, since 1560 the bishop of Nicastro and the future Innocent IX, was an excellent choice. He was a lawyer by training, ambitious, loyal, and well seasoned from the experience he had already gained on a number of delicate and demanding embassies. The pope's instructions to his new ambassador were clear. Facchinetti was to do all he could to stamp out heresy. And he was to do so not only through the reinvigoration of the Holy Office but through the application of the reforms that had been decided upon at the Council of Trent. By reforming all manner of clergy, secular and regular, the nuncio, it was hoped, would be able to show up the heresies of the day as false and once again to provide "a good example . . . to the people, and to persuade them more easily to follow the Catholic and Apostolic Church." [6]

Even before leaving Rome, Facchinetti went to work. He met with Tiepolo and made plain his wish that the Holy Office in Venice would do more in an overt and public manner to repress the heretical movements in the city. Eventually, despite some resistance to his innovations from the Venetian senators, the nuncio was able to put at least aspects of his plan into effect. He was tireless in his effort to eradicate heresy. He struggled to have the Venetian patriarch publish the bull *in coena Domini*, a decree that was to be read from every pulpit to the faithful each year on Holy Thursday but that—although it called for the repression of heresy—the Venetian government found prejudicial to its interests (the bull insisted that no Catholic state had the right to provide shelter to Protestants) and refused finally to publish. [7] In other

5. "Relazione in tempo di Pio IV e di Pio V," in Eugenio Alberi, ed. *Le Relazioni degli ambasciatori veneti al Senato* (Florence: Società Editrice Fiorentina, 1857), 10:172.

6. Michele Bonelli, Instruttione per Venezia, data a mons. di Nicastro [= Giovanni Antonio Facchinetti], March 1566, in Stella, ed., *Nunziature di Venezia*, 8:35. On Facchinetti's career, see ibid., ix–xiv as well as Pastor, *The History of the Popes*, 22:409–427.

7. Giovanni Antonio Facchinetti, letter to Michele Bonelli, 1 June 1566, in Stella, ed., *Nunziature di Venezia*, 8:51–55; and Bouwsma, *Venice and the Defense of Republican Liberty*, 327–329.

areas, however, he was more successful. In October 1566—nearly twenty years after the reorganization of the local tribunal of the Roman Inquisition in Venice—he persuaded the Venetian state, long opposed to making its repression of heresy a conspicuous matter, to allow a public penance. As a consequence, one Sunday morning that fall a certain Zuangiacomo Mocaiati—a fifty-four-year-old native Venetian, who hawked goods such as leather jackets, illustrated books, and knives at the Rialto for a living—was dressed in a penitential gown and made to stand in front of the church of San Geminiano, holding in his hands a lighted candle. From the vantage point of Facchinetti, who had pressed for such a penance, the location was ideal. The parish church opened onto the piazza San Marco, the city's ritual center, and a crowd would easily be attracted. "This act of penance," Facchinetti wrote after learning that the Venetian government had given its blessing to a public ritual, "will serve as a check and instill fear in the others." He planned to send familiars of the Holy Office "who shall observe with care the movements, the gestures, the expressions, and the words of those who go to witness this spectacle."[8] Facchinetti was not disappointed. "This demonstration," he noted a few days later in his official correspondence, "was of great edification such that all the people in common consent shouted out that he should be burned and stoned."[9] Yet such a response was not automatic. And the nuncio continued to lobby for even more repressive measures. In a speech before the Venetian Collegio several years later, he cautioned his audience that heretics were the "hidden enemies" of the state. Furthermore, he argued, as a republic Venice was especially vulnerable. Even given the city's natural defenses, little could be done to protect Venice "were heresy (may God never permit such a thing) to spread within and the people to become divided and hostile toward one another."[10] The popular hostility occa-

8. "Questa penitentia sarà freno et terrore a gli altri; onde domatina si farà questa essecutione et io manderò persone a posta, che osserveranno diligentemente i moti, i gesti, i cenni et le parole di coloro che andaranno a veder questo spettacolo" (Giovanni Antonio Facchinetti, letter to Michele Bonelli, 5 October 1566 in Stella, ed., *Nunziature di Venezia*, 8:116). For the trial itself, see ASV, *Sant'Uffizio*, b. 12, doss. "Contra Maximum de Maximis ingenerium et complices"; as well as Achille Olivieri's useful essay on this case, "L' 'ecclesia' di Massimo Massimi: Ricerche sul movimento ereticale del Cinquecento," *Miscellanea Gilles Meerseman* (Padua: Antenore, 1970), 2:817–827. The church of San Geminiano no longer stands.

9. "Questa dimostrazione . . . fu di grand'edificatione ché il popolo tutto di commun consenso gridava che si dovesse abbruggiare et lapidare" (Facchinetti, letter to Bonelli, 12 October 1566, in Stella, ed., *Nunziature di Venezia*, 8:119).

10. Facchinetti, letter to Tolomeo Galli, 21 June 1572, in Stella, ed., *Nunziature di Venezia*, 10:221–222.

sioned by Zuangiacomo Mocaiati's public penance heartened Facchinetti; he even believed (mistakenly, it turned out) that the favorable popular response would convince the Venetian government to allow public executions of heretics in lieu of the secretive drownings of dissidents that had been its policy thus far.[11]

But the evidence for the papacy's success in intensifying the activity of the Inquisition in these years immediately after Trent is more than anecdotal. After an early wave of religious repression that crested in 1551, only a few years after the reorganization of the Venetian Holy Office, the business of the Inquisition slackened. But in 1565—the year before Facchinetti's arrival in Venice—it crested again. In that year alone, some eighty individuals were either denounced or implicated as heretics. And throughout Facchinetti's nunciature, the activity of the Holy Office remained high. As we note in figure 1, the decade running from 1565–1574 proved to be the busiest by far in the tribunal's history.

The intensification of the Inquisition's activity depended on far more than decisions reached in Rome. The new pope, Pius V, gave Facchinetti all the support he could muster. But the papal ambassadors also needed the cooperation of the local authorities. There was nothing automatic about the act of denouncing an individual for heresy. Ordinary Venetian men and women needed encouragement to do this. Thus the nuncios turned to their allies in the Church. At first, as we have seen, the preponderance of denunciations had come from the clergy. But by the mid–1560s the laity had begun to police itself.

This change had come about through a variety of avenues. Preachers were urged to speak out against the new religious ideas that seemed heretical. Teachers, many of whom were *sfratati* (former friars) and believed to be disaffected with the traditions of the Church, were required to make professions of their faith.[12] But by far the most influential ally in this war on heresy was the confessional. While serving as a much needed psychological outlet for the dilemmas and frustrations of everyday life, it could be used to ensure the piety of both the workplace and the household and to prohibit the spread of heresy. Carlo Borromeo made the connection between confession and orthodoxy explicit. He even listed personal knowledge of heretics as one of the

11. Facchinetti, letter to Bonelli, 12 October 1566, in Stella, ed., *Nunziature di Venezia*, 8:119.

12. For evidence of the importance of sermons in generating denunciations, see Eymeric, *Directorium Inquisitorum*, 408–409. And for an example of such influence, see ASV, *Sant'Uffizio*, b. 40, doss. "Negro Giorgio," denunciation of 23 April 1576. On the professions of faith, see Grendler, *Schooling in Renaissance Italy*, 42.

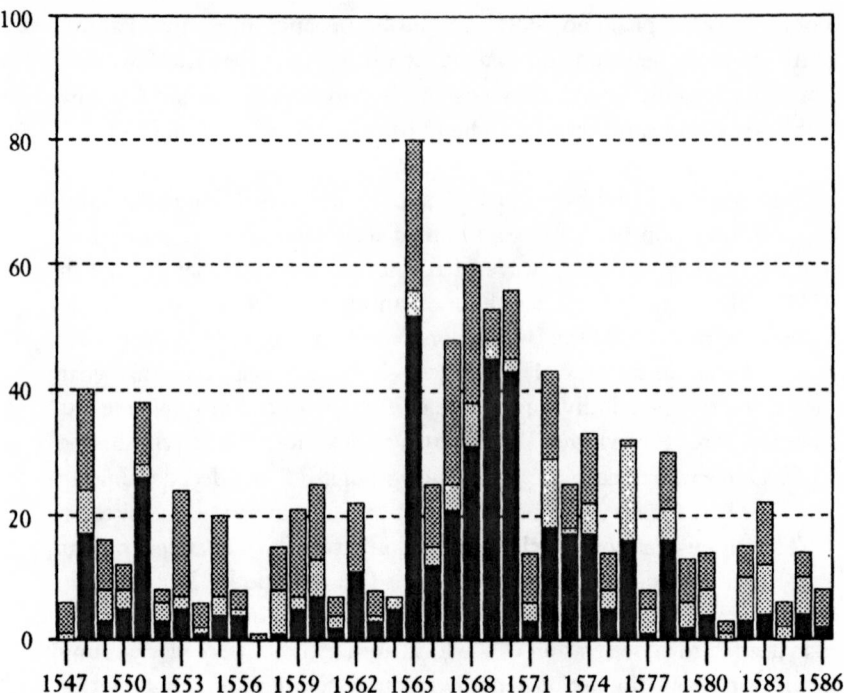

Fig. 1.   The business of the Inquisition, 1547–1586; ■ = number of suspects named in a denunciation or accused in a trial, but no action taken; ▨ = number of investigative hearings held concerning the suspects, but no further action taken; ▨ = number of suspects interrogated or tried *in absentia*. (Based on ASV, Sant'Uffizio, b. 6–59, 151–164; APV, *Criminalia Sanctae Inquisitionis*, b. 1–2. For the derivation of these figures, see the appendix.)

impediments to absolution. "Inquire if [the confessant] knows any heretic," Borromeo counseled the confessors, "or anyone suspected of heresy, or of any similar matter, since, according to our own Edicts and those of the Father Inquisitor, he is to denounce such a person, and discovering that he had such an obligation, be sure to have him carry it out."[13] And when the frequency of lay denunciations appeared to increase rapidly in 1565, there is considerable evidence that this shift was in response to the pressures that confession brought to bear on the faithful. In fact, during the Lenten season of 1565 its role seems to have

---

13. Carlo Borromeo, "Avvertenze di Mons. Illustrissimo Cardinale di S. Prasseede, Arcivescovo di Milano, ai Confessori nella Città, et Diocese soa," in *Acta ecclesiae mediolanensis* (Milan: Sanctus Joseph, 1892), vol. 2, col. 1893.

become systematic. It was then, for instance, that the confessor of a certain Jacomo di Vielmi instructed him to denounce the carder Paolo Gaiano (or da Campogalliano)—long known to members of his guild as "Polo luterano" and evidently so tolerated—to the Inquisition, and that a certain woman by the name of Andriana, also sent by her confessor, presented five denunciations to the Sant'Uffizio. Similarly, the birder Andrea Ballao, sent by his confessor, presented denunciations against several of his fellow workers to the Inquisition at this time.[14] At times the accuser was uneasy, caught between the loyalties to friends and the obligations of conscience. "These things, I tell them reluctantly," the scale maker Marcantonio de Simon, asserted in the midst of his denunciation against his fellow craftsman Antonio called "Melon," "because I am a friend of this man whom I have named, but when I made my confession during this most holy Jubilee and also before Christmas, the confessor told me on both occasions that I am obligated, under penalty of excommunication, to say this to the Holy Office of the Inquisition, and I have wished to say it as a matter of conscience." And Vienna Bertapaia, after denouncing her own son-in-law to the Sant'Uffizio for his heretical outbursts, made her ambivalence about the act quite plain: "And truly if my confessor had not advised me of this obligation of mine," she told the members of the tribunal, "I would never have come to do this."[15]

Spectacle too played a role. Although the Venetian state never engaged in anything like the full-scale, infamous autos-da-fé of Spain and Portugal or even the public executions in Rome's campo dei Fiori, it did find ways to make heresy a public matter. From the very beginning, abjurations and sentences had been read aloud in parish churches. And then in the mid–1560s, the Inquisition entered a decidedly more theatrical period. Zuangiacomo Mocaiati's public penance

14. ASV, *Sant'Uffizio*, b. 15, doss. "Andrea ormesiner, Marangon Iseppo, Martinello Pietro," denunciation of 15 April 1565; ibid., b. 20, doss. "Moian Vettore, Pizzamano Catterina, fra Felice da Padova, Rado Francesco, Marcello Francesco," denunciation of 27 May 1565; and ibid., b. 7, doss. "Pre Alvise de Michiel," denunciation of 17 April 1565.

15. "Queste son cose che io dico malvolentieri, perché son amico di questo che ho nominato, ma perché mi son confessato per pigliar questo Santissimo Giubileo, et anco avanti questa Natale. Et sempre el confessor mi ha ditto che son obligato sotto pena di escomunicatione a dirlo al Santo Officio dell'Inquisitione et mi l'ho voluto dire per scarico della mia conscientia" (ibid., b. 40, doss. "Antonio ditto Melon," testimony of 13 March 1576). "Et veramente si il mio confessore non mi avisava di questo mio obligo, io non sarei mai venuta a far questo officio" (ibid., b. 43, doss. "Cromeri Guglielmo," denunciation of 30 May 1578).

was only the first of several. In May 1567 Alessandro Riva, a young lawyer with close ties to many evangelicals in the city, was made to stand, as Zuangiacomo had the previous fall, in front of the centrally located church of San Geminiano.[16] And in June a master cobbler by the name of Giacomo da Sacile made a public penance in front of his parish church of Santa Sofia where there was also a *frequenza grandissima di popolo*.[17] Evangelicals were not the only ones so punished. In September 1573 four followers of the millenarian sect of Benedetto Corazzaro were pilloried for two hours in the piazza San Marco.[18] And in 1582, in a celebrated case involving necromancy and a hunt for buried treasure in the Veronese, the four principals involved were made to confess publicly in the Basilica San Marco. The papal nuncio Alberto Bolognetti argued that "this . . . enhanced the reputation of our tribunal and it increased also the fear in those who by chance might have an inclination to similar superstitions."[19] Public punishment had, therefore, become central to inquisitorial practice.

Such spectacles served two purposes. First, they undoubtedly encouraged many Venetians to identify more intensely with both Church and state, and to believe that it was both proper and obligatory to denounce those whose religious behavior offended them. In its symbolism, a public penance made a traditionally private religious act a public event and thereby encouraged spectators to see religion as a matter of the state. Second, this display of ecclesiastical justice appears to have intimidated the heretics themselves. Granted, to the chagrin of *zelanti* such as Facchinetti, the Venetian state—still preferring to drown relapsed or recalcitrant dissenters quietly at night, with only a few prison guards and a priest in attendance—never permitted the staging of a public execution of a heretic. But secrecy was no less effective than spectacle in this as in other stages of inquisitorial practice. Indeed, secrecy induced fear.[20]

16. Facchinetti, letter to Bonelli, 17 May 1567, in Stella, ed., *Nunziature di Venezia*, 8:217. On Alessandro's ties to other lawyers in Venice, see ASV, *Sant'Uffizio*, b. 22, doss. "Matteo degli Avogari; Alessandro degli Avogari; Andrea Pasqualigo."

17. Facchinetti, letter to Bonelli, 7 June 1567, in Stella, ed., *Nunziature di Venezia*, 8:227. For the trial: ASV, *Sant'Uffizio*, b. 22, doss. "Giacomo da Sacil."

18. Ginzburg, "Due note sul profetismo cinquecentesco," 211–212.

19. "Questo . . . accresceva riputatione al nostro tribunale et accresceva insieme il terrore a quelli che per avventura havessero havuto inclinatione a simili superstitioni" (Bolognetti, "Dello stato et forma delle cose ecclesiastiche nel dominio dei signori venetiani," 288). For an excellent discussion of this case, see Ruth Martin, *Witchcraft and the Inquisition in Venice, 1550–1650*, 89–96.

20. The Venetian government's choice of secret execution for recalcitrant heretics is of considerable interest. Most executions for other types of capital crimes were public

And yet it would be misleading to suggest that the Inquisition was able to exercise absolute control over the minds of the Venetian heretics. Other considerations—economic especially—served to check the growing spiral of repression that Facchinetti had unleashed. Throughout the sixteenth century Venice's commercial interests made the appeal to blindly repressive controls impossible. If the Venetian government were to clamp down too harshly on members of a particular community, the city risked losing their participation in the Venetian economy. Accordingly, from the very beginning the Venetian ruling class, drawn from families that had made their fortunes in trade, was concerned that the operation of the Roman Inquisition in the city might damage its trading relations with Protestant states. Acting in part on this concern, the Venetian government insisted that three senators serve as *assistenti* on the tribunal, an arrangement that made the Roman Inquisition in Venice subject not only to the Holy Office in Rome but also to the Venetian Council of Ten. Thus in 1561, for example, in a celebrated case concerning a former secretary to the English ambassador to Venice, a certain Guido Giannetti da Fano, the Council of Ten at first refused to allow the Venetian Inquisition to honor a papal request for the extradition of Giannetti to Rome and stated explicitly that this refusal was based on commercial considerations:

We must have respect for the Queen, for our merchants do much business on her island . . . and are well treated there . . . and should [the English] understand that their servants are not only detained here but are even sent to Rome, they might well protest, as they are a people quick to anger, with harm to our merchants and their merchandise.[21]

Only in 1566 with a new pope and a more insistent nuncio was the Venetian government finally persuaded to extradite Giannetti to Rome.

---

spectacles. The papal ambassadors to Venice argued for similarly public executions of heretics when the Roman Inquisition was reorganized in Venice. In 1547 the nuncio Giovanni della Casa urged the state to allow a public decapitation and burning of fra Baldo Lupetino between the two columns on the piazza San Marco, "talmente che la pena sua sia exempio ad altri" (ASV, *Sant'Uffizio*, b. 10, doss. "Lupetino fra Baldo," sentence of 27 October 1547); but the Venetian government refused the request. Yet members of the ruling class disagreed about the method (public burning or secret drowning) (ibid. and Facchinetti, letter to Bonelli, 1 February 1567, in Stella, ed., *Nunziature di Venezia*, 8:166–167): the *vecchi* supported Facchinetti's plea for a public execution but the *giovani* prevailed. Bartolomé Bennassar notes secrecy's effect in *L'Inquisition espagnole, XVe–XIXe siècle* (Paris: Hachette, 1979), 123–130.

21. Cited in Stella, "Guido da Fano eretico," 196.

In a similar fashion, the Council of Ten sought to protect the Greek and Jewish communities from undue interference in their internal lives by the Roman Inquisition, and it extended this principle to others as well.[22] Thus, despite recurrent efforts to bring foreigners to trial, the Inquisition, with its lay representatives, often found itself defending them. The principle applied even to individuals with very little status. In a trial from 1575, for example, a French journeyman printer by the name of Sidrach was under suspicion of heresy, but the Inquisition acted not to prosecute but rather to protect him, as the following exchange between the inquisitor and a witness (a certain typefounder named Jacobo) indicates:

*Inquisitor*:  Have you ever spoken with Sidrach?

   *Jacobo*:  Yes, we've had our words, and I've even called him a Huguenot to his face.

*Inquisitor*:  Why?

   *Jacobo*:  Because he is French.

*Inquisitor*:  Then you think all Frenchmen are Huguenots?

   *Jacobo*:  Yes, my lord . . .

*Inquisitor*:  Have you heard that in France the Catholics are at war with the Huguenots?

   *Jacobo*:  Yes, I suppose I have.

*Inquisitor*:  Therefore, all Frenchmen cannot be Huguenots.

   *Jacobo*:  I won't disagree, my lord.[23]

Similarly, during this period the Holy Office came to the defense of a number of German merchants. Sometimes the matter was easily resolved if the merchants were demonstrably Catholic. This was the case in 1571, for example, when Johann Fugger, a member of the famed banking firm in Augsburg, was denounced for heresy; and, again in 1582, when Christoph Ott, also a Catholic Augsburger, and a member of a German firm that served as the Fugger's representative in Venice,

22. Fedalto, *Ricerche storiche sulla posizione giuridica ed ecclesiastica dei Greci a Venezia*; and Pullan, *The Jews of Europe and the Inquisition of Venice*.

23. "Et domandato, havete mai parlato con Sidrach in casa di Gionta, respondit, Signor, sì. Et domandato, che rasonamenti havete fatto con lui, respondit, se dicevemo villania, et io li diceva, che l'era Ugonoto. Interrogatus, dixit li diceva così perché l'era francese. Et domandato, adunque havete tutti li francesi per Ugonoti, respondit, Signor, sì . . . Et domandato, havete inteso a dir, che in la Francia li Cattolici habbiano combatuto con Ugonoti, respondit, Signor, sì che l'ho sentito a dir. Fuit domandatus, adunque tutti non sono Ugonotti, respondit, non digo altro mi Signor" (ASV, *Sant'Uffizio*, b. 39, doss. "D'Ochino Pietro," testimony of 1 September 1575).

was accused of irregular religious practices.[24] Yet even when the Germans were Lutherans, the Venetian government seems to have had little concern. In the early 1580s Alberto Bolognetti, papal nuncio to Venice, characterized the Venetian policy. The Venetian lords, he argued, agreed that they must punish egregious offenses, but they remained lenient when it came to foreign Protestants. "They only ask them not to cause any public scandal, permitting them to live as they wish in their own homes," Bolognetti complained.[25] Thus the Venetian Inquisition found ways to balance the religious concerns of Rome with the commercial interests of local mercantile elites.

Venetians were subject to other less explicitly repressive measures that placed tighter controls on local religious dissidents and that represented, therefore, a narrowing of the opportunity for dissent. The most important of these measures was expressed in the evolving history of the city's confraternities. These institutions, both large and small, played a decisive role in communicating the central values of the Counter-Reformation to their members. But those who did so most conspicuously were the *scuole grandi*, the very institutions that Alessandro Caravia attacked in his poem in the early 1540s. In order to merit charity, the poorer members of these brotherhoods had to give evidence of their piety—attending mass, making the sacraments of confession and communion central to their faith. Doubtless, their motives for membership in the *scuole grandi* were not purely or even primarily economic since the confraternities provided a sense of fellowship and community to many of their members.[26] Their success in doing so, despite their increasingly hierarchical structure, was often what kept various members from rejecting Catholic observance for heretical beliefs. Zuane Vancimuglia, for example, had been a devout Catholic, participating in the Oratorio of the Incurabili, a confraternity associated with

24. Ibid., b. 29, doss. "Contra Joannem Sfulgher Theutonicum," and b. 49, doss. "Otto, Cristofolo; Otto, Daniele; Otto, Girolamo." On the firm of the brothers Christoph and Hieronymus Ott, see Heinrich Kellenbenz, "Le déclin de Venise et les relations économiques de Venise avec les marchés au nord des Alpes (fin du XVIème–commencement du XVIIIème siècle)," in *Aspetti e cause della decadenza economica veneziana nel secolo XVII* (Venice: Istituto per la Collaborazione Culturale, 1961), 132.

25. Bolognetti, "Dello stato et forma delle cose ecclesiastiche nel dominio dei signori venetiani," 282.

26. Pullan, *Rich and Poor in Renaissance Venice*; see also, on the social and religious roles of confraternities throughout Italy in this period, Christopher F. Black, *Italian Confraternities in the Sixteenth Century* (Cambridge: Cambridge University Press, 1989).

one of the new hospitals of the city, and attending services with regularity at the Gesù, the Jesuit church.[27] But at some point in the mid–1560s his life began to fall apart. His wife died; he fell into economic hardship; and, for reasons that are unclear, he came to feel betrayed by the Jesuits. Then he took to expressing opinions that made him seem heretical. "There is no more charity or faith," he was reported to have said. "The faith is of greater value to those at Geneva, and, if I could, I would be in that city that would give me fifty *scudi* or more." But the confraternity was able to bring him back into the fold. As one member, Alvise Moro, explained to the Holy Office, they decided that Zuane was desperate; they gave him some charity or alms, and he returned, showing himself to be repentant.[28]

But of all the changes in Venice that encouraged orthodoxy in the late fifteenth and sixteenth centuries, the proliferation of the Confraternity of the Holy Sacrament was probably the most efficacious.[29] Unlike the citywide *scuole grandi* and unlike many of the smaller *scuole* as well, these institutions, dedicated to the body of Christ and drawn almost exclusively from artisans, were based in individual parishes. Although they did not exist in every parish, by 1581 at least twenty of the city's parishes—nearly one-third—had such an institution.[30] And their grip on the spiritual life of the parishioners was remarkable. In early 1581, fearing interference by Rome in Venetian affairs, several senators prepared a memorial for their ambassador to Rome, in which they attempted to discourage the proposed apostolic visitation of the Venetian churches. In their report they noted the relatively prominent role of the laity in governing their parishes. "Visiting the churches, both those of priests and those of the friars," they noted, "one will necessarily encounter many institutions which are joined of and dependent upon these churches, but which are established, maintained and governed by laymen, with their own funds contributed by them not out of any obligation but through pious devotion. . . . These are the Scuole del Santissimo Sacramento of which [and here the senators were

---

27. On the Oratorio degli Incurabili, see Pullan, *Rich and Poor in Renaissance Venice*, 235–236.

28. "Non vi è piu charità né fede. Serva più la fede quelli de Genevra et se mi volesse troveria in questa Terra che mi doverasse cinquanta scudi et più" (ASV, *Sant'Uffizio*, b. 21, doss. "Contra Joannem de Vancimugio," testimony of 9 July 1566).

29. On the fifteenth-century origins of these parish confraternities, see Pullan, *Rich and Poor in Renaissance Venice*, 253.

30. Silvio Tramontin, "La visita apostolica del 1581 a Venezia," *Studi veneziani* 9 (1967): 453–533.

exaggerating] there is one in every church."[31] These institutions were deeply woven into the fabric of the parish, serving charitable, social, and religious functions. Above all, the *scuole* sought to intensify devotion to the sacraments. Not only did they take communion to the sick, they also organized processions through the parish when the host (which had been consecrated earlier at the parish church and was therefore held to be in fact the body of Christ) was carried to the intended recipient. This public quality made these *scuole* nothing less than the arbiters of orthodoxy for the parishioners. Communion became a public good, and if artisans did not cease work to show reverence to the procession as it passed their shop, they could easily be suspected of heresy. This issue figured in the trial of the large groups of heretics at San Moisè who were brought before the Sant'Uffizio in 1548.[32] And throughout the next thirty years, there were numerous cases in which the accused were said to be heretics, in part at least because they refused to show proper reverence to the passing body of Christ.

To a large degree the Scuole del Corpus Christi were concerned with social control. But it must be remembered that these confraternities were not simply imposed from above, at least not in Venice. The jeweler Alessandro Caravia, otherwise so critical of the pomp and excesses of the *scuole grandi*, fully approved of these smaller and humbler institutions.[33] Moreover, the fact that they did not exist in every parish is an indication that they had grown out of the religious needs of various neighborhoods. Had they been consciously devoted to social control, the government, so quick to intervene in so many matters of the life of the Church, would likely have sought to institute them in every parish of the city.

Be that as it may, the Scuole del Corpus Christi were controversial. Not only did many artisans refuse to show reverence, in 1573 a group of *popolani* on the island of Sant'Erasmo—possibly gardeners or domestic servants—took part in a memorable protest against the Scuola del Santissimo Sacramento of their parish. Originally a procession was to be held on the feast of Saint Luke, but rain and bad weather inter-

31. Ibid., 478.
32. ASV, *Sant'Uffizio*, b. 7, doss. "Contra denuntiatos pro hereticis de contracta Sancti Moysis Venetarum"; testimony of 23 November 1548 from this doss. serves as epigraph in chap. 8. On the confraternities and the parish as units of social control, see Ronald Weissman, *Ritual Brotherhood in Renaissance Florence* (New York: Academic Press, 1982), 207.
33. Caravia, *Il sogno dil Caravia*, D iii.

fered, and the event was delayed a week. That Sunday the parishioners were informed of the delay. But at some time during the night before the procession, garbage was scattered along its route, in all probability by men who resented the influence that the *scuola* was acquiring over the parish.[34]

The process of criminalizing certain religious beliefs and practices was, therefore, a complex one. And the success of the Inquisition in this matter came from its embedment in a rather elaborate web of religious institutions that included not only the pulpit and the confessional but such lay organizations as the confraternities of the city as well. Ultimately, the gradual meshing together of the various strands of this web intensified the repression. The evidence of its progress is clear. By the mid–1560s, the annual business of the Inquisition was nearly double what it had been during the first two decades of its activity (as we note in fig. 1). The general population appears to have moved closer to the view that religious dissent was something criminal and worthy of punishment. The popular classes had grown less tolerant. Not surprisingly, the targets of denunciations were often foreigners, even when they were in fact devout Catholics. Asked if he knew why he had been called before the Holy Office, the master printer Pierre de Huchin responded, "My lord, no, nor can I even imagine it, but I will tell you one thing: I am a foreigner here in Venice, even though it's been nearly twenty-eight years." At about the same time another outsider, a pressman from Chiavenna, made a similar point at the start of his trial, telling the inquisitor that he had been accused of heresy, "because I'm from the Grisons."[35] In both cases the assertions caused the Holy Office to take great care, sorting out whether the denunciations were well founded or merely expressed popular xenophobia. Thus the Inquisition, which had done so much to encourage religious intolerance, now found itself in the role of adjudicating the consequences of hostilities it had helped to engender. It punished those who presented false denunciations, and to those who were accused of heresy it could even show mercy, with the consequence that certain men and women were now actually grateful for its occasional leniency. This was the ultimate proof

34. ASV, *Sant'Uffizio*, b. 35, doss. "Contra illos qui proiecerunt immunditias in via per quam processio S.mi Sacramenti facenda erat in loco Santi Erasmi."

35. "Signore no, né mi posso imaginar de niente, ma ve diro, son quà in Venezia forestiero, ancora che sia stato forsi venti otto anni" (ASV, *Sant'Uffizio*, b. 39, doss. "Pietro D'Ochino," testimony of 11 August 1575); and "perché son grison" (b. 45, doss. "Grison Giovanni," testimony of 7 May 1579).

of the tribunal's success in gaining the loyalty of the Venetian population.[36]

Like many other cities in Italy, Venice became a somewhat less tolerant place. Contemporaries were conscious of this. In the late 1540s, most observers suggested that repression was not particularly harsh. Certainly this was, we saw, the view of Vergerio, himself a victim of inquisitorial justice.[37] But by the 1560s there was a decided change in tone. The activity of the Inquisition had already intensified under Pope Paul IV in the 1550s, and even the relatively mild Pope Pius IV invested the Inquisition with new powers in 1562.[38] Yet only with the conclusion of the Council of Trent in 1563 and the elevation of Michele Ghislieri to the papacy as Pius V in 1566 was the Inquisition able to gain the upper hand in the pursuit of heretics. The use of torture, praised by Peña in his commentary on Eymeric's *Directorium Inquisitorum*, became more common; in Venice the nuncio Facchinetti was able to restore galley service as a punishment.[39] Moreover, trials resulted in the death penalty much more frequently. In the twenty-five-year period 1562–1587 there were nearly twenty executions. In the Inquisition's first fifteen years, by contrast, two men had been sentenced to die for their religious beliefs.[40] In 1569 don Basilio d'Istria, the prior of San Giorgio Maggiore in Venice, looked back on the Inquisition's early years with a certain nostalgia: "At that time, it did not proceed with the rigor that it does at present."[41] Cardinal Seripando made a similar observation. "At first this Institution was a temperate and lenient tribunal, . . . but above all when the superhuman reign of Carafa held sway, the Inquisition acquired such a reputation that from no other judgement seat on earth were more horrible and fearful sentences to be expected."[42]

36. Cf. Louis Gernet, "Law and Prelaw in Ancient Greece," in *The Anthropology of Ancient Greece*, trans. John Hamilton and Blaise Nagy (Baltimore: Johns Hopkins University Press, 1981), 176.

37. Vergerio to Bullinger, 1553, cited in Pastor, *The History of the Popes*, 13:219.

38. On Pius IV's reforms, see Pastor, *The History of the Popes*, 16:309.

39. On the increased use of torture, see Seidel Menchi, "Inquisizione come repressione o inquisizione come mediazione?" 77; on Peña's views, see Eymeric, *Directorium Inquisitorum*, 594: "Laudo equidem consuetudinem torquendi reos, maxime his temporibus"; on the restoration of galley service, see Pullan, *The Jews of Europe and the Inquisition of Venice*, 67. Pullan notes that this punishment was tantamount to a death sentence; see also Tedeschi, *The Prosecution of Heresy*, 149–150.

40. Grendler lists most of those executed by the Venetian Holy Office in *The Roman Inquisition and the Venetian Press*, 57 n.92; my figures here are also provisional.

41. Cited in Seidel Menchi, "Inquisizione come repressione o inquisizione come mediazione?" 76.

42. Cited in Pastor, *The History of the Popes*, 12:508–509.

## CHAPTER EIGHT

# Two Horsemen of the Apocalypse

*When you do not wish to follow the laws of God, the judges will make you follow them with an iron rod, with force.*

A prophecy of Benedetto Corazzaro, 1548

CV NATO MVLER LIBERATVR VRE DRACONIS

A fter the journeyman dyer Zuanbattista Sambeni was drowned on orders of the Inquisition in 1569, the Anabaptists no longer posed any threat at all to the Venetian authorities. Perhaps because theirs had been, in general, such a well-defined sect, these men and women who rejected infant baptism and dreamt of a more egalitarian world constituted a relatively easy target for inquisitorial repression. In any case, after 1569 not a single member of their group (at least not in Venice) was the object of the Holy Office's investigations.[1] Yet despite the intensification of repression, both the millenarians and the evangelicals managed to continue at least some of their activities in Venice, though they too would find their foothold in Venetian society grow more precarious in the course of the 1570s.

Ironically, the ultimate cause of their unraveling lay less in the actions of the Inquisition per se than in the repercussions of the two great events to which Venice was subjected in this decade. One was the war of Cyprus and the passions it ignited: the euphoria that followed the defeat of the Ottomans by the Most Christian Armada at Lepanto in 1571 (where the Venetian fleet performed splendidly); then the frustration, as this early victory turned out to be the exception and not the rule. At home this war for the control of the eastern Mediterranean entailed economic pressures that percolated through all levels of society. In 1573 Venice was forced to reach a humiliating separate peace with the sultan. Moreover, the war had been a holy one, and both religious hopes and anxieties readily rose to the surface. To some, this conflict even seemed to signal a turning point in human and divine history. To others, it justified a harsher attitude toward religious dissent, for heresy, they increasingly felt, might provoke divine retribution. Then, with the war barely concluded, Venice suffered its second major blow of the decade: plague. From 1575 to 1577 the epidemic

---

1. The last trial involving Anabaptists in Venice is in ASV, *Sant'Uffizio*, b. 22, doss. "Marosella Odorico." The final repression of the Anabaptist movement in Rovigo came only two years later, in 1571; see S. Ferlin Malavasi, "Sulla diffusione delle teorie ereticali nel Veneto durante il '500: Anabattisti rodigini e polesani," *Archivio veneto* 96 (1972): 23.

---

*Opposite.* This mosaic from the Basilica San Marco held a central role in the sect of Benedetto Corazzaro. It depicts "a woman clothed with the sun, with the moon under her feet, and upon her head a crown of twelve stars . . . [crying] out in her pangs of birth" and confronting a great dragon (Revelation 12:1–3). (Basilica San Marco; courtesy of Osvaldo Böhm)

ravaged the city, killing some forty thousand men, women, and children—nearly a quarter of the city's population.[2] For the second time in less than ten years, more traditional forms of popular piety rose to the surface. By the end of the 1570s, heretics found Venice far less receptive to their ideas than it had been in earlier, more confident times.

Not surprisingly, the impact of the war registered most fully in the millenarian sect of Benedetto Corazzaro. A cosmic struggle between Christians and Turks had long figured in the prophecies of Benedetto's followers. And a Christian defeat of the Turks such as occurred at Lepanto in 1571 was bound to be read as a sign of the coming of a new dispensation. One member of the sect later revealed to the Inquisition that a book, written out by hand, had circulated among the members. "It contained," the witness confessed, "prophecies that the Turks were to be defeated, that the Austrian empire was to meet its ruin, that Constantinople was to be taken, and that the Turks were to convert to Christianity and that there was to be one sheepfold and one shepherd."[3] Moreover, in the Basilica San Marco, where the followers of Benedetto often met at vespers, they were especially drawn to a mosaic depicting a famous scene from the Apocalypse over the west portal (the image they viewed is shown at the beginning of this chapter). The woman, wearing the crown of stars, the witness continued, represented the Holy Mother Church; the twelve stars were the twelve apostles; the dragon was both Martin Luther and the Turks; the child, "he who is to be born, who will defend the Church and bring about one sheepfold and one pastor"; the man, "he who is to come"; the seven candlesticks were the seven bishops who had traveled through the world spreading the Gospel; and the seven churches were the churches built in Venice by San Magno, bishop of Altin.[4] In reference to the same image another of Benedetto's followers would also testify, making the link between his hopes and the recent victory at Lepanto explicit.

2. On the war of Cyprus, see Samuele Romanin, *Storia documentata di Venezia* (Venice: Filippi, 1974), 16:164–216; on the plague, Ernst Rodenwaldt, *Pest in Venedig, 1575–1577: Ein Beitrag zur Frage der Infektkette bei den Pestepidemien West-Europas* (Heidelberg: Springer, 1953); and Paolo Preto, *Peste e società a Venezia nel 1576* (Vicenza: N. Pozza, 1978).

3. I cite this text in the original in chapter 4 note 49. In this testimony we also learn that "il Patriarcha di Venetia fece grand'instantia d'havere detto libro nelle mani." On Benedetto's sect, see the works by Ginzburg, Prosperi, and Niccoli listed in chapter 4 note 42.

4. "Anco dechiarava messer Benetto vivo che per la detta donna s'intende la santa madre Chiesa, et per le dodece stelle s'intendono li dodeci apostoli, per il dragone intende

That woman has twelve stars, signifying the twelve apostles and the sun signifies the Holy Spirit and the moon under her feet indicates that she will dominate that lord who carries the moon as his banner, that is, the Turks. And as
a sign God has given us victory and the moon has started to bleed.[5]

The year 1571, then, encouraged the followers of Benedetto, to whom
the victory at Lepanto seemed a validation of the armorer's prophecies.
Domenego di Lorenzo, for example—an elderly cobbler who, after the
death of Benedetto, emerged as something of the leader of the group—
certainly grew bolder. This man with a long white beard talked inces-
santly and openly about his dream of religious unity in Europe and the
Mediterranean. He proselytized in the shops of his fellow artisans. He

---

Martin Luthero et il Turco perché si come quel dragone tira la terza parte delle stelle con
la coda, così il Turco tira la terza parte del mondo. Et s'intende Martin Luthero per il
dragone perché ha assai teste, tra qual ve ne sono tre coronate, che significano secondo
loro i tre principi dell'Alamagna che sono contra la Chiesa; et il cruciamento della donna
intendono le travaglie della santa madre Chiesa dateli dal Turcho et da Martin Luthero,
et heretici; et il putto di sopra intendono quello che haveva a nascere, et che haveva da
defendere la santa madre Chiesa et fare che fusse un sol ovile et un sol pastore. . . .
Quanto all'espositione che loro facevano dall'angello in mezzo alli quattro evangelisti non
me ne ricordo l'huomo che ha la spada et le chiavi intendono quello medemmo che dicevano che haveva da venir, qual con la spada saria defensore della santa madre Chiesa, et
con le chiavi per esser un sol pastore et un solo ovile, li sette candelieri esponevano li sette
vescovi, quali andavano per il mondo predicando l'evangelio: le sette chiese intendevano
che fussero sette chiese che sono in Venetia fabricate da San Magno, vescovo d'Altin"
(APV, *Criminalia Sanctae Inquisitionis*, b. 2, doss. "Contra Joannem Baptistam Ravajoli
Friulanum," testimony of 6 October 1573). Venetian legend named San Magno a founder
of Venice during the barbarian invasions of the early Middle Ages. The seven churches
were those that this holy bishop, in obedience to God, built on the islands surrounding
the Rialto for the northern Italians' protection. In the early thirteenth century as the
commune's identity took shape, Magno's body was translated from Eraclea, an outlying
island of the lagoon, to the parish church of San Geremia; Magno became the protector
of masons and his cult diffused broadly. In the midfifteenth century his day—6 October—became a feast day for the whole city and he was depicted by the Venetian painter
Cima da Conegliano. Perhaps to keep the cult within politically orthodox boundaries, in
1563 the Venetian Senate set up the ceremonial annual translation of a reliquary containing his arm from San Geremia to San Marco for high mass. Benedetto's celebration of
the cult of San Magno drew on a deep current of Venetian spirituality that he linked
(consciously or not) to a splendid portrayal of the Apocalypse, combining popular prophecies of the future with an important popular history of the past and weaving Venice's
destiny into prophecies of human destiny. On the cult of San Magno in Venice, see
Flaminio Cornelio [= Cornaro], *Ecclesiae venetae antiquiis monumentis nunc etiam primum
editis illustratae*, 6:419ff.
    5. "Quella donna ha xii stelle, che vol dir li xii apostoli, et il sol vol dir il Spiritu
Sancto, et la luna sotto i piedi vuol dir, per quel che credo, che la dominerà quel signor
che porta la luna per insegna, che sono i Turchi, et per segnal Dio benedetto ha dato la
vittoria, et la luna ha commincià andar in sangue" (ASV, *Sant'Uffizio*, b. 35, doss. "Contra
Dominico di Lorenzo callegaro et al.," testimony of 15 September 1573).

expounded his beliefs to a tailor and a printer in a shop in the calle di Ca' Dolfin. He tried to convince a fellow cobbler, a certain Alessandro, of his views at Alessandro's shop at the Sign of the Compass. He held readings in his apartment at San Felice or in the home of a fellow crafts-man, who lived in calle di Cinque near the Rialto.[6] And at least two other members of the sect—the harpsichord maker Benedetto Florian and the carder Lunardo—were equally outspoken. After a certain Brother Cristofolo preached a sermon at the Carmeni denouncing their beliefs, they visited the prior's cell to debate their views with him. And Domenego, in a letter, demanded of the friar an apology—otherwise, he warned, he and the others would put up placards in protest.[7]

While there were many aspects of the beliefs of Benedetto's sect that may have worried the city's authorities, clearly the most disconcerting component of his followers' views was not so much their conviction that the millennium was at hand as their insistence that a new man, "he who is to come," would usher in a new dispensation. This temer-arious step of identifying the new age with someone outside the Roman church placed the greatest strains on orthodoxy. Certainly this was the aspect of their thought that most preoccupied the Inquisition as it be-gan proceedings against them in September 1573. Did they expect a new messiah? Did they believe that Jesus Christ had come into the world, or did they, like the Jews and even like some of the Venetian antitrinitarians, deny that Christ was the Lord? Or did they identify this "new man" with some this-worldly figure? The inquisitor, there-fore, would press each of the accused on these issues. When he did so, Benedetto Florian, for one, explained that the man they were awaiting would be "similar to Christ" but not Christ himself. When the inquis-itor encouraged him to clarify precisely who this would be, Benedetto was evasive, scrupulously vague. "I believe," he said, "that he will simply be the one who does the will of God."[8] Then, when the silk weaver Biasio di Cristoforo, another member of the sect, was interro-gated, the inquisitor again tried to know who precisely this son of man was. Biasio's answer recalled the ancient prophecy of an angelic pope. "We have spoken of that woman who will give birth to a man who, I believe, is the pope, who will make one sheepfold and one shepherd."[9]

6. Ibid., testimony of 5 September 1573.
7. Ibid., testimony of 5 and 7 September 1573.
8. "Credo che sarà noma quel servo che farà la volontà di Dio" (ibid., testimony of 5 September 1573).
9. "Havemo parlato di quella donna, che partorirà un homo, che credo sia il papa, che farà un ovil et un pastor" (ibid., testimony of 15 September 1573).

This strategy undoubtedly placed Biasio on safe ground. For by identifying the savior with the angelic pope—that imaginary figure who
had long been the hope of late medieval and Renaissance millenarians
struggling to reconcile their hope for a new age with an expressed faith
in the visible Roman church—Biasio suggested that his views were not
radical at all. But the most arresting testimony came from Domenego.
"There is a man whom God begets not as he begot Christ," Domenego
began:

> but rather He begets him, that is He chooses him, for the destruction of the
> Infidel and the heretics—in order to bring the whole world under one faith
> and to accomplish the words of Christ who said: There will be one sheepfold
> and one shepherd. And this man is not Christ, but he is the sun which Malachi
> speaks of, for Christ is the light and gives light to the sun, that is, to the man
> who is the son of God and of the Church, it is he to whom the Psalm refers
> where it is written, "Ask of me and I will give you your inheritance." This is
> not said of Christ, but of that captain general who will come to give fulfillment
> to the law of God, redeeming humanity and bringing all to God's law. And
> this will be the son of God and of the Church, which will give birth to him in
> great pain. It is like the death of a pope. The cardinals are pregnant and give
> birth to another. And similarly with the doge of Venice; when he dies, the
> Signoria gives birth to another. He is given birth to not as a child but as a
> grown man. And I believe that he is born as all of us are. And the heresies are
> the birth pains.[10]

While less circumspect before the inquisitor than his friends Benedetto
Florian and Biasio, Domenego was nonetheless cautious. To be sure,
Domenego's language—especially his reference to the *capitano generale*
(the title of the commander of the Venetian fleet) and to the Venetian
doge and Signoria suggested a potentially explosive combination of religious and political millenarianism. But Domenego managed to soften
any political suspicions. Christ himself, he noted, had prophesied that
such a shepherd would come into this world. Moreover, Domenego

10. "Questo è un homo che Dio genera non come ha generato Cristo, ma genera, coiè
eleze a destrution de infideli et de heretici, et far vegnir tutto il mondo sotto questa fede,
et far quel che ha ditto Cristo: Erit unum ovile et unus pastor. Et questo homo non è
Cristo ma è quel sol del qual parla Malachia quando parla del sole, perché Cristo è la luce
che dà lume al sole, cioè a questo homo, et questo homo è fiol de Dio et della Chiesa, et
quello che dice il Salmo: Postula a me et dabo tibi gentis hereditatem tuam. Non è ditto
di Cristo, ma di questo capitano generale, che dee venir a dar essecution alla leze di Dio,
alla redention dell'humana generation, et far venir tutti alla leze di Dio. Et questo sarà
figliuol di Dio et della Chiesa, la quale lo partorirà con gran dolore. Et è come quando
more il sommo pontifice, li cardinali restano gravidi et ne partoriscono un altro, et così il
dose di Venetia, che, quando more, la Signoria ne parturisce un altro, et non parturisce
un putto ma un homo fatto, et questo credo che nasce come nascemo tutti nui, et li dolori
sono le heresie" (ibid., testimony of 7 September 1573).

gave Jesus not only historical but also ontological primacy: the pastor would be the sun, but the light of this sun would derive from Christ. It was difficult therefore to detect a theological heresy in the cobbler's interpretation of a new dispensation. In addition, Domenego seems to have satisfied the Inquisition that his millenarianism was not tied to Venetian politics. No actual this-worldly figurehead existed, he claimed, to whom he and his friends were giving their support. Certainly, Domenego's metaphors of birth were puzzling to the inquisitor, but even here the cobbler was disarming in his knowledge of Scripture. And when the inquisitor seemed puzzled, the cobbler recalled Jesus' response to the literalism of Nicodemus, who could not comprehend Jesus' assertion that one who was not reborn would not be able to enter the kingdom of heaven. "If I have spoken to you of earthly things and you do not understand me, how will you understand me when I speak to you of divine and heavenly matters?"[11]

From the inquisitor's vantage point, to be sure, heresies and "foolishness" were involved. Domenego argued that the Council of Trent had accomplished no good whatsoever, that the church doctors misunderstood many things, and, perhaps most dangerously, that baptism was not necessary for salvation. Moreover, the men were guilty of reading the vernacular Bible (in Brucioli's translation) after this had been explicitly prohibited by the Council of Trent. But the millenarian views of these artisans, it must have seemed, did not amount to much of a threat to the stability of either the Church or the city. Moreover, such views were certainly not unfamiliar. Only three years earlier, in a memorial prepared for the Venetian Inquisition by the Ferrarese humanist Nascimbene Nascimbeni, the Holy Office had learned of a similar set of ideas in Brescia. There a certain monk by the name of Stefano claimed to have received visions from God, and he too pointed to the passage in the Book of Revelation where it was written: "I saw a woman with the moon under her feet, and she was to give birth to a son." And he maintained that this prophecy referred to him and that he was that child to whom the woman had given birth.[12] But in the end Stefano had proven harmless and the Inquisition in Venice must have felt the same way about the followers of Benedetto Corazzaro. The inquisitor and his colleagues, evidently, were satisfied that the political

11. "Se mi ti ho parlato delle cose terrene, et tu non mi intendi, a che modo me intenderastu se ti parlo delle cose divine et celeste?" (ibid.); Domenego was quoting John 3:12.

12. Ginzburg, "Due note sul profetismo cinquecentesco," 205–207.

overtones of the sect were rather moderate. Thus the sentence was light. Domenego was confined to prison in his own home, and all four were taken on 19 September to the piazza San Marco and placed in a cage on public display for two hours. A sign was affixed to this temporary prison of shame: "For having read the Bible, although it is prohibited, and for having wished to argue boldly about Scripture, although they are ignorant."[13]

The stories Domenego, Benedetto, Lunardo, and Biasio told the Holy Office must have been convincing. After all, they got off with a relatively light punishment. But in this case, through the discovery of transcripts of a hearing held by Giovanni Trevisan—though, inexplicably, without the knowledge of his colleagues on the Holy Office—we know they were lying. Just one month later they provided a much more forthcoming account of their beliefs to this Venetian patrician, the patriarch of the city. Thus we know that the suspicions of the inquisitors were well founded. Some six months earlier they had in fact made the leap the Holy Office suspected but could not prove. They had identified the "new man," the "shepherd," the "captain general" with a this-worldly figure. "A man has appeared here in Venice," the carder Lunardo had written in April 1573 in a personal letter to his father-in-law Zuanbattista, a former resident of Venice who had moved to Forlì.

And this man is he who has come. He had told me all those things we are awaiting through Scripture. He has made me see the truth of it all. He showed me his portrait in the Basilica San Marco . . . and he has shown to me and to messer Benedetto [Florian?] it is he, and he has shown us his lineage through Holy Scripture. And look yourself in the Song of Solomon where it says: "Buon cipro diletto mio"; and then the Gospel where it says: "This is my son who is my diletto"; and in the song again where it says: "Viene, diletto mio, viene capriolo mio." "Viene" signifies Venice, and "capriolo" signifies Ca' Priuli, and he was born miraculously in the house of Priuli, the branch at San Stefano, as was his father, and his mother is from Cyprus, of the royal house of Cyprus . . . and the Song of Solomon also tells us that he will be nourished among the lilies until the new day, and the lilies are the king of France, and he is a knight of the king and has his rents in France, and thus he is being nourished in France until the new day, that is until dawn . . . which is Alba.[14]

13. "Per haver letto Bibie volgari prohibite, et voluto contendere temerariamente delle cose della scrittura sacra essendo ignoranti" (ASV, *Sant'Uffizio*, b. 35, doss. "Contra Dominico di Lorenzo callegaro et al.," report of the execution of the sentence, 19 September 1573).

14. "Si che vi ho scritto suso la lettera di alcun ligrece che ne s'è apparso qui in Venetia de un huomo, il qual huomo si è quello che die vegnire, il qual m'ha detto di

Just as the inquisitor feared but would never know, the members of the sect of Benedetto Corazzaro identified their "savior." He was a Venetian nobleman, born in the house of Priuli. His portrait was in the Basilica San Marco. And his coming fulfilled all their expectations and constituted for the sect of Benedetto Corazzaro a time of great joy. That Benedetto's followers would go out of their way to conceal this "revelation" from the Venetian Inquisition was perfectly sensible. A full disclosure of what they meant by "he who is to come" might well have cost them their lives. But they were doubly fortunate, for Lunardo's letter along with other equally incriminating material had fallen into the hands of Giovanni Trevisan, the Venetian patriarch and one of the three clerical judges who sat on the Holy Office. But Trevisan, for reasons we shall never know, held this material back from his colleagues on the tribunal. Perhaps the patriarch sought to avoid compromising the Priuli, his fellow patricians, or perhaps he recognized that the matter was hardly threatening. For, paradoxically—as we shall see—the views of the millenarians were increasingly consonant with those of their oppressors.

On one level, these particular millenarian beliefs reflected a general tendency in apocalyptic thought to see contemporary history in light of Scripture and, conversely, Scripture in light of contemporary history. As one recent student of apocalyptic thought observed, apocalypticism is less a response to crisis than an attitude that is always "on the lookout for crisis." [15] This attitude appeared especially in Lunardo's al-

---

tutte quelle cose che noi aspettamo per la Scrittura, il quale ne ha fatto vedere la verità del tutto et ne ha insegnado la sua figura in chiesa di San Marco dela quale figura il somea tutto et el ne ha fatto vedere a m. Beneto et a me a che modo che è lì lui et di che discendentia che'l è disceso per la scrittura santa, et guardate anche voi in nela Cantica del Salamone al primo, che el disi: Buon cipro dileto mio; et il Vangelo dice: Questo è il mio fiolo il quale l'è il mio diletto; et in essa cantica quando dice: Viene, diletto mio, viene capriolo mio. Viene vol dire Venetia, capriolo vol dire in Ca' Priuolo, et lui è nassuo in Ca' Priuolo a San Stefano miracolosamente, et suo padre et sua madre è di Cipro di casa Rege di Cipro, et sua madre è stata annunciada dal'angelo Gabriele il nascimento suo et in essa Cantica di Salamone dice ancora che'l se nudrise fra li cigli persin che si leva il giorno, li cigli si è il re di Francia, et lui è cavaliero del re di Francia et ha le sue intrade in Francia, et però el si nudrisce fra li cigli persin che si leva il giorno, adonché el speta l'alba el quale aspetta l'Alba" (APV, *Criminalia Sanctae Inquisitionis*, b. 2, doss. "Contra Joannem Baptistam Ravajoli Friulanum," letter of Lunardo to Zuanbattista, dated 10 April 1573).

15. Bernard McGinn, introduction to *Apocalyptic Spirituality* (New York: Paulist Press, 1979), 8.

lusions to the king of France and the duke of Alba; many men and women living in the sixteenth century must have taken the actions of these two political leaders in 1572 for a prophetic completion of the struggle of the Catholic forces over its enemies that began with the victory of the Christian fleet over the Turks the previous October at Lepanto. In August 1572 Catholic forces gained the advantage in Europe when, on Saint Bartholomew's Day, French Catholics attacked the Huguenots, killing nearly a thousand in Paris alone; similar massacres took place throughout the realm. At this same time Fernando Alvarez de Toledo, the duke of Alba, intensified his campaign against the Dutch Protestants in the Netherlands.[16] Everywhere in Europe and the Mediterranean, it seemed, Catholicism was victorious. Moreover, to many—among them the followers of Benedetto Corazzaro—the fact that these events coincided with the reign in France of King Charles IX hardly seemed accidental. For years prophecies had circulated, in Europe and in Venice as well, that the millennium, an age of religious peace and unity, would be ushered in under a French monarch with this name.[17] Despite decades of religious tension and conflict and the proliferation of new sects and confessions, there was hope for the restoration of a world empire under one faith.

Significantly, however, the hope was no longer one that challenged—as perhaps the earlier currents of Venetian millenarianism had done—the order of things. To the contrary, by the early 1570s the Venetian prophetic tradition had become profoundly conservative. How else do we explain this cryptic allusion to a Priuli, a Venetian nobleman, as a savior? Thus Venetian millenarianism, at one time a current of expectations that looked for a profound transformation of the social and political order, had been transformed into a movement

16. On the Saint Bartholomew's Day massacre, see Barbara Diefendorf, "Prologue to a Massacre: Popular Unrest in Paris, 1557–1572," *American Historical Review* 90 (1985): 1067–1092, and the bibliography. According to Donald R. Kelley, "The massacres of St. Bartholomew . . . set off an unprecedented firestorm of propaganda, perhaps the most sensational and most seminal in modern history" (*The Beginning of Ideology* [Cambridge: Cambridge University Press, 1981], 287). On the duke of Alba, see William S. Maltby, *Alba: A Biography of Fernando Alvarez de Toledo, Third Duke of Alba, 1507–1582* (Berkeley: University of California Press, 1983).

17. The hopes placed in King Charles related to the extremely popular "second Charlemagne" prophecy developed by the mysterious Francophile Telesphorus of Cosenza (Reeves, *Joachim of Fiore and the Prophetic Future*, 68–69). On a revival of this legend in France after the Saint Bartholomew's Day massacre, see Kelley, *The Beginning of Ideology*, 286.

of only moderate expectations.[18] Formerly hopeful that the "birth pangs" of heresy would bring forth a new dispensation, the Venetian millenarianism now identified the new dispensation with the apparently triumphant Catholicism of the early 1570s. Perhaps in Venice, with the increasingly repressive climate that the war brought into existence and that Facchinetti encouraged, such a view virtually forced itself upon these millenarians. And in the conservative scheme a Priuli made perfect sense. The Priuli family gave Venice two doges in the sixteenth century, Lorenzo and Girolamo, whose consecutive rules lasted from 1556 to 1567.[19] Moreover, this Venetian savior—a knight of the king of France and a young man (he was about twenty-five years old at the time Domenego's group met him in 1573)—seemed especially suited to bring about a restoration of traditional Venetian values. For the Cavaliere Priuli in question was a descendant of two families who, it turns out, played key roles in the Venetian conquest of Cyprus at the end of the fifteenth century.[20] On the maternal side, he could claim as an ancestor Caterina Cornaro, the Venetian noblewoman who

---

18. For an analysis of similar shifts in the expectations of another millenarian movement, see E. P. Thompson, *The Making of the English Working Class* (New York: Vintage Books, 1966), 375–400.

19. On the Priuli, see Romanin, *Storia documentata di Venezia*, 6:164–184.

20. The most likely candidate for the cavalier-messiah Lunardo claims to have encountered is Alvise di Zuanfrancesco Priuli. Of the many Priuli noblemen in Renaissance Venice, only two married women from the Cornaro family. In 1549 Domenego di Girolamo Priuli married Catarina di Girolamo Cornaro (widow of Girolamo di Anzolo Contarini); they never had children. Possibly the parents were Elisabetta di Giacomo Cornaro (grandniece of Queen Caterina) and Zuanfrancesco di Francesco Priuli (great-grandson of the capitano generale da mar Francesco Priuli); they were married in 1534 (Marco Barbaro, *Libro di nozze patrizie* [*Marciana*: It. VII. 156(8492)]). Elisabetta and Zuanfrancesco had three sons: Francesco, born in 1532, Federigo in 1538, and Alvise (Barbaro, *Genealogie delle famiglie patrizie venete* [*Marciana*: It. VII. 925–928 (8594–97)], vol 4, f. 168r; Girolamo Alessandro Capellari Vivaro, *Il Campidoglio Veneto* [*Marciana*: It. VII. 15–18 (8304–7)], vol. 3; Emmanuele Cicogna, *Delle inscrizioni veneziane* [Venice: Giuseppe Orlandelli, 1824–53]); but Cicogna lists only Francesco and Federigo. Alvise is elusive: unlike Francesco, he is not mentioned in Federigo's will (ASV, *Testamenti, Atti Ziliol*, 211 c 180, 13 July 1569); and he is not listed with his brothers in the *Libro d'oro* (ASV, *Avogaria di comun, Nascite*)—an omission that suggests illegitimate birth.

Nothing indicates that either Federigo or Francisco was a knight of the French king. But was Alvise? In his will (ASV, *Testamenti, Atti Ziliol*, 1250.III.134 of 21 March 1614) he makes no reference to France or a knighthood. An Alvise di Priuli (but we cannot be sure he was the same person) was listed among those present at the entrance of Henry III into Venice in 1574, and during the French wars of religion the monarch often knighted Italian nobles as allies (see the dispatch of the Venetian ambassador to France for 16 February 1568; and the "Relatione di Franza di messer Alvise Contarini, Kavalier,

married the king of Cyprus in 1472 and became the island's queen. Although her rule there was broken by 1488, and she was forced to return to the Venetian republic the following year, she became something of a local heroine and was allowed to continue the life of a monarch at Asolo, a hilltop town northwest of Treviso, where she held her court. Her funeral in Venice was a magnificent affair.[21] On the paternal side, a Priuli also had an important role in the conquest of Cyprus. Indeed, it was Francesco Priuli who served as the *capitano generale da mar* and who managed to bring the island under the military control of Venice—in light of which Domenego di Lorenzo's reference, nearly a hundred years later, to the "savior" as a *capitano generale* hardly seems accidental.[22] In his very descent, therefore, this Priuli recalled a time of Venetian glory, a time when Venice was the undisputed naval power of the Mediterranean—a glory that many in Venice hoped to regain during their present conflict with the Ottomans. The Priuli household, that is, directly connected the late sixteenth-century city to an age of Venetian self-confidence and imperial power. And the belief—even if fleeting—in a Priuli savior displayed an additional conservative trait of the Venetian millenarians: they believed that the millennium would be ushered in by men higher in prestige and more powerful than themselves. Accordingly, they did not place their hopes in a lowborn peasant or a humble artisan as had more radical millenarians of the early sixteenth century such as Albert of Trent or Francesco Meleto.[23] To the contrary, they looked to a king, a duke, and a Venetian nobleman as the agents for the transformation of their society. In this sense, they would have found little disagreement with the most orthodox spokesmen of their society. And in this choice they moved significantly closer to the orthodoxy of the authorities.

---

del 1571" in Alberi, *Relazioni degli ambasciatori veneti al Senato*, 5:234, where he notes, "di cavalleria francese il re si è servito d'italiani e di raitri").

Even if we found that the French king knighted Alvise di Zuanfrancesco Priuli and could prove that Alvise was present in Venice in 1572 and 1573, we still would not know whether he seriously presented himself as the messiah to Lunardo and his friends. Perhaps he was simply jesting, playing on the heightened credibilities of the millenarians? What matters is Lunardo's belief that the man encountered in the Basilica San Marco was a descendant of the Priuli and the Cornaro, and it is this angle of analysis that I stress here.

21. Sanuto, *I diarii*, vol. 10, cols. 764–765.

22. On Francesco Priuli, see Pio Paschini, *Un amico del cardinale Pole: Alvise Priuli* (Rome: Pontificio seminario romano maggiore, 1921).

23. Weinstein, *Savonarola and Florence: Prophecy and Patriotism in the Renaissance*.

The war of Cyprus took its toll on the evangelical community as well. Certainly by 1572 there was much talk of heresy not only in the Collegio but in the streets as well. In the summer of that year on the Rialto, the rumor that fresh charges for heresy had been presented to the Inquisition leaked out and then swept through the shops that crowded the bridge, even before the arrests began. Perhaps the shop-keeper Bernardino, a haberdasher on the Rialto bridge, had boasted too freely of his denunciation against the talkative Prospero, a cap vendor who came to the bridge daily to hawk his wares. More likely, it was the visit of an "official" of the Holy Office to Prospero's home, ostensibly to buy half a dozen caps, that alerted neighbors and others that Prospero was in danger. Women who lived nearby (Prospero was away from home) warned him, and he wisely took the opportunity to leave the city for the fairs, in the hope that the matter would simply blow over. Other shopkeepers expressed their outrage at Bernardino's action. The Rialto, after all, with its constant confluence of foreigners and merchants, had traditionally been tolerant of religious diversity. The denunciation of a poor vendor did not sit well with those who put commerce far above religious concerns. Vincenzo, a mercer with a shop on the bridge, was one of several who made his disapproval plain, even asserting that "if he had known who the denounced man was, he would have warned him so that he might escape."[24] Yet disapproval of the accusation brought little protection. It was a clear sign that Venice had become a less tolerant place. In late July, two weeks after the de-nunciation, Prospero was back in Venice; he was soon picked up on the piazza San Marco and taken off to jail. Six weeks later Battista Amai, another heretic, a man for whose youngest son Prospero had stood as godfather some three years earlier, was arrested on the Rialto bridge—again, despite warnings that he was in danger. But sympathy for the religious beliefs of these men was not widespread. When the authori-ties grabbed Battista, this itinerant mercer and enameler who spent much of his time at Rialto was dragged off to prison amid jeers calling for the destruction of "luterani."[25] There can be no doubt that the

24. "Si savesse chi fusse el denonciato, gli lo adverteria, acciò che'l scampasse" (ASV, *Sant'Uffizio*, b. 33, doss. "Contra Prosperum Capellarium et Battista Amai dalle Bam-bine" testimony of Bernardino, 12 July 1572). The mercer Camillo also warned Prospero to flee; see Camillo's testimony of 21 October. The denunciation was presented on 11 July. On the visit of the "offizial" to Prospero's home, see Prospero's interrogation of 4 July.

25. "Dum duceretur in carceribus populus clamabat, 'Bisogna destruzer i lutherani'" (ASV, *Sant'Uffizio*, b. 33, doss. "Contra Prosperum Capellarium," report of the arresting officer, 20 September 1572). Prospero's arrest was reported on 2 August.

crowd's hostility to Prospero and Battista was inflamed by the experience of a war that made Venetians far more suspicious of the hidden enemies at home.

But it was the plague that put the piety of the Venetians to its severest test. Indeed, not since the War of the League of Cambrai had the morality of the city's inhabitants been so clearly called into question. Even the evangelical physician Girolamo Donzellino, now back in Padua practicing medicine, surmised that the plague was divine punishment for human sins, and he saw prayer as an essential remedy for deliverance from the epidemic.[26] The patriarch Giovanni Trevisan was equally convinced that the epidemic was a manifestation of God's wrath for the vices of the Venetians, and he made his belief clear in a decree that "all should attend mass, preparing themselves by fasting on Wednesdays, Fridays, and Saturdays, that they should pray privately in their homes, their shops, or in the streets, and kneel and recite the Lord's Prayer and the Hail Mary three times a day." And he enforced the Tridentine canon that made religion more somber than ever, by prohibiting "vain or profane conversations, strolling, noise making, and shouting" in the churches of the city.[27] It was a view that was undoubtedly widely shared. A poem from the period—we do not know the author—saw the plague as a purely religious affair. No medical remedy would work. Fasts, prayers, vigils, and alms were recommended. And the poet included in his list of sins his fellow Venetian's traditional tolerance of religious nonconformity. Of course God was angry. We have failed to denounce to the Church those who do not go to communion.[28]

The response to the epidemic cut through all levels of Venetian society. The Senate organized a series of public processions in hopes of the collective expiation of the sins believed responsible for the tragedy, and it was during the ravages of this epidemic that the Venetian government undertook a vow to build a church to the Redeemer, if the city were delivered. The completion of Palladio's Church of the Redentore is evidence of the deeply Catholic piety of these years. On a popular level, there was a noted increase in the devotion to San Rocco, the patron saint of those suffering from the plague. And the printer Pietro

26. Preto, *Peste e società*, 62–63. Preto includes an excerpt from Donzellino's *Discorso nobilissimo e dottissimo preservativo et curativo della peste* (Venice, 1577) on 180–183.

27. Cited in Orazio Pugliese, ed., *Venezia e la peste (1348/1797)* (Venice: Marsilio, 1979), 138.

28. Preto, *Peste e società*, 80–81.

de Faris published a prayer sheet—at the urging of certain *gentildonne*, he claimed—which would protect against the plague those who recited its prayers several times a day. The practice was no doubt a common one, though Pietro's version brought him to the attention of the Inquisition because of his superstition that it was possible to manipulate stellar influences for medical benefits. He advised an invocation to the Virgin Mary as a means of tapping the benefits of the stars.[29]

For the millenarians, already a small group, the plague's devastation was especially direct. By 1578, in the sect of Benedetto Corazzaro apparently only the cobbler Domenego survived. Benedetto Florian—and in all likelihood many of his other companions—died in the plague. Domenego, now very old and suffering from palsy, was an isolated dreamer, the last surviving member of Benedetto's millenarian sect. Nonetheless, as before he was able to visit the shops of a few fellow artisans, including that of the master sword smith Piero who worked in the Spaderia (a narrow street virtually in the shadow of the Basilica San Marco) where he shared, quietly now, some of his prophetic ideas with whoever might listen.[30]

But the climate created both during and after the pestilence was hardly supportive of the evangelicals either. Because of the proximity of death, Venetians applied themselves to more regular devotions that held less room for dissenting views. Indeed, the plague seems to have been the immediate backdrop to a number of denunciations. Particularly in these years of plague, family members turned against one another, even reporting their own spouses to the Holy Office; artisans turned against their shop mates whom they too denounced to the Inquisition. Thus in 1576, one recently married Catholic made it clear to the Inquisition that he had to struggle a great deal to convince his wife, the daughter of the heretical tailor Paolo di Albori, to say her devotions. "[Her father] never taught her to pray," the young man testified, "and I have had to exert myself considerably to get her to do so. But now she says her prayers."[31] In the same year, the tailor Zorzi Gebler

29. ASV, *Sant'Uffizio*, b. 39, doss. "De Faris Pietro," testimony of 15 November 1575. On the shifts in popular piety in this period see, in addition to Preto, Paolo Ulvioni, "Cultura politica e cultura religiosa a Venezia nel secondo Cinquecento: Un bilancio," *Archivio storico italiano* 141 (1983): 591–651.

30. ASV, *Sant'Uffizio*, b. 43, doss. "De Lorenzi Domenico," testimony of 31 March and 28 June 1578.

31. "Mia mogier non vorrà dir niente per esser sua fia. E vero che lui non ghe ha mai insegnado a dir oration et ho habudo gran fadiga a farga [ = farghe] dir oration. Ma adesso la le disse" (ASV, *Sant'Uffizio*, b. 40, doss. "Paolo di Albori," testimony of 5 January 1576).

was accused of heresy by his shop companion; the mercer Bernardino Palavicino was denounced by his apprentice for keeping three Flemings in his shop—men who, it was alleged, kept a maidservant from attending mass; and a certain Roberto was denounced by his shop mate for, among other things, forcing his wife to prepare meat for him during Lent. "Many times," the shop mate asserted, "he has beaten her black, because she did not wish to cook meat for him on fast days."[32] And in 1578, when donna Bertapaia testified against her son-in-law, she first noted that her devotional practices assumed a more regular rhythm with the onset of the plague. "And in our house," she told the Holy Office, "whenever I, together with the others, say the litanies—as I have been accustomed to do with my women servants for a long time, that is, since the beginning of the plague until now—[Guglielmo] makes fun of us."[33]

In general, it was the wife who brought the denunciation against her husband or who was at least willing to testify against him. In a trial from 1577 Valeria, the wife of a man originally denounced by her step-father, freely offered testimony against her husband who had spoken out against sacerdotal confession, the giving of alms for the dead, and the effort to prohibit the printing and selling of certain works. "[My husband] told me the first night that he slept with me," she revealed to the Inquisition, "that I had had my eyes closed until that time and that he wished to open them for me and make me know the true light and the true faith." The following year Laura, the wife of a cobbler who worked on the piazza San Marco, denounced her husband for heresy.[34] In 1581 it was again a cobbler's wife who spoke against her husband, Franceschin. In her testimony about a man she had not seen for ten years, she spoke of how he had attempted to impose his religious beliefs on her and their children. He took down the images of the Madonna that she had placed in their house, opposed her teaching their children to make the sign of the cross, forced her to prepare and to eat meat on

32. "Et molte volte l'ha fatto nera battendola perché non li vol cosinar carne in giorni prohibiti" (ibid., b. 43, doss. "Roberto fiamengo," testimony of 1 May 1576); see also b. 40, doss. "Gebler Giorgio," denunciation of 7 April 1576 and doss. "Palavicino Bernardo et al.," denunciation of 1 April 1576.

33. "Et quando in casa nostra io o altri dicemo le litanie, come qualche volte usavo di dire per longo tempo con le mie massare, cioè dal principio del contagio sino a l'altro giorno, costui se ne ride" (ASV, *Sant'Uffizio*, b. 43, doss. "Cromeri Guglielmo," testimony of 30 May 1578).

34. "El mi disse anchora la prima notte che'l dormì con mi che io haveva fino alhora imbedadi gl'occhi et che'l voleva aprirmeli et farme conoscer el vero lume et la vera fede" (ASV, *Sant'Uffizio*, b. 47, doss. "Capuano Alvise," testimony of 18 July 1577); ibid., b. 42, doss. "Paese Giovanni," testimony of 5 May 1576.

fast days, beat her for attending confession, and taught her the Lord's Prayer. Asked to recite this prayer before the Holy Office, she did so, adding that Franceschin "wanted me to teach this same [prayer] to the children."[35] Holy battles between husband and wife—battles that had perhaps been simmering for a long time—came to the fore with the plague and the intensification of Catholic piety it entailed. In 1582 Caterina, the wife of Valentino, a furrier, denounced her husband, informing the Inquisition that "last Easter . . . because I had been to mass in my parish, San Zuane Nuovo, my husband—for this reason—began to spit on me when I came home." And as their differences continued, the husband refused to sleep with her.[36]

By the late 1570s, therefore, neither household nor shop was the haven for heretics that it had been at midcentury or even as late as the 1560s. In the 1560s such minuscule institutions of family and work often afforded especially safe settings for the evangelizing of friends, neighbors, and fellow workers. During the next decade, though less extroverted, they nonetheless remained centers of heretical discussion, clandestine foci of heretical activity. But by the late 1570s even these centers had begun to come apart. The pressures on them were too great. For one thing, both family and shop became targets of the Counter-Reformation offensive. Thus Carlo Borromeo not only argued that fathers had an obligation to ensure that their wives and children remained devout Catholics, he also maintained that the shop was to be a pious institution, with the shop master disciplining any apprentice or journeyman who failed to go to communion or to give his confessions at Easter.[37] For another, both the war and the plague made people less tolerant. Fellow workers and even family members who had once turned a deaf ear to the religious views of their spouses or masters seemed increasingly reluctant to do so. The stakes, in a time of plague, were too high.

The result was a world in which the evangelicals grew largely isolated from one another as well. Again and again in the trials from this

35. "Voleva che insegnasse questo medismo alli figlioli" (ASV, *Sant'Uffizio*, b. 48, doss. "Franceschino da Trieste," testimony of 17 August 1581).

36. "Il giorno de Pasqua de la ressuretione del nostro Signor proximo passato, perché io era stata a comunicarmi nella mia parochia di San Zuane Nuovo, el ditto mio marito per questo quando fui tornata a casa, el mi comenzò a spudermi drio" (ASV, *Sant'Uffizio*, b. 49, doss. "Valentino da Lubiana," testimony of 19 April 1582). Caterina also testified that her husband had beaten her on several occasions.

37. Carlo Borromeo, Litterae pastorales in *Acta ecclesiae mediolanesis*, vol. 3, col. 666.

period, those accused of heresy appeared to stand entirely alone. When four artisans testified against the tailor Paolo di Albori in 1576, not one of these accusers was able to identify anyone who shared the views of this heretical tailor. The following year Costantino Tessera, a Greek gold-leaf worker who lived "alla latina," was accused of heresy by no less than five individuals, but again no fellow heretics—the harvest of the heterodox that inquisitors hoped their proceedings would bring— were uncovered. And in 1580 the dyer Battista Grisolan, an immigrant worker who came to Venice via Lyon from Vicenza, was the object of considerable consternation among a large number of textile workers who lived in his parish of San Fosca. Although his wife may have shared his convictions, Battista too, like Paolo di Albori and Costantino Tessera, was isolated. Indeed, almost three out of every four individuals brought to trial for heresy in the decade after 1575 were tried alone, with no apparent connections to other heretics.[38]

To be sure, the number may be misleading. By their very nature, heretics sought to conceal their ties to one another. Nonetheless the contrast with the 1550s and 1560s, when well over half of those implicated in heresy were part of an identifiable group of dissenters in Venice, is telling. The heretical world of sixteenth-century Venice had begun to come undone. And the attention of the Inquisition had begun to shift elsewhere. In the early 1580s the papal nuncio Bolognetti recalled the time "when it was necessary to do a considerable amount [against heresy]," whereas in his own time, "nothing of consideration has been heard of unless from certain little villages located on the borders [of the republic], and not even in these cases have the accusations been verified."[39]

38. ASV, *Sant'Uffizio*, b. 40, doss. "Paolo di Albori"; b. 41, doss. "Tessera Costantino"; and b. 46, doss. "Grisolan Gio: Battista." On trials against individuals in this decade, see John Martin, "In God's Image: Artisans and Heretics in Counter-Reformation Venice" (Ph.D. diss., Harvard University, 1982), 248.

39. Bolognetti, "Dello Stato et forma delle cose ecclesiastiche nel dominio dei signori venetiani," 286.

# The Final Executions

*By the grace of God there are no heretics in this city.*
Paolo Sarpi, 1622

POENITENTIA.

Ceruetus. Bernardinus Ochinus. Ioannes Caluinus.

M yths have lives of their own. Traveling through Italy in the 1570s, Claude Banière—after visiting Naples, Rome, Florence, and Genoa—came to settle in Venice. Perhaps Claude (an alchemist from the Savoy) had heard it was a particularly tolerant place. In any case, he was quickly disillusioned when, shortly after his arrival, he was denounced for his Calvinist beliefs. The whole affair took him by surprise; as he explained to the inquisitor, he had been of the view that Venice "was a free country where each could live as he wished."[1]

Even after the wave of repression that Facchinetti unleashed in the 1560s and the apparent ascendancy of Catholicism that followed upon the heels of war and plague in the next decade, the idea that Venice offered its subjects a greater measure of freedom than did most other European states enjoyed considerable currency. It was in the 1580s, for example, that the French philosopher Jean Bodin would write, "One can live there with the greatest freedom."[2] And early in the seventeenth century the myth would find its most forceful proponent in fra Paolo Sarpi. Defending Venetian customs during the crisis of the papal interdict of 1606–1607, this Servite friar became a remarkably articulate spokesman for the tradition of Venetian liberty.[3] Sarpi was not isolated. Though a commoner, he was associated with a group of men known collectively as the *giovani*—often younger nobles, whose political vision was deeply republican and who, in the 1570s, came to hope for the recovery of many of the republic's customary freedoms that they believed had been eroded over the course of the century. In particular, they sought to curtail the authority of the Council of Ten that, since

1. "Libera patria de poter viver ciascun in modo suo" (ASV, *Sant'Uffizio*, b. 42, doss. "Soccino Cornelio, Textor Claudio," testimony of 15 January 1579). See also ibid., b. 59, doss. "Claudio (francese) Savoia." For an excellent discussion of Claude Banière [ = Claudio Textor] and Cornelio Sozzini, see Stella, *Dall'anabattismo al socinianesimo*, 144–187.

2. Bodin, *Colloquium of the Seven about Secrets of the Sublime*, 3.

3. The best introduction to Sarpi remains Gaetano Cozzi, *Paolo Sarpi tra Venezia e l'Europa* (Turin: Einaudi, 1979), 235–281; but see also Bouwsma, *Venice and the Defense of Republican Liberty*, chaps. 8, 9.

---

*Opposite.* This illustration from Luca Bertelli's *Typus Ecclesiae Catholicae*, published in Venice in 1574, shows the close interplay of the redemptive and repressive characteristics of the Counter-Reformation church. While penance is held up as an ideal, four "heretics" are drowned: Servetus, Ochino, Viret, and Calvin. (Galeria degli Uffizi)

the War of the League of Cambrai, had concentrated power in the hands of a small number of wealthy patrician families. In the view of the *giovani*, the traditional authority of the Senate had been eclipsed to the detriment of the republic. Through a series of constitutional maneuvers in 1582 and 1583, they enacted a correction of the Ten and restored power to the Senate. The republicanism of the *giovani* caused repercussions in the religious life of the city as well. They were by temperament antipapal and sought to check Rome's ever-growing claims to jurisdiction in Venetian territory.[4] On this matter in particular the Venetian doge Nicolò da Ponte appears to have offered leadership.

Even before his election in 1578, da Ponte was well known as an anticlerical. In 1560 Pope Pius V, recalling Nicolò's defense of a prominent Venetian heretic years earlier, had refused to recognize him as the republic's ambassador to the curia. Da Ponte acquired his reputation both from his long-standing efforts to defend the activity of Venetian printers and publishers against papal interference and from the fact that his own brother Andrea was the most outspoken of the patrician heretics in the city. Upon news of his election, his reputation seemed confirmed when the papal nuncio Alvise da Capua remarked that he found him "little disposed and perhaps even hostile to the Church's jurisdiction." But Nicolò's anticlericalism—and this would prove typical of the *giovani*—by no means entailed his unwillingness to crack down on heresy when necessary. Once, in the early 1560s, he took a crucial role in the decision to have two Anabaptists burned for their beliefs. And in 1578, largely as part of his effort to assure the pope that the Venetian government would be cooperative in matters of heresy, he permitted the extradition of Cornelio Sozzini (Lelio's eccentric brother) to Rome. "I hope," he told the papal nuncio after agreeing to this de-

---

4. On the *giovani*, see esp. Cozzi, *Il doge Nicolò Contarini*, the best discussion of this group (not a political party). Martin J.C. Lowry's essay, "The Reform of the Council of Ten, 1582–3: An Unsettled Problem?" *Studi veneziani* 13 (1971): 275–310, shows how little we know about the *giovani*, though he presents the issues rather more schematically than Cozzi does. The literature on Venice often reduces sixteenth- and seventeenth-century political history to conflicts between *giovani* and *vecchi*. On the risks of such an approach, which goes back to Leopold von Ranke (*Venezianischen Geschichte* [Leipzig: Duncker, 1878]) and is exemplified by Bouwsma (*Venice and the Defense of Republican Liberty*), see Grubb, "When Myths Lose their Power." For a sophisticated approach to Renaissance republican ideology that might apply to Venice, see John Najemy, *Corporatism and Consensus in Florentine Electoral Politics, 1280–1400* (Chapel Hill: University of North Carolina Press, 1982).

cision, "that His Holiness will see by our actions that we are more cooperative than he seems to believe."[5]

Nonetheless—while da Ponte was doge and perhaps in keeping with the views of the *giovani*—the Inquisition showed certain signs of leniency. To be sure, men like Claude Banière who had trouble keeping their views to themselves risked a trial. Thus in 1583 when the silk worker Achille Rubini began to talk too openly of his religious beliefs, he was brought to trial for heresy.[6] And in August 1578 Girolamo Donzellino, the Brescian physician who had been so active in Venetian evangelical circles since the 1540s, was sent back to jail after a fifteen-month period of freedom during which he was permitted to care for the victims of the plague.[7] But in general the business of the Inquisition slowed in these years, and not a single heretic was sent to his death.[8]

In 1585 the situation changed quickly. Not only was the new doge Pasquale Cicogna admired for his piety and well respected in Rome, there was a new pope as well: the Franciscan Felice Peretti, a gardener's son and a former inquisitor in Venice who took the name Sixtus V. This pope proved as rigorous as Ghislieri in his oversight of the Inquisition. Perhaps his most lasting contribution in this area came in 1588, in the midst of his far-reaching reorganization of the Vatican bureaucracy; he decided to make the Inquisition one of the fifteen secretariats of the Curia—the Congregation of the Holy Roman and Universal Inquisition or Holy Office—and thus to continue the process of centralizing jurisdiction over heresy in Rome. But his zeal was consequential in Venice as well. Old cases were reopened, and every possible effort was made to eradicate even the final and isolated remnants of what had once been a movement for religious reform.[9]

Our information from this period is fragmentary. But the general

---

5. Cited in Stella, *Dall'anabattismo al socinianesimo*, 157. The remark of da Capua is reported in Stella, *Chiesa e stato nelle relazioni dei nunzi pontifici a Venezia*, 15. On da Ponte see ibid., 12–16; and William Archer Brown, "Nicolò da Ponte: The Political Career of a Sixteenth-Century Venetian Patrician" (Ph.D. diss., New York University, 1974).

6. ASV, *Sant'Uffizio*, b. 50, doss. "Robino Achille," denunciation of 25 April 1583.

7. Nicolas Davidson, "Rome and the Venetian Inquisition in the Sixteenth Century," *The Journal of Ecclesiastical History* 39 (1988): 28; and Marie-Louise Portmann, "Der Venezianer Artz Girolamo Donzellini (etwa 1527–1587) und seine Beziehungen zu Basler Gelehrten," *Gesnerus* 30 (1973): 5–6.

8. See fig. 1 on the business of the Inquisition in chapter 7.

9. On Pasquale Cicogna, see Bouwsma, *Venice and the Defense of Republican Liberty*, 267–268; on Pope Sixtus V (Felice Peretti), Pastor, *The History of the Popes*, vol. 21.

drift of things is clear. On 10 April 1587 Donzellino, aged beyond his sixty years, was taken out to sea and drowned—in the eyes of the Inquisition he was known to be unrepentant, a recidivist, and therefore deserved this ultimate punishment.[10] But the madness had just begun. The previous night, Claude Banière (now known in Venice as Claudio Textor) had been arrested. Rumors of Donzellino's execution doubtless frightened him. He had reason for concern. The wheels of justice turned with unusual rapidity. On 17 April he too was drowned by the Venetian authorities. About two weeks later the Venetian Holy Office reinitiated a proceeding that, in an earlier time, it might well have forgotten: the case of the silk worker Achille Rubini. On 31 July he was executed by drowning.[11] On the same day five women—Laura Spadoni, Orsola Bortot, Valeria Brugnalesco, Splandiana Mariano, and Elisabetta Giantis, having been found guilty of witchcraft—were publicly mocked, chased, and whipped, as they stumbled during a forced run from the Rialto to the piazza San Marco, where they were put on display.[12] In August Pietro Longo, a book trader, was arrested for heresy and book smuggling; at the very end of January 1588 he became the last of the Venetian heretics to be executed. He too was drowned.[13] That the Inquisition turned each of these men over to the secular arm was certainly justified on technical grounds. All had been tried earlier, and inquisitorial law made it clear that such individuals could be put to death as *relapsi*, or backsliders.[14]

10. Salvatore Bongi, *Annali di Gabriele Giolito de' Ferrari da Trino, stampatore in Venezia* (Rome, 1890–1897), 1:351.

11. ASV, *Sant'Uffizio*, b. 59, doss. "Claudio (francese) Savoia," report of execution, 18 April 1587; ibid., b. 50, doss. "Robino Achille," report of execution, 31 July 1587.

12. Ibid., b. 59, doss. "Spadon Laura," "Bortot Orsola," "Brugnalesco Valeria, Mariano Splandiana," and "Giantis Elisabetta," all sentences of 31 July 1587. Whipping seems to have been a relatively common punishment for women convicted of witchcraft in early modern Italy; see John Tedeschi, "The Question of Magic and Witchcraft in Two Unpublished Inquisitorial Manuals of the Seventeenth Century," *Proceedings of the American Philosophical Association* 131, no. 1 (1987): 103–104.

13. Grendler, *The Roman Inquisition and the Venetian Press*, 188. There is no record of Longo's execution in the Venetian archives, but Grendler reports certain evidence that Longo was drowned.

14. Inquisitorial law specified cases for releasing a convicted heretic to the secular arm for execution. Death at the stake (or by drowning, we might add) faced three categories of offenders listed by John Tedeschi: "the obstinate and unrepentant who refused to be reconciled to the Church; the relapsed, those who had suffered a previous sentence for formal heresy; and individuals convicted of attempting to overturn such central doctrines of the Church as the Virgin Birth and the full divinity of Christ" (*The Prosecution of Heresy*, 151).

The technical aspects of the law are hardly enough to account for this final moment of institutional violence. By the 1580s the heretical community in Venice was a shadow of what it had been in earlier decades. The Anabaptists had been extirpated; the millenarians tamed; and the evangelicals, at least those who were committed to the ideals of the Protestant Reformation, reduced to a few isolated figures. Certainly they offered very little threat to Venetian Catholicism. What seems to have been at work was a bureaucratic rigor entirely out of touch with local realities. More and more of the Holy Office's authority was centered in Rome; the reasoning that caused the authorities to send these four final heretics to their deaths is not clear. Already in the early 1580s, the central concern of the Inquisition had begun to shift away from heresy to manifestations of witchcraft and to a variety of other superstitious beliefs and practices.

It is true that these heretics, isolated both from one another and from Venetian society as a whole, shared an enormous amount of self-confidence in their views—a conviction that their beliefs, even if now officially unorthodox, were justified. Donzellino, for example, continued to correspond with Protestants abroad and to read prohibited books.[15] Nor could Achille Rubini be easily moved from his convictions. Achille first encountered evangelical ideas in the early 1570s in Vicenza, where, as he told the Inquisition, "I was consumed in reading the Bible." And like Claude, Achille placed great emphasis on one's internal life: it was what was believed on the inside that mattered. Material things were not important. "The Church is only a structure of stone and wood," he said, "and this is not the true temple of God, but the true temple is the heart."[16] Pietro Longo, whom Donzellino no doubt knew, went even further. He made something of an effort to revive the clandestine book trade that Pietro Perna had put into place a generation earlier. He was in close contact with Perna, and he traveled regularly to the Frankfurt book fairs as well as to Strasbourg, another important printing center. To be sure, he was cautious about his activities. When packing up the books he would carry back to Venice, he worked apart from the other Venetian merchants who traveled with him. One of them accused Pietro of duplicity, of pretending to be a Catholic at home and a Protestant abroad: "You have two faces," he

15. Portmann, "Der Venezianer Artz Girolamo Donzellini," 6.

16. "Io me consumavo nel legger. . . . La chiesa è solamente un tempio materiale di pietre e di legni e che questo non è il vero tempio, ma il vero tempio è nel cuore" (ASV, *Sant'Uffizio*, b. 50, doss. "Robino Achille," testimony of 30 April 1582).

said, "you present one face in your own country and another in other lands."[17]

Such deceptions did not come easily to Claude Banière. Angered by his loss of religious freedom, he told Marcello de Juliis da Salerno, a fellow alchemist who was staying with him in the parish of Santi Apostoli, "The Inquisition is nothing but an extreme tyranny."[18] Later when his house was searched and several heretical titles by such reformers as Calvin and Beza were found with a variety of alchemical texts by Raymund Lull and Paracelsus, among others, Claude admitted his frustration at not feeling free to express his beliefs. Not, he explained to the Inquisition, that he believed there was anything wrong in keeping such books. "Since from the very beginning I was brought up on the doctrines contained in these works, that is, according to the way Calvin teaches the Gospel in France and Germany, I think it is a good thing to keep [the books]."[19] And now caught red-handed, Claude began to express his misgivings about his earlier abjuration—misgivings that recalled Francesco Spiera's dilemma of more than a quarter-century earlier. Claude too became deeply conscious of the difference between what one did externally out of fear and obedience and what was in one's heart. Like Spiera, he was worried that his earlier abjuration might compromise his salvation; finally he admitted to his judges, "The last time I was a prisoner, I said what I did in order to get out of prison, and I am most sorry for this, and I hope Christ will have mercy on me for having abjured."[20]

In the early seventeenth century, the Venetian theologian and statesman Paolo Sarpi could write: "By the grace of God there are no heretics

17. "Tu hai due fazzie. Tu nelli paesi de l'altra ne fai a una foggia et in altri paesi a un'altra" (ibid., b. 59, doss. "Valgrisio Giorgio," testimony of 20 September 1587).

18. "L'Inquisitione non è altro che un'estrema tirannia" (ASV, *Sant'Uffizio*, b. 59, doss. "Claudio [francese] Savoia," testimony of 28 March 1587); cited also in Stella, *Dall'anabattismo al socinianesimo*, 174.

19. "Essendo instituito da la prima mia età in la dottrina compresa e conforme a questi libri sudetti secondo la dottrina de l'evangelio come insegna Calvino in Francia et Alemagna, io non posso far altro in conscientia mia di tenerla per bona" (ASV, *Sant'Uffizio*, b. 59, doss. "Claudio (francese) Savoia," testimony of 11 April 1587); cited also in Stella, *Dall'anabattismo al socinianesimo*, 183.

20. "Et io l'altra volta che fui preggione dissi altramente perché non poteva far altro per uscir de preggione et ne son pentitissimo, et spero che Christo me havera misericordia d'haver abiurato el contrario de quel che credeva" (ASV, *Sant'Uffizio* b. 59, doss. "Claudio (francese) Savoia," testimony of 18 April 1587); cited also in Stella, *Dall'anabattismo al socinianesimo*, 185.

in this city, and for some decades there has been no trial for formal heresy, but only for the licentiousness of some who have spoken of the faith without due reverence and understanding, and for a few cases of herbal magic and sorcery."[21]

Considerable irony attends Sarpi's defensive observation about the piety of his fellow Venetians, for his own faith or orthodoxy was a matter of some suspicion, and not only in Rome. Sir Henry Wotton, the English ambassador to Venice, called him "a Protestant in a monk's habit," and many of Sarpi's Calvinist correspondents in France took him for one of their own.[22] While we shall probably never know Sarpi's personal convictions, many of his attitudes—an emphasis on the importance of grace in salvation, a stress on Scripture, a deep skepticism about the universal claims of the Roman church—suggest an affinity with the evangelical currents that had characterized Venetian spirituality since the early sixteenth century.[23] This is not to say that Sarpi had much in common with evangelicals such as Girolamo Donzellino and Pietro Longo who were executed in the late 1580s. On the contrary, he explicitly repudiated any public effort to establish a Protestant church in Venice.[24] His evangelism, like that of patricians such as Andrea Morosini, Nicolò Contarini, and Leonardo Donà, was an expression of personal piety.

Nonetheless, these men shared a certain openness to the Protestant world, both politically and intellectually.[25] It is even possible that their personal religious views had a part in the fiercely independent posture that Venice assumed in its relations with Rome in the last two decades of the sixteenth and the first two decades of the seventeenth century.[26] But we should not exaggerate the nature of their evangelical commitments. On the one hand, the decisive factors at work in the growing tensions between Venice and Rome were juridical, fiscal, and political. At issue were navigational rights in the Adriatic, the incorporation of

---

21. Sarpi, "In materia di crear novo inquisitor di Venezia," in *Opere*, ed. Gaetano Cozzi and Luisa Cozzi (Milan: R. Ricciardi, 1969), 1210 (the first phrase is this chapter's epigraph).

22. Pastor, *History of the Popes*, 25:131. On Sarpi and his French correspondents, see Cozzi, *Paolo Sarpi tra Venezia e l'Europa*, 235–281.

23. Bouwsma, *Venice and the Defense of Republican Liberty*, 583–591.

24. David Wootton, *Paolo Sarpi between Renaissance and Enlightenment* (Cambridge: Cambridge University Press, 1983), 93–104.

25. Cozzi, *Il doge Nicolò Contarini*, esp. chap. 1.

26. Such is the thesis of Cozzi's *Il doge Nicolò Contarini* and of Bouwsma's *Venice and the Defense of Republican Liberty*. On the limits of this view, see discussion in note 4 above.

Ferrara into the papal states, the extensive properties held by the Church within Venetian territories at a time of economic hardship for the Venetian ruling class, and Rome's claims to clerical immunity from lay jurisdiction for all priests and religious in the republic.[27] On the other hand, the *giovani* (even if they were evangelicals) had made their peace with Catholicism, a faith whose ideals and traditions seemed to them an essential support for the hierarchical arrangements of Venetian society and a guarantor of order; they explicitly attacked Protestantism as a source of political upheaval.[28] As Sarpi wrote: "The Venetian republic has always held that the most important support for all government and authority comes from true religion and piety. By the singular grace of God Venice was born, educated and has developed to the present day in practice of the true worship of God."[29] Thus the evangelism of the Venetian patriciate, in itself, never implied an underlying disagreement with Rome over matters of heresy. Indeed many Venetian patricians, even those who were evangelical in their personal piety, found little contradiction between their personal beliefs and the reforming programs of Tridentine Rome. What made them bristle was not religious reform or doctrine but Rome's attempt to encroach on the traditional rights of Venice and the Venetian church.

But what about the religious beliefs of non-nobles that had been such a central concern to the Venetian Inquisition in the middle decades of the sixteenth century? Here, the history of evangelism and of heresy more generally remains elusive. The records of the Inquisition do not allow us to assess either the extent or the nature of religious dissent in the last decade of the sixteenth and the first two decades of the seventeenth centuries: virtually no trial records survive from 1592 to 1615.[30] Even if they were available, they might not be useful. From 1585 on, with the Protestant Reformation a fait accompli, inquisitors occupied themselves with an assault on popular beliefs and practices of

27. Aldo Stella, "La proprietà ecclesiastica nella Repubblica di Venezia dal secolo XV al XVIII," *Nuova rivista storica* 42 (1958): 50–77; Grendler, *The Roman Inquisition and the Venetian Press*, 201–205.

28. On Catholicism's role in preserving the social order, see Cozzi, *Il doge Nicolò Contarini*, 41. In *Venice and the Defense of Republican Liberty*, Bouwsma sees no conflict between the *giovani's* broad concerns on the one hand and their fear of Protestantism's possible political consequences on the other; see his comments on the writings of Andrea Morosini (559), Nicolò Contarini (562), and Enrico Davila (568).

29. Cited in Wootton, *Paolo Sarpi*, 119.

30. ASV, *Indice 303: Santo Ufficio Processi (Tre Savi all'eresia)* has records of only a few trials from these years.

magic and witchcraft that became in Venice, as elsewhere in Italy, the primary business of the Inquisition.[31] During the years of jurisdictional conflict with the elites, the Venetian government found itself less willing to accommodate Rome's concerns over heresy. In 1595 the Great Council even acted to place the election of the three lay *assistenti* to the Inquisition in the hands of the Senate (their appointments had formerly been controlled by the doge)—legislation explicitly designed to reduce Rome's capacity to prosecute heretics within Venetian territory.[32]

The shifting behavior of the Inquisition should not lead us to suspect that popular heresies no longer existed. Certainly the foreign communities of Protestant merchants—especially the German, Dutch, and English—made it likely that Venetians would still have the opportunity to learn about the teachings of Luther and Calvin. In addition, traffic in illicit books brought many Protestant texts to Venetian readers.[33] In many wills from this period an evangelical emphasis was apparent, though the Augustinian stress on grace was often balanced by an invocation to the saints and by a bequest to monastic institution.[34] Perhaps this equivocation reflected the fears the Inquisition had instilled in the Venetians; perhaps too it stemmed from Nicodemite attitudes that were so widespread in the late sixteenth century. But many of the heresies in this period were new. We can only imagine the conversations in the early 1580s between Venetians and travelers such as Menocchio, the Friulian miller who developed a spiritualist and materialist cosmology that led to his conviction by the Inquisition of Concordia and Aquileia in 1599. A generation later the itinerant jester and distiller Costantino Saccardino, who was to be hanged for heresy in Bologna in 1622, visited Venice and tried to convince other workers and artisans that religion was a ruse forced on them by their rulers.

31. E. William Monter and John Tedeschi, "Toward a Statistical Profile of the Italian Inquisitions, Sixteenth to Eighteenth Centuries," in Gustav Henningsen and John Tedeschi, eds., *The Inquisition in Early Modern Europe* (DeKalb: Northern Illinois University Press, 1986), 134. On this same tendency in Venice, see Ruth Martin, *Witchcraft and the Inquisition in Venice*, 259–261. Mary O'Neil is completing a study of witchcraft in Modena; for preliminary results, see her "Magical Healing, Love Magic and the Inquisition in Late Sixteenth-Century Modena," in Stephen Haliczer, ed., *Inquisition and Society in Early Modern Europe* (London: Croom Helm, 1987), 88–114.

32. Grendler, *The Roman Inquisition and the Venetian Press*, 219.

33. Ibid., 280–285; see also Grendler, "Books for Sarpi: The Smuggling of Prohibited Books into Venice during the Interdict of 1606–1607," in S. Bertelli and G. Ramakus, eds., *Essays Presented to Myron Gilmore* (Florence: La Nuova Italia, 1978), 105–114.

34. O.M.T. Logan, "Grace and Justification: Some Italian Views of the Sixteenth and Early Seventeenth Centuries," *Journal of Ecclesiastical History* 20 (1969): 67–78.

"You're baboons if you believe in them," he said. "Princes want you to believe, so that they can have their way, but . . . finally the whole dovecote [Costantino's metaphor for the popular classes] has opened its eyes."[35] These examples suggest that certain ideas of materialism and libertinism came to replace evangelism as the popular "heresies" of this period, but we must admit that we still know next to nothing about popular religious culture in these years.

Nonetheless, we do know that the atmosphere or conditions that permitted ordinary Venetians in the sixteenth century to dream of religious reform no longer existed. The heresy trials, the executions, the exile of many of the most important leaders had eroded all hope that such a movement would ever succeed. When, shortly after the lifting of the papal interdict in 1607, several foreign Protestants thought that Venice might be brought into the Protestant camp and even sent representatives to try to work out such a "reformation" through the mediation of Paolo Sarpi, they were quickly disillusioned. Yes, many in Venice accepted the value of the teachings of Luther and Calvin, but few believed it necessary or advisable to abandon the structure of the Catholic church.[36] The era in which hope for a fundamental change seemed realistic had come to an end, even as Venice grew more tolerant. In the early seventeenth century, the Venetian Inquisition never even bothered to investigate the activities of a well-known group of noble libertines and atheists, who established the Accademia degli Incogniti in 1630.[37]

Like republicanism with which it was often associated, evangelism proved to be extremely malleable. There may well have been continuities between the evangelical thought of Gasparo Contarini in the early sixteenth century and the ideals of Sarpi nearly a hundred years later; there may even have been affinities between the thought of both these figures and the republican ethos of Venice.[38] But we ought not to con-

35. Cited in Carlo Ginzburg, "The Dovecote Has Opened Its Eyes: Popular Conspiracy in Seventeenth-Century Italy," in Gustav Henningsen and John Tedeschi eds., *The Inquisition in Early Modern Europe*, 193. On the now celebrated figure of Menocchio, see Ginzburg, *The Cheese and the Worms*; and Andrea del Col, ed., *Domenico Scandella detto Menocchio: I processi dell'Inquisizione* (Pordenone: Biblioteca dell'Immagine, 1990).

36. Wootton, *Paolo Sarpi*, 93–104.

37. Giorgio Spini, *Ricerca dei libertini: La teoria dell'impostura delle religioni nel Seicento italiano* (Rome: Editrice Universale di Roma, 1950), 139–163.

38. Bouwsma argued thus in *Venice and the Defense of Republican Liberty*.

clude from such linkages that the content and significance of evangelism were ever in any way fixed. On the contrary, the pervasiveness of evangelical ideas (much like the pervasiveness of republican ideas) lay in their flexibility and in their openness to diverse interpretation. Just as the *giovani* and their oligarchic opponents, who had long dominated the Council of Ten and favored a close association with the papacy, pressed separate claims to represent the Venetian republican tradition, so the men and women who called for a reformation of the Church in Venice and those who stressed the importance of a purely personal and interior reform of the individual stood, equally, in the broad currents of Renaissance evangelism.

In religion, as in politics, class appears to have been the decisive factor in shaping the interpretation of tradition. Evangelical ideals, as I have argued, attracted a broad cross section of the Venetian population: patricians and *popolani*, rich and poor, clerical and lay. But as we have seen, the social and political experiences of their new adherents often transformed the original message. In the late 1530s and the early 1540s, under the influences of both the Protestant reformers and a number of the Italian *spirituali*, a more dogmatic and a more civic evangelism emerged that challenged the basic assumptions of Venetian Catholicism. Yet men like Francesco Donà, the doge of Venice from 1545 to 1553, who might well have been sympathetic with the more individualistic ideas of reform, did not hesitate to cooperate with Rome in the persecution of heresy and assisted in the critical reorganization of the Venetian tribunal of the Roman Inquisition in 1547.

But there were forces at work that not even the Inquisition could contain. The rapid expansion of manufactures and the intensification of investments by the Venetian nobility in properties on the mainland called many of the traditional notions about hierarchy and status into question. Elite artisans and professionals especially experienced an erosion of their privileges and standing. Accordingly they turned to evangelical teachings in order to recover a more egalitarian and open world that was slipping away, and they crafted an evangelical vision that was far more consequential for the public practice of religion than was the evangelism of many members of the Venetian patriciate. Underlying their efforts were the close trading ties that Venice maintained with Germany, the city's large publishing and printing industry, and the steady arrival of immigrants and refugees who came to Venice with the hope of finding the freedoms denied to them in their homelands.

The forces at work in cultural life were more complex than in the economic sphere: they included a tradition of active lay participation in the religious life of the city and a certain intimacy with the sacred; a measure of cultural autonomy in informal settings such as the shop and the tavern, places that were often beyond the reach of secular and religious authorities alike; and, above all, the widespread availability of evangelical propaganda. This last point was critical. As long as the great meetings at Trent went on, the Italian humanists and publishers who were largely responsible for the diffusion of the evangelical teachings offered to their public a language for envisioning and for preserving the more participatory religious arrangements that had nourished the Renaissance republics. This language—derived from writers such as Luther, Calvin, and Valdés as well as from Ochino, Curione, and the anonymous authors of the *Beneficio di Cristo*—created only a small niche for itself within the religious culture of Venice. Nonetheless, evangelical teachings enjoyed a considerable following in Venice, as a generation of friars, artisans, and professionals kept alive hope for a world in which churches would be transformed into inns for preaching, and shops and *piazze* would become churches.

Yet in Venice the consolidation of such a reform never had a chance. For in the end the evangelicals were unable to garner the public support of the patriciate. Most Venetian nobles never saw the need for reform; collectively, they had considerable control over the existing ecclesiastical institutions and a vested interest in maintaining them. The bishoprics in Venetian territories were often lucrative benefices, and the Venetian patricians who occupied them frequently put loyalty to Venice ahead of Rome. In addition, the state exercised considerable fiscal and jurisdictional authority over the clergy. Even when some of the local Venetian nobles did embrace evangelical teachings, they tended to do so, as we have seen, privately. They warmed to that aspect of the evangelical message that encouraged a deepening of personal piety but kept at arm's length any aspect of such teachings that called the fundamental order into question.

Consequently, heresy in Venice had few repercussions on the institutional history of the city. Its story is rather that of a hidden history that played itself out on the level of popular ideas—both in the remarkable endurance of certain evangelical ideas and simultaneously in the gradual development of breakaway sects within the evangelical community. The first major shift came in the late 1540s and early

1550s, when several members of various evangelical circles in Venice developed a sympathy for more radical religious perspectives and decided finally to cross over and to embrace Anabaptist and even antitrinitarian ideas. Among these individuals, both social and cultural forces shaped their more radical posture. The social gap between many of the poorer artisans and the elite leadership of the republic kept the artisans from feeling comfortable with evangelical teachings that placed such confidence in the patriciate for a reform. Accordingly they forged their own small communities of faith. We have only an occasional glimpse of the culture of those men and women who chose Anabaptist beliefs; their values were both more collectivist and more egalitarian than those of the evangelicals. But the Anabaptists were far more willing than the evangelicals to subject the received teachings of Christianity to a radical critique. This culture managed to make itself felt only down to the late 1560s when its last remnants were either executed or forced into exile.

Finally, the millenarians. Here too was a sect consisting of individuals uncomfortable with the Augustinianism of the evangelicals; its social and cultural origins are still quite obscure. We know only that the members—while not as privileged as the majority of those who adhered to evangelical teachings—were nonetheless somewhat more prosperous than the Anabaptists. Yet their culture was in some sense the most archaic of all. As their dream of one sheepfold and one shepherd demonstrates, they longed for a degree of unity that was no longer possible and probably never had been, in the European world. Yet the hope that all people might worship the same god and that conflict and economic disruption might give way to peace and prosperity was (and remains) one of humanity's most deeply rooted hopes. Ultimately, the millenarians were perhaps the most fortunate of all the heretics. They suffered repression yet in the long run, by the early 1570s, were able to accommodate their beliefs to a seemingly triumphant Catholicism.

Thus even Venice—the Most Serene Republic—had its share of dissenting voices. But this study does more, I hope, than illuminate an aspect of the history of Venice that has for too long remained in the shadows. I also argue that the development of religious ideas is continually subject to both social and cultural forces. Certainly, at times one of these forces may outweigh the other. But the way in which peoples' lives are structured by the realities of their workplace, their families, and their place in the social hierarchy *as well as* the way people think about and imagine their world (both as it is and as it might be) directly shape religious beliefs and practices. The balance that results is a complex dialectic between material life and material interests that ultimately renders religious life so varied, so rich in ideals and in prejudices.

Finally, this study seeks to reshape the way we think about the history of the Reformation in Italy. Scholars no longer view that history as the simple story of the penetration into the Italian peninsula of the ideas of such reformers as Luther or Calvin. Rather they try, through careful analyses of the writings of the Italian reformers, to discern what was distinctive about the Italian Reformation. In general, they portray a reform movement that was far more radical than that of either Luther or Calvin. The Italian reformers, they argue, tended to draw more directly on the writings of such towering Renaissance humanists as Valla and Pico, with the result that they envisioned a religious culture that was more optimistic, more rational, freer from dogma (such as the traditional teachings on the Trinity), more devoted to the ethical teachings of Christianity, and ultimately more tolerant of religious diversity than were the confessional movements that had begun to take shape around Luther and Calvin. And, while this reform was never successful in any of the Italian states, it would eventually exercise considerable influence in the early modern European world through the writings of those thinkers who, fleeing Italy, established close contacts with intellectuals elsewhere in Europe. Thus the literature on the Italian Reformation places the greatest emphasis on the thought of such exiles as Bernardino Ochino, Pier Martire Vermigli, Pier Paolo Vergerio, Andrea da Ponte, Lelio and Fausto Sozzini, and Francesco Pucci.

Certainly, both views of the religious history of sixteenth-century Italy—the one that stresses the influence of Luther and Calvin as well as the one that underlines the originality of the Italian reformers— contain a measure of truth. Indeed, it is only when we take both seriously that we come close to capturing something of the complexity of the intellectual currents of the age. Yet this book moves away from a nearly exclusive concern with great ideas. My focus is deliberately closer to the ground. I listen to the many voices of artisans and merchants, conversing in their shops or in the piazza, in a particular city. The result is a view of the Italian Reformation that, in stressing the social and political contexts in which it developed, sees evangelism as its central idiom. But the evangelism that held sway proved especially malleable. For some, it was purely a matter of personal spirituality; for others, it served as the basis of the hope for a renewed Church and a more inclusive society. For still others—the Anabaptists and the anti-trinitarians—it would be remembered as a point of departure for far more radical hopes and expectations.

# Appendix:
# A Note on the Quantitative
# Study of the Inquisition

In this book I make use of as few tables and statistics as possible, but for the few that do appear and for the occasional quantitative observations—all of which I believe to be impressionistic, certainly, but nonetheless indicative of various trends—I owe some further explanation.

In recent years the quantitative study of history has become fashionable, and it was inevitable that such an approach would become part of studies devoted to the inquisitions of early modern Europe. This is particularly true of recent histories of the Spanish Inquisition, the records of which seemingly lend themselves to such analysis.[1] But in Italy quantification of inquisitorial archives has developed rather more slowly. Certain Italian intellectual traditions (historicism, for example, or the more recent interest in *microstoria*) may in part account for this, but the primary reason is the state of the documentation itself. In the Italian archives of the Roman Inquisition opened thus far (in Bologna, Imola, Modena, Naples, Pisa, Rovigo, Siena, Udine, Venice, and so on), the scholar rarely finds a convenient summary of cases. Rather he or she confronts a massive and largely undigested collection of dossiers—some containing an entire trial from start to finish, the majority

1. Jaime Contreras and Gustav Henningsen, "Forty-Four Thousand Cases of the Spanish Inquisition (1540–1700): Analysis of a Historical Data Bank," in Gustav Henningsen and John Tedeschi, eds., *The Inquisition in Early Modern Europe: Studies on Sources and Methods*, 100–129, provides a superb introduction to the quantitative history of the Spanish Inquisition. On various approaches scholars have taken to the study of the Italian and the Spanish Inquisition, see Andrea del Col and Giovanna Paolin, eds., *L'Inquisizione romana in Italia nell'età moderna: Archivi, problemi di metodo e nuove ricerche* (Rome: Ministero per i beni culturali e ambientali, 1991).

containing fragments: an investigative hearing perhaps, the interrogation of an accused individual, correspondence from Rome or one of the provincial tribunals, a denunciation, and so on. Moreover, in the case of such tribunals as Venice, the records concern not only heresy and various other forms of religious "deviance" in Venice itself but similar cases in other cities, towns, and villages that fell under the jurisdiction of the Venetian tribunal. As a consequence, the Roman Holy Office in Venice operated not only as the Inquisition for the city of Venice but also as the district court for the entire republic. Thus, it oversaw the activity of inquisitorial courts in Padua, Treviso, Verona, Rovigo, Vicenza, Udine, and Brescia. Furthermore, it was subject to a variety of directives and pressures from Rome.

About a third of the Inquisition's routine business concerned Venetian matters and I concentrated on these. Accordingly, I went through all the surviving Venetian inquisitorial records from 1547 (the year the Holy Office was reorganized in Venice) to 1586 (a point of arrival determined by the fact that by the mid–1580s the tribunal's predominant concerns had shifted from heresy to cases of witchcraft, magic, and superstition). I quantified *only* those cases in which the suspect was a resident of Venice itself (including Murano) and was accused of some form of evangelical, Anabaptist, or millenarian beliefs and practices. On the positive side, this selection made my work more manageable. And I did not try to cover topics that might benefit from more specialized studies. Thus on the history of the relation of the Inquisition to the Jews in Venice, readers should look to the works of Brian Pullan and Pier Cesare Ioly Zorattini; those interested in the Venetian Inquisition and witchcraft will find much of interest in the recent work of Ruth Martin; and finally, those concerned with the history of the Venetian Inquisition and book publishers and printers should examine Paul Grendler's *The Roman Inquisition and the Venetian Press*. For the more provincial manifestations of heresy in more rural settings, readers may consult a vast range of works that includes Carlo Ginzburg's *The Cheese and the Worms*.[2]

On the negative side, this process of selection must occasionally

2. On the Venetian Inquisition and the Jews, for example, see Pullan, *The Jews of Europe and the Inquisition of Venice*; and Pier Cesare Ioly Zorattini, "Note sul S. Uffzio e gli Ebrei a Venezia nel Cinquecento," *Rivista di storia della Chiesa in Italia* 33 (1979): 500–508. Ioly Zorattini has also edited and published all the Venetian heresy trials involving Jews and Judaizers; see his *Processi del S. Uffizio di Venezia contro Ebrei e giudaizzanti*, 8 vols. (Florence: Olschki, 1980–1990). On witchcraft, see Ruth Martin, *Witchcraft and the Inquisition*. For the booktrade and heresy, in addition to Grendler, *The Roman Inquisition and*

have something arbitrary about it. To be sure, I tried to follow a set of empirically established criteria in distinguishing among the various heresies studied. Because sixteenth-century observers held a relatively clear idea of the characteristic attributes of anabaptism and millenarianism, I had little difficulty in determining which individuals either belonged or were believed to belong to these groups. Evangelism is a more elastic category, and in it I included individuals whose assertions (on such matters as devotion to saints, sacerdotal confession, the doctrine of the real presence, and salvation through faith alone) made them appear more Protestant than Catholic in outlook as well as those individuals whose behavior (the refusal to show devotion to a passing crucifix, the failure to observe fasts, a repeated pattern of working on holy days, and a refusal to take communion or give one's confession to a priest) also brought them under suspicion of holding evangelical ideas. When at least one of these traits was present, I counted the individual as an evangelical. This process of labeling admittedly required considerable latitude for my own judgment, as is likely inevitable in all quantitative analysis. As David Herlihy has written,

In designing the questionnaire, the researcher is often prone to include questions which, albeit of great interest, yet require a judgment on the part of the persons conducting the inquiry. . . . The researcher is not truly collecting the objective data of history, but his own interpretations of the historical account. He is conducting a survey of the opinions of present-day observers: what do I, or my assistants, think a passage means? In selecting some accounts over others, and in interpreting their meanings, he runs the risk of introducing biases into the machine-readable files, which will be beyond the powers of men or machines subsequently to rectify. He may strive to be scrupulously objective, but the need to select and to interpret at this early stage in the processing of his records will inevitably weaken the precision of the analysis and lower the credibility of the conclusions.[3]

Various issues remain that a quantitative approach can help illuminate. In the course of my research, I developed a simplified typology of information for each suspect (whether formally accused or named as an

---

*the Venetian Press*, see del Col, "Il controllo della stampa a Venezia e i processi di Antonio Brucioli," 457–510. Finally, on heresy in more rural settings, in addition to Ginzburg, *The Cheese and the Worms*, see Ester Zille, *Gli eretici a Cittadella nel Cinquecento* and Andrea del Col, "Eterodossia e cultura fra gli artigiani di Porcia nel secolo XVI," *Il Noncello* 46 (1978): 9–76.

3. David Herlihy, "Numerical and Formal Analysis in European History," *The Journal of Interdisciplinary History* 12 (1981): 127.

"accomplice" during a trial), a card on which I indicated the individual's name, the type of heresy involved, the location of the archival document or documents, and then the place of origin, the place of residence (that is, the parish), and the place of work (again the parish) for each of the suspects. Moreover, I developed information on the relation of the court to each person accused. I indicated whether or not the suspect was merely named as such, either through a formal accusation or through another form of implication; whether a hearing was held concerning his or her beliefs and behavior; and, finally, whether or not the suspect was either forced to testify or tried *in absentia*.[4] I also kept a tally of those who abjured their heresies, of those who were tortured, and of the sentences that were handed down.

These data were entered into a computer and (with SPSS-X) cross-tabulated and analyzed from a variety of perspectives. The results form the basis not only for each table in chapter 6 and for the graph in chapter 7 but also for most of the observations throughout the book about the social context of heresy and its repression. The reader should bear in mind that the tables present profiles of those *accused* of heresy and not of actual heretics. While neither the precise nature nor the magnitude of the distortions is easy to assess, the most probable inaccuracy stems from the Holy Office's tendency to concern itself primarily with the cultural elite and with individuals with close ties to the city. As a consequence, poorer workers and artisans as well as foreigners are probably underrepresented in the data derived from Venetian inquisitorial records. About many heretics in Venice we know absolutely nothing.[5] But it remains my conviction nonetheless that heresy was especially widespread among elite artisans.

To be sure, there are several difficulties in the use of occupation or trade as a key to understanding the place of heresy in the complex social hierarchy of early modern Venice. The main problem lies in the coexistence of several overlapping and even competing hierarchies in every complex society. An individual's relative standing often varies according to the criteria used to establish a particular model. Education and

4. Clearly, actual proceedings were more complex. For an excellent introduction to heresy trials, see Ruth Martin, *Witchcraft and the Inquisition*, esp. chaps. 1, 2; and John Tedeschi, "The Organization and Procedures of the Roman Inquisition: A Sketch," in Tedeschi, *The Prosecution of Heresy*, 127–203.

5. See John Martin, "Per un analisi quantitativa dell'Inquisizione veneziana," in del Col and Paolin, eds., *L'Inquisizione romana in Italia nell'età moderna*.

prestige might yield one set of results, and wealth would yield another. Moreover, because trades and professions have their own internal hierarchies, comparisons are often difficult. In a hypothetical world we might be inclined to attribute greater standing to a mercer than to a cobbler, but would we do so if we knew the mercer to be a journeyman who did not own his own shop and the cobbler to be a prosperous businessman who had a fine shop on the piazza San Marco and employed several assistants? When other variables such as sex, age, clerical versus nonclerical status are introduced, the problem of occupational ranking seems insurmountable.

Despite this difficulty, many sociologists and historians put forth the merits of the use of occupation as an index of hierarchy in both preindustrial and industrial societies. One sociologist even claims to have developed a "standard occupational prestige scale" that is able to predict accurately the prestige a particular occupation has or had in any complex society nine times out of ten.[6] He argues that such consistency, though perhaps at first surprising, is consistent with the inevitable inequalities in the distribution of power, wealth, and prestige in any advanced society. But, as other scholars attempting to develop their own occupational hierarchies note, the claim to have developed a "standard scale" is exaggerated. What has been discovered, they argue, is the obvious. Certain professions—those that require the greatest amount of education and control the greatest amount of wealth—are always at the top, while others—that require virtually no skills at all—are always at the bottom.[7] Nonetheless, there are significant variations in between, variations that relate to political, technical, cultural, and economic shifts.

In late medieval and early modern Italy, this "in-between" world appears to have been especially fluid. The constitutional history of Florence, for example, can be written in terms of the oscillating status of various guildsmen who now held, now lost political power. The debate of the relative dignity among the arts and the rise of academies

6. Donald J. Treiman, "A Standard Occupational Prestige Scale for Use with Historical Data," *Journal of Interdisciplinary History* 7 (1976): 283–304.

7. See Michael Katz, "Occupational Classification in History," *Journal of Interdisciplinary History* 3 (1972): 63–88; see also William H. Sewell, Jr., "The Working Class of Marseille Under the Second Republic: Social Structure and Political Behavior," in Peter N. Stearns and Daniel J. Walkowitz, eds., *Workers in the Industrial Revolution: Recent Studies of Labor in the United States and Europe* (New Brunswick: Rutgers University Press, 1974), 75–116.

both indicate subtle shifts in Italian conceptions of the "nobility" of certain professions. And, in the sixteenth century, the volatility of the discussion over the proper place of the mechanical arts demonstrates that the status of artisans was by no means settled. On the contrary, artisans in this period inhabited a world of shifting values and status, a fact that is itself central to understanding the sociology of the Renaissance.

In Venice, too, this "in-between" world was highly fluid. There were two reasons for this. One lay in the structure and the character of the guilds themselves. Unlike guilds in Florence, which tended to be monopolized by merchants who excluded producers and workers from their corporations, the Venetian guilds were usually structured in such a way as to prevent merchants from monopolizing control of production. This meant that individual guildsmen, even in humble trades, tended to manage their own affairs. They enjoyed a certain level of economic independence that their Tuscan counterparts did not know. At the upper levels of the artisan world, craftsmen and merchants were often indistinguishable.[8]

A second difficulty is more specific to Venice. In part, the sheer number of guilds—there were over one hundred—may have masked some of the harsher realities of hierarchy. Venetian artisans felt that their individual guilds conferred a certain status and privilege upon their members, in much the same way that voluntary societies in nineteenth-century America, as Tocqueville observed, gave citizens a sense of place and importance even though in reality they were alienated from the republic's centers of governance and decision making. A more decisive factor in concealing hierarchy was the fact that, unlike many other late medieval and early modern cities that made their hierarchical structure at the popular level explicit through processions that ranked the guilds, Venice subordinated guilds to confraternities (which drew their memberships from a wide variety of trades). Consequently, the consciousness of occupational status was perhaps lower in Venice than elsewhere in Europe, not only in Florence but also in such cities as Coventry or Rouen.[9]

8. This contrast between Florentine and Venetian guilds is underlined in Mackenney, "Arti e stato a Venezia."

9. See Benedict, *Rouen During the Wars of Religion*; and Charles Phythian-Adams, "Ceremony and the Citizen: The Communal Year at Coventry, 1450–1550," in Peter Clark and Paul Slack, eds., *Crisis and Order in English Towns, 1500–1700* (London: Routledge and Kegan Paul, 1972), 57–85.

Nonetheless, an occupational analysis of the distribution of heresy in Venice proves useful. In addition to a number of professions, there were over one hundred *arti* (incorporated crafts or trades) in sixteenth-century Venice, representing an extreme diversity of occupations. I consolidate these crafts and professions into five broad categories, here hierarchically arranged by status.

1. Clergy
2. Professions
3. Commerce
4. Elite Crafts
5. Skilled Crafts and Services

This categorization is unsatisfactory on a number of counts. It does not distinguish between craftsmen and retailers as well as I would like. For example, it cannot tell us whether specific hatters or coopers both made and sold their products; or whether they were craftsmen who produced them, either independently or under contract, for retailers; or whether they themselves were retailers. Nor does it distinguish between masters and journeymen.

Nonetheless, workers in early modern Venice did not conceive of themselves as a labor force or proletariat in contradistinction to a capitalist class; rather they were most conscious of themselves as members of a particular corporation or guild in which aspects of entrepreneurship and craftsmanship often combined. But this extremely diversified world was not infinitely varied. Shopkeepers of all kinds had more in common with one another than they did with spinners or carders. And the elite artisans in Venice, like their counterparts elsewhere in preindustrial Europe, had far more in common with one another then they did, for example, with street vendors or with textile workers. Perhaps we might test this categorization by analyzing marriage patterns and economic mobility among the *popolani*, a project that we could undertake for the late sixteenth century through the use of parish and notarial records.[10]

The additional advantage of this classification is that it often lets us estimate the approximate number of individuals working in most of the

---

10. As has been done, for example, by Samuel Kline Cohn in *The Laboring Classes in Renaissance Florence* (New York: Academic Press, 1980), and by James R. Farr in *Hands of Honor: Artisans and Their World in Dijon, 1550–1650* (Ithaca: Cornell University Press, 1988).

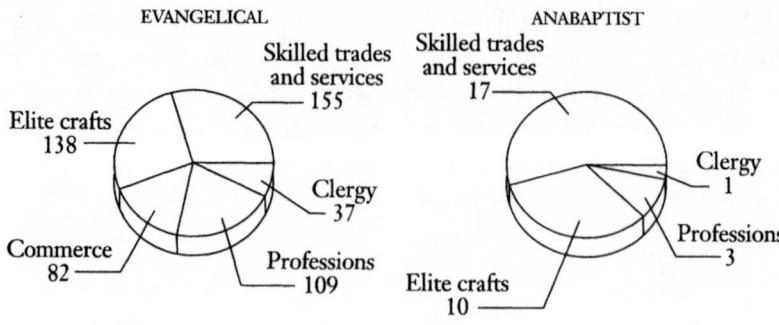

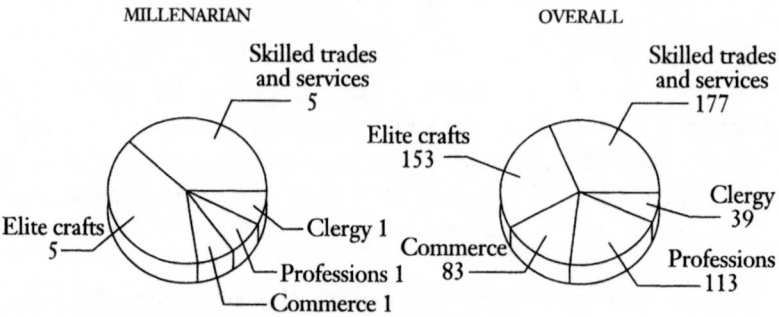

Fig. A1.   The social bases of the Venetian heresies.

Venetian trades and occupations in the sixteenth century, and we can, therefore, derive not only the absolute number of men or women accused of heresy according to their occupational status but also rates of accusations for heresy by occupational status in relation to the size of occupational groupings.

Chapter 6 uncovered the general pattern that we note in figure A1: the clergy, professionals, merchants, and elite artisans had by far the largest role among the evangelicals. By contrast, skilled workers figured prominently among the Anabaptists. Though the sample is small, the millenarians seem to have included individuals from all levels of Venetian society.

Furthermore, this pattern holds even when we examine the social distribution of heresy in relation to the size of each occupational category. The evangelicals came predominantly from the professions (at a rate of 4.9 percent), commerce (at a rate of 3.6 percent), and the elite crafts (at a rate of 3.2 percent). By contrast, the Anabaptists came primarily from the elite crafts (at a rate of .23 percent) and the textile trades (at a rate of .16 percent). The millenarians were too few for meaningful analysis here, though again the elite crafts (at a rate of .12 percent) appear to have predominated (see table A1, pp. 244–247). Thus, while each of the three major currents of heresy may have had quite different constituencies, they shared a social base as well. This fact may help explain some of the fluidity in the boundaries that existed among the various group; it certainly helps explain the close relation that existed between evangelism and anabaptism in the late 1540s.

Unless otherwise specified, the number of individuals in each trade or profession indicated in the table below is derived from Richard Til-den Rapp, *Industry and Decline in Seventeenth-Century Venice*. Rapp provides a list of all the Venetian *arti* and the 1595 *Milizia da Mar* census of their membership. Since Venice in the sixteenth century was characterized by rapid economic growth and was devastated by a major epidemic in 1575–1577, Rapp's numbers are to be taken as rough guides only. Moreover, the numbers represent membership in one year only, while the accusations are spread out over forty years. Thus, though for simplicity's sake I calculated the rates of accusation for the various heresies as percentages, they are not true percentages but rather indicators of the proportional rates with which heresy occurred in each occupation. Only occupations in which at least one individual was either denounced or implicated are specified.

Table A1. *Number of Persons Accused of Heresy in Venice, 1547–1586*
*(with the rate of accusation for each belief in parentheses)*

| Occupation[a] | N | Evangelical Beliefs | Anabaptist Beliefs | Millenarian Beliefs |
|---|---|---|---|---|
| Clergy and Religious[b] | | | | |
| Secular priests | 536 | 17 | | 1 |
| Monks and friars | 1,238 | | | |
| Augustinians | — | 4 | | |
| Carmelites | — | 1 | | |
| Carthusians | — | 1 | | |
| Dominicans | — | 3 | | |
| Observant Franciscans | — | 1 | 1 | |
| Conventual Franciscans | — | 4 | | |
| Friars (no order) | — | 4 | | |
| Servites | — | 1 | | |
| Female religious | 2,403 | 1 | | |
| Total | 4,177 | 37 ( .9) | 1 (.024) | 1 (.024) |
| Professions | | | | |
| Clerks, notaries | — | 25 | | |
| Engineers | — | 1 | | |
| Lawyers, solicitors | — | 29 | | |
| Physicians | — | 18 | 1 | |
| Attendants | — | 3 | | |
| Tutors, humanists | — | 33 | 2 | 1 |
| Total | 2,243[c] | 109 (4.9) | 3 (.13) | 1 (.04) |
| Commerce | | | | |
| Cotton, linen merchants | 79 | 4 | | |
| Wine merchants | 197 | 3 | | |
| Drapers | 541 | 4 | | |
| Mercers | 567 | 9 | | |
| Wool-cloth merchants | — | 1 | | |
| Brokers | 243 | 11 | | |
| Publishers | — | 1 | | |
| Booksellers | — | 10 | | |
| Used-clothing dealers | 140 | 5 | | |
| Cotton merchants | 104 | 4 | | |
| Silk merchants | 273 | 5 | | |
| Furriers | 128 | 1 | | |
| Merchants (unspecified) | — | 24 | | 1 |
| Total | 2,272[c] | 82 (3.6) | | 1 (.04) |

| Occupation[a] | N | Evangelical Beliefs | Anabaptist Beliefs | Millenarian Beliefs |
|---|---|---|---|---|
| **Elite Crafts** | | | | |
| Gold-leaf beaters | 138 | 3 | 1 | |
| Painters | 432 | 11 | 1 | |
| Instrument makers | — | 10 | | 1 |
| Jewelers | 415 | 29 | | 1 |
| Engravers | — | 1 | | |
| Enamelers | — | 2 | | |
| Moneyers | — | 2 | | |
| Shipwrights[d] | 1,024 | 5 | | |
| Tailors | 642 | 22 | 7 | |
| Musicians | 61 | 5 | | |
| Sword smiths | 103 | 4 | 1 | 1 |
| Apothecaries | 509 | 23 | | 1 |
| Printers[e] | 500 | 11 | | |
| Correctors, illuminators | — | 3 | | |
| Pressmen, letter casters | — | 2 | | |
| Glass makers | 30 | 3 | | |
| Armorers | 8 | 2 | | 1 |
| Others | 429 | | | |
| *Total* | 4,291 | 138 (3.2) | 10 (.23) | 5 (.12) |
| | | | | |
| **Skilled Trades and Services** | | | | |
| Miscellaneous trades | | | | |
| Potters | 91 | 7 | | |
| Hatters | — | 5 | | |
| Basket makers | 58 | 1 | | |
| Blind makers | — | | 1 | |
| Smiths | 503 | 3 | | |
| Rope makers | 146 | 6 | | |
| Glovers | — | 2 | 1 | |
| Ribbon makers | — | 2 | | |
| Rosary-bead makers | 52 | 1 | | |
| Comb makers | 84 | 1 | | |
| Soap makers | 111 | 2 | | |
| Tin workers | — | 1 | | |
| Others | 1,493 | | | |
| *Subtotal* | 2,538 | 31 (1.2) | 2 (.08) | |

Table A1. *Continued*

| Occupation[a] | N | Evangelical Beliefs | Anabaptist Beliefs | Millenarian Beliefs |
|---|---|---|---|---|
| Textile and leather trades | | | | |
| Purse makers | — | 2 | | |
| Cobblers | 727 | 18 | 7 | 2 |
| Belt makers | 49 | 2 | | |
| Tenterers | 52 | | | 1 |
| Raw-wool shearers | 1,124 | 6 | | |
| Tanners | 128 | 1 | | |
| Silk throwsters | 249 | 5 | 1 | |
| Teaselers | — | 2 | | |
| Carders | 1,222 | 1 | | 1 |
| Linenworkers | 142 | 1 | | |
| Dyers | 393 | 4 | 2 | |
| Wool-cloth weavers | 856 | 2 | | |
| Silk weavers | 1,541 | 33 | 1 | 1 |
| Others | 541 | | | |
| *Subtotal* | 7,024 | 77 (1.1) | 11 (.16) | 5 (.07) |
| Building trades | | | | |
| Turners | 84 | 4 | | |
| Dike builders | — | 1 | | |
| Carpenters | 340 | 1 | | |
| Stone cutters | 224 | 1 | | |
| Others | 511 | | | |
| *Subtotal* | 1,159 | 7 (.6) | | |
| Provisions | | | | |
| Distillers | — | 1 | | |
| Butchers | 71 | 3 | | |
| Flour sellers | 57 | 2 | 1 | |
| Bakers | 580 | | | |
| Fruit vendors | 438 | 1 | | |
| Pork butchers | 209 | 1 | | |
| Cooks | 60 | 1 | | |
| Biscuit makers | 143 | 4 | | |
| Wine vendors | — | 1 | | |
| Birders | — | 1 | | |
| Others | 1,329 | | | |
| *Subtotal* | 2,887 | 15 (.5) | 1 (.03) | |

| Occupation[a] | N | Evangelical Beliefs | Anabaptist Beliefs | Millenarian Beliefs |
|---|---|---|---|---|
| General services | | | | |
| Barbers | 282 | 4 | | |
| Boat men | 2,654 | 2 | | |
| Stevedores | 56 | 1 | | |
| Couriers | 62 | 1 | | |
| Porters | — | 6 | | |
| Innkeepers | 96 | 2 | 1 | |
| Knife grinders | 44 | 4 | 1 | |
| Servants[f] | 9,385 | 5 | | |
| Soldiers/sailors | 985 | | 1 | |
| *Subtotal* | 13,564 | 25 (.18) | 3 (.02) | |
| *Total* | 27,172 | 155 (.57) | 17 (.06) | 5 (.02) |
| *Total all occupations* | 40,155 | | | |

[a]Of the 730 individuals accused of heresy, I have been able to identify the occupation in only 565 cases. We know the occupations of 521 out of 676 individuals accused of evangelical beliefs and practices; of 31 out of 37 accused of Anabaptist beliefs; and of 13 out of 17 accused of millenarian beliefs.

[b]The figures on the size of the clergy in 1586 are reported by Beloch, *Bevölkerungsgeschichte Italiens*, 3:22.

[c]There is no accurate estimate of the size of either the professional or the merchant class in sixteenth-century Venice. I assume that most of the professionals and many merchants were either nobles or *cittadini*. As Luca di Linda observed in the seventeenth century, "The nobleman employs his talents in letters or public office, sometimes in the affairs of Mars. . . . The *cittadino* of lower standing either takes up the career of government secretary or is employed in trade (cited in Ugo Tucci, "The Psychology of the Venetian Merchant," in John R. Hale, ed., *Renaissance Venice*, 360). Since there were 2,147 adult male nobles and 2,312 adult male *cittadini* in Venice in 1595, I sum these groups for a total of 4,559. Rapp's figures for the merchants yield 2,316, leaving 2,243 for the professionals. The figures are probably low and very rough (some *popolani* who were neither of noble nor of *cittadino* status made it into these ranks).

[d]Rapp's figures for shipwrights are taken from 1595, when the industry was depressed; by contrast, 1550–1575 was a boom period. I use Robert C. Davis's figures for these years; note that the figure of 1,024 represents the total number of shipwrights with the privilege of working in the Arsenal and that probably only some 600 actually worked there on a given day (*Shipbuilders of the Venetian Arsenal*, 13, 21).

[e]Leonardo Donà estimated that the Venetian printing industry employed four to five hundred men in 1596 (Grendler, *The Roman Inquisition and the Venetian Press*, 3).

[f]The number of servants is from Beltrami (*Storia della popolazione di Venezia*, 213); this figure, from the 1581 census, postdates the plague.

# Sources and Bibliography: Heresy and Reform in Sixteenth-Century Italy

In part I intend this book to challenge the traditional meanings of the terms Renaissance and Reformation. Neither concept, at least as each is normally used in English-speaking countries, does much to capture or to illuminate the reform movements in sixteenth-century Venice, or in Italy generally. The reasons for this are quite obvious. Italy ceases to be the focus of Renaissance studies after the 1520s; Reformation scholarship, by contrast, stresses developments in Germany, Switzerland, France, Holland, and England. As a consequence, British and American readers, whose traditions rely on the twin lenses of Renaissance and Reformation studies, are likely to find the problems that are central to my arguments and exposition somewhat marginal to the chronological and geographical conventions of these fields.

This situation is changing. Since the late 1930s scholarship on the reform movements in sixteenth-century Italy has become a major current in the exploration of early modern history. The work of those (primarily Italian) historians who have contributed to this scholarship is the subject of this essay. Although considerations of space limit my references and remarks, I hope that this effort to bring together in one place an overview of a rapidly growing field will demonstrate that the *apparently* marginal quality of certain of my arguments results primarily from academic habits and does not reflect historical experience. In short, this essay explores alternative ways of thinking about sixteenth-century Italy. When one chooses to look at the past through the lenses such as the ones I mention below, previously quite secondary figures and movements on the early modern landscape leap to the foreground.

249

We are reminded how selective, if not distortive, our customary ways of viewing the past can become, even under the rubrics of such old friends as the Italian Renaissance, on the one hand, and the Protestant Reformation, on the other.

## Primary Sources

---

### THE ROMAN INQUISITION

Because the Roman Inquisition had such a large jurisdiction, from the papal states to Venice, its records occupy a central place in the study of the heresies of sixteenth-century Italy. The Archives of the Congregation of the Holy Office (since 1965 the Congregation for the Doctrine of the Faith) and of the Congregation of the Index, both in Rome, have remained closed to all but a handful of scholars, but many other collections are accessible. For a recent inventory of these *fondi*, of which there are more than twenty currently known, see Andrea del Col and Silvana Seidel Menchi, "Elenco dei fondi inquisitoriali italiani attualmente noti," in Andrea del Col and Giovanna Paolin, eds., *L'Inquisizione romana in Italia nell'età moderna: Archivi, problemi di metodo e nuove ricerche* (Rome: Ministero per i beni culturali e ambientali, 1991), 80–85. As del Col and Seidel Menchi correctly emphasize, given the current state of interest in inquisitorial records, each effort at an inventory is necessarily provisional. New sources will continue to come to light.

The inquisitorial documents I have used are located in the Archivio di Stato in Venice, in the series *Sant'Uffizio*. Altogether, this collection consists of 164 *buste* (boxes or bundles of materials) covering the period ca. 1541–ca. 1794. I have concentrated on buste 6–59, which include the denunciations along with the transcripts of hearings, trials, sentences, and so on, arranged more or less chronologically and covering the period 1547–1586, as well as on buste 151–164, which consist of letters, edicts, and dispatches either generated by the Venetian inquisitors or sent to them and of various extracts from trials and registers of inquisitorial proceedings. A manuscript index to this collection is available in the reading room of the Archivio di Stato in Venice: *Indice 303: Santo Ufficio Processi (Tre Savi all'eresia): Indici alfabetico, cronologico e geografico dei Processi del Sant'Uffizio 1541–1794*. This index, compiled in 1870 by Luigi Pasini and Giuseppe Giomo, is neither complete nor without errors, but it proved an essential point of departure for my research. Another collection of inquisitorial materials—whose relationship to the *fondo* in the Archivio di Stato in Venice remains problematic—is located in Venice in the Archivio della Curia Patriarcale in the series *Criminalia Sanctae Inquisitionis*. This includes four buste of documents from the period 1461–1622.

Dozens of trials have been edited by scholars and are available for consultation. For examples of Venetian trials and other archival materials such as the ones on which my study is based, see Franco Gaeta, "Documenti da codici vaticani per la storia della Riforma in Venezia," *Annuario dell'Istituto storico italiano per l'età moderna e contemporanea* 7 (1955): 5–53; Enrica Benini Clementi, "Il processo del gioielliere veneziano Alessandro Caravia," *Nuova rivista storica* 65 (1981): 628–652; Carlo Ginzburg, ed., *I costituti di don Pietro Manelfi* (DeKalb: Northern Illinois University Press; Chicago: Newberry Library, 1970); Domenico Berti, "Di Giovanni Valdes e di taluni suoi discepoli secondo nuovi documenti tolti dall'Archivio veneto," *Atti della R. Accademia dei Lincei* 275(1877–78), 3d s., *Memorie della classe di scienze morali, storiche e filologiche*, vol. 2, 61–81; M. E. [Edouard] Pommier, "L'itinéraire religieux d'un moine vagabond italien au XVIe siècle," *Mélanges d'archéologie et d'histoire de l'Ecole française de Rome* 66 (1954): 293–322; Andrea del Col, "Il secondo processo veneziano di Antonio Brucioli," *Bollettino della Società di studi valdesi* 146 (1979): 85–100; Aldo Stella, "Il processo veneziano di Guglielmo Postel," *Rivista di storia della Chiesa in Italia* 22 (1968): 425–466; Gaetano Cozzi, "Vita avventurosa di un setaiolo eretico," *Archivio storico lombardo* 80 (1954): 244–251; John Martin, edited trial of Paolo Gaiano, from "In God's Image: Artisans and Heretics in Counter-Reformation Venice" (Ph.D. diss., Harvard University, 1982), 415–518. The most comprehensive publishing project of Venetian inquisitorial materials (though not central to my study) involves the trials against Jews and judaizing Christians; see Pier Cesare Ioly Zorattini, ed., *Processi del S. Uffizio di Venezia contro Ebrei e giudaizzanti*, 8 vols. (Florence: Olschki, 1980–1990).

The trials of prominent heretics have also been the subject of scholarly editions. Of these, two in particular have significance for the history of the reform movement in Italy: the trial of the Florentine Pietro Carnesecchi, who had extensive contacts with many reformers throughout Italy, is published in Giacomo Manzoni, ed., "Estratto del processo di Pietro Carnesecchi," *Miscellanea di storia italiana* 10 (1870): 187–573; and that of Giovanni Morone, in Massimo Firpo, ed., *Il processo inquisitoriale del cardinal Giovanni Morone: Edizione critica*, 5 vols.

(vols. 2–5 edited in collaboration with Dario Marcatto) (Rome: Istituto Storico Italiano per l'Età Moderna e Contemporanea, 1981–1989). Firpo's splendid edition of Morone's trial is important in light of its extensive scholarly apparatus, which illuminates many aspects of the reform movements in sixteenth-century Italy. Another recently published trial of great interest is Andrea del Col's edition of the proceedings against the northern Italian miller Domenico Scandella, a figure previously made famous by Carlo Ginzburg's *The Cheese and the Worms*, cited below; see del Col, ed., *Domenico Scandella, detto Menocchio: I Processi dell'Inquisizione (1583–1599)* (Pordenone: Biblioteca dell'Immagine, 1990).

In order to understand the structure of inquisitorial law and practice, it is useful to begin with the manuals of inquisitors. Two of these, both widely used in the sixteenth century, are of special importance: Nicolau Eymeric, *Directorium Inquisitorum . . . cum commentariis Francisci Pegnae . . . in hac postrema editione iterum emendatum et auctum, et multis litteris apostolicis locupletatum* (Rome: in aedibus Populi Romani, 1578); and the *Repertorium Inquisitorum Pravitatis Haereticae, In quo omnia quae ad haeresum cognitionem, ac S. Inquisitionis forum pertinent, continentur* (Venice: Apud D. Zenarum, 1588).

Rome provided direction to the struggles against heresy throughout the peninsula. There is considerable material available for consultation in the collections of both the Archivio Segreto Vaticano and the Biblioteca Apostolica Vaticana. For a general orientation, see the documents collected by B. Fontana, ed., "Documenti vaticani contro l'eresia luterana in Italia," *Archivio della società romana di storia patria* 15 (1892): 71–165, 365–474; and by Ludwig von Pastor, *Allgemeine Dekrete der römischen Inquisition aus den Jahren 1555–1597: Nach dem Notariatsprotokoll des S. Uffizio zum ersten Male veröffentlicht* (Freiburg im Breisgau: Herdersche Verlagshandlung, 1912). See also Franco Gaeta et al., eds., *Nunziature di Venezia* (Rome: Istituto Storico Italiano per l'Età Moderna e Contemporanea, 1958–), vols. 1, 2, 5, 6, 8, 9, 10, and 11; and Alberto Bolognetti, "Dello stato et forma delle cose ecclesiastiche nel dominio dei signori venetiani, secondo che furono trovate et lasciate dal nunzio Alberto Bolognetti," in Aldo Stella, ed., *Chiesa e Stato nelle relazioni dei nunzi pontifici a Venezia* (Vatican City: Biblioteca Apostolica Vaticana, 1964), 105–318. Bolognetti devoted a chapter to the Holy Office. The correspondence of several other nunciatures are also published; see John Tedeschi, *The Prosecution of Heresy: Collected Studies on the Inquisition in Early Modern Italy* (Binghamton: Medieval and Renaissance Texts and Studies, 1991), 76 n.69 for further information. In both its richly annotated notes and its bibliography, this volume of Tedeschi's collected essays now provides the most authoritative guide to the institutional and legal history of the Roman Holy Office.

### THE LITERATURE
### OF THE ITALIAN REFORMATION

Many of the works of the Italian reformers are available only as *cinquecentine* (rare sixteenth-century editions). An especially important collection of these texts is located in the *fondo Guicciardini* in the Biblioteca Nazionale Centrale in Florence. On this collection, see the *Catalogo e suo supplemento del dicembre 1875 della collezione de' libri relativi alla riforma religiosa del secolo XVI, donata dal conte Piero Guicciardini alla città di Firenze* (Florence: Pellas, 1877) (this catalogue also contains a 2d supplement of 1881 and a 3d of 1887; see also Lia Invernizi, ed., *Il fondo Guicciardini nella Biblioteca Nazionale Centrale di Firenze: Catalogo* [Florence: La Nuova Italia, 1984–], for a newly edited guide to this collection, though it should be noted that Invernizi begins with the nineteenth-century works in the collection). Anne Jacobson Schutte, *Printed Italian Vernacular Religious Books 1465–1550: A Finding List* (Geneva: Librairie Droz, 1983), gives 3,678 titles as well as a list of printers and publishers of interest to students not only of the Italian reform movements but also of lay religious life generally in the late fifteenth and the first half of the sixteenth century. Paul Grendler has published eleven inventories of confiscated titles, primarily taken from inquisitorial records in Venice, in *The Roman Inquisition and the Venetian Press, 1540–1605* (Princeton: Princeton University Press, 1977), 304–324; these too may be used as a preliminary guide to the heretical literature circulating in Italy. Another "guide" to this literature is J.M. De Bujanda, ed., *Index des livres interdits*, vol. 3: *Index de Venise 1549; Venise et Milan 1554* (Sherbrooke, Québec: Centre d'Etudes de la Renaissance, 1987). The Newberry Library in Chicago holds an outstanding collection of materials relative to the Italian Reformation; see *The Literature of the Italian Reformation: An Exhibition Catalogue* (Chicago: Newberry Library, 1971), compiled, with an introduction, by John Tedeschi.

Two important early editions of the works of various Italian reformers include Giuseppe Paladino, ed., *Opuscoli e lettere di riformatori italiani del Cinquecento*, 2 vols. (Bari: Laterza, 1913–1927); and Delio Cantimori and Elisabeth Feist, eds., *Per la storia degli eretici italiani del secolo XVI in Europa* (Rome: Reale Accademia d'Italia, 1937). Recent initiatives have led to modern critical editions of several of the most important works. Among these, the most useful are those included in the series *Corpus Reformatorum Italicorum*, begun under the general editorship of Luigi Firpo, Giorgio Spini, Antonio Rotondò, and John Tedeschi. Unhappily, this series has thus far brought out only a portion of its projected volumes: see Camillo Renato, *Opere: Documenti e testimonianze*, ed. Antonio Rotondò (DeKalb: Northern Illinois University Press; Chicago: Newberry Library, 1968); Carlo Ginzburg, ed., *I costituti di don Pietro Manelfi*, cited above; Benedetto da Mantova, *Il Beneficio di Cristo con le versioni del secolo XVI: Documenti e testimonianze*, ed. Salvatore Caponetto (DeKalb: Northern Illinois University Press; Chicago: Newberry Library, 1972) (this volume includes various editions of the *Beneficio* as well as an edition of Ambrogio Catarino Politi, *Compendio d'errori, et inganni Luterani, contenuti in un Libretto, senza nome de l'Autore, intitolato, Trattato utilissimo del benefitio di Christo crucifisso*); Mino Celsi, *In haereticis coërcendis quatenus progredi liceat: Poems—Correspondence*, ed. Peter G. Bietenholz (Naples: Prismi; Chicago: Newberry Library, 1982); Antonio Brucioli, *Dialogi*, ed. Aldo Landi (Naples: Prismi; Chicago: Newberry Library, 1982); and, finally, though the focus here is the seventeenth century, Emidio Campi and Carla Sodini, eds., *Gli oriundi lucchesi di Ginevra e il cardinale Spinola* (Naples: Prismi; Chicago: Newberry Library, 1988). Antonio Rotondò's edition of Lelio Sozzini, *Opere: Edizione critica* (Florence: Olschki, 1986) in the series *Studi e testi per la storia religiosa del Cinquecento* appears to represent a new initiative.

Finally, Claudiana Editrice in Turin is publishing a series of works relating to the Italian Reformation in its series *Testi della Riforma*, edited by Giorgio Tourn and Ermanno Genre. See, for example, Benedetto da Mantova and Marcantonio Flaminio, *Il beneficio di Cristo*, ed. Salvatore Caponetto (Turin: Claudiana, 1975); Bernardino Ochino, *I "Dialogi sette" e altri scritti del tempo della fuga dall'Italia*, ed. Ugo Rozzo (Turin: Claudiana, 1985); *Il Sommario della santa Scrittura e l'ordinario dei cristiani*, ed. Cesare Bianco, with an introduction by Johannes Trapman (Turin: Claudiana, 1988); Giulio da Milano, *Scritti sul martirio*, ed. Ugo Rozzo (Turin: Claudiana, forthcoming in 1993); and Pietro Martire Vermigli, *Scritti del periodo italiano*, ed. Luigi Santini (Turin: Claudiana, forthcoming).

# Secondary Sources

## STUDIES ON THE ROMAN INQUISITION

On the history of inquisitorial records, John Tedeschi's "The Dispersed Archives of the Roman Inquisition," in Gustav Henningsen and John Tedeschi, eds., *The Inquisition in Early Modern Europe: Studies on Sources and Methods* (DeKalb: Northern Illinois University Press, 1986), 13–32 (and reprinted in John Tedeschi, *The Prosecution of Heresy*, cited above, 23–45) is fundamental. The use of such records as sources has generated considerable discussion in recent years. Perhaps best known are Carlo Ginzburg's methodological observations on the use of heresy trials for the reconstruction of popular beliefs and culture; see *The Night Battles: Witchcraft and Agrarian Cults in the Sixteenth and Seventeenth Centuries*, trans. John and Anne Tedeschi (Baltimore: Johns Hopkins University Press, 1983; reprint, New York: Penguin, 1985), xiii–xxii; *The Cheese and the Worms: The Cosmos of a Sixteenth-Century Miller*, trans. John and Anne Tedeschi (Baltimore: Johns Hopkins University Press, 1980; reprint, New York: Penguin, 1982), xi–xxvi; and, finally, his essay "The Inquisitor as Anthropologist" in his volume *Clues, Myths, and the Historical Method*, trans. John and Anne Tedeschi (Baltimore: Johns Hopkins University Press, 1989), 156–164. But see also Andrea del Col on inquisitorial records as sources: del Col, "I processi dell'Inquisizione come fonte: Considerazioni diplomatiche e storiche," *Annuario dell'Istituto storico italiano per l'età moderna e contemporanea* 35–36 (1983–1984): 29–49; and John Tedeschi, "Inquisitorial Sources and Their Uses" in Tedeschi, *The Prosecution of Heresy*, 47–88. Both del Col and Tedeschi have correctly stressed the necessity to take into account a great variety of inquisitorial and related sources (trials; sentences; manuals of inquisitors; the official correspondence generated by the Sacred Congregation in Rome, the provincial tribunals and the episcopal courts; nunciatures; monastic records; papal legislation, instructions, and decrees; as well as related secular and even artistic sources) not only to shed light on inquisitorial law and practice but also for the interpretation of the surviving records of this court. On manuals of inquisitors that were widely used in this period, see Agostino Borromeo, "A proposito del *Directorium Inquisitorum* di Nicolás Eymerich e delle sue edizioni cinquecentesche," *Critica storica* 20 (1983): 499–547; as well as Edward Peters, "Editing Inquisitors' Manuals in the Sixteenth Century: Francisco Peña and the *Directorium inquisitorum* of

Nicholas Eymeric," *The Library Chronicle* 40 (1974): 95–107. Finally, for the proceedings of a conference at which several methodological issues in the use of inquisitional sources were debated, see Andrea del Col and Giovanna Paolin, eds., *L'Inquisizione romana in Italia nell'età moderna*, cited above.

The legal and institutional history of the Inquisition has by now far surpassed the work of Ludwig von Pastor, whose multivolume *History of the Popes from the Close of the Middle Ages*, translated under the supervision of and edited by Frederick Ignatius Antrobus and Ralph Francis Kerr, 40 vols. (St. Louis: Herder, 1923–1933; reprint, Wilmington, N.C.: Consortium, 1978) still provides a compelling narrative of the policies and activities of the Inquisition as seen from Rome. Camillo Henner's *Beiträge zur Organisation und Competenz der päpstlichen Ketzergerichte* (Leipzig: Duncker und Humbolt, 1890) remains an authoritative discussion of the Roman Inquisition as a legal body. In terms of institutional history, scholars have generally favored the study of the Spanish Inquisition, whose operations are now quite well known, especially as the result of two recent works that decisively advance our understanding of inquisitorial law and practice: Jean-Pierre Dedieu, *L'Administration de la foi: L'Inquisition de Tolède (XVIe–XVIIIe siècle)* (Madrid: Casa de Velázquez, 1989); and William Monter, *Frontiers of Heresy: The Spanish Inquisition from the Basque Lands to Sicily* (Cambridge: Cambridge University Press, 1990), though Henry Charles Lea's *History of the Inquisition of Spain*, 4 vols. (New York and London: Macmillan, 1906–1907; reprint, 1922) remains both a mine of information and a classic of its genre.

The institutional history of the Inquisition in Venice has attracted considerable attention, noticeable in the recent work of several scholars, who have explored diverse aspects of the Holy Office in Venice: Paul Grendler in both *The Roman Inquisition and the Venetian Press* and "The Tre Savii sopra Eresia 1547–1605: A Prosopographical Study," *Studi veneziani* n.s. 3 (1979): 283–340; Brian Pullan in *The Jews of Europe and the Inquisition of Venice, 1550–1670* (Totowa, New Jersey: Barnes and Noble, 1983); and Ruth Martin in *Witchcraft and the Inquisition in Venice, 1550–1650* (Oxford: Blackwell, 1989), but these works should be supplemented by Andrea del Col's masterful "Organizzazione, composizione e giurisdizione dei tribunali dell'Inquisizione romana nella repubblica di Venezia (1500–1550)," *Critica storica* 25 (1988): 244–294, as well as "L'Inquisizione romana e il potere politico nella repubblica di Venezia (1540–1560)," *Critica storica* 28 (1991): 189–250, articles that fundamentally alter the received understanding of the relations of the Venetian government both to the problem of heresy and the activity of the Inquisition in Venice and its subject territories. In particular, del Col demonstrates on the basis of a thorough analysis of the records of the Council of Ten that the Venetian government (its secular magistrates) took an active role in the suppression of heresy not only well before the defeat of the Schmalkaldic League in 1547 but even before the establishment of the Roman Inquisition in 1542. Nicolas Davidson is completing a monograph on the institutional and legal history of the Holy Office in Venice. For some preliminary results, see N. S. Davidson, "Il Sant'Uffizio e la tutela del culto a Venezia nel '500," *Studi veneziani* n.s. 6 (1982): 87–101; and, by the same author, "Rome and the Venetian Inquisition in the Sixteenth Century," *Journal of Ecclesiastical History* 39 (1988): 16–36. In addition, there are numerous studies of other tribunals. The most distinguished of these include Luigi Amabile, *Il Santo Officio della Inquisizione in Napoli*, 2 vols. (Città di Castello: S. Lapi, 1892); and Antonio Battistella, *Il Santo Officio e la riforma religiosa in Friuli: Appunti storici documentati* (Udine: P. Gambiersi, 1895). For other comparable works on Italy, consult the excellent select bibliography in Tedeschi, *The Prosecution of Heresy*, 355–400; and, for a more general overview, though it is weak on Italian scholarship, Emil Van der Vekene, *Bibliotheca bibliographica historiae Sanctae Inquisitionis*, 2 vols. (Vaduz: Topos, 1982–1983).

## STUDIES OF THE ITALIAN REFORMATION

### General Studies

Several general studies of the Italian Reformation appeared in the nineteenth century. The most readable of these is the work of the eminent Scottish historian Thomas M'Crie, *History of the Progress and Suppression of the Reformation in Italy in the Sixteenth Century, Including a Sketch of the Reformation in the Grisons* (Edinburgh and London: Blackwood and Sons, 1856) (a posthumous edition, edited by M'Crie's son; the original edition appeared in 1827). See also Cesare Cantù, *Gli eretici d'Italia: Discorsi storici*, 3 vols. (Turin: UTET, 1865–66); both these works were written in the heroic mode and are monuments to nineteenth-century liberalism. A useful overview of the early scholarship on the Italian Reformation is available in Frederic C. Church, "The Literature of the

Italian Reformation," *Journal of Modern History* 3 (1931): 457–473; and, more recently, in Adriano Prosperi, "Riforma in Italia, Riforma italiana?" preface to Manfred Welti, *Breve storia della Riforma italiana*, trans. Armido Rizzi (Casale Monferrato: Marietti, 1985), vii–xvi (the original German edition of Welti's book, cited below, does not include Prosperi's essay).

Among early twentieth-century works, Frederic C. Church, *The Italian Reformers: 1534–1564* (New York: Columbia University Press, 1932) far surpassed G.K. Brown, *Italy and the Reformation to 1550* (Oxford: Blackwell, 1933). But by far the most significant work was that of Delio Cantimori, whose magisterial *Eretici italiani del Cinquecento: Ricerche storiche* (Florence: Sansoni, 1939; reprint, 1967) led to a fundamental transformation in approaches to the Reformation in Italy. Cantimori's work made it possible for scholars to go beyond the question of a *riforma mancata*, a failed Protestant Reformation in Italy, and to focus instead on what is now called "the Italian Reformation," the specific ways in which Italian intellectuals (whether artisans or humanists) contributed to the general religious ferment of the sixteenth century. Most of the *eretici* Cantimori examined fled Italy for Switzerland and later left Switzerland (where the Reformed churches and the Lutherans were seen as growing increasingly intolerant) for Poland and England. But Cantimori's later work examined in greater detail the experience of heretics in Italy. On the latter theme, see in particular *Prospettive di storia ereticale italiana del Cinquecento* (Bari: Laterza, 1960) as well as "Le idee religiose del Cinquecento: La storiografia," in Emilio Cecchi and Natalino Sapegno, eds., *Storia della letteratura italiana*, vol. 5: *Il Seicento* (Milan: Garzanti, 1967), 7–87. In addition, several of his more important essays are available in Delio Cantimori, *Umanesimo e religione nel Rinascimento* (Turin: Einaudi, 1975). Unfortunately, few of Cantimori's writings have been translated into English, but readers may wish to consult his "Italy and the Papacy," in G.R. Elton, ed., *The New Cambridge Modern History*, vol. 2: *The Reformation 1520–1559* (Cambridge: Cambridge University Press, 1958; reprint, 1975), 251–274; "The Problem of Heresy: The History of the Reformation and of the Italian Heresies and the History of the Religious Life in the First Half of the Sixteenth Century—the Relation Between Two Kinds of Research" in Eric Cochrane, ed. and trans., *The Late Italian Renaissance, 1525–1630* (London: Macmillan, 1970), 211–225; and "Submission and Conformity: 'Nicodemism' and the Expectations of a Conciliar Solution to the Religious Question," in ibid., 244–265. Giovanni Miccoli, *Delio Can-*

*timori: La ricerca di una nuova critica storiografica* (Turin: Einaudi, 1970) offers an overview of Cantimori's contributions, but see also Marino Berengo, "La ricerca storica di Delio Cantimori," *Rivista storica italiana* 79 (1967): 902–943; Alberto Tenenti, "Delio Cantimori storico del Cinquecento," *Studi storici* 9 (1968): 3–29; and Michele Ciliberto, *Intellettuali e fascismo: Saggio su Delio Cantimori* (Bari: De Donato, 1977). For a sense of the new directions in Italian Reformation studies since Cantimori's death, see the review articles by Silvana Seidel Menchi, "Lo stato degli studi sulla Riforma in Italia," *Wolfenbütteler Renaissance Mitteilungen* 5 (1981): 35–42, 89–92; and, more recently, by Anne Jacobson Schutte, "Periodization of Sixteenth-Century Italian Religious History: The Post-Cantimori Paradigm Shift," *Journal of Modern History* 61 (1989): 269–284. Both essays provide helpful insights into recent research; Schutte's is valuable for its detailed bibliography. The indefatigable John Tedeschi, in collaboration with Andrea del Col and Jim Lattis, is preparing a comprehensive bibliography on the reform movements of sixteenth-century Italy; it will be published by SUNY Binghamton in the Medieval and Renaissance Texts and Studies Series, and copublished by the Istituto di Studi Rinascimentali, Ferrara.

The most recent general analyses of the reform movement in Italy are Achille Olivieri, *La Riforma in Italia: Strutture e simboli, classi e poteri* (Milan: Mursia, 1979); and Manfred Welti, *Kleine Geschichte der italienischen Reformation* (Gütersloh: G. Mohn, 1985) (its Italian translation, *Breve storia della Riforma italiana*, is cited above). It is best to begin with Welti's synthesis, which provides a brief overview of several major issues and developments in the reform movements both within the various regions of Italy and among the exiles. Olivieri's provocative but idiosyncratic work requires some expertise on the part of the reader.

### Intellectual History

A central problem in the intellectual history of the Italian Reformation is the relative influence of the ideas of such ultramontane reformers as Luther, Calvin, and Erasmus on the development of reform ideas in Italy. Luther's ideas were certainly known early through much of the peninsula; scholars point out that, like the writings of Calvin and Erasmus, they were never received uncritically in Italy. For a general orientation to Luther's influence, see Silvana Seidel Menchi, "Le traduzioni italiane di Lutero nella prima metà del Cinquecento," *Rinascimento* 17 (1977): 31–108; Carlos Gilly, "Juan de Valdés: Übersetzer und Bear-

beiter von Luthers Schriften in seinem *Diálogo de Doctrina christiana*,"
*Archiv für Reformationsgeschichte* 74 (1983): 257–305; and Elisabeth Gleason, "Sixteenth-Century Italian Interpretations of Luther," *Archiv für
Reformationsgeschichte* 60 (1969): 160–173; for Calvin, Tommaso Bozza,
"Italia Calvinista: Traduzioni italiane di Calvino nel secolo XVI," *Miscellanea in onore di Ruggero Moscati* (Naples: Edizioni Scientifiche Italiane, 1985), 237–251; for Erasmus, Silvana Seidel Menchi, "Sulla for-
tuna di Erasmo in Italia: Ortensio Lando e altri eterodossi della prima
metà del Cinquecento," *Schweizerische Zeitschrift für Geschichte* 24 (1974):
537–634; and, most recently, by the same author, *Erasmo in Italia,
1520–1580* (Turin: Bollati Boringhieri, 1987); for Melanchthon, Salvatore Caponetto, "Due opere di Melantone tradotte da Lodovico Castel-
vetro: 'I principii de la Theologia di Ippophilo da Terra Negra' e 'Del-
l'autorità della Chiesa e degli scritti degli antichi,'" *Nuova rivista storica*
70 (1986): 253–274. A general overview is offered by Carlo De Frede,
*Ricerche per la storia della stampa e la diffusione delle idee riformate nell'Italia
del Cinquecento* (Naples: De Simone, 1985). The issue of the influence
of the ultramontane reformers on the ideas of the Italian heretics has
been especially contested in the case of the *Beneficio di Cristo*, a work
that continues to occupy a central position in the interpretation of the
reform movements in Italy. On this debate, see Tommaso Bozza, *Nuovi
studi sulla Riforma in Italia*. vol. 1: *Il Beneficio di Cristo* (Rome: Edizioni
di Storia e Letteratura, 1976); Paolo Simoncelli, "Nuove ipotesi e studi
sul 'Beneficio di Cristo,'" *Critica storica* 12 (1975): 320–388; and, by the
same author, "Noterelle sul *Beneficio di Cristo* nella letteratura religiosa
della controriforma," *Rivista di storia e letteratura religiosa* 19 (1983): 63–
83 as well as Mario Rosa, "'Il Beneficio di Cristo': Interpretazioni a
confronto," *Bibliothèque d'humanisme et Renaissance* 40 (1978): 609–620.
This debate does little to illuminate the ways in which sixteenth-century Italians read and understood a text like the *Beneficio*, as Carlo Ginzburg and Adriano Prosperi persuasively argue in their *Giochi di pazienza: Un seminario sul "Beneficio di Cristo"* (Turin: Einaudi, 1975).
See also Carlo Ginzburg and Adriano Prosperi, "Le due redazioni del
'Beneficio di Cristo,'" in *Eresia e riforma nell'Italia del Cinquecento: Miscellanea I del Corpus Reformatorum Italicorum* (DeKalb: Northern Illinois
University Press; Chicago: Newberry Library, 1974), 135–204.

It is the work of Silvana Seidel Menchi and of Massimo Firpo, above
all, that offers the most sophisticated approach to the ways in which
the ideas of non-Italian scholars were read in Italy. Seidel Menchi's
*Erasmo in Italia*, cited above, despite its modest title offers a compre-

hensive analysis of reform movements in Italy in the sixteenth century, though the reader should also consult Seidel Menchi's articles on the subject that are listed in her bibliography. Useful also are the articles by Massimo Firpo on Juan de Valdés and his followers throughout the peninsula; see "Juan de Valdés e l'evangelismo italiano: Appunti e problemi di una ricerca in corso," *Studi storici* 26 (1985): 733–754; "Valdesianesimo ed evangelismo: alle origini dell'*ecclesia Viterbiensis* (1541)," *Schifanoia* 1 (1986): 152–168—these articles are now reprinted and published with a new essay in Massimo Firpo, *Tra Alumbrados e "spirituali": Studi su Juan de Valdés e il valdesianesimo nella crisi religiosa del '500 italiano* (Florence: Olschki, 1990).

The reader can also approach the intellectual history of the Italian Reformation through a variety of issues that have dominated the discussion of the reform movements. Especially important are the discussions on Italian evangelism. This topic was given its original formulation by Eva-Maria Jung, "On the Nature of Evangelism in Sixteenth-Century Italy," *Journal of the History of Ideas* 14 (1953): 511–527; the latest comprehensive study is that of Paolo Simoncelli, *Evangelismo italiano del Cinquecento: Questione religiosa e nicodemismo politico* (Rome: Istituto Storico Italiano per l'Età Moderna e Contemporanea, 1979). On Simoncelli, see the perceptive remarks of Rita Belladonna and Andrea del Col, "Per una sistemazione critica dell'evangelismo italiano e di un'opera recente," *Critica storica* 17 (1980): 264–276. However, unlike Simoncelli as well as Belladonna and del Col, who use the term "radical" to refer to the current of evangelism represented by such figures as Flaminio and Vergerio, I prefer the use of the term "popular." The disagreement is not merely semantic. After the publication of George H. Williams's *The Radical Reformation*, cited below, historians have generally reserved the term "radical" for those movements and individuals who rejected the teachings of the Roman Catholic church and those of the major Protestant reformers and who sought in their place sects of "true believers." On this issue, see John Martin, "Salvation and Society in Sixteenth-Century Venice: Popular Evangelism in a Renaissance City," *Journal of Modern History* 60 (1988): 205–233. For two useful specialized studies on evangelism in English, see Anne Jacobson Schutte, "The *Lettere Volgari* and the Crisis of Evangelism in Italy," *Renaissance Quarterly* 28 (1975): 639–688; and O. M. T. Logan, "Grace and Justification: Some Italian Views of the Sixteenth and Early Seventeenth Centuries," *Journal of Ecclesiastical History* 20 (1969): 67–78. The meaning of the term "evangelism" and its usefulness are much debated. For overviews of the historiography and the issues involved, see Elisabeth Gleason, "On the Nature of Sixteenth-Century Italian Evangelism: Scholarship, 1953–1978," *Sixteenth-Century Journal* 9, no. 3 (1978): 3–25; and Susanna Peyronel Rambaldi, "Ancora sull'evangelismo italiano: Categoria o invenzione storiografica?" *Società e storia* 18 (1982): 935–967. In the near future, research is likely to veer away from studies of evangelism as a general category and to focus more specifically on the reception and the development of the ideas of such major figures as Erasmus and Valdés—for example, in the studies I have cited above by Silvana Seidel Menchi and Massimo Firpo. Yet, as the argument of my book should make clear, I am by no means convinced that we should abandon the term "evangelism." It is an acceptable term if the reader keeps in mind the various meanings it assumes in different periods (before and after 1542, for example), as well as in varying social and intellectual contexts. In my view, its very ambiguities and tendencies make it the best available lens through which we can observe the popular movements for reform in sixteenth-century Italy.

Another important current of beliefs in sixteenth-century Italy was that of anabaptism and antitrinitarianism. Friedrich Trechsel first explored the history of antitrinitarianism in *Die protestantischen Antitrinitarier vor Faustus Socin*, 2 vols. (Heidelberg: K. Winter, 1839–1844); and, for a relatively early work on the Anabaptists, see Karl Benrath in "Wiedertäufer im Venetianischen um die Mitte des 16. Jahrhunderts," *Theologische Studien und Kritiken* 58 (1885): 9–67. The more recent works of Aldo Stella are essential; see *Dall'anabattismo al socinianesimo nel Cinquecento veneto: Ricerche storiche* (Padua: Liviana, 1967), and *Anabattismo e antitrinitarismo in Italia nel XVI secolo: Nuove ricerche storiche* (Padua: Liviana, 1969), which are both rich in the author's use of archival sources, with the second volume providing a useful selection of documents in its appendix. Stella's volumes are summarized in George H. Williams, "The Two Social Strands in Italian Anabaptism, ca. 1526–ca. 1565," in Lawrence P. Buck and Jonathan W. Zophy, eds., *The Social History of the Reformation* (Columbus: Ohio State University Press, 1972), 156–207. For two significant studies that focus in part on this subject, see Earl Morse Wilbur, *A History of Unitarianism*, vol. 1: *Socinianism and Its Antecedents* (Cambridge, Mass.: Harvard University Press, 1945); and George H. Williams, *The Radical Reformation* (Philadelphia: Westminster, 1962).

As repression intensified in the mid-sixteenth century, Italian heretics could either go into exile or try to conceal their beliefs from their neighbors and co-workers. This latter strategy, known as Nicodemism, has generated a large literature. Despite the earlier work on this problem in its French context by Albert Autin, *La Crise du Nicodémisme, 1535–1545* (Toulon: Faculté des lettres de Montpellier, 1917), Delio Cantimori's work was decisive in defining Nicodemism as a historical problem. In addition to *Eretici italiani del Cinquecento*, cited above, see "'Nicodemismo' e speranze conciliari nel Cinquecento italiano," in Cantimori, *Studi di storia* (Turin: Einaudi, 1959), 518–536 (an English translation of this work is in Cochrane, ed., *The Late Italian Renaissance*, cited above); "Spigolature per la storia del nicodemismo italiano," in Cantimori et al., eds., *Ginevra e l'Italia* (Florence: Sansoni, 1959), 177–190, as well as the relevant chapters in *Prospettive di storia ereticale italiana del Cinquecento*. Carlo Ginzburg's ambitious *Il Nicodemismo: Simulazione e dissimulazione religiosa nell'Europa del '500* (Turin: Einaudi, 1970), which sought to describe Nicodemism as a phenomenon that developed throughout Europe in response to the conservative turn of the Reformation in the 1520s, has been soundly criticized by Carlos M.N. Eire, "Calvin and Nicodemism: A Reappraisal," *Sixteenth-Century Journal* 10, no. 1 (1979): 45–69. Rather more successful approaches to the topic have been taken by Albano Biondi, "La giustificazione della simulazione nel Cinquecento," in *Eresia e riforma nell'Italia del Cinquecento*, previously cited, 7–68, while Antonio Rotondò, "Atteggiamenti della vita morale italiana del Cinquecento: La pratica nicodemitica," *Rivista storica italiana* 79 (1967): 991–1030 is a judicious account of Nicodemite theory and practice in Italy. Rich new perspectives on this subject are offered by Rita Belladonna in a series of articles on Bartolomeo Carli Piccolomini: "Bartolomeo Caroli, nobile senese, imitatore di Juan de Valdés," *Critica storica* 10 (1973): 514–528; "Cenni biografici su Bartolomeo Carli Piccolomini," *Critica storica* 11 (1974): 507–510; "Pontanus, Machiavelli, and a Case of Religious Dissimulation in Early Sixteenth-Century Siena (Carli's *Trattati nove della prudenza*)," *Bibliothèque d'humanisme et Renaissance* 37 (1975): 377–385; "Bartolomeo Carli Piccolomini's Attitude towards Religious Ceremonies Compared to That of Erasmus and That of Luther," *Bibliothèque d'humanisme et Renaissance* 42 (1980): 421–425; and "Aristotle, Machiavelli, and Religious Dissimulation: Bartolomeo Carli Piccolomini's *Trattati Nove Della Prudenza*," in J.C. McLelland, ed., *Peter Martyr Vermigli and Italian Reform* (Waterloo, Ontario: Wilfrid Laurier University Press,

1980), 29–41; as well as Paolo Simoncelli in *Evangelismo italiano del Cinquecento*, cited above. See also Massimo Firpo, "Gli 'spirituali,' l'Accademia di Modena e il Formulario di fede del 1542: Controllo del dissenso religioso e Nicodemismo," *Rivista di storia e letteratura religiosa* 20 (1984): 40–111. Unfortunately, the most extensive discussion of Italian Nicodemism in English, Perez Zagorin, *Ways of Lying: Dissimulation, Persecution and Conformity in Early Modern Europe* (Cambridge, Mass.: Harvard University Press, 1990), 83–99, is largely derivative and, following Cantimori, exaggerates the significance of Giorgio Siculo's *Epistola . . . alli cittadini di Riva di Trento* (Bologna: Anselmo Giaccarello, 1550)—for a more thorough reading of Siculo, see Barry Collett, *Italian Benedictine Scholars and the Reformation: The Congregation of Santa Giustina of Padua* (Oxford: Clarendon, 1985), 213–245.

As noted, Cantimori gave considerable emphasis to the exiles *religionis causa* in *Eretici italiani del Cinquecento*. This tradition of scholarship has remained an important focus in Italian Reformation studies. See, for example, the studies by Antonio Rotondò in *Studi e ricerche di storia ereticale italiana del Cinquecento* (Turin: G. Giappichelli, 1974), as well as the monographs of Domenico Caccamo, *Eretici italiani in Moravia, Polonia, Transilvania (1558–1611)*, Biblioteca del "Corpus Reformatorum Italicorum" (Florence: Sansoni; Chicago: Newberry Library, 1970); Massimo Firpo, *Antitrinitari nell'Europa orientale del '500* (Florence: La Nuova Italia, 1977); and, by the same author, *Pietro Bizzarri: esule italiano del Cinquecento* (Turin: G. Giappichelli, 1971).

On the millenarian and prophetic currents, Marjorie Reeves offers a useful starting point in both *The Influence of Prophecy in the Later Middle Ages: A Study in Joachimism* (Oxford: Oxford University Press, 1969), and *Joachim of Fiore and the Prophetic Future* (New York: Harper and Row, 1976); but see also Bernard McGinn, *Visions of the End: Apocalyptic Traditions in the Middle Ages* (New York: Columbia University Press, 1979). For Savonarola, Donald Weinstein's *Savonarola and Florence: Prophecy and Patriotism in the Renaissance* (Princeton: Princeton University Press, 1970) is a model of clarity in its study of the profound connections between Florentine political traditions and Savonarola's religious messages. For the resonances of the prophectic tradition in sixteenth-century Italy, see Ottavia Niccoli, *Prophecy and People in Renaissance Italy*, trans. Lydia G. Cochrane (Princeton: Princeton University Press, 1990). In my view, the terminus ad quem that Niccoli has imposed on the prophetic fervor of the period is rather too early, at least for Venice. For a relatively late expression of prophetic ideals in Venice, see Carlo Ginzburg, "Due note sul profetismo cinquecentesco," *Rivista storica italiana* 78 (1966): 184–227. Marion L. Kuntz's current researches on prophecy in sixteenth-century Venice should also somewhat modify Niccoli's interpretation. Finally, see Cesare Vasoli, *Profezia e ragione: Studi sulla cultura del Cinquecento e del Seicento* (Naples: A. Morano, 1974).

### Biographies

Biographical approaches to the Italian Reformation have long been central to the study of the field, and there are several excellent such works. Among the most important are—on Valdés, José C. Nieto, *Juan de Valdés and the Origins of the Spanish and Italian Reformation* (Geneva: Librairie Droz, 1970); and Domingo de Santa Teresa, *Juan de Valdés, 1498(?)–1541: Su pensamiento religioso y las corrientes espirituales de su tiempo* (Rome: Apud Aedes Universitatis Gregorianae 1957);—on Gasparo Contarini, Franz Dittrich, *Gasparo Contarini, 1483–1542: Eine Monographie* (Braunsberg: Druck und Verlag der Ermländischen Zeitungs- und Verlagsdruckerei, 1885) remains the most comprehensive study, but for an *aggiornamento*, see Gigliola Fragnito, *Gasparo Contarini: Un magistrato veneziano al servizio della Cristianità* (Florence: Olschki, 1988), which is less a biography than a collection of specific studies on central aspects of Contarini's thought and contributions;—on Giberti, for a striking example of the ambiguous positions many highly placed clerics held in relation to the ideals of the reform, see Adriano Prosperi, *Tra evangelismo e Controriforma: G.M. Giberti (1495–1543)* (Rome: Edizioni di Storia e Letteratura, 1969);—on Ochino, Roland Bainton, *Bernardino Ochino: Esule e riformatore senese del Cinquecento, 1487–1563*, trans. E. Gianturco (Florence: Sansoni, 1940) (the English manuscript of this work was never published); and Karl Benrath, *Bernardino Ochino of Siena: A Contribution towards the History of the Reformation*, trans. H. Zimmern (New York: Robert Carter and Bros., 1877); both studies should now be analyzed in light of Ugo Rozzo, "Nuovi contributi su Bernardino Ochino," *Bollettino della Società di studi valdesi* 146 (1979): 51–83;—on Vermigli, Philip McNair, *Peter Martyr in Italy: An Anatomy of Apostasy* (Oxford: Clarendon, 1967); see also Salvatore I. Camporeale, "Lo studio di McNair su Pietro Martire Vermigli: Giustificazione per fede o teologia umanistica?" *Memorie Domenicane* 3 (1972): 180–197, as well as several of the essays in J.C. McLelland, ed., *Peter Martyr Vermigli and Italian Reform*, cited above;—on Pole,

Dermot Fenlon, *Heresy and Obedience in Tridentine Italy: Cardinal Pole and the Counter Reformation* (Cambridge: Cambridge University Press, 1972); and Paolo Simoncelli, *Il caso Reginald Pole: Eresia e santità nelle polemiche religiose del Cinquecento* (Rome: Edizioni di Storia e Letteratura, 1977);—on Flaminio, Alessandro Pastore, *Marcantonio Flaminio: Fortune e sfortune di un chierico nell'Italia del Cinquecento* (Milan: Franco Angeli, 1981); and, in English, Carol Maddison, *Marcantonio Flaminio: Poet, Humanist and Reformer* (Chapel Hill: University of North Carolina Press, 1965);—on Vergerio, Fulvio Tomizza's *Il male viene dal nord: Il romanzo del vescovo Vergerio* (Milan: A. Mondadori, 1984) is full of human interest, but Anne Jacobson Schutte's *Pier Paolo Vergerio: The Making of an Italian Reformer* (Geneva: Librairie Droz, 1977) (now in an Italian version, with an updated preface and bibliography) remains the most authoritative scholarly biography;—and on Carnesecchi, Oddone Ortolani, *Per la storia della vita religiosa italiana nel Cinquecento: Pietro Carnesecchi* (Florence: Le Monnier, 1963);—on Paleario, with many insights on the reform movement in Tuscany, see Salvatore Caponetto, *Aonio Paleario (1503–1570) e la Riforma protestante in Toscana* (Turin: Claudiana, 1979);—finally, on Postel, see William James Bouwsma, *Concordia Mundi: The Career and Thought of Guillaume Postel (1510–1581)* (Cambridge, Mass.: Harvard University Press, 1957); Marion L. Kuntz, *Guillaume Postel: Prophet of the Restitution of All Things* (The Hague: Martinus Nijhoff, 1981); and Kuntz, ed., *Postello, Venezia e il suo mondo* (Florence: Olschki, 1988).

Aristocratic women also played an important role in the Italian Reformation. For a general introduction to such major figures as Giulia Gonzaga, Caterina Cibo, Vittoria Colonna, Isabella Bresegna, Renée of Ferrara, and Olympia Morata, see Roland Bainton, *Women of the Reformation in Germany and Italy* (Minneapolis: Augsburg, 1971). Issues of gender have attracted surprisingly little attention among students of the Italian Reformation, but see Nancy L. Roelker, "The Appeal of Calvinism to French Noblewomen in the Sixteenth Century," *Journal of Interdisciplinary History* 2 (1972): 391–418, whose conclusions might also explain the interest of certain Italian noblewomen in the ideas of the reformers. Finally, many entries in the *Dizionario biografico degli Italiani*, now completed through the letter *D* (Rome: Società Grafica Romana, 1960–), discuss individual reformers and heretics.

### The Italian Reformation
### in Its Social and Political Contexts

For the most part, the social and political histories of the reform movements in Italy have considered the experience of various groups of heretics in an urban context. An influential work is Federico Chabod's "Per la storia religiosa dello Stato di Milano durante il dominio di Carlo V: Note e documenti." This essay was published in the *Annuario dell R. Istituto storico per l'età moderna e contemporanea*, 2–3 (1936–1937): 1–261. It subsequently appeared twice as a single volume (Bologna: Zanichelli, 1938, and Rome: Istituto Storico per l'Età Moderna e Contemporanea, 1962) but is now most accessible in Chabod, *Opere*, vol. 3: *Lo stato e la vita religiosa a Milano nell'epoca di Carlo V* (Turin: Einaudi, 1971). Chabod's work shows the influence of the scholarship of Lucien Febvre; to understand the particular historiographical context in which Chabod was working, see Giorgio Spini, "Qualche riflessione su 'Per una storia religiosa dello Stato di Milano' di Federico Chabod," in Brunello Vigezzi, *Federico Chabod e la "nuova storiografia" italiana dal primo al secondo dopoguerra* (Milan: Jaca Book, 1984), 233–241.

The Venetian heretics have been the subject of many studies, without which my attempts to make sense of the reform movements in the city would have been in vain. Early general studies stem from those of Karl Benrath, *Geschichte der Reformation in Venedig* (Halle: Verein für Reformationsgeschichte, 1887), and Emilio Comba, *I nostri Protestanti*, vol. 2: *Durante la Riforma nel Veneto e nell'Istria* (Florence: Claudiana, 1897), and more recently, Edouard Pommier, "La société vénitienne et la Réforme protestante au XVIe siècle," *Bollettino dell'Istituto di storia della società e dello Stato veneziano* 1 (1959): 3–26, and Adriano Prosperi, "Ortodossia, diversità, dissenso: Venezia e il governo della religione intorno alla metà del Cinquecento," in André Chastel and Renato Cevese, eds., *Andrea Palladio, Nuovi contributi: Settimo Seminario Internazionale di Storia dell'Architettura, Vicenza 1–7 settembre 1988* (Milan: Electa, 1990), 27–31. On Venetian anabaptism, the studies of Stella, cited above, are essential and greatly deepen our understanding of the phenomenon in Venice and the Veneto. My work has been informed by Stella, who has also charted the more moderate currents of the reform movements in Venetian politics in the sixteenth century. See "L'Orazione di Pier Paolo Vergerio al Doge Francesco Donà sulla riforma della chiesa

(1545)," *Atti dell'Istituto veneto di scienze, lettere ed arti: classe di scienze morali, lettere ed arti* 128 (1970): 1–39; "Utopie e velleità insurrezionali dei filoprotestanti italiani (1545–1547)," *Bibliothèque d'humanisme et Renaissance* 27 (1965): 133–82; and "Guido da Fano eretico del secolo XVI al servizio dei re d'Inghilterra," *Rivista di storia della Chiesa in Italia* 13 (1959): 196–238. Andrea del Col's exquisitely documented work also significantly deepens our knowledge of the intellectual history of heresy in the city. His articles are too numerous to list in their entirety, but see—in addition to "Organizzazione, composizione e giurisdizione dei tribunali dell'Inquisizione romana nella repubblica di Venezia," and "L'Inquisizione romana e il potere politico nella repubblica di Venezia," both cited above—the following: "Note sull'eterodossia di fra Sisto da Siena: I suoi rapporti con Orazio Brunetto e un gruppo veneziano di 'spirituali,'" *Collectanea Franciscana* 47 (1977): 27–64; "Due sonetti inediti di Pier Paolo Vergerio il giovane," *Ce fastu?* 54 (1978): 70–85; "Lucio Paolo Rosello e la vita religiosa veneziana verso la metà del secolo XVI," *Rivista di storia della Chiesa in Italia* 32 (1978): 422–459; and "Il controllo della stampa a Venezia e i processi di Antonio Brucioli (1548–1559)," *Critica storica* 17 (1980): 457–510.

Del Col has also extensively researched the history of reformers and heretics in the Friuli, territory that was subject to the Venetian state. See "Eterodossia e cultura fra gli artigiani di Porcia nel secolo XVI," *Il Noncello* 46 (1978): 9–76; "La storia religiosa del Friuli nel Cinquecento: Orientamenti e fonti, parte prima," *Metodi e ricerche* n.s. 1 (1982): 69–87; and "La storia religiosa del Friuli nel Cinquecento: Orientamenti e fonti, seconda parte," *Metodi e ricerche* n.s. 2 (1983): 39–56. Other excellent studies by del Col as well as by such scholars as Silvano Cavazza, Stefania Ferlin Malavasi, and Giovanna Paolin, who also work on the history of heresy in the territories of the Venetian republic, are listed by Schutte in her essay "Periodization of Sixteenth-Century Italian Religious History," 280–281. Achille Olivieri's "Sensibilità religiosa urbana e sensibilità religiosa contadina nel Cinquecento veneto: suggestioni e problemi," *Critica storica* 9 (1972): 631–650, inspired by the *mentalité* studies of the *Annales* school, is frustratingly vague but suggests possibilities for future research.

Other cities and regions have also received considerable attention, though here I can list only some of the more influential works. See, for Siena, Valerio Marchetti, *Gruppi ereticali senesi del Cinquecento* (Florence:

La Nuova Italia, 1975). On Lucca, in addition to Marino Berengo, *Nobili e mercanti nella Lucca del Cinquecento* (Turin: Einaudi, 1965), chap. 6, see Simonetta Adorni Braccesi, "Giuliano da Dezza caciaiuolo: Nuove prospettive sull'eresia a Lucca nel XVI secolo," *Actum Luce* 9 (1980): 89–138; "Maestri e scuole nella repubblica di Lucca tra Riforma e Controriforma," *Società e storia* 33 (1986): 559–594; "Libri e lettori a Lucca tra Riforma e Controriforma: Un'indagine in corso," in *Libri, idee e sentimenti religiosi nel Cinquecento italiano: 3–5 aprile 1986* (Modena: Panini, 1987), 39–46; and "Il dissenso religioso nel contesto urbano lucchese della Controriforma" in *Città italiane del '500 tra Riforma e Controriforma: Atti del Convegno Internazionale di Studi, Lucca 13–15 ottobre 1983* (Lucca: Maria Pacini Fazzi, 1987), 225–239. On Modena, see Cesare Bianco, "La comunità di 'fratelli' nel movimento ereticale modenese del '500," *Rivista storica italiana* 92 (1980): 621–679; and Susanna Peyronel Rambaldi, *Speranze e crisi nel Cinquecento modenese: Tensioni religiose e vita cittadina ai tempi di Giovanni Morone* (Milan: Franco Angeli, 1979). On Bologna, see Antonio Rotondò, "Per la storia dell'eresia a Bologna nel secolo XVI," *Rinascimento* 13 (1962): 107–154. All these works show a considerable diffusion of religious ideas among the popular classes. It should be noted that Berengo's work is a model for those interested in the interrelation of religious and social life. For other cities and regions, see the bibliographies provided in Schutte's "Periodization of Sixteenth-Century Italian Religious History," and in Tedeschi's *Prosecution of Heresy*.

In his review of *Città italiane del '500 tra Riforma e Controriforma*, Samuel Cohn was certainly correct to observe that "Italy still lacks its Bernd Moeller" (*Renaissance Quarterly* 42 [1989]: 558). There simply is no work for the Italian context that corresponds to Moeller's now classic *Imperial Cities and the Reformation*, ed. and trans. Mark Edwards and H.C. Erik Midelfort (Philadelphia: Fortress, 1972). Nonetheless there is much of general interest in Luigi Donvito, "La 'Religione cittadina' e le nuove prospettive sul Cinquecento religioso italiano," *Rivista di storia e letteratura religiosa* 19 (1983): 431–474, which goes further than any work I know in its effort to trace the recurrent social and political forces of religious reform in sixteenth-century Italy. Unhappily for both social and cultural history, there is little dialogue between students of the Italian Reformation and scholars who work on the reform movements in Germany, France, and England; nationalist perspectives, it appears, continue to limit our view of widespread contemporaneous movements. The one conspicuous exception is Silvana Seidel Menchi's magisterial *Erasmo in Italia*. Seidel Menchi manages not only to offer the most comprehensive interpretation we have yet of the reform movements in Italy but also to consider various substantive and methodological discussions about the circulation of religious ideas, especially in the German context. An important discussion of this work, with *interventi* by Andrea del Col, Silvano Cavazza, and Adriano Prosperi, was published in *Quaderni storici* 70 (1989): 269–296. In my view, Prosperi's reservations exaggerate Seidel Menchi's departure from Cantimori's teachings. For an excellent introduction to recent approaches to the social history of the German Reformation, see R. Po-Chia Hsia, ed., *The German People and the Reformation* (Ithaca: Cornell University Press, 1988).

## For Students

In addition to the works cited above, there are texts and documents available in English translations that should prove particularly useful to students. Several important texts by Juan de Valdés are included in George H. Williams and Angel M. Mergal, eds., *Spiritual and Anabaptist Writers* (Philadelphia: The Westminster Press, 1957). See also Bernardino Ochino, *Seven Dialogues*, trans. and ed. Rita Belladonna (Ottawa: Dovehouse Editions, 1988). Elisabeth Gleason provides a rich collection of texts, including *The Beneficio di Cristo*, in *Reform Thought in Sixteenth-Century Italy*, American Academy of Religion, Texts and Translations Series, no. 4 (Chico, Calif.: Scholars Press, 1981). For certain essential Catholic Reformation writings from late fifteenth- and sixteenth-century Italy (including texts by Savonarola, Contarini, and Giberti), see John C. Olin, *The Catholic Reformation: Savonarola to Ignatius Loyola* (New York: Harper and Row, 1969).

Students may also benefit from an analysis of trials that have been translated into English: see John Tedeschi and Josephine von Henneberg, eds. and trans., "Contra Petrum Antonium a Cervia relapsum et Bononiae concrematum," in Tedeschi, ed., *Italian Reformation Studies in Honor of Laelius Socinus* (Florence: Le Monnier, 1965), 243–268; David Chambers and Brian Pullan, eds., *Venice: A Documentary History, 1450–1630* (Oxford: Blackwell, 1992), 228–237; and Carlo Ginzburg, *Night Battles: Witchcraft and Agrarian Cults in the Sixteenth and Seventeenth Cen-*

*turies*, 147–171, including the trials of two *benandanti*. Moreover, John and Anne Tedeschi are preparing an English translation of Andrea del Col's edition of the trial of Domenico Scandella, cited above, to be published in the series Medieval and Renaissance Texts and Studies at SUNY Binghamton. Finally, there are brief selections from Nicolau Eymeric's *Directorium Inquisitorum* in Alan C. Kors and Edward Peters, eds., *Witchcraft in Europe, 1100–1700: A Documentary History* (Philadelphia: University of Pennsylvania Press, 1972), 84–92.

# General Index

Here as in the text, first names appear in variant forms—Giacomo and Jacomo, for example, or Giovanni and Zuane—in accordance with early modern practice; however, a single form is used for each individual. Patronyms are given when these were clearly established by the sixteenth century or when they have become conventional in the historiography. In the matter of names, consistency is neither possible nor desirable—especially in a book that discusses not only popes and monarchs but also artisans and workers in the textile and other trades.

# Index of Secondary Authors

Adorni Braccesi, Simonetta, 8n, 269
Alberi, Eugenio, 183n
Amabile, Luigi, 257
Ambrosini, Federica, 160n, 181
Autin, Albert, 263

Bainton, Roland, 41n, 265–266
Bakhtin, Mikhail, 13n, 15n
Baron, Hans, 31n
Battistella, Antonio, 257
Baudrier, Henri Louis, 135n, 136n
Baum, G., 131n
Belladonna, Rita, 261, 263, 270
Beloch, Karl Julius, 25n, 153n, 247n
Beltrami, Daniele, 25n, 153n, 247n
Benedict, Philip, 151n, 240n
Benini Clementi, Enrica, 80n, 158, 251
Bennassar, Bartolomé, 189n
Benrath, Karl, 4, 5n, 7, 27n, 141, 262,
   265, 267
Berchet, Federico, 28n, 163
Berengo, Marino, 8n, 28n, 48n, 156n,
   259, 269
Bertelli, Sergio, 34n, 227n
Berti, Domenico, 16n, 251
Bianco, Cesare, 8n, 87n, 254, 269
Bietenholz, Peter G., 254
Biondi, Albano, 126n, 130n, 263
Bishop, Morris, 3n
Bistort, Giulio, 61n
Black, Christopher F., 191n

Bloch, Marc, 177n
Bongi, Salvatore, 222n
Borromeo, Agostino, 13n, 255
Borsa, Gedeon, 135n
Bossy, John, 19n, 169n
Bouwsma, William James: on Calvin,
   127n; on evangelism, 228n; on Postel,
   29n, 115n, 119n, 122n, 266; on Ven-
   ice, 34n, 183n, 219n, 220n, 221n,
   225n, 226
Bozza, Tommaso, 84n, 260
Brady, Thomas A., Jr., 17n, 48n, 151n
Braudel, Fernand, 161n, 162n, 164n
Brown, G. K., 258
Brown, Horatio, 25n, 78n
Brown, Patricia Fortini, 168n
Brown, William Archer, 221n
Buck, Lawrence P., 100n, 262
Burckhardt, Jacob, 20
Burke, Peter, 11n, 18n

Caccamo, Domenico, 133n, 142n, 143n,
   264
Campana, Lorenzo, 53n, 66n, 68n
Campi, Emidio, 254
Camporeale, Salvatore I., 265
Camporesi, Piero, 153n
Cantimori, Delio: on antitrinitarianism,
   107n; editor, 254; on exiles, 264; his-
   toriographical contribution of, 5–9,
   258–259; on Melanchthon, 26n; on

Printed in the United States
100443LV00001B/168/A

9 780801 878770